P9-DMJ-564

WEST'S LAW SCHOOL
ADVISORY BOARD

JESSE H. CHOPER
Professor of Law,
University of California, Berkeley

DAVID P. CURRIE
Professor of Law, University of Chicago

YALE KAMISAR
Professor of Law, University of Michigan

MARY KAY KANE
Dean and Professor of Law, University of California,
Hastings College of the Law

WAYNE R. LaFAVE
Professor of Law, University of Illinois

ARTHUR R. MILLER
Professor of Law, Harvard University

GRANT S. NELSON
Professor of Law, University of California, Los Angeles

JAMES J. WHITE
Professor of Law, University of Michigan

CHARLES ALAN WRIGHT
Charles Alan Wright Chair in Federal Courts
The University of Texas

LEGAL RESEARCH

IN A NUTSHELL

SEVENTH EDITION

By

MORRIS L. COHEN
Librarian (Retired) and Emeritus Professor of Law
Yale Law School

KENT C. OLSON
Assistant Librarian and Lecturer in Legal Research
University of Virginia School of Law

CHING CHIH CHUANG

WEST
GROUP

ST. PAUL, MINN.
2000

West Group has created this publication to provide you with accurate and authoritative information concerning the subject matter covered. However, this publication was not necessarily prepared by persons licensed to practice law in a particular jurisdiction. West Group is not engaged in rendering legal or other professional advice, and this publication is not a substitute for the advice of an attorney. If you require legal or other expert advice, you should seek the services of a competent attorney or other professional.

Nutshell Series, In a Nutshell, the Nutshell Logo and the West Group symbol are registered trademarks used herein under license.

COPYRIGHT © 1968, 1971, 1978, 1985, 1992, 1996 WEST PUBLISHING CO.
COPYRIGHT © 2000 By WEST GROUP
                            610 Opperman Drive
                            P.O. Box 64526
                            St. Paul, MN 55164–0526
                            1–800–328–9352

All rights reserved
Printed in the United States of America

ISBN 0–314–23885–9

 TEXT IS PRINTED ON 10% POST CONSUMER RECYCLED PAPER

PREFACE

Legal Research in a Nutshell has seen considerable change since it was first published in 1968. Each edition has focused increasingly on electronic methods of research. Lexis and Westlaw were first introduced in the 1978 edition, followed by CD-ROM in 1992. The 1996 edition added the first references to the Internet, but it did not provide any web addresses to assist researchers in finding resources. In this seventh edition, Internet resources are integrated into a discussion once dominated by books and commercial databases.

Yet in some respects the *Nutshell* of 1968 is not so distant. This edition continues to devote much of its attention to printed, or "traditional," legal resources. While electronic methods are essential in today's legal research, they have not yet supplanted the sophisticated editorial tools that form the basis of our legal literature. Many online sources are based on printed works and thus incorporate their structure and logic. An understanding of these works is required for effective research, whether in print or electronic media. Successful research also requires an appreciation for the computer's ability to execute searches which are impossible with print materials, and for its power to retrieve information unavailable on a local library's shelves. An integrated approach to print and electronic sources pervades most of the chapters that follow and shapes the actual practice of legal research today.

This book presents legal materials in the order in which they are often consulted by beginning researchers.

Part I, Basic Sources, provides an introductory overview and covers essential secondary and primary sources in American law. General background sources such as legal encyclopedias and law review articles are discussed at the outset, just as they are usually the first sources consulted in research. Case law publication and research are discussed next, in keeping with the central place of court decisions in the American legal system and in legal education. The first part concludes with a discussion of constitutional and statutory law. Part II, Advanced Topics, covers sources such as legislative history, administrative regulations, court rules, looseleaf services, and directories. While these materials are somewhat more specialized than the basic case law and statutory sources, they are no less important in many research situations. Part III, Beyond the Borders, provides a brief introduction to research in international and foreign law. These chapters may be beyond the scope of many introductory courses in legal research, but we feel that no consideration of legal resources is quite complete without recognizing the place of the United States in a larger community. Our discussion of international and foreign law resources reflects their increased role in practice and in scholarship.

Throughout the book, we note which materials are available online as well as in print. Electronic research methods have grown increasingly diverse, and as a result this edition has less about the specific mechanics of online searching than its predecessors. No longer is there one simple search method, but a range of sophisticated options that change almost daily. Even the names for online databases have become fluid, depending on whether access is through software or website. One person's

"GENFED" or "ALLFEDS" is another's "Federal Legal - U.S." It may be necessary to consult online or print database directories to identify the current locations of particular resources.

Using an Internet search engine to find a resource can be considerably more troublesome than scanning a Westlaw or Lexis-Nexis database list, so the book does provide a substantial number of website addresses. Many of the websites mentioned are valuable starting points, with links to research materials beyond those discussed in this book. All addresses were rechecked and still valid as of April 2000.

This book is designed not as a reference work but as a practical teaching tool, for use by individuals or in legal research courses. In either case, simply reading its text will not make you an effective researcher. Skill in legal research can only be achieved by combining knowledge with experience. Reading in the *Nutshell* should be accompanied by practice. Ruth McKinney's *Legal Research — A Practical Guide and Self-Instructional Workbook* (2d ed. 2000) can be used as a companion volume to this work and contains extensive cross-references to relevant sections of *Legal Research in a Nutshell*.

The authors wish to express their gratitude to law library colleagues at Yale and the University of Virginia for supporting the preparation of this new edition, and to students in Advanced Legal Research courses for suggesting ways to improve this text. The exhibits in chapter 6 were selected in honor of Gloria Greene, a very generous friend of the Olson family.

We hope that with the extensive revisions incorporated in this new edition, this *Nutshell* will continue to provide an effective introduction to American legal research in the 21st century.

MORRIS L. COHEN
KENT C. OLSON

New Haven, Connecticut
Charlottesville, Virginia
April 2000

OUTLINE

APPENDICES

LEGAL RESEARCH

IN A NUTSHELL

SEVENTH EDITION

*

CHAPTER 1

THE RESEARCH PROCESS

―――――――

§ 1–1. INTRODUCTION

Legal research is an essential component of legal practice. It is the process of finding the law that governs an activity and materials that explain or analyze that law. These resources give lawyers the knowledge with which to provide accurate and insightful advice, to draft effective documents, or to defend their clients' rights in court. Ineffective research wastes time, and inaccurate research leads to malpractice.

Determining what law applies to a particular situation is a skill requiring expertise in legal analysis. Lawyers need to be able to analyze factual situations, determine the relevant fields of legal doctrine, and apply rules developed by courts, legislatures, and administrative agencies. Finding these rules requires expertise in legal research, and that demands an understanding of which

1

resources to consult in each situation, as well as the relative value of the resources available. Experienced legal researchers know which sources are authoritative or useful for what purposes.

Legal research involves the use of a variety of resources, some created by lawmaking bodies such as courts and legislatures, and others by scholars and practicing lawyers. Many of these resources are accessible in both print and electronic forms, affecting the means of research but not changing the essential purpose of the task. For each problem, the researcher must choose the appropriate tools and tactics. There are as many procedures as there are problems, and no single approach can work every time.

§ 1–2. THE SOURCES OF THE LAW

The law consists of those recorded rules that society will enforce and the procedures that can implement them. These rules and procedures are created in various ways. Statutes are enacted by elected representatives, while common law doctrines have been shaped over many years in court decisions. These are just two of many sources of the law, but the distinction between statutory and common law forms one of several dichotomies and classifications that characterize the legal system.

The law has numerous sources, from the United States Constitution to the pronouncements of municipal agencies. Both the federal government and the states have lawmaking powers, and in each case the three branches—legislative, executive, and judicial—share in this responsibility. As the elected voice of the citizens, the

legislature raises and spends money, defines crimes, regulates commerce, and generally determines public policy by enacting statutes.

The executive branch is charged with enforcing the law, but in doing so it too creates legally binding rules. The president and most governors can issue executive orders, and administrative agencies provide detailed regulations governing activity within their areas of expertise. Agencies also act in a "quasi-judicial" capacity by conducting hearings and issuing decisions to resolve particular disputes. These *administrative law* sources are less studied by law students than statutes and court decisions, but they are no less important in the areas they govern.

The judicial branch plays a complex role in this system. The courts apply the language of constitutions and statutes to circumstances that may not have been foreseen when they were enacted. In most instances, these judicial interpretations become as important as the text of the provisions they interpret. Through the power of *judicial review*, asserted by Chief Justice Marshall in *Marbury v. Madison*, the courts also determine the constitutionality of acts of the legislative and executive branches.

Judges also create and shape the *common law*. In a common law system such as ours, the law is expressed in an evolving body of doctrine determined by judges in specific cases, rather than in a group of prescribed abstract principles. As established rules are tested and adapted to meet new situations, the common law grows and changes over time.

An essential element of the common law is the doctrine of precedent, or *stare decisis* ("let the decision stand"). Under this doctrine, courts are bound to follow earlier decisions. These provide guidance to later courts faced with similar cases, and aid in preventing further disputes. People can study earlier cases, evaluate the legal impact of planned conduct, and modify their behavior to conform to existing rules. Although the law changes with time, precedent provides both fairness and stability. It is the importance of judicial decisions as precedent that gives them such a vital place in American legal research.

The first year law school curriculum sorts legal issues another way, into distinct areas of doctrine such as contract, tort, and property. In doing so, it provides law students with a framework for analyzing legal situations and applying a particular body of rules. Real life does not divide so neatly into issues of contract or tort, but legal materials generally follow this paradigm. A researcher with a breach of warranty problem, for example, will find answers by turning to texts and articles on contracts.

Other distinctions that pervade legal thinking include *civil* and *criminal law*, *substance* and *procedure*, and *state* and *federal jurisdiction*. Law students must learn how legal issues fit into these dichotomies, not only to solve problems but to know where to look for answers. It is necessary, however, to learn how to classify a question without pigeonholing the situation too narrowly. Analysis within a particular doctrinal area can clarify a specific issue, but most situations contain issues from a number of areas. A lawyer who does thorough research on causation issues but forgets about the statute of limitations or service of process is a losing lawyer.

§ 1–3. THE FORMS OF LEGAL INFORMATION

Effective legal research requires more than knowledge of the nature of the legal system. An understanding of the ways in which legal information is disseminated is also needed. Several characteristics have affected the research process. Laws are published chronologically, requiring tools to provide access by subject. Legal literature comprises both official, primary statements of the law and an extensive body of unofficial secondary writings. Information is accessible both in print and electronically, creating a wide range of choices in research methods.

a. Access to Chronological Publications

The legal system is created over the course of time, and the law in force today is a combination of old and new enactments and decisions. The United States Constitution has been in force for more than 200 years, and many judicial doctrines can be traced back even farther. Other laws are just days or weeks old, as legislatures, courts, and executive agencies address issues of current concern.

These laws have been published as they were issued, whether in volumes of legislative acts or court reports, or through electronic dissemination. They retain their force and effect until they are expressly repealed or overruled. To determine the law that governs a particular situation, the researcher may need access to all of these sources, no matter how old or how new they may be.

This has led to the creation of a complex collection of resources designed to provide topical access to this vast body of material. Today the most widely used approach is keyword searching in databases containing the full text of thousands of court decisions or other documents. More

traditional means of access to court opinions include digests classifying summaries of points from cases; texts and reference works summarizing and comparing similar cases; and citators allowing researchers to trace doctrines forward in time. For access to statutes and regulations, laws in force are arranged by subject in codes and accompanied by extensive indexes. Much of legal research involves mastering these various means of access to the law.

It is just as important for lawyers and others interested in the legal system to keep up with new developments, and an extensive body of resources exists to provide current information. New statutes, regulations, and court decisions are issued by the government and by commercial publishers, both in print and through electronic means. Newsletters and looseleaf services provide notice of and analyze these new developments. In addition, the codes and texts lawyers use are updated regularly to reflect changes. One of the most common forms of updating print publications is the *pocket part,* a supplement designed to fit inside the back cover of a bound volume. Many publications are issued in binders so that they can be updated with supplementary inserts or replacement pages. Electronic updating is even faster and more efficient.

b. Primary and Secondary Sources

Legal sources differ in the relative weight they are accorded. Some are binding authority; some are only persuasive in varying degrees; and some are useful only as tools for finding other material. Researchers must evaluate the sources they find, and place them in the hierarchy of authority. A decision from one's state su-

preme court has more force than a scholarly article, but that article may be more valuable than rulings of courts in other jurisdictions.

The most important distinction is between *primary* and *secondary sources*. Primary sources are the court decisions, statutes, and regulations that form the basis of the legal doctrine. These are the official pronouncements of the governmental lawmakers. Not all primary sources have the same force for all purposes. A decision from a state supreme court is mandatory authority in its jurisdiction and must be followed by the lower state courts. A state statute also must be followed within the state. Other primary sources are only persuasive authority; a court in one state may be influenced by decisions in other states faced with similar issues, but it is free to make up its own mind. A statute or regulation from one state may not even have persuasive authority in another state.

Works which are not themselves the law, but which discuss or analyze legal doctrine, are considered secondary sources. These include treatises, hornbooks, restatements, and practice manuals. Much of the most influential legal writing is found in the academic journals known as *law reviews*. Secondary sources serve a number of important functions in legal research. Scholarly commentaries can have a persuasive influence on the law-making process by pointing out flaws in current legal doctrine or suggesting solutions. More often, they serve to clarify the sometimes bewildering array of statutes and court decision, or provide current awareness about developing legal doctrines. Finally, their footnotes provide extensive references to both primary sources and other secondary material.

Some resources, such as digests or citators, have no secondary authority at all. The purpose of these finding tools is not to persuade, but simply to facilitate access to other sources. Those sources must then be read to determine their applicability to a particular situation.

c.   Print and Electronic Resources

Most of the resources to be discussed in this book first appeared in printed form, and developed as print publications over several decades or even centuries. Detailed editorial systems such as digests, citators, and annotated codes have standardized access to the jumble of primary sources. In recent years, of course, more and more material has become available electronically. The computer has not, however, replaced the book, and the astute researcher knows how to take advantage of both media.

Electronic research has significantly affected the process of legal research. The computer can integrate a variety of tasks that are conducted with separate print sources, such as finding cases, checking the current validity of their holdings, and tracking down secondary commentary. The ability to search the full text of documents for specific combinations of terms has freed researchers from total reliance on the editors who create indexes and digests. Each research situation presents a unique set of factual and legal issues, and the computer makes it possible to find documents which address this specific confluence of issues.

Yet editors have hardly been put out of work. Researchers forced to work only with an uncontrolled mass of electronic data would quickly find themselves drowning in unsorted information. Tools such as digests and in-

dexes continue to provide the invaluable service of sorting material by subject and presenting it in a comprehensible fashion.

Computerized research has also blurred the distinctions among different types of information and broadened the scope of legal inquiry. Research in case law, for example, was traditionally a process quite distinct from research in secondary commentary or social sciences. Using electronic databases, it is much more convenient and natural to switch from one source to another and back again, bringing to legal research more empirical experience and a wider range of scholarly commentary. Hypertext links between documents make it possible to follow various leads and ideas as they arise, rather than following one linear research path.

Two major commercial database systems, Lexis–Nexis and Westlaw, are widely used in law schools and in legal practice as comprehensive legal research tools. Originally designed for access through proprietary software, both of these systems are now also accessible through the World Wide Web (<www.lexis.com> and <www.westlaw.com>). Through either method, however, they are available only to subscribers and other paying customers. Law students generally have access through their school's subscriptions, but for other researchers these can be expensive tools.

Free sites on the Internet are increasingly important sources of legal information. Some provide access to recent case law, but the Internet is more important as a source of statutes, legislative documents, and administrative agency materials. It also provides an invaluable

means of linking scholars and researchers through websites, discussion groups, and electronic mail.

§ 1–4. LEGAL LANGUAGE

One of the tasks facing law students is mastering a new way of speaking and writing. The law has developed its own means of expression over the centuries. Latin words and phrases remain prevalent, from the familiar writs of *certiorari* or *habeas corpus* to doctrines such as *res ipsa loquitur*, and even familiar words such as *instrument* or *intent* may have specialized meanings in legal documents.

A good law dictionary is needed to understand the language of the law. For many years, the definitions in most law dictionaries have been almost as obscure and archaic as the terms defined. Fortunately for researchers, the leading work, *Black's Law Dictionary* (7th ed. 1999), has recently undergone a major revision under the editorship of Bryan A. Garner and now provides much more clarity in its definitions. The new *Black's* has numerous new entries, but it continues to define older terms found in historical documents as well. In addition to definitions for nearly 25,000 terms, it includes pronunciations and more than 2,000 quotations from scholarly works. *Black's* can also be searched on Westlaw. *Ballentine's Law Dictionary* (3d ed. 1969) was once the major competitor to *Black's*, but it is considerably out of date.

Several shorter dictionaries can also be found in law libraries and bookstores. Among the best are Bryan A. Garner, ed., *Black's Law Dictionary: Pocket Edition* (1996); Steven H. Gifis, *Law Dictionary* (4th ed. 1996); and Daniel Oran, *Oran's Dictionary of the Law* (2d ed.

2000). *Oran's* is also the most extensive law dictionary available free on the Web <www.lawoffice.com/pathfind/orans/orans.asp>.

Bryan A. Garner, editor of the new *Black's Law Dictionary*, is also author of *A Dictionary of Modern Legal Usage* (2d ed. 1995), which focuses on the way words are used in legal contexts. It is an entertaining guide to legal language's complexities and nuances, and an articulate advocate for clear and simple writing. *Mellinkoff's Dictionary of Legal Usage* (1992) is a somewhat similar work by the late David Mellinkoff, author of *The Language of the Law* (1963), a learned and often witty introduction to the history and peculiarities of legal expression.

A variety of other language reference works exist. William C. Burton, *Burton's Legal Thesaurus* (3d ed. 1998) helps writers choose correct terms, and can aid researchers in identifying and choosing words when searching in indexes or preparing online searches. Fred R. Shapiro, *Oxford Dictionary of American Legal Quotations* (1993) is the most scholarly of several sources providing access to the most memorable uses of legal language. It is arranged topically, with precise citations to original sources and indexes by keyword and author.

§ 1–5. LEGAL CITATION

A second hurdle in understanding legal literature is understanding the telegraphic citation form used in most sources. Before reading *Brown v. Board of Education*, a researcher must be able to decipher "347 U.S. 483 (1954)" and understand that "347" is the volume number, "483"

the page number, and "U.S." the abbreviation for the *United States Reports*, official source of United States Supreme Court opinions.

This citation form is centuries old, but the standard guide to its present use is *The Bluebook: A Uniform System of Citation* (16th ed. 1996), published by the Harvard Law Review Association. *The Bluebook* establishes rules both for proper abbreviations and usage of signals such as "cf." and "But see." A few journals follow the somewhat simpler rules in the *University of Chicago Manual of Legal Citation* (1989), known as the *Maroon Book*; and the new *ALWD Citation Manual* (2000) from the Association of Legal Writing Directors may challenge the *Bluebook*'s supremacy in law school use.

In recent years there has been a trend towards citations to legal authorities that does not depend on reference to a particular volume and page number, and that thus can be as relevant whether documents are retrieved in printed volumes, through subscription databases, or from free Internet sites. A *public domain citation* system assigns official numbers to documents such as court decisions sequentially as they are issued, and also numbers each paragraph to allow references to specific portions of the text. This approach has only been adopted in a few jurisdictions, but it has been endorsed by the American Bar Association. The American Association of Law Libraries has issued a *Universal Citation Guide* (1999) providing rules for public domain citation formats.

No matter what citation rules are followed, part of the puzzle is simply deciphering the abbreviations used. *Black's Law Dictionary* and the *Bluebook* contain tables

listing the major abbreviations found in legal literature, but neither is comprehensive. Cases and law review articles contain numerous abbreviations and citations that are cryptic even to experienced researchers. Two specialized abbreviations sources, Mary Miles Prince, *Bieber's Dictionary of Legal Abbreviations* (4th ed. 1993) and Donald Raistrick, *Index to Legal Citations and Abbreviations* (2d ed. 1993) provide extensive coverage of both common and obscure abbreviations. *Bieber's Dictionary* is also available electronically on Lexis–Nexis.

§ 1–6. BEGINNING A RESEARCH PROJECT

Often the hardest part of the research process is finding the first piece of relevant information. Once one document is found, it usually can lead to a number of other sources. Cases cite earlier cases as authority; a statute's notes provide useful leads to decisions, other statutes, legislative history, and secondary sources; and periodical articles cite a wide variety of sources. Finding the first piece of the puzzle, though, can be a challenge.

Where does a researcher begin when working on a new problem? To some extent, this is a matter of personal preference and relative familiarity with particular tools. It makes sense to start with material which you can use most effectively. There are, however, some guidelines that can make for better choices.

Before looking anywhere, step back and study the problem carefully. If possible, determine whether the jurisdictional focus is federal or state. Be sure you understand the terms in which the problem is stated; if not, consult a good dictionary or other reference source. For-

mulate *tentative* issues, but be prepared to revise your statement of the issues as research progresses and you learn more about the legal background.

It is generally best to begin research by going to a trustworthy secondary source—a legal treatise or a law review article. The mass of primary sources can seem forbidding, and using a subject index or digest to find cases or statutes on point is often frustrating. Primary sources by themselves often are not very straightforward. Secondary materials, on the other hand, try to *explain* and *analyze* the law. They offer easier access, while providing food for thought. They summarize the basic rules and the leading primary sources and place them in context, allowing the researcher to select the most promising primary sources to pursue.

The choice of the appropriate starting point should be influenced by the nature of the problem. When researching a new or developing area of law, start by looking for a recent periodical article. A law review article can provide an overview of the field, references to important cases and statutes, and a relatively current perspective. Moreover, the indexes to periodicals are among the easiest and most useful tools for subject access to legal literature.

When researching an issue that fits within a traditional area of legal doctrine, begin by consulting a subject treatise or hornbook in the area. A good treatise explains the major issues and terminology, and provides a context in which related matters might be raised or considered. The names of some of the most famous treatises, such as *Corbin on Contracts* or *Prosser and Keeton on Torts*, are

familiar to any law student. Treatises in other areas can be found by checking a law library's catalog or asking a reference librarian.

If no treatise is available, a legal encyclopedia such as *American Jurisprudence 2d* or *Corpus Juris Secundum* can be a useful first step. These works attempt to cover the entire field of legal doctrine, so their focus is rather diffuse. They do, however, outline the basic rules in each area and provide extensive references to court decisions.

There are times when the first research step will be the major case-finding tools to be discussed in this book, such as digests and annotations. These tools are specifically designed to gather together cases with similar facts or issues, and they can be great resources for finding relevant court decisions. It is not always easy, however, to find the appropriate place to look. For that reason it is often easier to use digests or annotations once a few cases have been found by other means. These cases will provide easy leads into the digest system or annotated reports.

When it is apparent that the issue to be researched is one of public law (i.e., involves substantial governmental regulation), it may be most efficient to begin with the statute underlying the area of regulation. Public law includes areas such as administrative law, antitrust, banking, labor, and taxation. The statutory language may not provide a clear overview of the field, but an annotated code leads directly to most of the other relevant primary sources. Looseleaf services often combine the statutory text with editorial explanatory notes.

In most situations it is best to begin research by using printed resources, in order to get an overview of an area and to clarify relevant doctrines and issues. There are times, though, when the computer databases of Lexis–Nexis or Westlaw may be the best starting point. If you are generally familiar with an area of law and are researching a narrow question or a particular combination of issues, use of the databases may be the most effective way of focusing your research. Because the researcher defines the terms to be searched, computers provide far more flexibility than other tools.

Free Internet sites are not comprehensive, but they can provide places to start if more thorough resources are not readily available. Several websites provide directories organizing legal material by jurisdiction and topic. Among the most popular are the commercial site Find-Law <www.findlaw.com> and Cornell Law School's Legal Information Institute <www.law.cornell.edu>. These sites provide links to primary sources, directories, journals, and numerous other sources. Internet search engines can also be useful, although it may be difficult to evaluate results and weed out superficial or misleading information. Search engines limited to legal sites (such as LawCrawler <www.lawcrawler.com> or LawRunner <www.lawrunner.com>) may yield more focused results.

Finally, sometimes the first step of research does not involve using either books or databases. Instead it may be more efficient to make a telephone call or two. Government agencies and professional associations are staffed with experts who can answer questions, provide invaluable references, or send essential documents. There are several directories of government agencies, and resources

such as the *Encyclopedia of Associations* list professional and trade groups by subject.

These various options are the sorts of choices one must make in any research process. It is important to remember that there may be professional help available to guide you in the choice of the first resource. Most law libraries are staffed with librarians trained to provide just this sort of assistance. While law librarians are not permitted to interpret the law or provide legal advice to library users, they are trained to assist patrons in determining how best to track down the relevant sources.

§ 1–7. COMPLETING A RESEARCH PROJECT

It can be just as difficult to know when to stop researching as it is to know where to begin. In every research situation, however, comes a time when it is necessary to synthesize the information found and produce the required memorandum, brief, or opinion letter.

Sometimes the limits to research are set by the nature of the project. An assignment may be limited to a specified number of hours or a certain amount of money. If so, the ability to find information quickly and accurately is essential.

A more difficult decision must be made when there is no clear limit to the amount of research to be done. In such cases you must do enough research to be confident that your work is based on information that is complete and accurate. The surest way to achieve this confidence is to try several approaches to the research problem and compare results. If a review of the secondary literature, a digest search, and online queries produce different conclusions, more research is necessary. When these various

approaches lead to the same primary sources and a single conclusion, chances are better that a key piece of information has not eluded you.

No matter what criteria are used in determining when to stop researching, it is essential to verify that sources to be relied upon are still in force and "good law." No research is complete if the latest supplements haven't been checked, current-awareness sources haven't been searched for new developments, and the status of cases to be relied upon hasn't been determined.

Confidence in your research results is a result of confidence generally in your research skills. Familiarity with legal resources and experience in their use will produce the confidence that your research is complete and accurate.

§ 1–8. CONCLUSION

As we will see in the following chapters, the law has a voluminous literature and a wide range of highly developed research tools. Many of these are unfamiliar even to experienced scholars in other disciplines. Learning to use these tools requires patience and effort, but in time you should become aware of the different functions they serve and they ways they fit together.

Too many practitioners of legal research understand little about the tools they use. As a result, they spin their wheels and overlook aids and shortcuts designed to help them. If you learn how legal resources work as you encounter them, and hone your skills through practice, this mastery will save you valuable time and effort.

CHAPTER 2

BACKGROUND AND ANALYSIS

---

§ 2–1. INTRODUCTION

While it is the primary sources of law—the constitutional provisions, legislative enactments, and judicial decisions—that determine legal rights and govern procedures, these primary sources can be a notoriously labyrinthine place to do research. The prudent researcher looks first for an explanation and analysis of the governing legal doctrines.

Many of the sources discussed in this chapter perform more than one function. One of their most important purposes is to set forth and analyze established legal doctrine, explaining its nuances and leading researchers to understand how a problem fits into this doctrinal structure. They provide the context necessary to see how a particular issue relates to other concerns. They can also provide an introduction to a new area of law or refresh a reader's recollection of a familiar area.

Some secondary sources, particularly treatises and law review articles, contain influential insights that can shape law reform or stimulate new legislation. Others are more practical, providing a straightforward overview of the law as it is without advocating what it should be. Some sources are written primarily for law students and spell out basic doctrines, while others are designed for practicing lawyers and provide guidelines and forms to simplify common procedures.

One function that most secondary sources share is that they provide references to the primary sources which are the next step in research. Most texts and articles discuss the leading cases and major statutes, and contain extensive footnotes leading directly to these and numerous other sources. For the reader these footnote references may be among the more mundane aspects of a secondary source, but for the researcher they can be invaluable.

§ 2–2. OVERVIEWS

Even basic resources such as legal encyclopedias can be daunting to someone new to legal literature. For a start in understanding a legal problem, it may be helpful to begin with resources written for a more general audience.

Several works explain the nature of the American legal system and provide a broad outline of basic institutions and doctrines. Two of the most respected of these are Alan B. Morrison, ed., *Fundamentals of American Law* (1996), and E. Allan Farnsworth, *An Introduction to the Legal System of the United States* (3d ed. 1996). They explain common legal concepts and procedures, survey doctrinal areas such as contract law, corporations, and labor law,

and provide references to major cases and other sources. Farnsworth's book is quite short, but it includes "Suggested Readings" of basic texts in each area it discusses.

Several encyclopedias provide basic coverage of legal issues. One of the broadest and most accessible for general readers is *West's Encyclopedia of American Law* (12 vols. 1998, supplemented by an annual *American Law Yearbook*). *West's Encyclopedia* has more than 4,000 entries, including articles on basic legal doctrines and terminology, major court decisions, government agencies, and influential jurists and lawyers. Its articles are a mix of legal theory, history, and politics. A 15–page overview of "Contracts," for example, is followed by a page on the Republican Party's "Contract with America."

Other reference works cover more specific topics in greater depth. Some, such as Sanford H. Kadish, ed., *Encyclopedia of Crime and Justice* (4 vols. 1983), or Leonard W. Levy et al., eds., *Encyclopedia of the American Constitution* (6 vols., 2d ed. 2000), are well-respected interdisciplinary treatments with contributions from legal scholars as well as historians and political scientists. David M. Walker's *Oxford Companion to Law* (1980) is a one-volume British work providing thorough coverage of major legal concepts and historical figures, including American references.

Works such as these provide a broad perspective on legal issues, and can place these issues in the context of other political or societal concerns. They generally will not, however, answer more specific questions about particular legal situations, and they contain references to

relatively few primary sources. For more detailed coverage, we must turn to works designed specifically for lawyers and law students.

§ 2–3. LEGAL ENCYCLOPEDIAS

Legal encyclopedias are not simply general encyclopedias about legal topics, but works that attempt to describe systematically the entire body of legal doctrine. Articles are arranged alphabetically, and most cover very broad areas such as constitutional law or criminal law.

Encyclopedias are relatively easy to use and provide straightforward summaries of the law, and thus they are among the first law library resources consulted by many students. In most instances, however, their perspective is quite limited. Legal encyclopedias tend to emphasize case law and neglect statutes and regulations, and they rarely consider the historical or societal aspects of the rules they discuss. They are generally not viewed as persuasive secondary authority, but rather as introductory surveys and as tools for case-finding. Their extensive citations to judicial decisions give encyclopedias their major value in legal research.

a. *American Jurisprudence 2d* and *Corpus Juris Secundum*

Two national legal encyclopedias were once competing works but are now both published by West Group: *American Jurisprudence 2d* (*Am. Jur. 2d*) and *Corpus Juris Secundum* (*C.J.S.*). Each of these sets contains more than 120 volumes, with articles on more than 400 broad legal topics. Some articles, such as "Cemeteries" or "Dead Bodies," are narrowly defined and cover just a few dozen pages, but more extensive articles such as "Corporations" or "Evidence" can occupy two or three volumes. Each

article begins with a topical outline of its contents and an explanation of its scope. This is followed by an exhaustive text divided into numbered sections, explaining concepts and providing references to cases and other sources.

While *Am. Jur. 2d* and *C.J.S.* are quite similar, there are differences between these two works. Exhibits 1 and 2 show pages from *Am. Jur.* and *C.J.S.* discussing the scope of the crime of homicide. In *C.J.S.*, but not *Am. Jur. 2d*, each section or subsection begins with a "black letter" summary of its major legal principle. Generally, the discussion in *Am. Jur. 2d* tends to focus a bit more on federal law, while *C.J.S.* seeks to provide an overall synthesis of state law. (Until the 1980s, in fact, it claimed to restate "the entire American law as developed by all reported cases"; recently published volumes are more selective.) Both encyclopedias contain references to West digest key numbers, which can be used to find more cases. *Am. Jur. 2d* also includes footnote references to *ALR*, another case-finding tool, and *C.J.S.* provides cross-references to major treatises.

The discussion in both works is accompanied by copious footnotes to court decisions, but neither work cites any state statutes. The case references provide citations, but most do not indicate the dates of the decisions; only *Am. Jur. 2d* volumes published since 1997 include this useful piece of information.

Volumes in both sets are updated annually with pocket part supplements providing notes of new developments, and each encyclopedia publishes several revised volumes each year. In the instance of Exhibits 1 and 2, the *Am. Jur. 2d* volume was published in 1999 while the *C.J.S.* volume dates from 1991. Some volumes are much older,

used, the size and strength of the party using it, and the person on whom it is used, must all be taken into consideration.[53] A pocketknife, a stone, a walking stick, or the like, may be made a deadly weapon when used with great or furious violence, and especially if the party assailed has comparatively less power than the assailant, or is helpless and feeble.[54]

II. ELEMENTS OF CULPABLE HOMICIDE [§§ 8-11]

Research References

ALR Digest: Homicide §§ 8.5, 23
ALR Index: Criminal Law; Homicide
West Digest, Homicide ☞ 1, 2

§ 8. Killing of human being

Culpable homicide consists in the felonious killing of a human being.[55] Thus, for example, it is not criminal homicide to shoot a dead body.[56] It is not necessary, however, that the indictment describe the deceased as a human being; this may rest in implication arising from other language.[57]

§ 9. —Infant

At common law and in the absence of statute, it is the general rule that if a child dies before birth, the act causing its death is not a crime,[58] although there is also authority to the contrary.[59] If the child is born alive and thereafter dies from the effects of the defendant's felonious act, the culpability is the same as

Annotations: Fact that gun was unloaded as affecting criminal responsibility, 68 A.L.R.4th 507.

53. State v. Sinclair, 120 N.C. 603, 27 S.E. 77 (1897).
The trial court did not err in a murder prosecution by giving a deadly weapon instruction to the jury where the evidence was that defendant had kicked or stomped the victim in the abdomen while wearing cowboy boots. Cowboy boots may be a deadly weapon when worn to kick or stomp an elderly man. State v. Jennings, 333 N.C. 579, 430 S.E.2d 188 (1993), cert. denied, 510 U.S. 1028, 114 S. Ct. 644, 126 L. Ed. 2d 602 (1993) and related reference, 337 N.C. 804, 452 S.E.2d 588 (1994).

54. Acers v. U.S., 164 U.S. 388, 17 S. Ct. 91, 41 L. Ed. 481 (1896) (stone).
An ordinary pocketknife used to stab a four-year-old child in the chest nine times was a deadly weapon. Longoria v. State, 53 Del. 311, 168 A.2d 695 (1961), appeal dismissed, cert. denied, 368 U.S. 10, 82 S. Ct. 18, 7 L. Ed. 2d 18 (1961).
Annotations: Pocket or clasp knife as deadly or dangerous weapon for purposes of statute aggravating offenses such as assault, robbery, or homicide, 100 A.L.R.3d 287.

Walking cane as deadly or dangerous weapon for purpose of statutes aggravating offenses such as assault and robbery, 8 A.L.R.4th 842.

55. Askew v. State, 439 N.E.2d 1350 (Ind. 1982), related reference, 500 N.E.2d 1219 (Ind. 1986), reh'g denied, (Feb. 10, 1987).

56. People v. Dlugash, 41 N.Y.2d 725, 395 N.Y.S.2d 419, 363 N.E.2d 1155 (1977), on remand to, 59 A.D.2d 745, 398 N.Y.S.2d 560 (2d Dep't 1977); State v. Simpson, 244 N.C. 325, 93 S.E.2d 425 (1956).

57. § 217.

58. People v. Ryan, 9 Ill. 2d 467, 138 N.E.2d 516 (1956) (distinguished on other grounds by, People v. Doss, 214 Ill. App. 3d 1051, 158 Ill. Dec. 693, 574 N.E.2d 806 (1st Dist. 1991)); Jackson v. Commonwealth, 265 Ky. 295, 96 S.W.2d 1014 (1936); State v. Gyles, 313 So. 2d 799 (La. 1975); Bennett v. State, 377 P.2d 634 (Wyo. 1963).

59. Com. v. Lawrence, 404 Mass. 378, 536 N.E.2d 571 (1989) (a viable fetus is a human being for the purpose of the common-law crime of murder).

Exhibit 1. 40 Am.Jur.2d *Homicide* §§ 8–9 (1999).

---

the act is voluntary or involuntary.[20] Motive is not an element of any degree of homicide.[21]

§ 3. Persons Subject of Homicide

   a. In general
   b. Unborn child

a. In General

Any living human being may be the subject of a felonious homicide.

Library References

Homicide ⟸1.

LaFave & Scott Substantive Criminal Law Vol. 2 § 7.1(c).

Any human being may be the subject of a felonious homicide.[22] A person ceases to be a human being at death, and no injury to a corpse can be homicide,[23] but the erroneous belief of a murderer that his victim was already dead is immaterial.[24]

A person may be the subject of homicide, although affected with an incurable disease which would have in all probability caused his death within a short time.[25]

b. Unborn Child

Although there is authority to the contrary, generally, an unborn fetus cannot be the subject of a homicide.

Research Note

The killing of a fetus as murder is treated infra § 44. The killing of an unborn child as manslaughter in the first degree is discussed infra § 72.

Under common law,[26] and under some homicide statutes,[27] which have been construed as not including a fetus within the definition of a "person" or "human being" as they use the terms,[28] an unborn fetus, viable or otherwise, cannot be the subject of a homicide. However, if the child is born alive it may be the subject of homicide although its death was caused by injuries inflicted before its birth.[29]

In order to be considered born alive, an infant must have an existence independent of its mother, and derive none of its power of living through any connection with her.[30] Ordinarily, a child becomes fully born so as to be a subject of homicide when the body of the child has been completely delivered and an independent circulation established.[31] According to some authorities, the umbilical cord must have been severed,[32] but, according to others, this is not necessary.[33]

Ordinarily, independent life may be shown by the fact that the child has breathed.[34] However, this test is not infallible,[35] and the fact that the child has breathed is not conclusive of independent life since children sometimes breathe before complete delivery and while placental circulation is still going on;[36] nor is the fact that the child

---

20. Tex.—Simpkins v. State, Cr.App., 590 S.W.2d 129.

21. Ind.—Coleman v. State, 354 N.E.2d 232, 265 Ind. 357.

22. Miss.—State v. Jones, 1 Miss. 83.
Tex.—Perryman v. State, 36 Tex. 321.

Corporations

A corporation cannot be the victim of a homicide.

N.Y.—People v. Ebasco Services Inc., 354 N.Y.S.2d 807, 77 Misc.2d 784.

23. Ky.—Jackson v. Commonwealth, 38 S.W. 422, 100 Ky. 239, rehearing denied 38 S.W. 1091, 100 Ky. 239.

24. Ky.—Jackson v. Commonwealth, 38 S.W. 422, 100 Ky. 239, rehearing denied 38 S.W. 1091, 100 Ky. 239.

25. Cal.—People v. Lanagan, 22 P. 482, 81 C. 142.

26. Cal.—Keeler v. Superior Court of Amador County, 87 Cal.Rptr. 481, 470 P.2d 617, 2 C.3d 619.

Fla.—State v. Gonzalez, App. 3 Dist., 467 So.2d 723, petition denied 476 So.2d 675.

La.—State v. Gyles, 313 So.2d 799.

Ohio—State v. Dickinson, 263 N.E.2d 253, 23 Ohio App.2d 259, 52 O.O.2d 414, affirmed 275 N.E.2d 599, 28 Ohio St.2d 65, 57 O.O.2d 255.

27. Ark.—Meadows v. State, 722 S.W.2d 584, 291 Ark. 105.

Conn.—State v. Anonymous (1986–1), 516 A.2d 156, 40 Conn.Sup. 498.
Ky.—Hollis v. Commonwealth, 652 S.W.2d 61.

W.Va.—State ex rel. Atkinson v. Wilson, 332 S.E.2d 807.

28. Ark.—Meadows v. State, 722 S.W.2d 584, 291 Ark. 105.

Conn.—State v. Anonymous (1986–1), 516 A.2d 156, 40 Conn.Sup. 498.

Ky.—Hollis v. Commonwealth, 652 S.W.2d 61.

N.Y.—People v. Vercelletto, 514 N.Y.S.2d 177, 135 Misc.2d 40.

Utah—State v. Larsen, 578 P.2d 1280.

29. N.J.Super.—State v. Anderson, 343 A.2d 505, 135 N.J.Super. 423, affirmed 413 A.2d 611, 173 N.J.Super. 75, certification denied 425 A.2d 282, two cases, 85 N.J. 124, appeal after remand 426 A.2d 1019, 177 N.J.Super. 334.

Tenn.—Morgan v. State, 256 S.W. 433, 148 Tenn. 417.

30. Ky.—Jackson v. Commonwealth, 96 S.W.2d 1014, 265 Ky. 295.

La.—State v. Gyles, 313 So.2d 799.

Tenn.—Morgan v. State, 256 S.W. 433, 148 Tenn. 417.

31. Tenn.—Morgan v. State, 256 S.W. 433, 148 Tenn. 417.

32. Tenn.—Morgan v. State, 256 S.W. 433, 148 Tenn. 417.

33. Ky.—Jackson v. Commonwealth, 96 S.W.2d 1014, 265 Ky. 295.

34. Tenn.—Morgan v. State, 256 S.W. 433, 148 Tenn. 417.

35. Tenn.—Morgan v. State, 256 S.W. 433, 148 Tenn. 417.

36. Ky.—Jackson v. Commonwealth, 96 S.W.2d 1014, 265 Ky. 295.
Tenn.—Morgan v. State, 256 S.W. 433, 148 Tenn. 417.

Exhibit 2.   40 C.J.S. *Homicide* § 3 (1991).

and researchers may need to be careful not to rely on obsolete information. *Am. Jur. 2d* also includes a *New Topic Service* binder, covering a few newer areas of law which are not covered in the bound volumes. Both encyclopedias, however, are slow to reflect subtle changes in the law or to cover significant trends in developing areas.

The basic means of access to the encyclopedias are the multivolume softcover indexes published annually for each set. It might be possible to browse through an article outline and find a relevant issue, but legal encyclopedias have lengthy articles covering extensive areas of legal doctrine. A pinpoint reference from the index usually saves considerable time. The indexes are very detailed and extensive, but finding the right section may require patience and flexibility. It may be necessary to rethink the terms used or to follow leads in cross-references. Some of these cross-references even refer to separate indexes in the volumes containing specific articles. Each encyclopedia also includes a tables volume listing the federal statutes, regulations, court rules, and uniform laws discussed in the set. Only two *C.J.S.* articles (Insurance and Internal Revenue) are available electronically, through Westlaw, but *Am. Jur. 2d* can be searched through both major database systems.

Am. Jur. 2d is often shelved with several related publications. The *Am. Jur. Deskbook* provides a variety of reference information about the legal system, including outlines of government structure, standards of the legal profession, financial tables, and demographic data of legal interest. There are also several multivolume adjunct sets to *Am. Jur. 2d*, some focusing on trial preparation and practice (*Am. Jur. Trials* and *Am. Jur. Proof of Facts*)

and others providing legal forms (*Am. Jur. Legal Forms 2d* and *Am. Jur. Pleading and Practice Forms*).

b. Jurisdictional Encyclopedias

Several states have multivolume encyclopedias specifically focusing on the law of those jurisdictions. These state encyclopedias often do a better job of tying together statutory and case law than the national encyclopedias. Again, while not generally viewed as authoritative, they can provide both a good general overview of state law and extensive footnotes to primary sources.

Fewer than half of the states have their own legal encyclopedias, but these include the eight most populous jurisdictions (California, Florida, Illinois, Michigan, New York, Ohio, Pennsylvania, and Texas). Several of these sets are available through Lexis–Nexis or Westlaw, as well as in print. Many states have other reference works that provide extensive coverage of their law, although not necessarily made up of alphabetically arranged articles like the national encyclopedias. Sets such as *Kentucky Jurisprudence* and *New Jersey Practice*, for example, contain separate volumes for doctrinal areas such as criminal procedure, domestic relations, and evidence. They may not cover all legal topics comprehensively, but they do address most major areas.

West Group also publishes an encyclopedia focusing specifically on federal law, *Federal Procedure, Lawyers' Edition*. It emphasizes procedural issues in civil, criminal and administrative proceedings, but many of its eighty chapters also discuss matters of substantive federal law. Because it deals exclusively with federal law rather than attempting to generalize about fifty state jurisdictions, it

is often more precise and useful than *C.J.S.* or *Am. Jur. 2d* and includes helpful pointers for federal practice.

§ 2–4.   TEXTS AND TREATISES

Thousands of texts and treatises written by legal scholars and practitioners address topics of substantive and procedural law. These range from multivolume specialized treatises and detailed surveys to short monographs on specific issues or limited aspects of practice in particular jurisdictions.

For centuries, legal treatises have played a vital role in legal research. They analyze the developing common law and contribute their own influence to this development. By synthesizing decisions and statutes, texts and treatises help to impose order on the chaos of individual precedents. Although they lack legal authority and effect, some are written by scholars of outstanding reputation and are well respected by the courts. Other texts offer convenient guides by which practitioners can familiarize themselves with particular fields of law, and often contain practice checklists and sample forms.

There are several distinct types of legal texts:

• Multivolume scholarly surveys of particular fields in depth (e.g., *Moore's Federal Practice*, *Wigmore on Evidence*) provide exhaustive coverage of specific subjects. Many of the original multivolume treatises were written by leading scholars (such as James William Moore or John H. Wigmore), but many today are produced by editorial staffs at publishing companies. While these are not accorded the same level of deference as the work

of a respected scholar, they nonetheless provide extensive commentaries and numerous references to primary sources.

• Hornbooks and law school texts (e.g., *Prosser and Keeton on Torts* or West's Nutshell Series), while written primarily for a student audience, can also be of value to anyone seeking an overview of a doctrinal area. They vary widely in the extent of citations they provide to cases and other sources. These are distinct from the *casebooks* designed as teaching tools, which reprint cases for analysis and discussion and tend to provide less straightforward summary and explanation.

• Practitioners' handbooks and manuals, many published by groups such as the American Law Institute–American Bar Association (ALI–ABA) Joint Committee on Continuing Legal Education or the Practising Law Institute (PLI), are less useful for students but can be invaluable in real life. They tend to address practical concerns, and many provide useful features designed to simplify routine aspects of law practice. Many of these focus on the law of a specific jurisdiction, making them particularly useful in determining quickly the law in force and finding relevant primary sources.

• Scholarly monographs on relatively narrow topics (e.g., Robert H. Bork's *The Antitrust Paradox* or John Hart Ely's *Democracy and Distrust*) are most useful for understanding the history or policy background of a particular area. They are often published by university presses and are similar to scholarly works in other disciplines. Because they are generally not exhaustive in

their coverage of doctrinal issues and are rarely updated on a regular basis, such works are usually not the best sources for current research leads.

• Self-help publications, such as those published by Nolo Press (e.g., *Patent It Yourself* and *Your Rights in the Workplace*), can be useful starting points and often provide clear introductions to areas of law. They may over-simplify complex issues, and they tend to provide fewer leads to primary sources than works designed specifically for lawyers.

For any of these publications to be reliable for coverage of current legal issues, it is important that changes in the law be reflected promptly and accurately. Some form of updating, whether by looseleaf inserts, pocket parts or periodic revision, is usually essential to preserve a treatise or text's value. An outdated text may be of some historical or intellectual interest, but it cannot be relied upon as a statement of today's law.

Although printed texts remain the norm, an increasing number are available electronically. Westlaw provides access to more than 200 treatises, including major works such as and LaFave & Scott's *Substantive Criminal Law*, *McCarthy on Trademarks and Unfair Competition*, Rotunda & Nowak's *Treatise on Constitutional Law*, and Wright & Miller's *Federal Practice and Procedure*. Lexis–Nexis has several Matthew Bender treatises, including *Chisum on Patents*, *Collier on Bankruptcy*, *Moore's Federal Practice*, and *Nimmer on Copyright*. A number of treatises are also available in CD–ROM products focusing on specialized areas of practice. Electronic texts are not necessarily more up-to-date than their print counter-

parts, but full-text searching allows means of access beyond browsing and subject indexes.

There are several ways to find relevant and useful texts and treatises. Usually the basic starting place is a law library's online catalog. A subject search may turn up a large number of publications, but most catalogs allow searches to be limited to recent publications or to books kept in a reserve collection. Online catalogs from other libraries can also be helpful in identifying what resources are available for purchase or interlibrary loan. No law library has every possible text, so research limited to one library's holdings may miss important works. FindLaw's list of law schools by state <lawschools.findlaw.com/schools/bystate.html> includes direct links to library websites. (Union catalogs and other more extensive bibliographic sources will be discussed in Chapter 10, at page 297.)

Following research leads provided by other sources is usually a reliable way to find useful works. Treatises are often cited in cases and law review articles, and such references are likely to lead to works which are considered well-reasoned and reputable. Note in Exhibit 2 on page 25, for instance, that *C.J.S.* provides a cross-reference to LaFave & Scott's *Substantive Criminal Law*, a leading treatise in the area.

There are several printed guides listing legal publications by subject. Most, unfortunately, do not differentiate between major treatises and obscure monographs, and few are updated regularly. James A. McDermott, ed., *Recommended Law Books* (2d ed. 1986) is a useful list of basic materials in over fifty subject areas, annotated with

practitioners' and reviewers' comments. Although it is quite dated, it can still be useful in identifying major respected works. Kendall Svengalis, *Legal Information Buyer's Guide and Reference Manual* (annual) is a more current work with annotated listings of treatises in about 50 subject areas. Its annotations are more descriptive than critical, but they provide useful information about the scope and expense of the treatises works listed. Brian L. Baker & Patrick J. Petit, eds., *Encyclopedia of Legal Information Sources* (2d ed. 1993) provides an unannotated listing of texts, periodicals and looseleaf services in over 400 law-related subjects. Most state legal research guides (listed in Appendix B at page 392) describe or list the treatises and practice materials focusing on the law of particular jurisdictions.

It may be difficult to evaluate texts without extensive use and expertise in the subject area, but several considerations may aid in deciding whether a particular work would be of value in research. These include a text's purpose and intended audience; the reputation of the author and publisher, based on such factors as the value of their previous publications; the organization and scope of the work; the clarity, comprehensiveness and usefulness of its scholarly apparatus (footnotes, tables, index, bibliography, etc.); and the adequacy and timeliness of supplementation.

§ 2–5. RESTATEMENTS OF THE LAW

Some of the most important commentaries on American law are found in the series called *Restatements of the Law*. These American Law Institute texts attempt to organize and articulate the common law rules in selected subject fields. The Restatements' reporters and advisors

are well-known scholars and jurists, and their work is perhaps more persuasive in the courts than any other secondary material.

Each Restatement covers a distinct area of law. The first series of nine Restatements (*Agency, Conflict of Laws, Contracts, Judgments, Property, Restitution, Security, Torts,* and *Trusts*) was published between 1932 and 1946, and after several years a second series (of all the original topics except restitution and security, as well as *Foreign Relations Law*) was issued to reflect new developments or later thinking. Several components of the *Restatement of the Law (Third)* have been published: *Foreign Relations Law* (1987), *Trusts—Prudent Investor Rule* (1992), *Unfair Competition* (1995), *Suretyship and Guaranty* (1996), *Property—Mortgages* (1997), *Torts—Products Liability* (1998), and a portion of *Property—Wills and Other Donative Transfers* (1999). The process of drafting a Restatement is a long one, usually involving the publication of several preliminary and tentative drafts. Projects in progress include two that have reached the "proposed final draft" stage: *The Law Governing Lawyers* and *Torts—Apportionment of Liability*.

The Restatements are divided into sections, each of which contains a basic "black letter" statement of law, followed by explanatory comments and illustrations of particular examples and variations on the general proposition. Exhibit 3 shows a page from the recent Restatement on products liability, illustrating the use of black-letter rule, comment, and illustration.

The comments and illustrations are followed in recent Restatements by Reporter's Notes providing background information on the development of the section. In the

§ **11.** Liability of Commercial Product Seller or Distributor for Harm Caused by Post–Sale Failure to Recall Product

One engaged in the business of selling or otherwise distributing products is subject to liability for harm to persons or property caused by the seller's failure to recall a product after the time of sale or distribution if:

(a)(1) a governmental directive issued pursuant to a statute or administrative regulation specifically requires the seller or distributor to recall the product; or

(2) the seller or distributor, in the absence of a recall requirement under Subsection (a)(1), undertakes to recall the product; and

(b) the seller or distributor fails to act as a reasonable person in recalling the product.

Comment:

a. Rationale. Duties to recall products impose significant burdens on manufacturers. Many product lines are periodically redesigned so that they become safer over time. If every improvement in product safety were to trigger a common-law duty to recall, manufacturers would face incalculable costs every time they sought to make their product lines better and safer. Moreover, even when a product is defective within the meaning of § 2, § 3, or § 4, an involuntary duty to recall should be imposed on the seller only by a governmental directive issued pursuant to statute or regulation. Issues relating to product recalls are best evaluated by governmental agencies capable of gathering adequate data regarding the ramifications of such undertakings. The duty to recall or repair should be distinguished from a post-sale duty to warn about product hazards discovered after sale. See §§ 10 and 13.

Illustration:

1. MNO Corp. has manufactured and distributed washing machines for five years. MNO develops an improved model that includes a safety device that reduces the risk of harm to users. The washing machines sold previously conformed to the best technology available at time of sale and were not defective when sold. MNO is under no common-law obligation to recall previously-distributed machines in order to retrofit them with the new safety device.

b. Failure to recall when recall is specifically required by a governmental directive issued pursuant to statute or other governmental regulation. When a product recall is specifically required by a governmental directive issued pursuant to a statute or regulation, failure reasonably to comply with the relevant directive subjects the seller or other distributor to liability for harm caused by such failure. For the product seller or other distributor to be subject to liability

Exhibit 3. RESTATEMENT (THIRD) OF TORTS—PRODUCTS LIABILITY § 11 (1998).

three earliest Restatements in the second series (*Agency*, *Torts*, and *Trusts*), the Reporter's Notes are not printed after each section but appear in separate appendix volumes. The appendices for these and the other Restatements in the second and third series also contain annotations of court decisions which have applied or interpreted each section. Cases and law review articles citing Restatements can also be found in *Shepard's Restatement of the Law Citations*.

There has been no general index to the Restatements since the first series, but each Restatement includes its own index. The current editions of all Restatements are also accessible online through both Westlaw and Lexis–Nexis. The American Law Institute website <www.ali.org> has information on publications and pending projects, but not the full text.

§ 2–6. LAW REVIEWS

Some of the most influential scholarly commentary in American law appears in the academic legal journals known as law reviews. Some articles have led directly to major changes in legal doctrine. Because several hundred law reviews are published, however, making effective use of these resources requires learning several means of access and evaluating articles carefully.

The law review, edited by law students rather than established scholars, is a form of scholarly publication unknown to most disciplines. Most reviews follow a fairly standard format, containing lengthy *articles* and shorter *essays* by professors and lawyers, as well as *comments* or *notes* by students. Articles and essays by established scholars are more influential, but even the student contributions are usually accompanied by extensive foot-

notes citing to primary sources and other secondary sources. These footnotes help to make law reviews very useful research tools.

Exhibit 4 shows a page from a student comment in a recent law review issue, on a related topic to that discussed in the encyclopedia pages shown earlier in this chapter. Note that one footnote includes a quotation from an 1897 article by Oliver Wendell Holmes, and that others provides citations to statutes from fifteen states and cases from five states.

In addition to general law reviews, there is an ever growing number of specialized academic journals, focusing on topics from animal rights to pharmacy law. Some law schools publish several general and specialized journals. While a few specialized journals have prestigious reputations in their subject areas, for many the primary purpose is to give students the "law review experience." Most specialized journals are student-edited, but a few, such as *Florida Tax Review* and *Supreme Court Review*, are edited by faculty members.

Articles in periodicals and journals can be found through a variety of means. For many students, the most frequently used approach is the full-text databases available through Lexis–Nexis and Westlaw. In addition, however, indexes available in print and online can expand retrieval and focus it more specifically on a topic in question. Other means of finding articles require knowing about a particular case or statute being discussed, and use tools to be discussed in later chapters. Resources such as *Shepard's Citations* or KeyCite (Chapter 4) and annotated codes (Chapter 5) provide references to articles citing cases, statutes, or other documents.

B. Survey of Fetal Rights in the States

Without ever seeing the light of day, or extracting a breath of fresh air, a fetus is gradually acquiring legal protection as a "person" in the United States.[29] By way of legislation[30] or court decisions, half the fifty states prohibit the killing of a fetus outside the domain of legal abortion.[31] In every state, infanticide, the killing of a newborn, is considered homicide.[32] If an infant takes one breath, the infant is legally a child who has been murdered.[33]

---

forbade charging a defendant with homicide for the death of a fetus, Chief Justice Edward Hennessey, quoting Justice Oliver Wendell Holmes, stated:

> [T]he antiquity of a rule is no measure of its soundness. "It is revolting to have no better reason for a rule of law than that so it was laid down in the time of Henry IV. It is still more revolting if the grounds upon which it was laid down have vanished long since, and the rule simply persists from blind imitation of the past."

Id. at 1328 (quoting Oliver Wendell Holmes, *The Path of the Law*, 10 HARV. L. REV. 457, 469 (1897)).

  29. *See* Epstein, *supra* note 12, at A10.

  30. *See* ARIZ. REV. STAT. ANN. § 13-1103(A)(5) (West 1989) (defining "manslaughter" to include "[k]nowingly or recklessly causing the death of an unborn child . . . by any physical injury to the mother"); CAL. PENAL CODE § 187(a) (West 1988); GA. CODE ANN. § 16-5-80 (1988) (stating that feticide is the willful killing of a child "quick," or alive in the mother's womb); 720 ILL. COMP. STAT. ANN. 5/9-1.2 (West 1996) (creating the crime of "intentional homicide of an unborn child"); IND. CODE ANN. § 35-42-1-6 (West 1985) (imposing criminal liability for causing death of a fetus at any state of development); IOWA CODE ANN. § 707.7 (West 1979) (stating that any person who intentionally terminates a pregnancy after the end of the second trimester in which the death of the fetus results commits feticide); LA. REV. STAT. ANN. §§ 14:2(7), 14:32.5-.8 (West 1991); MICH. STAT. ANN. § 28.554 (Law. Co-op. 1990) (prohibiting the "willful killing of an unborn, 'quick' child"); MINN. STAT. ANN. § 609.266-8 (West 1987) (establishing separate homicide statutes encompassing unborn children); N.D. CENT. CODE §§ 12.1-17.1-.01-12.1-17.1-04 (1991); S.C. CODE ANN. § 16-3-10 (Law. Co-op. 1976); S.D. CODIFIED LAWS § 22-17-6 (Michie 1988) (setting up penalty for intentional killing of fetus); TENN. CODE ANN. § 39-13-214 (1990) (including viable fetus within protection of criminal homicide laws); UTAH CODE ANN. § 76-5-201 (1990) (including unborn child within protections of criminal homicide law); WASH. REV. CODE § 9(A) .32.060 (1996) (stating that the intentional and unlawful killing of an unborn, "quick" child by inflicting injury upon the mother is manslaughter).

  31. *See* People v. Davis, 872 P.2d 591, 599 (Cal. 1994) (ruling that it is murder to kill a fetus when the fetus has progressed beyond embryonic state of seven-cight weeks); Commonwealth v. Lawrence, 536 N.E.2d 571, 575-76 (Mass. 1989) (stating that a viable fetus is a person for purposes of common law crime of murder); State v. Merrill, 450 N.W.2d 318, 321 (Minn. 1990) (deciding that unborn child homicide statute was not unconstitutional under the Equal Protection Clause); State v. Horne, 319 S.E.2d 703, 704 (S.C. 1984) (holding that the killing of a viable fetus constituted homicide); Hughes v. State, 868 P.2d 730, 731 (Okla. Crim. App. 1994).

  32. *See* Delsite, *supra* note 11, at F1.

  33. *See id.*

Exhibit 4. Cari L. Leventhal, Comment, *The Crimes Against the Unborn Child Act: Recognizing Potential Human Life in Pennsylvania Criminal Law*, 103 DICK.L.REV. 173, 177 (1998).

Both Westlaw and Lexis–Nexis provide databases containing the text of thousands of articles from several hundred law reviews, with coverage for some reviews extending back to the early 1980s and many more beginning in the 1990s. The two major search methods, natural language and Boolean, will be discussed more extensively in Chapter 4, but both can be useful in searching for law reviews. A natural language search ranks articles for relevance, and finds those that discuss search concepts at greatest length. A Boolean keyword search can be used to find articles using any particular combination of words, including phrases, case names, or titles of other articles or books. Even if an article retrieved is not directly on point, footnote references matching the query can often lead to relevant treatises and articles in law review volumes predating online coverage or in journals outside the legal field.

Free Internet sites provide some access to recent law review literature, as the number and quality of law review websites improve. Some websites feature only tables of contents or abstracts, but a growing number are making the full text of articles available. A few law reviews, such as *Michigan Telecommunications and Technology Law Review* <www.mttlr.org>, are published only electronically. Lists of journals, such as those at FindLaw <lawschools.findlaw.com/journals/> and the University of Southern California <www.usc.edu/dept/law-lib/legal/journals.html> note which reviews provide the full text of articles.

At this point, searching of law reviews on the Internet is rather primitive. Some reviews allow full-text searching of their articles, but searches limited to a specific review are too narrow for most purposes. A few sites, such

as the University Law Review Project <www.lawreview. org>, permit searches of multiple sources, but coverage is quite slim compared to the huge databases available through Lexis–Nexis or Westlaw. It may be possible, however, to find one or two useful articles and gain entry into the broader scholarly literature.

Fulltext searches are powerful tools, but they do have drawbacks. Searching for particular terms can retrieve too many extraneous articles that only mention these terms in passing, not just those that focus specifically on a particular subject. In addition, there remain thousands of law review articles that are not available electronically and might never be found through online searches. For these reasons, periodical indexes remain valuable resources.

Two general indexes to English-language legal periodical literature are published. Both are available in printed volumes with monthly updating pamphlets, on CD–ROM, and online through Westlaw, Lexis–Nexis, and subscription Internet sites.

The older of the two indexes is *Index to Legal Periodicals and Books* (*ILP*), which began publication in 1908. (Earlier articles are covered by the Jones–Chipman *Index to Legal Periodical Literature*, with indexing back to 1803.) *ILP* indexes more than 700 legal periodicals by subject and author, in a format similar to the *Readers Guide to Periodical Literature*. (Books were added to *ILP*'s coverage, and title, in 1994.) Since 1983 articles have been indexed under both subject and author; earlier volumes have bibliographic information only under the subject entries, with cross-references from author entries to the subject headings. *ILP* also includes tables of cases

and statutes that are the focus of articles, and a book review section. Exhibit 5 shows a page from its subject/author index, with an entry under the "Homicide" heading for the student comment shown in Exhibit 4.

The newer index, which began publication in 1980, is issued in several formats under various names: *Current Law Index* (*CLI*), *LegalTrac*, and *Legal Resource Index* (*LRI*). It provides access to more than 800 legal and law-related periodicals, using detailed Library of Congress subject headings with extensive subheadings and cross-references. The printed version, *Current Law Index*, has separate indexes for subjects and authors, as well as case and statute tables.

The electronic versions of both indexes combine several annual volumes into one database, with coverage back to 1980 (*LegalTrac*, *LRI*) or 1981 (*ILP*). *ILP* is part of the WilsonDisc and WilsonWeb systems, and *LegalTrac* operates on Gale Group's InfoTrac CD–ROM and Internet platforms. Both databases are also available through Westlaw and Lexis–Nexis, although not all subscribers have access. *LegalTrac* and *LRI* are somewhat broader in scope than *CLI*, and include citations to several legal newspapers and to relevant articles in non-law periodicals. Any of these electronic versions allow the researcher either to use the subject headings assigned by the indexers or to create customized keyword searches that would be impossible with printed sources. Exhibit 6 shows records for three articles found by searching for "homicide" and "unborn children" (including the comment in Exhibit 4) through the Internet version of *LegalTrac*.

Law reviews are but one of several types of legal periodicals. More specialized and practice-oriented

74 INDEX TO LEGAL PERIODICALS & BOOKS

History—*cont.*
  Historical development of the year 2000 problem: challenging the conventional wisdom. R. D. Williams, B. T. Smyth. 16 no2 *Computer Law.* 7-15 F '99; 16 no3 *Computer Law.* 25-30 Mr '99; 16 no4 *Computer Law.* 10-20 Ap '99
  Reflection on the Treaty of Guadalupe Hidalgo and the border it established. R. I. Rochín. 5 no1 *Sw. J.L. & Trade Am.* 141-6 Spr '98
  The use and abuse of history: the Supreme Court's interpretation of Thomas Jefferson's influence on the patent law. E. C. Walterscheid. 39 no2 *IDEA: J.L. & Tech.* 195-224 '99

    Greece
  The politics of law, language, & morality: Thucydides & the abortion debate. P. Hau, student author. 8 no2 *S. Cal. Interdisc. L.J.* 711-42 Spr '99

    Rwanda
  A lesson unlearned: the unjust revolution in Rwanda, 1959-1961. L. C. Marlin. 12 no3 *Emory Int'l L. Rev.* 1271-329 Fall '98

Hitchings, Paul
  Access to international telecommunications facilities. 19 no2 *Eur. Compet. L. Rev.* 85-98 F '98
HIV Infection *See* AIDS (Disease)
HMOs *See* Health care industry
Ho, Victoria M.
  A seven-step analysis of equitable distribution in Florida. Classification and valuation of marital property. Distributing marital property (Pt2); by V. M. Ho, J. R. Brigman. 73 no5 *Fla. B.J.* 62-8 My '99; 73 no6 *Fla. B.J.* 94-8 Je '99
Hoberman, Lori S.
  Receipt of partnership interest in exchange for services: still polishing the Diamond [Diamond v. Commissioner, 492 F.2d 286 (1974)] 15 no4 *J. Partnership Tax'n* 336-53 Wint '99
Hochberg, Melanie
  Protecting students against peer sexual harassment: Congress's constitutional powers to pass Title IX. 74 no1 *N.Y.U. L. Rev.* 235-76 Ap '99
Hodge, James Blythe
  Legal aspects of the year 2000 problem; by J. B. Hodge, G. P. Fondo, C. F. Van den Bosch. 39 no3 *Santa Clara L. Rev.* 657-718 '99
Hodgson, Douglas
  See/See also the following book(s):
  The human right to education. Ashgate 1998 233p
    ISBN 1-85521-909-3   LC 98-3167
Hoefling, Tricia A.
  The (draft) WIPO arbitration rules for administrative challenge panel procedures concerning Internet domain names. 8 no2 *Am. Rev. Int'l Arb.* 271-301 '97
Høegh, Katja
  The EU directives on public procurement—Danish experiences; by J. Jordahn, K. Høegh. 15 pt1 *Int'l Constr. L. Rev.* 5-13 Ja '98
Hogan, Gerard
  The cabinet confidentiality referendum. 4 no2 *Eur. Pub. L.* 160-5 Je '98
Hogan, Sarah B.
  To Net or not to Net: Singapore's regulation of the Internet. 51 no2 *Fed. Comm. L.J.* 429-47 Mr '99
Hogler, Raymond
  The law, economics, and politics of right to work: Colorado's Labor Peace Act and its implications for public policy; by R. Hogler, S. Shulman. 70 no3 *U. Colo. L. Rev.* 871-951 Summ '99
Holden, James P.
  1999 Erwin N. Griswold Lecture before the American College of Tax Counsel: dealing with the aggressive corporate tax shelter problem. 52 no2 *Tax Law.* 369-80 Wint '99
Holding companies
  See also
  Bank holding companies
Hollingsworth, Danny P.
  Beware of FLP traps. 30 no4 *Tax Adviser* 256-61 Ap '99
  Why give an IRA to charity? by D. L. Chesser, M. J. Gulig, D. P. Hollingsworth. 30 no3 *Tax Adviser* 162-7 Mr '99
Holly, Wayne D.
  Criminal and civil consequences of false oaths in bankruptcy help ensure reliable information. 71 no3 *N.Y. St. B.J.* 38-45 Mr '99
Holmes, Oliver Wendell, 1841-1935
    about
  Holmes and the romantic mind. A. C. Dailey. 48 no3 *Duke L.J.* 429-510 D '98
  Non-representational jurisprudence: a centennial reading of "The path of the law". [O. W. Holmes. 110 *Harv. L. Rev.* 991-1009 '97] R. E. Rodes, Jr. 42 *Am. J. Juris.* 263-75 '97

Oliver Wendell Holmes and the decline of the American lawyer: social engineering, religion, and the search for professional identity. M. P. Schutt. 30 no1 *Rutgers L.J.* 143-208 Fall '98
Holmwood, Amy
  Split-dollar life insurance: an old friend with new wrinkles; by B. H. London, L. Kreisberg, A. Holmwood. 138 no4 *Tr. & Est.* 48-52 Mr '99
Home rule
    Massachusetts
  Home rule, potholes and preemption. D. M. Moore. 83 no4 *Mass. L. Rev.* 137-46 Spr '99
    Washington (D.C.)
  Federal influence on sentencing policy in the District of Columbia: an oppressive and dangerous experiment. R. L. Wilkins. 11 no3 *Fed. Sentencing Rep.* 143-8 N/D '98
Homestead
  See also
  Bankruptcy exemptions
    California
  First-to-file, last-in-line: after Jones v. Heskett [106 F.3d 923 (9th Cir. 1997)], creditors dragged into bankruptcy lose the state law race of the diligent. P. Epstein, student author. 33 no2 *U.S.F. L. Rev.* 285-312 Wint '99
Homicide
  Children and guns. S. DeFrancesco. 19 no2 *Pace L. Rev.* 275-84 Wint '99
  Murder by premeditation. M. A. Pauley. 36 no2 *Am. Crim. L. Rev.* 145-69 Spr '99
    Canada
  Latimer [R. v. Latimer [1998] 121 C.C.C.3d 326], Davis and Doerksen: Mercy killing and assisted suicide on the Op. Ed. page. B. Sneiderman. 25 no3 *Man. L.J.* 449-66 '98
    England
  Can you forgive her?: Legal ambivalence toward infanticide. K. Lewicki, student author. 8 no2 *S. Cal. Interdisc. L.J.* 683-710 Spr '99
    Missouri
  Clemency: doing justice to incarcerated battered children. R. Hegadorn. 55 no2 *J. Mo. B.* 70-83 Mr/Ap '99
    Pennsylvania
  The crimes against the Unborn Child Act: recognizing potential human life in Pennsylvania criminal law. C. L. Leventhal, student author. 103 no1 *Dick. L. Rev.* 173-97 Fall '98

  See/See also the following book(s):
  Pohlman, H. L. The whole truth; a case of murder on the Appalachian Trail. University of Mass. Press 1999 249p
Homosexuality and lesbianism
    See also
    Domestic partners
    Employment discrimination—Gays and lesbians
    Sexual orientation discrimination
    Transsexualism
    Pennsylvania
  See/See also the following book(s):
  Pohlman, H. L. The whole truth; a case of murder on the Appalachian Trail. University of Mass. Press 1999 249p
Hopkins, John
  Devolution from a comparative perspective. 4 no3 *Eur. Pub. L.* 323-33 S '98
Horizontal antitrust restraints
  The extraterritorial application of the U.S. antitrust laws to criminal conspiracies. R. M. Reynolds, J. Sicilian, P. S. Wellman. 19 no3 *Eur. Compet. L. Rev.* 151-5 Mr '98
Horowitz, Darryl J.
  See/See also the following book(s):
  California mechanic's lien law. Coleman & Horowitz 1998 93p
    LC 98-141453
Horvath, RoseMarie R.
  Recent developments affecting self-insurers and risk managers; by K. D. Smith, R. R. Horvath. 34 no2 *Tort & Ins. L.J.* 655-67 Wint '99
Horwich, John L.
  Environmental planning: lessons from New South Wales, Australia in the integration of land-use planning and environmental protection. 17 no3 *Va. Envtl. L.J.* 267-356 Spr '98
Hospices *See* Hospitals
Hospital records *See* Medical records
Hospitals
    See also
    Nursing homes
  Sales of not-for-profit hospitals to for-profit corporations. C. D. Fox, C. Kelly. 137 no11 *Tr. & Est.* 38+ O '98
  The use of the nonprofit "defense" under Section 7 of the Clayton Act. A. J. Vaughn, student author. 52 no2 *Vand. L. Rev.* 557-98 Mr '99

Exhibit 5. INDEX TO LEGAL PERIODICALS & BOOKS, July 1999, at 74.

Dickinson Law Review, Fall 1998 v103 i1 p173-197

The Crimes Against the Unborn Child Act: recognizing potential human life in Pennsylvania criminal law. *Cari L. Leventhal.*

Subjects　　Unborn children (Law) - Laws, regulations, etc.
　　　　　　　　Fetal death - Laws, regulations, etc.
　　　　　　　　Homicide - Laws, regulations, etc.
　　　　　　　　Pregnant women - Laws, regulations, etc.

Locations　Pennsylvania

Article A54690561

Hastings Constitutional Law Quarterly, Spring 1998 v25 i3 p457-481

Fetal homicide laws: shield against domestic violence or sword to pierce abortion rights? *Alison Tsao.*

Subjects　　Homicide - Laws, regulations, etc.
　　　　　　　　Unborn children (Law) - Protection
　　　　　　　　Abortion - Comparative method

Locations　States

Article A53405045

Journal of Criminal Law, Feb 1997 61 n1 p86-94

The unborn child and the limits of homicide. (United Kingdom) *John Beaumont.*

Subjects　　Homicide - Litigation
　　　　　　　　Unborn children (Law) - Litigation

Cases　　　Attorney General's Reference No. 3 of 1994 - (1996) 2 All E.R. 10 (C.A.)

Locations　United Kingdom

Article A19305724

Exhibit 6. Legal Trac website printout.

sources such as bar magazines, legal newspapers, and newsletters, as well as tools providing notice of newly published articles, are considered below in Chapter 9.

§ 2–7. CONCLUSION

This brief survey of major secondary sources focuses on general resources that are likely to be of the most assistance to beginning researchers. Encyclopedias, texts, Restatements, and law review articles are essential tools for someone starting out in analyzing a legal problem. They provide a broad introductory overview of legal doctrine and provide references to the primary sources that must be examined.

Secondary legal literature is much more extensive than these few materials, and additional resources will be discussed in later chapters. These general tools, however, can provide a solid basis for successful research of most legal issues.

CHAPTER 3

CASE LAW SOURCES

----

§ 3–1. INTRODUCTION

Reports of judicial decisions are among the most important sources of legal authority in the common law system. Over the course of time, judges shape legal doctrines to address the complex issues of changing society. Despite the ever increasing scope of legislative enactments, case law continues to retain its vitality. Even statutes which may appear straightforward must be read in light of the court decisions which construe and apply their provisions.

To use court reports effectively, it is necessary to understand the hierarchical structure of the American judicial system. Litigation usually begins in a *trial court*. The jurisdiction of these courts may be based on geography (the U.S. District Courts in the federal system, or county courts in many states) or subject (the U.S. Tax Court, or

state family courts and probate courts). In the trial court, *issues of fact* (such as which of two cars entered an intersection first) are decided by the fact finder, either the judge or a jury. These findings are binding on the parties and cannot be appealed. *Issues of law* (such as whether a witness's statement is admissible at trial) are decided by the judge, and a party who disagrees with these rulings can appeal them to a higher court.

Appeals from the decisions of trial courts are generally taken to an *intermediate appellate court* (the U.S. Courts of Appeals and similar state tribunals). An appellate court usually consists of three or more judges, who confer and vote on the issues after considering written briefs and oral argument by the lawyers for each side. One of the judges writes an opinion summarizing the question and stating the court's holding. Dissenting judges may write separate opinions outlining their views.

The *court of last resort* in each jurisdiction (called the Supreme Court in the federal system and in most states) usually reviews cases from the intermediate appellate courts, but may take appeals directly from the trial court. Most courts of last resort have discretion in deciding which cases they will hear. Their role in the judicial system is not to resolve every individual dispute, but rather to establish rules, review legislative and administrative acts, and resolve differences among intermediate appellate courts. A court of last resort's decisions on issues of law are binding on all trial and intermediate appellate courts in its jurisdiction.

Numerous works provide more extensive discussions of the role of judges in deciding cases and creating legal doctrine. Among the more concise introductory works are

two books by Daniel John Meador, *American Courts* (1991) and *Appellate Courts in the United States* (1994, with Jordana Simone Bernstein).

Most court reports consist of the decisions of appellate courts on issues of law. Very few trial court decisions are published. Trial court decisions on issues of fact have no precedential effect and usually do not even result in written judicial opinions. A jury verdict at the end of a trial, for example, produces no published decision unless the judge must decide a motion challenging the verdict on legal grounds. Some trial court decisions on issues of law are published, but they are generally less important than appellate court decisions. Selected intermediate appellate court decisions and nearly all decisions from courts of last resort are published both in printed volumes and electronically.

A bit of history may help in understanding court reports. The American colonies inherited the English legal system and its common law tradition. No decisions of American courts were published during the colonial period, so lawyers and judges had to rely on English precedents. The first volume of American decisions, *Kirby's Reports* in Connecticut, was published in 1789. Reports from other states, and from the new Supreme Court of the United States, soon followed. *Official* series of court reports (published pursuant to statutory direction or court authorization) began in several states in the early 1800s. Many of these early reports were cited by the names of their reporters and are known as *nominative reports*.

As the country grew in the 19th century, the number of reported decisions increased dramatically and official

reporting systems began to lag further and further behind. The need for improved and more timely access to cases was met by commercial publishers. In 1876, John B. West began publishing selected decisions of the Minnesota Supreme Court in a weekly leaflet, the *Syllabi*. Three years later he launched the *North Western Reporter*, covering five surrounding states as well as Minnesota. By 1887 West published cases from every state and the federal system, in what became West Group's National Reporter System. These reporters continue to be widely used today. Exhibit 7 shows the beginning of a case in *West's Pacific Reporter*.

In recent years the major development in access to court decisions has been electronic dissemination, through a variety of computerized means. New decisions can be made available electronically before they are published in print form. The most widespread electronic resources are the commercial databases Westlaw and Lexis–Nexis, but a number of smaller commercial providers and numerous government and law school Internet sites also provide access to court decisions.

The first appearance of a new decision is the official *slip opinion* issued by the court itself, usually an individually paginated copy of a single decision. Slip opinions provide the text of new cases and are often available free from official court websites, but they have two major drawbacks for research purposes. They rarely provide editorial enhancements summarizing the court's decision and facilitating the research process, and they must be cited by docket number and date rather than to a permanent published source. Several jurisdictions have ameliorated this second problem by assigning public domain citations to their recent cases. Such opinions are numbered se-

1999 UT App 089

STATE of Utah, Plaintiff and Appellee,

v.

Kalob Ted KEPPLER, Defendant and Appellant.

No. 981182–CA.

Court of Appeals of Utah.

March 25, 1999.

Defendant, who had previously pled guilty to possession of drug paraphernalia, entered conditional guilty plea to possession of methamphetamine in the First District Court, Brigham City Department, Ben H. Hadfield, J., and he appealed. The Court of Appeals, Billings, J., held that prosecution of defendant for possession of methamphetamine was not barred by single criminal episode statute.

Affirmed.

1. Criminal Law ⚖ 1134(3), 1158(1)

The Court of Appeals reviews the trial court's interpretation of a statute for correctness and accords no deference to its conclusions of law.

2. Criminal Law ⚖ 29(8)

Prosecution of defendant for possession of methamphetamine following his guilty plea to possession of drug paraphernalia was not barred by "single criminal episode statute,"even though paraphernalia and methamphetamine were found at the same time and in the same location their possession did not satisfy the same criminal objective requirement of the statute; crimes were separate statutory offenses and property implicated was not the same quality. U.C.A.1953, 58–37–8(2), 58–37a–5(1), 76–1–401.

Kevin McGaha, Brigham City, for Appellant.

Jan Graham, Atty. Gen. and James Beadles, Asst. Atty. Gen., Salt Lake City, for Appellee.

Before WILKINS, P.J., GREENWOOD, Associate P.J., and BILLINGS, J.

OPINION

BILLINGS, Judge:

¶ 1 Kalob Ted Keppler (defendant) appeals from a conditional guilty plea for possession of a controlled substance, a third degree felony. We affirm.

BACKGROUND

¶ 2 On April 5, 1997, in a search incident to an arrest, defendant was found in possession of marijuana, methamphetamine, and a pipe with marijuana residue. Defendant was cited for possession of drug paraphernalia and on April 14, 1997, he pleaded guilty to that offense, a class B misdemeanor, and was sentenced to probation. That same day, the State filed an information charging defendant with possession of methamphetamine, possession of a controlled substance, and possession of drug paraphernalia. These charges all arose from the evidence discovered during the April 5th search.

¶ 3 Defendant filed a motion to dismiss, arguing that his guilty plea to possession of paraphernalia barred the district court prosecutions because the offenses were all part of the same criminal episode under Utah Code Ann. § 76–1–403(1)(a) (1995). The trial court denied the motion to dismiss and defendant subsequently entered a conditional guilty plea to possession of methamphetamine, reserving his right to appeal. The State had already dismissed the other charges.

ANALYSIS

[1] ¶ 4 This appeal presents a single question: Whether, under the "single criminal episode" statute, *see id.* § 76–1–403(1), a prosecution for possession of methamphetamine is barred when defendant had already pleaded guilty to possession of drug paraphernalia found at the same time and in the same location as the methamphetamine. We review the trial court's interpretation of a statute for correctness and accord no deference to its conclusions of law. *State v. Brooks,* 908 P.2d 856, 859 (Utah 1995).

Exhibit 7.   *State v. Keppler,* 976 P.2d 99 (Utah App. 1999).

quentially as they are issued, and each paragraph is numbered so that a particular point in an opinion can be identified. The public domain citation for the case in Exhibit 7, *State v. Keppler*, is 1999 UT App 089, indicating that this is the 89th decision delivered in 1999 by the Court of Appeals of Utah. The page shown includes the first four numbered paragraphs of the court's opinion.

The next form of court reports provides the editorial summaries and easily cited sources lacking in slip opinions. These usually appear first in weekly or biweekly pamphlets known as *advance sheets*, containing a number of decisions paginated in a continuous sequence, and then in bound volumes. The volumes consolidate the cases from several advance sheets, and most contain alphabetical tables of the cases reported as well as subject indexes or digests. They are numbered consecutively, often in more than one series. When the volumes of a reporter reach an arbitrary number (such as 100 or 300), publishers frequently start over with volume 1, second series. Some reporters are now in their third or fourth series. If a reporter is in a second or later series, that must be indicated in its citation in order to distinguish it from the same volume number in the first series. The case in Exhibit 7, for example, is on page 99 of volume 976 of the second series of the *Pacific Reporter*. It is cited as *State v. Keppler*, 976 P.2d 99 (Utah App. 1999).

Court reports generally include editorial features which make it easier to find and understand the court decisions. In West's National Reporter System series, each case is prefaced with a one-paragraph summary of its holding, called a *synopsis*, and with numbered editorial abstracts, or *headnotes*, of the specific legal issues. Each headnote is assigned a legal topic and a number

indicating a particular subdivision of that topic. This classification plan, known as the *key number system*, allows uniform subject access to the cases of different jurisdictions. The headnotes are reprinted by subject in digests, which will be discussed in Chapter 4. *State v. Keppler* in Exhibit 7 has two numbered headnotes, both in the Criminal Law topic. The first headnote corresponds to the last paragraph on the page, as is indicated by the bracketed [1] that precedes the paragraph.

Exhibit 7 includes several other standard features of court reports. Immediately below the names of the parties is the docket number, useful for tracking down briefs and other information. At the bottom of the left column are the names of the lawyers representing the parties. The right column begins with the names of the judges who heard the case, and identifies the judge writing the majority opinion.

§ 3–2.　SUPREME COURT OF THE UNITED STATES

The Supreme Court of the United States stands at the head of the judicial branch of government, and determines the scope and interpretation of the Constitution and federal statutes. Its decisions are studied not only by lawyers but by political scientists, historians, and citizens interested in the development of social and legal policy.

The Supreme Court is the court of last resort in the federal court system and also has the final word on federal issues raised in state courts. The Court exercises a tight control over its docket and has wide discretion to decline review, or to *deny a writ of certiorari* as it is called in almost all cases. The Supreme Court usually accepts for consideration only those cases that raise significant

policy issues. In recent years it has issued opinions in fewer than 100 cases during its annual term, which begins on the first Monday of October and ends in late June or early July.

Numerous reference works explain the history and role of the Supreme Court in the American political and legal system. Leonard W. Levy et al., eds., *Encyclopedia of the American Constitution* (6 vols., 2d ed. 2000), and Kermit L. Hall, ed., *Oxford Companion to the Supreme Court* (1992), both provide encyclopedic coverage of the Court, including articles on major cases, doctrinal areas, and individual justices. Joan Biskupic & Elder Witt, *Guide to the U.S. Supreme Court* (2 vols., 3d ed. 1996) is arranged thematically rather than alphabetically, but it too explains major doctrines and provides historical background. The major practical guide for lawyers bringing a case before the Court is Robert L. Stern et al., *Supreme Court Practice* (7th ed. 1993).

Reference works are useful for historical and general background, but they cannot cover the latest developments and they are no substitute for reading the opinions of the Supreme Court. The Court makes law through its decisions in individual cases. These decisions are available in a variety of printed and electronic means. They are published in three permanent bound reporters and in a weekly newsletter providing prompt access to new decisions, and they can be searched and retrieved through several commercial databases and free Internet sites.

a.   The *United States Reports*

Begun in 1790 as a private venture, the *United States Reports* (cited as U.S.) became official in 1817 and continues today as the official edition of United States Supreme

Court decisions. Several volumes of *U.S. Reports* are published every year. Following the general pattern of publication, the decisions appear first in slip opinion form, followed by an official advance sheet (called the "preliminary print"), and finally the bound *U.S. Reports* volume. Unfortunately, as with many government publications, the *U.S. Reports* tends to be published quite slowly. More than a year passes before a decision appears in the preliminary print, and two more years before its inclusion in a bound volume. (In contrast, the decisions are available electronically within minutes of their issuance.)

The early volumes of Supreme Court decisions are now numbered sequentially as part of the *U.S. Reports* series, but for many years they were cited only by the names of the individual reporters. Even now citations to these early cases include a parenthetical reference to the nominative reporter volume, as in *Marbury v. Madison*, 5 U.S. (1 Cranch) 137 (1803). Some familiarity with the following reporters' names and their periods of coverage will make it easier to read and understand older citations:

Nominative Reports			**U.S. Reports**
Dallas	1–4	(1790–1800)	1–4
Cranch	1–9	(1801–1815)	5–13
Wheaton	1–12	(1816–1827)	14–25
Peters	1–16	(1828–1842)	26–41
Howard	1–24	(1843–1860)	42–65
Black	1–2	(1861–1862)	66–67
Wallace	1–23	(1863–1874)	68–90

After volume 90 (1874), cases are cited only by volume number of the *U.S. Reports*. Thus the official citation of the Supreme Court's decision in *Oncale v. Sundowner Offshore Services, Inc.* is 523 U.S. 75 (1998), meaning the

case beginning on page 75 of volume 523 of the *U.S. Reports*. The opening pages of the official report of *Oncale* appear in Exhibits 8 and 9. This version does not include numbered headnotes, but the Court's reporter of decisions prefaces the text of each decision with a *syllabus* summarizing the case and the Court's holding. This syllabus is shown in Exhibit 8. Exhibit 9 identifies the attorneys in the case and shows the beginning of the majority opinion by Justice Scalia.

b.   *Supreme Court Reporter* and *Lawyers' Edition*

Because the *U.S. Reports* is published so slowly, the need for more timely publication is met by several commercial versions. Two of these publications, West Group's *Supreme Court Reporter* (cited as S. Ct.) and Lexis Publishing's *United States Supreme Court Reports, Lawyers' Edition* (known simply as *Lawyers' Edition*, and cited as L. Ed.) are not only published in advance sheets within a few weeks of decision; they also have a permanent value because they are later published in bound volumes with editorial research aids not in the official edition.

The *Supreme Court Reporter* began in 1882, with cases from volume 106 of the *U.S. Reports*. As a component of West's National Reporter System, it includes the publisher's editorial synopses and headnotes. Each headnote is designated by topic and assigned to a classified key number within the topic. Subject access to the headnotes is provided in the *United States Supreme Court Digest*, a companion set to the reporter. Since the same key number system is used for court decisions throughout the country, the same point of law can also be researched in digests covering other federal courts and state courts. The opening page of *Oncale v. Sundowner Offshore Services, Inc.* as

Syllabus

ONCALE *v.* SUNDOWNER OFFSHORE SERVICES, INC., ET AL.

CERTIORARI TO THE UNITED STATES COURT OF APPEALS FOR THE FIFTH CIRCUIT

No. 96–568.   Argued December 3, 1997—Decided March 4, 1998

Petitioner Oncale filed a complaint against his employer, respondent Sundowner Offshore Services, Inc., claiming that sexual harassment directed against him by respondent co-workers in their workplace constituted "discriminat[ion] . . . because of . . . sex" prohibited by Title VII of the Civil Rights Act of 1964, 42 U. S. C. § 2000e–2(a)(1).   Relying on Fifth Circuit precedent, the District Court held that Oncale, a male, had no Title VII cause of action for harassment by male co-workers.   The Fifth Circuit affirmed.

Held: Sex discrimination consisting of same-sex sexual harassment is actionable under Title VII.   Title VII's prohibition of discrimination "because of . . . sex" protects men as well as women, *Newport News Shipbuilding & Dry Dock Co. v. EEOC,* 462 U. S. 669, 682, and in the related context of racial discrimination in the workplace this Court has rejected any conclusive presumption that an employer will not discriminate against members of his own race, *Castaneda* v. *Partida,* 430 U. S. 482, 499.   There is no justification in Title VII's language or the Court's precedents for a categorical rule barring a claim of discrimination "because of . . . sex" merely because the plaintiff and the defendant (or the person charged with acting on behalf of the defendant) are of the same sex.   Recognizing liability for same-sex harassment will not transform Title VII into a general civility code for the American workplace, since Title VII is directed at discrimination because of sex, not merely conduct tinged with offensive sexual connotations; since the statute does not reach genuine but innocuous differences in the ways men and women routinely interact with members of the same, and the opposite, sex; and since the objective severity of harassment should be judged from the perspective of a reasonable person in the plaintiff's position, considering all the circumstances.   Pp. 78–82.

83 F. 3d 118, reversed and remanded.

SCALIA, J., delivered the opinion for a unanimous Court.   THOMAS, J., filed a concurring opinion, *post,* p. 82.

Exhibit 8. *Oncale v. Sundowner Offshore Services, Inc.,* 523 U.S. 75 (1998).

76   ONCALE *v.* SUNDOWNER OFFSHORE SERVICES, INC.

Opinion of the Court

Nicholas Canaday III argued the cause for petitioner. With him on the briefs were *Andre P. LaPlace* and *Eric Schnapper.*

Deputy Solicitor General Kneedler argued the cause for the United States as *amicus curiae* urging reversal. On the brief were *Acting Solicitor General Dellinger, Acting Assistant Attorney General Pinzler, Deputy Solicitor General Waxman, Beth S. Brinkmann, C. Gregory Stewart, J. Ray Terry, Jr., Gwendolyn Young Reams,* and *Carolyn L. Wheeler.*

Harry M. Reasoner argued the cause for respondents. With him on the brief were *John H. Smither, Marie R. Yeates, Thomas H. Wilson,* and *Samuel Issacharoff.*[*]

JUSTICE SCALIA delivered the opinion of the Court.

This case presents the question whether workplace harassment can violate Title VII's prohibition against "discriminat[ion] . . . because of . . . sex," 42 U. S. C. § 2000e–2(a)(1), when the harasser and the harassed employee are of the same sex.

I

The District Court having granted summary judgment for respondent, we must assume the facts to be as alleged by petitioner Joseph Oncale. The precise details are irrelevant

---

[*]Briefs of *amici curiae* urging reversal were filed for the Association of Trial Lawyers of America by *Ellen Simon Sacks* and *Christopher P. Thorman;* for the Lambda Legal Defense and Education Fund et al. by *Beatrice Dohrn, John Davidson, Ruth Harlow, Steven R. Shapiro, Sara L. Mandelbaum,* and *Minna J. Kotkin;* for the National Employment Lawyers Association by *Margaret A. Harris* and *Anne Golden;* for the National Organization on Male Sexual Victimization, Inc., by *Catharine A. MacKinnon;* and for Law Professors by *Nan D. Hunter.*

Briefs of *amici curiae* urging affirmance were filed for the Equal Employment Advisory Council by *Robert E. Williams* and *Ann Elizabeth Reesman;* and for the Texas Association of Business & Chambers of Commerce by *Jeffrey C. Londa* and *Linda Ottinger Headley.*

Exhibit 9.   *Oncale v. Sundowner Offshore Services, Inc.,* 523 U.S. 75, 76 (1998).

it appears in the *Supreme Court Reporter* at 118 S. Ct. 998 is shown in Exhibit 10 and the synopsis and first few headnotes.

Lawyers' Edition contains all Supreme Court decisions since the Court's inception in 1790. It is now in a second series, and its version of *Oncale* is cited as 140 L. Ed. 2d 201 (1998). Like the *Supreme Court Reporter*, *Lawyers' Edition* contains editorial summaries and headnotes for each case. Its headnotes are reprinted, arranged by topic, in the companion set to the reports, *United States Supreme Court Digest, Lawyers' Edition*. The *Lawyers' Edition* classification system, however, does not appear in other reports, so it is useful only for Supreme Court research. The headnotes are followed by "Research References," providing citations to relevant coverage in legal encyclopedias, digests, annotations, and the *United States Code*.

At the back of each *Lawyers' Edition* volume are two features not found in the *U.S. Reports* or the *Supreme Court Reporter*: legal analyses, or *annotations*, on issues arising in about four decisions per volume; and short summaries of selected briefs submitted by the lawyers who argued the cases. Another useful *Lawyers' Edition* feature is the "Citator Service," with summaries of later Supreme Court cases citing a particular decision. These summaries are found in annual pocket parts for each volume since 32 L. Ed. 2d (1972), and in separate *Later Case Service and Citator Service* volumes for 1 to 31 L. Ed. 2d (1956–72).

Both the *Supreme Court Reporter* and *Lawyers' Edition* are published first in biweekly advance sheets, long before the official preliminary print is available. At the

U.S. 927, 115 S.Ct. 1914, 131 L.Ed.2d 976 (1995), we concluded that the common-law principle of announcement is "an element of the reasonableness inquiry under the Fourth Amendment," but noted that the principle "was never stated as an inflexible rule requiring announcement under all circumstances." *Id.,* at 934, 115 S.Ct., at 1918. In *Richards v. Wisconsin,* 520 U.S. ——, 117 S.Ct. 1416, 137 L.Ed.2d 615 (1997), we articulated the test used to determine whether exigent circumstances justify a particular no-knock entry. *Id.,* at ——, 117 S.Ct., at 1419. We therefore hold that § 3109 includes an exigent circumstances exception and that the exception's applicability in a given instance is measured by the same standard we articulated in *Richards.* The police met that standard here and § 3109 was therefore not violated.

We accordingly reverse the judgment of the Court of Appeals and remand this case for further proceedings consistent with this opinion.

It is so ordered.

⊙ KEY NUMBER SYSTEM

Joseph ONCALE, Petitioner,

v.

SUNDOWNER OFFSHORE SERVICES, INCORPORATED, et al.

No. 96–568.

Argued Dec. 3, 1997.

Decided March 4, 1998.

Male employee brought Title VII action against former employer and against male supervisors and co-workers, alleging sexual harassment. The United States District Court for the Eastern District of Louisiana, 1995 WL 133349, G. Thomas Porteous, Jr., J., granted summary judgment for defendants, and plaintiff appealed. The United States Court of Appeals for the Fifth Circuit, No. 95-30510, 83 F.3d 118, affirmed. Certiorari was

granted. The Supreme Court, Justice Scalia, held that sex discrimination consisting of same-sex sexual harassment is actionable under Title VII.

Reversed and remanded.

Justice Thomas filed concurring opinion.

1. Civil Rights ⇐145

When workplace is permeated with discriminatory intimidation, ridicule, and insult that is sufficiently severe or pervasive to alter conditions of victim's employment and create abusive working environment, Title VII is violated. Civil Rights Act of 1964, § 703(a)(1), as amended, 42 U.S.C.A. § 2000e–2(a)(1).

2. Civil Rights ⇐158.1

Title VII's prohibition of discrimination "because of sex" protects men as well as women. Civil Rights Act of 1964, § 703(a)(1), as amended, 42 U.S.C.A. § 2000e–2(a)(1).

3. Civil Rights ⇐104.1

Because of the many facets of human motivation, it would be unwise to presume as matter of law that human beings of one definable group will not discriminate against other members of that group. Civil Rights Act of 1964, § 703(a)(1), as amended, 42 U.S.C.A. § 2000e–2(a)(1).

4. Civil Rights ⇐158.1

Title VII does not bar claim of discrimination "because of sex" merely because plaintiff and defendant, or person charged with acting on behalf of defendant, are of the same sex. Civil Rights Act of 1964, § 703(a)(1), as amended, 42 U.S.C.A. § 2000e–2(a)(1).

5. Civil Rights ⇐167

Sex discrimination consisting of same-sex sexual harassment is actionable under Title VII; statutory prohibition against discrimination "because of sex" in terms or conditions of employment includes sexual harassment of any kind that meets statutory requirements. Civil Rights Act of 1964,

Exhibit 10.   *Oncale v. Sundowner Offshore Services, Inc.,* 118 S.Ct. 998 (1998).

end of the annual term they are then published in "interim editions" bound volumes. The permanent bound volumes are not published until the cases appear in the *U.S. Reports* volumes, so that the commercial editions can include *star paging* with references to the official *U.S. Reports* page numbers. Star paging allows the researcher to use the commercial volumes while citing directly to the official text. This feature is shown in a state court decision below, in Exhibit 15 on page 74.

Even for researchers without access to online databases, it is usually quite easy to find a case in either the *Supreme Court Reporter* or *Lawyers' Edition* if one has the official *U.S. Reports* citation. Each of the commercial volumes indicates on the spine which U.S. volumes it covers, and tables in the beginning of the volumes match up the starting pages of particular cases. For researchers with the name of a decision, but not its citation, the digests accompanying both reporters include extensive case tables listing Supreme Court cases by name. *Lawyers' Edition* is also accompanied by a *Quick Case Table with Annotation References*, a paperback volume listing opinions by name and providing references to the U.S., L. Ed. and S. Ct. citations. This table is less extensive than others, because it omits the numerous cases in which the Supreme Court denied review.

c. *United States Law Week*

While *Supreme Court Reporter* and *Lawyers' Edition* are published much sooner than the official *United States Reports*, there is still a lag of several weeks while their synopses and headnotes are prepared. Another publication provides access to Supreme Court cases much sooner in a newsletter format, reproducing the official slip opin-

ions without adding its own headnotes and mailing them to subscribers the day after they are announced. This service, *The United States Law Week* (cited as U.S.L.W.), published by the Bureau of National Affairs, also provides information about the Supreme Court's docket, arguments, and other developments, making it a comprehensive source of current information about the Court's activities.

U.S. Law Week is the standard source for information on cases pending on the Court's docket. Its Topical Index and Table of Cases can be confusing at first, because they provide page references only if an opinion has been issued. Other entries (for cases which are pending on the docket or for which review has been denied) simply provide a docket number; to find more information it is necessary to turn to a Case Status Report table for page references. These index features are indicated in Exhibit 11, showing entries referring to *Oncale v. Sundowner Offshore Services, Inc.* in the 1997–98 *U.S. Law Week* volume.

U.S. Law Week also provides weekly coverage of other legal developments in a separate "General Law" binder. The "Case Alert" section of this binder summarizes major new decisions from federal and state courts, and the "Legal News" section notes legislative and administrative actions and includes various special reports and analyses. Two "Legal News" features are of particular interest to law students. A monthly Circuit Split Roundup summarizing conflicts among the Courts of Appeals may suggest paper or note topics, and announcements of new judicial nominations and confirmations provide leads for students seeking clerkships.

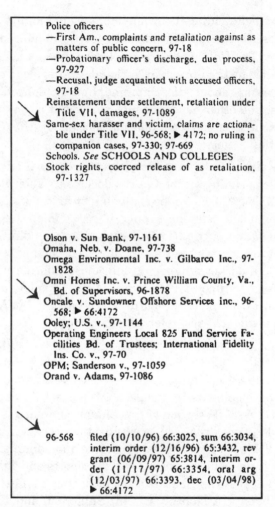

Police officers
—First Am., *complaints and retaliation against as matters of public concern*, 97-18
—Probationary officer's discharge, due process, 97-927
—Recusal, judge acquainted with accused officers, 97-18
Reinstatement under settlement, retaliation under Title VII, damages, 97-1089
Same-sex harasser and victim, claims are actionable under Title VII, 96-568; ▶ 4172; no ruling in companion cases, 97-330; 97-669
Schools. *See* SCHOOLS AND COLLEGES
Stock rights, coerced release of as retaliation, 97-1327

Olson v. Sun Bank, 97-1161
Omaha, Neb. v. Doane, 97-738
Omega Environmental Inc. v. Gilbarco Inc., 97-1828
Omni Homes Inc. v. Prince William County, Va., Bd. of Supervisors, 97-1878
Oncale v. Sundowner Offshore Services inc., 96-568; ▶ 66:4172
Ooley; U.S. v., 97-1144
Operating Engineers Local 825 Fund Service Facilities Bd. of Trustees; International Fidelity Ins. Co. v., 97-70
OPM; Sanderson v., 97-1059
Orand v. Adams, 97-1086

96-568   filed (10/10/96) 66:3025, sum 66:3034, interim order (12/16/96) 65:3432, rev grant (06/09/97) 65:3814, interim order (11/17/97) 66:3354, oral arg (12/03/97) 66:3393, dec (03/04/98) ▶ 66:4172

Exhibit 11. Excerpts from THE UNITED STATES LAW WEEK Supreme Court Index, Table of Cases, and Case Status Report (1997–98).

U.S. Law Week is also available online, as a subscription-based Internet site and through Lexis–Nexis and Westlaw. Supreme Court developments are reported in an electronic-only daily edition, directly from BNA as *Supreme Court Today* or through the major database systems. Westlaw and Lexis–Nexis users should note that Supreme Court information since July 1997 is available *only* in the daily edition databases, and not in the regular *U.S. Law Week* databases.

d. Electronic Resources

The Supreme Court's official website <www.supremecourtus.gov>, launched in April 2000, has general information, selected documents, and new opinions in Adobe Acrobat's PDF format, which reproduces the appearance of the printed slip opinions. Opinions are also transmitted electronically as soon as they are announced to several organizations, including Westlaw and Lexis–Nexis. The major source for free Internet access to all opinions since 1990 is Cornell Law School <supct.law.cornell.edu/supct/>, with decisions since October 1997 in PDF format.

In addition to speedy access to the latest opinions, Lexis–Nexis and Westlaw also provide complete historical coverage of the Supreme Court since 1790, so that every Supreme Court case since its inception can be searched by keyword, parties' names, or names of justices.

Older Supreme Court opinions are also available at free Internet sites. One of the most extensive and useful sources is FindLaw, which has all opinions since 1893 <www.findlaw.com/casecode/supreme.html>, fully searchable and with hypertext links between cases. The Cornell site, above, provides access to several hundred major decisions. A number of subscription Internet sites, includ-

ing USSC+ <www.usscplus.com/>, Loislaw.com <www. loislaw.com>, and V. <www.versuslaw.com>, also provide access to older decisions.

Several publishers offer CD–ROM versions of Supreme Court opinions. Some of these include only recent cases, but West's *Supreme Court Reporter* and Lexis's *Federal Law on Disc* provide complete coverage since 1790.

§ 3–3.   LOWER FEDERAL COURTS

The federal court system has grown extensively from the thirteen District Courts and three Circuit Courts created by the Judiciary Act of 1789. The general trial courts in the federal system, the United States District Courts, are divided into ninety-four districts, with one or more in each state. In addition, there are several specialized trial courts, such as the Bankruptcy Courts, the Court of Federal Claims, and the Court of International Trade. The intermediate appellate courts, the United States Courts of Appeals, are divided into thirteen circuits, consisting of the First through Eleventh Circuits (each covering several states), the District of Columbia Circuit, and the Federal Circuit. The map in Exhibit 12 shows the jurisdiction of these circuits.

There is no counterpart to the *U.S. Reports* for the decisions of the U.S. District Courts and Courts of Appeals. The only officially published sources are the individual slip decisions issued by the courts themselves. Federal court decisions are widely available, however, in commercially published reports and electronic sources.

The only comprehensive printed sources for lower federal court decisions are reporters published by West

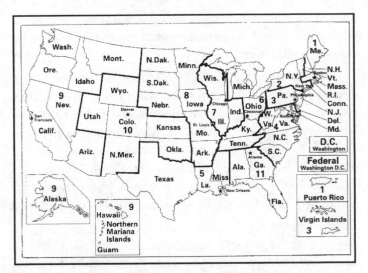

Exhibit 12. Map of the 13 federal judicial circuits.

Group. In 1880 West's *Federal Reporter* began covering decisions of both the district and circuit courts. More than 1,500 volumes later it is still being published, and is now in its third series (cited as F.3d). In 1932, with the increasing volume of litigation in the federal courts, West began another series called *Federal Supplement* (F. Supp.) for selected U.S. District Court decisions, leaving the *Federal Reporter* to cover the decisions of the U.S. Courts of Appeals. *Federal Supplement* is now in its second series (F. Supp. 2d), and also includes decisions of the U.S. Court of International Trade and rulings from the Judicial Panel on Multidistrict Litigation. Like the *Supreme Court Reporter*, both of these reporters contain

editorial synopses and headnotes with key numbers, allowing researchers to find cases through West's series of digest publications.

Because the *United States Reports* is limited to Supreme Court decisions, any citation to *U.S.* clearly indicates the deciding court. Citations to the *Federal Reporter* or *Federal Supplement* must identify the specific circuit or district in parentheses, as in *Oncale v. Sundowner Offshore Services*, 83 F.3d 118 (5th Cir. 1996). This is vital information in evaluating the scope and precedential value of a decision, but it is often omitted by beginning researchers.

The *Federal Reporter* and *Federal Supplement* publish thousands of new decisions each year. Unlike Supreme Court decisions, however, not every case considered by the lower federal courts is represented by a decision published in one of the reporter series. Some matters are settled or tried to a jury verdict and do not result in any written opinions. Decisions in many cases are issued as slip opinions but are not published in the reporters. Some of these are available in topical looseleaf services, and many more can be found online, but others can be obtained only from the clerk of the court. In an attempt to limit the proliferation of court opinions, each circuit has rules establishing criteria to determine whether decisions are published (e.g., establishing a new rule of law, resolving a conflict in the law, or involving issues of continuing public interest) and restricting the citation of "unpublished" decisions. These vary from circuit to circuit, but some courts prohibit citation of such decisions; some allow citation, but with restrictions; and some limit their precedential value.

Cases from the lower federal courts before 1880 are found in a separate West publication called *Federal Cases*. Before the inception of the *Federal Reporter* in 1880, federal court decisions were issued in more than 100 different series of nominative reports. *Federal Cases*, a thirty-volume series published in 1894–97, reports over 20,000 of these decisions. This set incorporated virtually all available lower federal court decisions from 1789 to 1880, arranged in alphabetical sequence by case name.

In 1940, West began another series, *Federal Rules Decisions* (F.R.D.), containing a limited number of U.S. District Court decisions (not published in *Federal Supplement*) dealing with procedural issues under the Federal Rules of Civil Procedure and the Federal Rules of Criminal Procedure. *Federal Rules Decisions* also contains proceedings of judicial conferences and occasional speeches or articles dealing with procedural law in the federal courts.

West Group also issues a number of other reporters in specialized subject fields of federal law. These selective reporters include: *Military Justice Reporter* (1978–date), containing decisions of the U.S. Court of Appeals for the Armed Forces (formerly the U.S. Court of Military Appeals), as well as selected decisions of the four Courts of Criminal Appeals for the separate branches of the military; *Bankruptcy Reporter* (1980–date), containing decisions of the U.S. Bankruptcy Courts and bankruptcy decisions from the U.S. District Courts; *Federal Claims Reporter* (1982–date), containing decisions of the U.S. Court of Federal Claims (formerly U.S. Claims Court); and *Veterans Appeals Reporter* (1991–date), containing decisions of the U.S. Court of Veterans Appeals. These last three reporters also reprint decisions from the Courts

of Appeals and Supreme Court in their subject areas. West's National Reporter System does not include decisions from the U.S. Tax Court, which are published by the government, in *Reports of the United States Tax Court* (1942–date), and by the major commercial tax publishers.

Federal court decisions are also printed in a variety of other sources, including commercial topical reporters designed for practitioners in specialized subject areas. Some cases appearing in these sources are not available in the *Federal Reporter* or *Federal Supplement*, although there is extensive duplication. West publishes two more series of cases on procedural issues which are *not* part of its National Reporter System, *Federal Rules Service* (1939–date) and *Federal Rules of Evidence Service* (1979–date). Reporters in specialized areas include *American Maritime Cases* (1923–date), *Environment Reporter Cases* (1970–date), and *U.S. Patents Quarterly* (1929–date). Several topical reporters, such as BNA's *Fair Employment Practice Cases* (1969–date) and CCH's *Trade Cases* (1948–date), are published as adjuncts to looseleaf services on those topics.

Westlaw and Lexis–Nexis are major sources of lower federal court decisions. They provide full-text coverage of all federal court cases that appear in print in the various West reporters, back to the earliest decisions in *Federal Cases*. New decisions are available online well before they are published in the *Federal Reporter* or *Federal Supplement*. In addition, the online services also provide access to many decisions which never appear in the reporters, making them the most comprehensive sources for current decisions. Both services include in their data-

bases thousands of decisions not available in any other form, except as slip opinions. These are identified by Westlaw or Lexis citations, as shown in Exhibit 16 on page 86.

Recent decisions from the each of the Courts of Appeals are also available from free Internet sites. In most instances, the circuit sites are hosted by law schools and have opinions going back to about 1995. Cases can generally be retrieved by party name, date, docket number, or through a full-text keyword search. Quick access to the sites for specific circuits is provided by sites such as the Federal Court Finder <www.law.emory.edu/FEDCTS/>, .

District and bankruptcy courts are also represented on the Internet, but most of these sites focus on local rules and procedures rather than the text of decisions. Individual courts can be found through listings at FindLaw <www.findlaw.com/casecode/district.html>, or the Federal Judiciary homepage <www.uscourts.gov/links.html>.

More extensive Internet access to Court of Appeals decisions is available through the commercial services V. and Loislaw.com. V. has coverage from 1930 for most circuits, while Loislaw coverage begins in 1971. Neither has very extensive coverage of other lower federal courts.

As with the Supreme Court, both West and Lexis publish CD–ROM discs containing decisions of lower federal court decisions. West publishes CD versions of its *Federal Reporter*, *Federal Supplement*, and *Federal Rules Decisions*, with coverage extending back to 1880. Lexis's *Federal Law on Disc* consists of separate discs for each circuit, with coverage of most circuits beginning with the court restructuring of 1891.

§ 3–4. STATE COURTS

Although federal law governs an increasingly wide range of activities, state courts have a vital lawmaking role in numerous areas. State courts determine the law in areas such as domestic relations, contracts, property, and substantive criminal law. A state's court of last resort has the final say in interpreting the state's constitution and statutes.

The structure of most state court systems roughly follows the federal paradigm, with various trial courts, intermediate appellate courts, and a court of last resort. There are, however, wide variations. A few states have no intermediate appellate courts, with appeals going directly from the trial court to the state supreme court. Other states have more complicated systems, with more than one appellate court for different subject areas. Some even have separate courts of last resort for civil and criminal matters.

A good way to develop a quick familiarity with a state court system is to examine a chart of its structure, such as these published in the U.S. Bureau of Justice Statistics publication *State Court Organization 1993* or the National Center for State Courts' *State Court Caseload Statistics* (annual). These tables are reprinted in several sources, such as *BNA's Directory of State and Federal Courts, Judges, and Clerks* (biennial), *Legal Researcher's Desk Reference* (biennial), and *WANT's Federal–State Court Directory* (annual).

Just as Supreme Court decisions are published both in the official *United States Reports* and in commercial reporters, so decisions from state appellate courts are traditionally published both in official reports, issued by

or under the auspices of the courts themselves, and in unofficial reports issued by commercial publishers. The major comprehensive commercial reports are West Group's National Reporter System. Lexis–Nexis and Westlaw provide comprehensive access to modern cases, and recent decisions are available on the Internet. Every state has at least one CD–ROM version of its cases, and some cases appear in topical reporters with specialized subject coverage.

a. Official Reports

Like the *U.S. Reports*, state official reports are the authoritative version of a court's decisions and must be cited in briefs before that court. In many instances they are less used than commercial reporters, which are usually published more quickly with superior research aids. In fact, 21 states have ceased publishing official reports series and have designated a commercial reporter as the authoritative source of state case law. Appendix A of this book, on page 371, gives information on the current status of the published reports in each state.

Forms of publication vary from state to state. Some states publish just one series of reports for decisions of the state supreme court; in some instances these include decisions of intermediate appellate courts as well. More than a dozen states issue two or more series of reports, with separate series for decisions of the supreme court, for intermediate appellate decisions, and in a few instances for selected trial court decisions. New York, for example, has three official series: *New York Reports*, covering the Court of Appeals; *Appellate Division Reports*, covering the Appellate Divisions of the Supreme Court; and *Miscellaneous Reports*, with decisions of various lower courts. Official slip decisions and advance sheets

are published for the courts of some states, but not for every state. Exhibit 13 shows the first page of *Commonwealth v. Maxim*, an opinion of the Massachusetts intermediate appellate court, in *Massachusetts Appeals Court Reports*. Instead of numbered headnotes, note that it simply has an introductory paragraph summarizing the decision.

Even though official reports do not generally provide links to a comprehensive digest system like West's, they can still provide a valuable perspective on the decisions of a state's appellate courts. If the summaries or headnotes are written by lawyers practicing in that state, they may be more attuned to local judicial developments than headnotes written by commercial editors. Some official reports include research leads not mentioned in the West reporters, and others provide their own classification and digest systems. Although official reports are less widely used than West's, in some jurisdictions they maintain a valuable research role.

As with the early *United States Reports* volumes, the early reports of several of the older states were once cited only by the names of their reporters. Many of these volumes have now been incorporated into the numbered series, but it may still be necessary to use a reference work such as *Bieber's Dictionary of Legal Abbreviations* (4th ed. 1993) to decipher some case citations.

b. National Reporter System

West's National Reporter System includes a series of *regional reporters* publishing the decisions of the appellate courts of the fifty states and the District of Columbia. The National Reporter System divides the country into seven regions, and publishes the decisions of the appel-

45 Mass. App. Ct. 49 (1998)   49

Commonwealth *v.* Maxim.

COMMONWEALTH *vs.* MICHAEL J. MAXIM
(and a companion case[1]).

No. 97-P-0010.

Barnstable. November 12, 1997. - June 11, 1998.

Present: BROWN, SMITH, & LAURENCE, JJ.

Municipal Corporations, By-laws and ordinances, Shellfish. *Shellfish.*

Discussion of native American fishing rights. [50-52]

Native Americans, charged with criminal offenses under a municipal by-law prohibiting the taking of shellfish by hand on certain days, were entitled to findings of not guilty, where their right to fish was protected by the Treaty of Falmouth of 1749 and where the Commonwealth did not prove beyond a reasonable doubt that the by-law was a reasonable and necessary conservation measure that did not discriminate against native Americans. [52-53]

COMPLAINTS received and sworn to in the Barnstable Division of the District Court Department on February 9, 1996.

The cases were heard by *George H. Lebherz, Jr.,* J.

Peter P. d'Errico for Michael J. Maxim.

Julia K. Holler, Assistant District Attorney, for the Commonwealth.

Robert T. Doyle, Jr., for David S. Greene, was present but did not argue.

BROWN, J. The Commonwealth sought and obtained convictions of two members of the Mashpee Wampanoag tribe for violating the town of Bourne's ordinance prohibiting recreational shellfishing on certain days of the week. The defendants, who were gathering clams by hand and rake to feed their families, claim that they were exercising their rights as native Americans (both aboriginal rights and rights reserved by their ancestors under certain treaties with Massachusetts) to fish for sustenance without restriction by town ordinance. This dispute, which

[1]Commonwealth *vs.* David S. Greene.

Exhibit 13. *Commonwealth v. Maxim,* 45 Mass. App. Ct. 49 (1998).

late courts of the states in each region together in one series of volumes. Six of these sets are now in their second series (*Atlantic* (A.2d), *North Eastern* (N.E.2d), *North Western* (N.W.2d), *Pacific* (P.2d), *South Eastern* (S.E.2d), *Southern* (So. 2d)); and one has just started its third series (*South Western* (S.W.3d)). These sets are supplemented by separate reporters for the two most litigious states, also in their second series: *California Reporter* (Cal. Rptr. 2d) and *New York Supplement* (N.Y.S.2d). (Cases from the highest courts of California and New York appear in both the regional and the state reporter, while lower court cases are not published in the *Pacific* or *North Eastern Reporter*.) These nine reporters, together with West's federal court reporters, comprise a uniform system tied together by the key number headnote and digest scheme. The map in Exhibit 14 shows which states are included in each region of the reporter system. Appendix A, on page 371, indicates the scope of coverage for each state appellate court in the regional reporters.

West also publishes individual reporters for over thirty additional states. Unlike the *California Reporter* and *New York Supplement*, however, most of these other series simply reprint a state's cases from its regional reporter, including the original regional reporter pagination. These "offprint" reporters are published for practitioners who need their own state courts' decisions but not cases from other states.

Exhibit 15 shows the first page of the Appeals Court of Massachusetts decision in *Commonwealth v. Maxim*, as printed in West's *North Eastern Reporter*. Note that this version includes an introductory synopsis and four num-

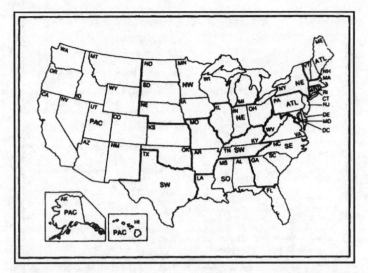

Exhibit 14. National Reporter System may, showing states included in each reporter.

bered headnotes. In addition, the *North Eastern Reporter* version includes star paging indicating the exact page breaks in the official *Massachusetts Appeals Court Reports*.

In most states, cases appear in both official and National Reporter System editions. Cases are traditionally cited to both of these sources, with the official reports cited first. Note in Exhibit 15 that the official citation is printed above the name of the case. The two citations for the same decision are known as *parallel citations*. For example, in *Commonwealth v. Maxim*, 45 Mass. App. Ct.

45 Mass.App.Ct. 49

⌐₄₉COMMONWEALTH

v.

Michael J. MAXIM (and a
companion case [1]).

No. 97–P–0010.

Appeals Court of Massachusetts,
Barnstable.

Argued Nov. 12, 1997.

Decided June 11, 1998.

Members of Native American tribe were
convicted in the District Court Department,
Barnstable Division, George H. Lebherz, Jr.,
J., of violating town ordinance prohibiting
recreational shellfishing on certain days of
the week. Tribe members appealed. The
Appeals Court, Brown, J., held that tribe
members' criminal convictions could not
stand.

Reversed.

1. Indians ⬅32.10(8)

Right of Native American tribe members to fish was protected by treaty, and
therefore tribe members who gathered clams
by hand and rake to feed their families could
not be convicted of violating town ordinance
prohibiting recreational shellfishing on certain days of the week, absent showing that
ordinance was reasonable and necessary conservation measure and that application of
ordinance to Native Americans was necessary and nondiscriminatory.

2. Indians ⬅3(3)

Any ambiguities in treaties with Native
Americans must be construed in favor of
Native Americans.

3. Indians ⬅3(3)

Practical construction in the sense in
which words would naturally be understood
by Native Americans may be considered in
interpreting treaties with Native Americans.

1. Commonwealth vs. David S. Greene.

4. Indians ⬅32.10(7)

Even where protected by treaty, fishing
rights of Native Americans may be regulated
by state in interest of conservation, provided
the regulation is reasonable and necessary
conservation measure, and that its application to Native Americans is necessary in
interest of conservation and does not discriminate against Native Americans.

Peter P. d'Errico, Amherst, for Michael J.
Maxim.

Julia K. Holler, Assistant District Attorney, for the Commonwealth.

Robert T. Doyle, Jr., Northampton, for
David S. Greene, was present but did not
argue.

Before BROWN, SMITH and
LAURENCE, JJ.

BROWN, Justice.

[1] The Commonwealth sought and obtained convictions of two members of the
Mashpee Wampanoag tribe for violating the
town of Bourne's ordinance prohibiting recreational shellfishing on certain days of the
week. The defendants, who were gathering
clams by hand and rake to feed their families, claim that they were exercising their
rights as native Americans (both aboriginal
rights and rights reserved by their ancestors
under certain treaties with Massachusetts) to
fish for sustenance without restriction by
town ordinance. This dispute, which ⌐₅₀would
have been ideally suited for resolution in a
civil action styled as a request for declaratory relief, has been inartfully forced into a
criminal proceeding, which perforce requires
us to employ the traditional standard of proof
beyond a reasonable doubt and the principle
that "ambiguity concerning the ambit of
criminal statutes should be resolved in favor
of lenity." *Rewis v. United States,* 401 U.S.
808, 812, 91 S.Ct. 1056, 1059, 28 L.Ed.2d 493
(1971). See *United States v. Bass,* 404 U.S.
336, 347–348, 92 S.Ct. 515, 522–523, 30
L.Ed.2d 488 (1971); *Commonwealth v. Hry-
cenko,* 417 Mass. 309, 317, 630 N.E.2d 258
(1994).

Exhibit 15. *Commonwealth v. Maxim,* 695 N.E.2d 212 (Mass. App. Ct.
1998).

49, 695 N.E.2d 212 (1998), the citation to the official *Massachusetts Appeals Court Reports* precedes the unofficial *North Eastern Reporter*.

The *Bluebook* requires parallel citations *only* for cases cited in documents submitted to that state's courts; in other documents such as law review articles and notes, only the National Reporter System citation is used. (One of the unfortunate consequences of this rule is that lawyers with official reports in their offices can easily find cases cited in briefs, but not those cited in their local law reviews.) If the cited reporter does not clearly identify the deciding court (e.g., Mass. App. Ct.), remember to include this information in parentheses with the date: *Commonwealth v. Maxim*, 695 N.E.2d 212 (Mass. App. Ct. 1998).

Frequently a researcher has a citation to only one report of a case and needs to find the other, either to complete the citation in a brief or to examine the other version. The parallel citation is not always printed at the beginning of the case, as it is in Exhibit 15. Many state reports are not published quickly enough for their citations to be included in the regional reporters. But parallel citations can be found in a variety of sources.

One of the simplest printed sources for finding parallel citations is a West publication called the *National Reporter Blue Book*, which is updated annually and lists the starting page of each case in the official reports and provides cross-references to National Reporter System citations. For some states, West also publishes a *Blue and White Book*, which has two sets of parallel citation tables. The blue pages duplicate the information provided in the *National Reporter Blue Book*, and the white pages provide references from the regional reporter back to the official

reports. Easy access to parallel citations is also provided by *Shepard's Citations* and KeyCite, resources to be discussed in the following chapter.

Not all cases have parallel citations. West's National Reporter System was not created until the late 19th century, so only the official reports exist for many older state cases. On the other hand, more than 20 states have discontinued their official reports in recent years and newer cases from these states are published only in the West reporters.

c.   Electronic Resources

The computer systems of Lexis–Nexis and Westlaw are increasingly comprehensive sources for state court decisions. New decisions from all state appellate courts are added to the databases before they are available in published form, and retrospective coverage of older case law is steadily expanding. Westlaw, for example, has all state supreme court decisions since the beginning of the National Reporter System in the 1880s, with coverage being extended to the earliest reported cases. The online systems include some opinions not printed in the official reports and commercial reporters, but for most jurisdictions online coverage is limited to the same courts for which reports are published. Very few state trial court decisions are available either in print or in online case databases.

Although the amount of information on the Internet has exploded in recent years, free sites still lag far behind the commercial services in coverage of state court opinions. For some states, only opinions from the most recent three months are maintained on official websites.

Other sites are much more extensive; Oklahoma's website <www.oscn.net> has cases back to the 1950s.

The easiest way to find state court opinions on the Internet is through a general legal resources site such as FindLaw. Its "State Cases and Codes" page <www. findlaw.com/casecode/state.html> provides direct access to opinions by date, case name or docket number, as well as links to official sites. Several law school sites, including Cornell's Legal Information Institute <www.law.cornell. edu/opinions.html>, have similar links, and Piper Resources State Court Directory <www.piperinfo.com/pl03/ statedir.html> has an annotated listing of both free and pay sites with court opinions.

Every state has at least one CD–ROM version of its opinions. Most have two or more, from West, Lexis and other publishers, and many of these products combine court decisions with current statutory codes and other materials.

§ 3–5. CONCLUSION

This chapter has introduced case law as it is published in the United States today, both in print and through a variety of electronic means. While publication methods are changing rapidly, the structure of court systems and the inherent nature of judicial decisions remain relatively constant. This chapter's focus has been on the cases themselves, leaving to subsequent chapters the methods of finding case law relevant to a research problem. Chapter 4 will discuss several of the most important means of case research.

In addition to their value as legal precedent and their importance in legal research, court reports constitute a

literary form with other values as well. They describe human problems and predicaments—domestic crises, moral failings, economic troubles. They reflect the larger social, political and economic trends and conditions of life in particular periods and places. And they frequently have a unique literary quality which adds to the tone and substance of the prose of their time. These judicial decisions have always been an influential part of our literature.

CHAPTER 4

CASE LAW RESEARCH

---

§ 4–1. INTRODUCTION

For the doctrine of precedent to operate effectively, lawyers must be able to find cases which control or influence a court's decisionmaking. This requires locating "cases on point," earlier decisions with factual and legal issues similar to a dispute at hand. It is then necessary to determine that these decisions are valid law and have not been reversed, overruled, or otherwise discredited. Judicial decisions, however, are published in chronological order. Court reports are not arranged by subject, and they

79

are generally not updated once they are published. Additional resources are therefore needed to provide subject access to decisions and to verify their current status.

This chapter discusses several major tools which perform these functions, but it is not exhaustive. Several resources discussed in other chapters—such as legal encyclopedias, law reviews, annotated codes, and looseleaf services—are also valuable in case research. Much of legal research revolves around finding cases, and its methods are not confined to just this one chapter.

We begin with an overview of online research methods. Although many law students begin by using printed methods, electronic case research is the approach most widely used in legal practice today. Online research methods change rapidly, so we offer only a brief survey. More in-depth knowledge comes from experience, training classes, and guides prepared for specific tools. It is easy to learn the basics of online research., but the expertise gained from practice and study will dramatically improve search effectiveness. Anyone can run an online search, but only a competent researcher can be confident that the results are accurate and complete.

The printed tools introduced in this chapter, West digests, *ALR* annotations, and *Shepard's Citations*, are complex resources unlike research materials in most other disciplines. At first they may seem more confusing than online research, but they can yield more thorough, accurate results and are basic and necessary parts of any case law research. The assistance of editors who have analyzed and classified related cases can lead to insights that a searcher using only full-text databases might never reach.

§ 4–2. ELECTRONIC RESEARCH

Electronic resources are powerful and effective tools in legal research. Full-text databases allow researchers to determine their own criteria for each search, freeing them from reliance on editors' indexing decisions, and hypertext links permit them to move effortlessly from one document or service to another and back again.

This discussion focuses primarily on the online databases Westlaw and Lexis–Nexis, the most powerful and comprehensive electronic resources. Law schools generally have subscriptions allowing their students unlimited use of these databases, and most larger law firms subscribe to at least one of these services.

For other researchers, however, these commercial online systems may be unavailable or prohibitively expensive. Other options are available. Many college and university libraries subscribe to Lexis–Nexis Academic Universe, with many of Lexis–Nexis's features, and other commercial services such as Loislaw.com and V. provide case research at relatively low cost. Some researchers may have access to their state's case law on CD–ROM rather than online. Generally these services and products provide access in similar ways to Westlaw and Lexis–Nexis, although approaches may be less flexible and sophisticated.

Free Internet sites, on the other hand, are generally not yet a viable option for most case research. They may offer a searchable database of a particular court's opinions, but most are limited in coverage to the past few years (or months), and opportunities to search multiple jurisdictions are limited. They may nonetheless be useful starting points, if they provide one or two cases that can lead

to other documents. The Internet is a more useful resource for obtaining copies of new decisions and monitoring recent developments.

Westlaw and Lexis–Nexis are available both through websites <www.westlaw.com> and <www.lexis.com> and by using proprietary software such as WESTMATE. These approaches access the same databases of court decisions, but the way information is presented can vary somewhat. Natural language searching is called "FREE-STYLE" on Lexis–Nexis software, for instance, but not on the lexis.com website. Lexis–Nexis software uses short names for sources, such as the GENFED library for federal materials, while the lexis.com website uses descriptive entries such as "Federal Legal—U.S." These differences make it difficult for a general overview to provide specific examples of research steps.

No matter what access method is used, the first choice confronting an online researcher is the selection of an appropriate database. Both systems have online directories that list the numerous available options. One can search databases with the decisions of a particular state or a specific court, databases limited to cases in specific subject areas, or comprehensive databases combining the decisions of all state and federal jurisdictions. Whether to limit research to a particular jurisdiction or topical area depends upon a variety of factors, including cost (searches in large databases are generally more expensive), the purpose of the research, and the value of precedent from other jurisdictions or in other subjects. Sometimes the only relevant cases for a research issue are those from a particular state or within a narrow doctrinal area. For other research questions, cases from other jurisdictions or in other fields may provide useful guidance.

a.   Basic Search Methods

Lexis–Nexis and Westlaw offer two methods of searching: natural language, and terms and connectors (or Boolean). Each of these search methods has its strengths.

A natural language search allows the researcher to enter a phrase, or a combination of words (e.g., "Is BASE jumping considered delivery by parachute?" or simply "BASE jump parachute delivery"). The computer assigns relative weights to the terms in a query, depending on how often they appear in the database. It then retrieves a specified number of documents which appear most closely to match the query, giving greater weight to the less common terms. Not all terms will necessarily appear in every document retrieved, but one can specify mandatory terms or "control concepts" that *must* appear in all documents.

Terms and connectors searching provides greater precision in retrieval, but it does require learning a structured search syntax. Specific terms or phrases are joined by logical connectors such as *or* and *and*. Frequently the most effective way to combine search terms is a *proximity connector* specifying the maximum number of words that can separate the search terms (e.g., /10 or w/10), or specifying that the words appear in the same sentence (/s or w/s) or the same paragraph (/p or w/p).

In either search method, the cases retrieved will match the terminology used. For most subjects of research, more than one word can be used to denote the same concept. One decision may use the word *ambiguous*, another *vague*, and a third *unclear*. Whether searching with terms and connectors or natural language, it is important to use synonyms and related concepts. Both systems provide

help in coming up with additional terms, through online thesauri and lists of related terms. In Lexis–Nexis, this feature lists not only related concepts but terms that regularly appear in close proximity to the term. For *parachute*, for example, it includes such terms as *airport*, *aircraft*, *employment agreement*, *executive*, and *merger*.

One major difference between the two types of searching is that a terms and connectors search can retrieve anywhere from nothing to thousands of cases, depending on how well the search is prepared and how often the terms appear in the database. The number of retrieved cases can be a useful indication of whether an appropriate search was performed. Unless a natural language search includes mandatory terms, it always retrieves the number of cases specified by the researcher (from 1 to 100 in Westlaw). The first few cases may be right on point, but the degree of relevance can drop off precipitously. It is important to recognize when relevance declines, and to be aware that reading every case retrieved will usually be a waste of time.

Researchers generally develop a preference for natural language or terms and connectors search methods, but they are best suited for different purposes. Because natural language searching retrieves documents based on relevance, it is ideal for finding documents that focus on issues such as summary judgment that are often mentioned but seldom discussed at length. Terms and connectors searches require documents to match a request exactly, so this approach is generally preferable when searching for a particular phrase. It is often fruitful to perform similar searches using both methods.

b. Case Formats

Westlaw and Lexis–Nexis display the same opinions, but these are accompanied by different editorial matter.

Westlaw includes the synopsis and headnotes for any case published in a West reporter. The synopsis is particularly useful as a quick guide to a case's relevance to a research issue. Lexis–Nexis provides a list of "core terms" indicating the nature of the document, and has announced plans to begin adding case summaries as well.

In addition to the full text of cases, both systems have ways to see the parts of the opinion that match the search query. This is done by choosing the KWIC (key words in context) display format on Lexis–Nexis, or by clicking on the *Term* button in Westlaw. Natural language searches can also zero in on that part of the document that most closely matches the query, called *Best* in Westlaw and SuperKWIC in Lexis–Nexis. Exhibit 16 shows the SuperKWIC display for *United States v. Oxx*, a U.S. Court of Appeals case retrieved with a query about BASE jumping and parachutes.

As part of the screen display of a case, both systems provide citations to published versions, whether in official reports, West's National Reporter System, or looseleaf topical reporters. They also provide *star paging* references showing the exact reporter page on which particular text is printed. In Exhibit 16, for example, the text shown is from pages 1279 of the *Federal Reporter* volume.

c. Fields and Segments

An important feature of online searching is the use of document *fields* (in Westlaw) or *segments* (in Lexis–Nexis). Fields or segments are specific parts of a case, such as the names of the parties, the judge writing the opinion, or the date of decision. Limiting a search to a field or segment can produce a much more specific result. A search for *brown* retrieves any cases where the color

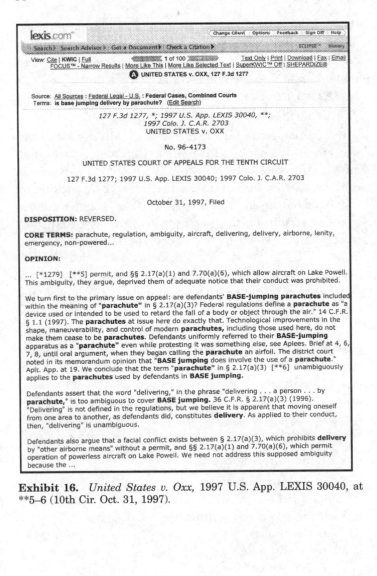

Exhibit 16. *United States v. Oxx,* 1997 U.S. App. LEXIS 30040, at **5–6 (10th Cir. Oct. 31, 1997).

brown or a person named Brown is mentioned. A search for *title(brown)* on Westlaw or *name(brown)* on Lexis–Nexis, however, retrieves only those cases where one of the parties is named Brown.

Some fields and segments allow research that is virtually impossible by other means. It would be a lengthy and tedious process manually to find all opinions written by a particular judge, but online databases can easily retrieve a complete list of a judge's opinions with commands such as *judge(kelly)* (on Westlaw) or *opinionby(kelly)* (on Lexis–Nexis). The researcher can even examine a judge's decisions on a particular topic by combining this request with other search terms.

In Westlaw, one can use the *synopsis* and *digest* fields to search only for words in West's introductory summary and headnotes. Limiting the search to words important enough to be mentioned in the synopsis or headnotes retrieves a smaller body of cases more precisely on point. West's digest topics and key numbers (which will be discussed below in § 4–3) can also be used in Westlaw searches, either alone or in combination with other search terms.

Fields and segments can be used in both terms and connectors and natural language searches. In natural language searches, however, they must be added as "field restrictions" on Westlaw or as "mandatory terms" on Lexis–Nexis.

d. Refining and Expanding Searches

If a completed search retrieves too many cases, the researcher can narrow the focus of inquiry in several ways. The features *Locate* (on Westlaw) and *Focus* (on Lexis–Nexis) allow the researcher to examine the re-

trieved set of documents for specific terms, whether or not they were included in the initial request. Instead of identifying a new set of cases replacing the original search result, *Locate* and *Focus* search for and highlight particular terms among the retrieved documents. These features are particularly valuable if each search costs money, because they do not incur additional charges.

It is also possible, of course, to edit a query to add new terms or to pursue new topics. Lexis–Nexis has a "more like this" feature which automatically builds a new search by using a computer-generated list of related terms. Choosing this feature when viewing the *Oxx* case shown in Exhibit 16, for example, leads to options to retrieve documents citing the same cases *Oxx* cites or to select from a list of core terms in *Oxx* (including *parachute*, *delivery*, *regulation*, *airborne*, *jumper*, and *ambiguity*), to find similar cases.

Most judicial opinions cite extensively to other cases, as well as to statutes and other documents. Cases in Westlaw and Lexis–Nexis include hypertext links to these other sources if they are available online. Researchers can thus follow leads as they arise rather than making notes for possible future reference.

Another way to find related cases is to use the services KeyCite or Shepard's Citations. These services provide annotated lists of cases and other documents which cite the case under study, making them an easy way to find related cases. These services perform several valuable functions in the research process, and will be discussed separately in § 4–5, beginning on page 114.

One valuable feature which many students overlook is the ability to save a search and have the system auto-

matically run it to check for new material on a daily or weekly basis. This is a convenient way to stay abreast of new developments in a specific case or in an area of interest. This feature is known as WESTCLIP on Westlaw, and as ECLIPSE on Lexis–Nexis.

§ 4-3. WEST KEY–NUMBER DIGESTS

Digests, publications reprinting in a subject arrangement the headnotes from court reports, are one of the most powerful methods of case-finding. Despite the ease and flexibility of keyword access, electronic searching may miss relevant cases that can be found in the digests. Editorial analysis in organizing and classifying cases may lead to relevant analogous cases that use different words from those that might occur to a researcher. Similar legal issues may arise, for example, in cases involving BASE jumping and scuba diving, but a researcher may not think to explore both in the air and underwater.

Several digest systems are published, but most focus on specific subject areas and will be discussed briefly in Chapter 9. The most comprehensive digest system is West Group's key number system, covering every case published in West's National Reporter System. The West digest system consists of over 400 topics, arranged alphabetically from Abandoned and Lost Property to Zoning and Planning. Each topic is divided into numbered sections designating specific points of law. These individual sections are called *key numbers*. Some narrow topics like Party Walls employ relatively few key numbers, while broader ones such as Taxation or Trade Regulation may have thousands.

The entries in West's digests come directly from the cases published in the National Reporter System. Editors

at West create short abstracts for every significant point of law discussed in each case in the West reporters. Each abstract is classified by topic and key number to designate its subject. These abstracts first appear as headnotes preceding the text of the opinion in the West reporter advance sheet. Exhibit 17 shows the first page of the Tenth Circuit decision in *United States v. Oxx*, at 127 F.3d 1277, with headnotes assigned to the topics Criminal Law, Statutes, and United States.

All headnotes for cases in an advance sheet or reporter volume are reprinted in a Key Number Digest in the front of the advance sheet or at the back of the bound reporter volume. These digests serve as subject indexes to the cases in the advance sheet or volume. Exhibit 18 shows the digest from the *Federal Reporter* volume containing the *Oxx* decision, including three *Oxx* headnotes under United States ⬤ 57, "Control, regulation, and use of public property, buildings, and places." Only a small percentage of the key numbers are used in this volume's decisions, but West then reprints these headnotes, arranged by key number, in multivolume digest series to provide subject access to the cases in hundreds of reporter volumes.

Although digests are valuable case-finders, they do have several shortcomings. They consist simply of case abstracts, with no explanatory text, and the researcher must often wade through many irrelevant entries to find citations to significant authorities. Digest entries may reflect dicta and may even misstate points of law in the cases they abstract. Unless a case has been directly reversed or modified, the digests don't indicate that it may no longer be good law. It is essential to locate and

U.S. v. OXX   **1277**
Cite as 127 F.3d 1277 (10th Cir. 1997)

**UNITED STATES of America,
Plaintiff–Appellant,**

v.

**William OXX, Jonathan Oxx, Martin Tilly,
Christopher Berke, David Katz, Steve
Mulholland, John M. Henderson, Aaron
M. Brennan, and Michael Kvale, Defen-
dants–Appellees.**

No. 96–4173.

United States Court of Appeals,
Tenth Circuit.

Oct. 31, 1997.

Defendants were charged by petty offense information with delivery of persons by
parachute in national park without a permit
and not in an emergency. The United States
District Court for the District of Utah dismissed information, and government appealed. The Court of Appeals, Paul J. Kelly, Jr.,
Circuit Judge, held that: (1) parachutes used
by defendants were covered by relevant regulation; (2) act of jumping from cliff into
national park was "delivery" of person by
parachute; (3) any ambiguity of regulations
as to landing of powerless aircraft on particular lake was irrelevant under instant circumstances; and (4) act of jumping off cliff with
parachute was not per se "emergency," within meaning of exception to regulation.

Reversed.

1. Criminal Law ⟐1139

Although Court of Appeals generally reviews dismissal of indictment or information
for abuse of discretion, Court reviews de
novo dismissal based on district court's interpretation of governing law.

2. United States ⟐57

Parachute used for jumping from buildings, antennae, spans, and earth forms was
"parachute" within meaning of regulation
prohibiting delivery of persons by parachute
in a national park without a permit and not
in an emergency, even if parachute had more
maneuverability and control than typical parachute, in view of separate regulation defining parachute as device used or intended to
be used to retard fall of body or object

through the air. 14 C.F.R. § 1.1; 36 C.F.R.
§ 2.17(a)(3).

> See publication Words and Phrases
> for other judicial constructions and def-
> initions.

3. United States ⟐57

Defendants' act of jumping from cliffs
into national park with parachutes was "delivery" of person by parachute within meaning of regulation prohibiting delivery of persons by parachute in a national park without
a permit and not in an emergency. 36
C.F.R. § 2.17(a)(3).

> See publication Words and Phrases
> for other judicial constructions and def-
> initions.

4. United States ⟐57

Alleged conflict between regulation prohibiting delivery of persons by parachute,
helicopter or other airborne means in national park without a permit and not in an emergency and regulations permitting powerless
aircraft on particular lake in national park
did not render former regulation ambiguous
as to defendants who were charged with
delivery by parachute, not delivery by other
airborne means. 36 C.F.R. §§ 2.17(a)(1, 3),
7.70(a)(6).

5. Statutes ⟐241(1)

Rule of lenity may not be invoked to
manufacture ambiguity.

6. Statutes ⟐241(1)

In absence of ambiguity, rule of lenity,
or strict construction, may not be applied.

7. United States ⟐57

Act of jumping off cliff with parachute is
not per se "emergency," within meaning of
exception to regulation prohibiting delivery
of persons by parachute, helicopter or other
airborne means in national park. 36 C.F.R.
§ 2.17(a)(3).

Lisa E. Jones, Department of Justice,
Washington, DC (Lois Schiffer, Assistant Attorney General, Washington, DC, Scott M.
Matheson, Jr., United States Attorney,
Wayne Dance, Assistant United States Attorney, Salt Lake City, UT, and M. Alice Thur-
ston, Department of Justice, Washington, DC

Exhibit 17.   *United States v. Oxx,* 127 F.3d 1277 (10th Cir. 1997).

⟜34 **UNITED STATES**

criminal scheme unless they were deposited in account of their corporation and made available for real estate and other financial transactions specified in indictment. 18 U.S.C.A. § 1956(a)(1)(A)(i).—Id.

Evidence that defendants concealed nature and source of embezzled funds by placing those funds in seemingly legitimate business account of their corporation and passing them off as funds of legitimate business and used embezzled funds to pay tax debt was sufficient to demonstrate intent to conceal their identity and relationship to funds, as required to support money laundering conviction, although defendants did not use false names in attempt to conceal their identity. 18 U.S.C.A. § 1956(a)(1)(B)(i).—Id.

Jury instructions on money laundering adequately instructed jury on each of two theories of money laundering charged; instruction permitted jury to enter general guilty verdict if it found either intent to promote carrying on of embezzlement or knowing concealment of source, ownership, or nature of embezzled funds. 18 U.S.C.A. § 1956(a)(1)(A)(i), (a)(1)(B)(i).—Id.

⟜39(15). **Pensions and retirement allowances.**

C.A.Fed. 1997. Importance of particular employee's contribution to law enforcement mission is not enough to render that employee a "law enforcement officer" within the meaning of law enforcement retirement benefit statutes. 5 U.S.C.A. §§ 8336(c)(1), 8412(d)(2).—Bingaman v. Department of Treasury, 127 F.3d 1431.

Employee waived issue of whether Merit Systems Protection Board erred by revising its original decision entitling employee to law enforcement officer retirement benefits so that decision would not be given prospective effect, by complying with Board's directive to file annual requests for benefits, rather than filing motion to enforce original decision. 5 U.S.C.A. § 8336(c)(1).—Id.

Department of the Treasury had no affirmative duty to advise employees on how to request law enforcement officer credit, and employees could not point to any deceit or malfeasance by Department, and thus Department would not be equitably estopped from applying, against employees, requirement that they make formal, written request for such credits within six months of either taking position or significant change in position. 5 U.S.C.A. § 8412(d)(2); 5 C.F.R. § 842.804(c).—Id.

Supervisory Detection Systems Specialist (Airborne) did not request law enforcement officer retirement credits for himself by signing letter requesting such credits for nonsupervisory Detection Systems Specialists. 5 U.S.C.A. § 8336(c)(1). —Id.

II. PROPERTY.

⟜57. **Control, regulation, and use of public property, buildings, and places.**

C.A.10 (Utah) 1997. Parachute used for jumping from buildings, antennae, spans, and earth forms was "parachute" within meaning of regulation prohibiting delivery of persons by parachute in a national park without a permit and not in an emergency, even if parachute had more maneuverability and control than typical parachute, in view of separate regulation defining parachute as device used or intended to be used to retard fall of body or object through the air. 14 C.F.R. § 1.1; 36 C.F.R. § 2.17(a)(3).—U.S. v. Oxx, 127 F.3d 1277.

Defendants' act of jumping from cliffs into national park with parachutes was "delivery" of person by parachute within meaning of regulation
(140)

prohibiting delivery of persons by parachute in a national park without a permit and not in an emergency. 36 C.F.R. § 2.17(a)(3).—Id.

Alleged conflict between regulation prohibiting delivery of persons by parachute, helicopter or other airborne means in national park without a permit and not in an emergency and regulations permitting powerless aircraft on particular lake in national park did not render former regulation ambiguous as to defendants who were charged with delivery by parachute, not delivery by other airborne means. 36 C.F.R. §§ 2.17(a)(1, 3), 7.70(a)(6).—Id.

Act of jumping off cliff with parachute is not per se "emergency," within meaning of exception to regulation prohibiting delivery of persons by parachute, helicopter or other airborne means in national park. 36 C.F.R. § 2.17(a)(3).—Id.

III. CONTRACTS.

⟜73(9). —— **In general.**

C.A.Fed. 1997. Final decision by contracting officer on "claim" under Contract Disputes Act (CDA) is prerequisite for jurisdiction in agency board of contract appeals. Contract Disputes Act of 1978, § 2 et seq., 41 U.S.C.A. § 601 et seq.— D.L. Braughler Co., Inc. v. West, 127 F.3d 1476.

To properly certify claim, contractor must make statement which simultaneously makes all assertions required by Contract Disputes Act. Contract Disputes Act of 1978, § 6(c)(1), 41 U.S.C.(1988 Ed.) § 605(c)(1).—Id.

If contractor's submission fails to meet all requirements of "claim" under Contract Disputes Act, contracting officer has no authority to issue final decision on submission, and any subsequent proceedings on submission have no legal significance. Contract Disputes Act of 1978, § 6(c)(1), 41 U.S.C.(1988 Ed.) § 605(c)(1).—Id.

Government contractor's letter to resident engineer, regarding contractor's claim for extra payment based on delay allegedly caused by government, was not "submitted to" contracting officer for final decision, within meaning of Contract Disputes Act (CDA), as letter gave no indication that contractor was seeking final decision from contracting officer, letter was not forwarded to contracting officer, and contractor sought to resolve matter with resident engineer. Contract Disputes Act of 1978, § 6(a), 41 U.S.C.A. § 605(a).—Id.

Government contractor's letter to contracting officer was claim submission, under Contract Disputes Act (CDA), even though letter was not accompanied by contemporaneous certification, where letter referred to valid certification included with previous letter to resident engineer, and claim was not altered since certification; thus, contracting officer's final decision on claim was valid, and contractor's failure to timely appeal from decision deprived Corps of Engineers Board of Contract Appeals of jurisdiction to review claim. Contract Disputes Act of 1978, § 6(a, b), (c)(1), 41 U.S.C.A. § 605(a, b), (c)(1).—Id.

V. LIABILITIES.

⟜78(12). **Execution of statutes or regulations; discretionary acts or functions.**

C.A.10 (N.M.) 1997. Where governmental conduct at issue falls within discretionary function exception to Federal Tort Claims Act (FTCA), district court lacks subject matter jurisdiction to hear suit. 28 U.S.C.A. § 2680(a).—Bell v. U.S., 127 F.3d 1226.

Exhibit 18. Key Number Digest, 127 F.3d app. at 140 (1998).

read the cases themselves in order to find those which are actually pertinent, and then to verify their status through other means.

a. Finding Cases in Digests

To use a digest, the researcher must identify the topic and key number relevant to the problem. Digest topics and key numbers can be found in several ways: (1) by using a Descriptive–Word Index after analyzing the factual and legal issues involved in a problem; (2) by surveying a relevant legal topic; or (3) from the headnotes of a case known to be on point. In addition, digests provide alphabetical tables of cases so that researchers can use names of known cases to find their citations.

Descriptive-Word Method. To find the appropriate key number under which relevant cases are digested, it is usually most productive to begin with a Descriptive–Word Index. These indexes, which list thousands of factual and legal terms, accompany each digest set.

One can approach a Descriptive–Word Index either by looking up legal issues, such as causes of action, defenses, or relief sought; or by looking up factual elements in an action, such as parties, places, or objects involved. For example, in a criminal action involving BASE jumping, the researcher might use the index to investigate some of the legal issues (ambiguity, lenity, misdemeanor) or, usually more effectively, some of the specific facts of the case (flight, national park, parachute). Exhibit 19 shows a page from a Descriptive–Word Index in a West digest, including a reference to the regulation and use of national parks. This entry refers to United States ☞ 57, while other

entries under "Parks" lead to Constitutional Law, Eminent Domain, Municipal Corporations, and several other topics.

Finding appropriate key numbers in the index can sometimes be a simple step. In using any legal index, however, the researcher should be prepared for some frustration. Even the most thorough index cannot list every possible approach to a legal or factual issue. It is often necessary to rethink issues, reframe questions, check synonyms and alternate terms, and follow leads in cross-references.

When turning from the index to the volume of digest abstracts, it may be helpful to look first at the outline of the topic to verify that the legal context is indeed appropriate. A researcher looking for cases on substantive negligence issues, for example, may find that a reference leads instead to a key number dealing with the standard of review for summary judgment. Exhibit 20 contains part of the outline for the United States topic, showing how ☞ 57 fits with other issues involving government property, contracts, and liabilities.

Topic Approach. An alternative approach used by some researchers bypasses the Descriptive–Word Index and goes directly to the West digest topic most relevant to the problem. Each topic begins with a scope note, indicating which subjects it includes and which are covered in related topics. The United States topic, for example, covers issues such as the management of federal property and actions in which the U.S. is a party, but it does not incorporate matters such as citizenship (Citizens, Civil Rights); separation of powers (Constitutional Law); rela-

PARKING

References are to Digest Topics and Key Numbers

PARKING LOTS—Cont'd
INVITEES, injuries to. Neglig 32(2.5)
LICENSEES, injuries to. Neglig 32(2.5)
NUISANCE. Nuis 3(1)
OPERATOR'S liability as bailee. Bailm 14(1)
OPERATOR'S liability for loss of vehicle or content. Autos 372
POLICE power. Mun Corp 600
USE and regulation. Mun Corp 721(1)
ZONING regulations. Zoning 77, 78
  Amendments or modifications. Zoning 170
  Construction and operation. Zoning 280, 303
  Injunctions. Zoning 776
  Permits and certificates. Zoning 411–423
  Variances or exceptions. Zoning 509
    Evidence. Zoning 540

PARKING RAMPS
Generally, see this index—
  Garages
  Parking Lots

PARKS
ACQUISITION of property. Mun Corp 223
ASSESSMENTS. Mun Corp 420
COMMISSIONERS, delegation of legislative power to. Const Law 63(4)
CONDEMNATION of property for. Em Dom 41
  Previously devoted to public use. Em Dom 47(6)
DEDICATION of property for park. Dedi 6
DEPARTMENT of municipal corporation. Mun Corp 210
DISTRICT of Columbia, use and regulation. Dist of Col 23
EQUAL protection of laws. Const Law 219
FOREST reservations. Woods 8
GRANTS of right to use, see this index Grants
HIGHWAYS, use of park lands for. High 103
INJURIES from condition or use. Mun Corp 851
  Damages for injuries from improvement. Mun Corp 389
  Establishment and maintenance. Mun Corp 734
↘ LEASE. Mun Corp 721(4)
NATIONAL parks—
  Regulation and use. U S 57
  Reservations to United States. Pub Lands 49
OFFICERS of municipal park department. Mun Corp 210
PROPERTY acquired for special purpose. Mun Corp 225(3)
PUBLIC improvements. Mun Corp 276
  Damages for injuries. Mun Corp 389
SOUND amplification guideline—
  First Amendment—
    Const Law 90.1(4)
    Mun Corp 596
STATES—
  Claims for injuries to visitors. States 184.22
  Tort liability, injuries in. States 112.2(6)
USE and regulations. Mun Corp 721

PARKWAYS
AUTOMOBILES, meeting of cars on streets divided by parkways. Autos 170(17)
DEFECTS, nature. Mun Corp 766

PARLIAMENTARY LAW
ADOPTION. Parl Law 3
APPLICATION. Parl Law 3
CONGRESS, rules of procedure. U S 18
CONSTITUTION of deliberative body. Parl Law 4
FORM of procedure. Parl Law 5
LEGISLATURE, rules of procedure and conduct of business. States 35
MODE of procedure. Parl Law 5
MUNICIPAL council, rules of procedure governing conduct of meetings. Mun Corp 92
NATURE in general. Parl Law 1
ORDER of procedure. Parl Law 5
ORGANIZATION of deliberative body. Parl Law 4

PARLIAMENTARY LAW—Cont'd
PRESIDING officer, rulings of. Parl Law 6
PRINCIPLES. Parl Law 2
REVIEW of proceeding. Parl Law 6, 7
RULINGS of presiding officer. Parl Law 6
SOURCES. Parl Law 2

PAROCHIAL SCHOOLS
See generally, this index Private Schools

PAROL AGREEMENTS
ACCEPTANCE of bill of exchange. Bills & N 69
AGENT, appointment of. Princ & A 12
ASSIGNMENTS. Assign 34
  Insurance. Insurance 208
  Leases. Land & Ten 77
BILLS and notes, acceptance of. Bills & N 69
CONSTRUCTION. Contracts 149
  Collateral to written contract. Contracts 165
  Of oral contracts and contracts partly oral as jury questions. Contracts 176(7)
CONSTRUCTIVE trusts arising from breach of oral agreements, see this index Constructive Trusts
EVIDENCE of separate or subsequent oral agreement to affect writing. Evid 439–445
INSURANCE—
  Assignment. Insurance 208
  Modification of policy. Insurance 144(4)
  Validity. Insurance 131
LEASES. Land & Ten 23
  Assignments or subletting. Land & Ten 77
  Construction and operation. Land & Ten 38
  Creating tenancy at will. Land & Ten 118(3)
    Effect of statute of frauds. Frds St of 123(1)
  Creating tenancy from year to year. Land & Ten 114
    Effect of statute of frauds. Frds St of 123(2)
  Month to month tenancy. Land & Ten 115(2)
    Effect of statute of frauds. Frds St of 123(3)
  Tenancy at will. Land & Ten 118(3)
LIMITATIONS, acknowledgment or new promise. Lim of Act 146(2)
MODIFICATION of written contracts. Contracts 238(2, 3)
MORTGAGES—
  Constituting absolute deed a mortgage. Mtg 34
PARTITION. Partit 5
SALES—
  Sales 26, 57
  Ven & Pur 19
SPECIFIC performance. Spec Perf 38
  Contracts partly performed. Spec Perf 40–47
    Acts constituting performance in general. Spec Perf 43
    Evidence of part performance. Spec Perf 121(5)
    Improvements and expenditures. Spec Perf 47
    Payment. Spec Perf 44
    Performance of services. Spec Perf 45
    Performance referable to contract. Spec Perf 42
    Possession. Spec Perf 46
  Statute of frauds, contracts within. Spec Perf 39
STATUTE of frauds—
  Agreement to reconvey property. Trusts 17(5)
  Contracts within evidence of part performance. Spec Perf 121(5)
  Damages for breach of. Frds St of 125(2)
  Gift of land. Gifts 25
  Objections to evidence of parol agreement. Frds St of 157
  Oral trusts, see this index Parol Trusts
  Specific performance, ante
  Writing subsequent to agreement. Frds St of 127
STIPULATION. Stip 7
SUBLETTING. Land & Ten 77
TRUSTS, see this index Parol Trusts

Exhibit 19. Descriptive-Word Index, 99 FEDERAL PRACTICE DIGEST 4TH, at 4 (1992).

UNITED STATES

I. GOVERNMENT AND OFFICERS.—Continued.

    ⊷50.10. —— Particular acts or claims.—Continued.

        (6). Medical malpractice claims.

        (7). Defamation, disclosure, and privacy claims.

    50.15. —— Relation to sovereign immunity.

    50.20. —— Actions.

    51. Liabilities on official bonds.

        (1). In general.

        (2). Enforcement.

    52. Criminal responsibility of officers, agents, and clerks.

    53. Corporations and special instrumentalities controlled by United States.

        (1). In general.

        (2). Power to create and regulate.

        (3). Constitutional and statutory provisions.

        (4). Organization, existence and status.

        (5). Officers, agents and employees.

        (6). Powers, liabilities and activities.

        (7). —— Agriculture and agricultural finance.

        (8). —— Financial instrumentalities in general.

        (9). —— Housing and home financing.

        (10). —— Maritime matters and shipbuilding.

        (11). —— Representation by officers, agents and employees, in general.

        (12). —— Liability for agents' and employees' torts.

        (13). Actions.

        (14). —— Power to sue and be sued.

        (15). —— Nature and form of remedy.

        (16). —— Parties, process and pleading.

        (17). —— Evidence and fact questions.

        (18). —— Relief granted, judgment and review.

        (19). —— Costs.

II. PROPERTY, CONTRACTS, AND LIABILITIES.

    ⊷55. Acquisition of property in general.

    56. Public improvements and works.

    57. Control, regulation, and use of public property, buildings, and places.

    58. Disposition of property.

        (1). In general.

        (2). Abandonment or loss.

        (3). Sale of realty, timber, and fixtures in general.

        (4). Sale of goods and surplus property in general.

        (5). Authority of government officers.

        (6). Quality and condition of property sold.

        (7). Vessels and aircraft.

        (8). Remedies and procedure.

    58½. Release of property held by legal proceedings.

    59. Capacity and authority to contract in general.

    60. Powers of particular boards or officers to contract.

    61. Individual interest of officer in contract.

    62. Appropriation or provision for payment as prerequisite of contract.

Exhibit 20.   United States, 93 Federal Practice Digest 4th, at 112 (1992).

tions with foreign countries (International Law, Treaties); or federal employees (Officers and Public Employees).

Once the correct topic is found, the outline of key numbers is analyzed to select the appropriate key number for a specific issue. An advantage of this method is that it provides the context of the individual key numbers; reading through the outline may help clarify issues or raise concerns the researcher had not yet considered. This can be a very time-consuming approach, however, and beginning researchers may not have the legal background to choose the right topic and determine the appropriate issues. In most instances, the index is a faster and more reliable starting point.

Case Headnotes. The easiest and most foolproof way to use the digest is to begin with the headnotes of a case on point. When you already know of a relevant case, you can find it in the National Reporter System, scan its headnotes for relevant issues, and then use the key numbers accompanying these headnotes in searching the digest. This eliminates the need to search through indexes or to analyze the digest's classification system, and reduces the likelihood of turning to the wrong issue or getting stuck in a dead end. This method, of course, requires that at least one initial case be found through other means, but several other case-finding resources— from legal encyclopedias to online databases—have already been discussed.

Tables of Cases. The digests serve another purpose, distinct from the topical arrangement of headnotes. Each digest is accompanied by a Table of Cases occupying one or more volumes, listing cases by their parties' names and providing citations so that the opinions can be found.

These tables are the starting point when one knows of a case but does not know where it is published, or wishes to see cases involving a particular party. Tables of Cases provide parallel citations to both official and unofficial reports, and information about a case's later history (whether it was affirmed, reversed, or modified). Beginning in 1999, new Tables of Cases volumes provide access under both parties' names. Older Tables volumes, however, generally list cases by the plaintiffs' or appellants' names, with separate Defendant–Plaintiff Tables listing cases under the defendants' or appellees' names.

b. *Decennial* and *General Digests*

West digests are available for the entire country, for some regions, for individual states, and for a few specific subjects. Choosing the right digest depends on the scope of the inquiry. A researcher may want to find cases from only one jurisdiction, or may be interested in developments throughout the country. A more focused digest obviously covers fewer cases but is usually easier to use.

The most comprehensive series of digests is known as the American Digest System. Its most current component, the *General Digest*, collects and publishes headnotes from all West advance sheets. The *General Digest* is published about once a month, with each volume covering the entire range of over 400 digest topics. One *General Digest* volume cumulates entries from about twenty reporter volumes from federal and state courts.

The entries in the *General Digest* do not cumulate, so one may have to look through several dozen volumes to search for recent cases. This search is eased somewhat by tables listing the key numbers found in each volume.

```
┌─────────────────────────────────────┐
│  UNITED STATES—Cont'd               │
│  ☞                                   │
│  47—12, 13, 15                       │
│  50.1—11, 12, 13, 14, 15, 16, 17, 18,│
│      19, 20                          │
│  50.2—18, 19                         │
│  50.3—11, 13, 15, 18, 19             │
│  50.5(1)—11, 12, 14, 15, 16, 18, 19  │
│  50.5(2)—18, 19                      │
│  50.5(3)—14, 15, 18                  │
│  50.5(4)—13                          │
│  50.5(5)—11, 14, 18                  │
│  50.10(1)—11, 12, 14, 15, 16, 17,    │
│      19                              │
│  50.10(2)—19                         │
│  50.10(3)—11, 12, 14, 16, 17, 18,    │
│      19                              │
│  50.10(4)—11, 13, 14, 15, 17, 18     │
│  50.10(5)—17, 20                     │
│  50.10(7)—13, 18                     │
│  50.20—11, 12, 13, 16, 17, 18, 19,   │
│      20                              │
│  53(6.1)—11                          │
│  53(9)—11, 12, 16                    │
│  53(13.1)—19                         │
│  53(17)—18                           │
│  57—12, 16, 17, 18, 19, 20           │
│  58(3)—14, 16, 17, 18                │
│  58(5)—12                            │
│  58(6)—12                            │
│  58(8)—17                            │
└─────────────────────────────────────┘
```

Exhibit 21. Table of Key Numbers, 20 GENERAL DIGEST 804 (1998).

These tables cumulate every tenth volume. If twenty-seven *General Digest* volumes have been published, for example, it would be necessary to check the tables in volumes 10, 20, and 27. An excerpt from one of these tables is shown in Exhibit 21.

After five years, West recompiles the headnotes from the *General Digest* and publishes them in a multivolume

set called a *Decennial Digest*. The name *Decennial* comes from the fact that these sets used to be published every ten years. The *Eighth Decennial*, for example, covers cases decided between 1966 and 1976. Due to the increased volume of case law, West now compiles these digests every *five* years. The *Tenth Decennial Digest* consists of separate parts for 1986–91 and 1991–96.

The first unit of the American Digest System, called the *Century Digest*, covers the long period from 1658 to 1896. It was followed by a *First Decennial Digest* for 1897 to 1906, and subsequent *Decennials* for each decade since. The topics and key numbers used for points of law are generally the same in each unit of the digest system, from the most recent back to the *First Decennial*. The *Century Digest* employs a slightly different numbering system, but the *First Decennial* provides cross-references between the two units. Thus research under a digest key number can turn up cases from the seventeenth century to the present.

The law, of course, has not remained static over these centuries. West attempts to stay abreast of new developments by revising and expanding old topics and by establishing new topics. When new or revised topics are introduced, they are accompanied by tables converting older topics and key numbers into those newly adopted and vice versa. For example, for 90 years after the publication of the *First Decennial Digest* in 1910 the organization of the Negligence topic did not change significantly. In 1999, it was completely revised to provide greater coverage of modern issues such as assumption of risk, comparative negligence, premises liability, and liability for the negligent or criminal acts of third parties.

The new topic includes tables so that researchers can find related cases in the older *Decennials* and the newest *General Digest* volumes.

The digest changes slowly, however, and it may take several years for new areas of legal doctrine to be recognized and to receive adequate coverage. The key number assigned to the *Oxx* headnotes, for example, deals with management of federal property generally, rather than more specific issues such as BASE jumping or delivery of persons by parachute. Because cases in newly developing areas of the law are often assigned to general key numbers, digest research may not be the best way to find cases in these areas.

c. Jurisdictional and Regional Digests

The American Digest System covers cases appearing in all of West's reporters, and is therefore a massive, sometimes unwieldy finding tool. West also publishes digests covering the decisions of smaller geographical or jurisdictional units. There are digests for four of the regional reporter series (*Atlantic*, *North Western*, *Pacific*, and *South Eastern*), and digests for every state but Delaware, Nevada and Utah. Each state digest is devoted to only one jurisdiction, except for the *Dakota Digest* and the *Virginia-West Virginia Digest*. The state digests include references to all the cases West publishes from the state's courts, as well as federal cases arising from the U.S. District Courts in that state. (Federal courts often interpret and apply state law, sometimes addressing issues that state courts have not yet addressed.)

One advantage of using a state digest instead of the American Digest System is that a single volume can contain all relevant headnotes from a century or more.

(For about a dozen states, the current digest only provides coverage of cases back to 1930 or later, and an earlier digest must be consulted for complete retrospective coverage to the earliest court decisions. Most research, however, requires consulting only the current set for cases on point.) Instead of being issued in ten-year installments, state digests cumulate and are kept up to date by annual pocket parts in the back of each volume, and by quarterly pamphlets between annual supplements.

Another significant advantage to state digests arises when classifications change, as happened with the Negligence topic in 1999. As part of the process West editors reclassified the headnotes in thousands of older negligence cases, but this change is reflected only on Westlaw and in newly recompiled state digest volumes. *Decennial Digests* are closed sets, and their headnotes remain locked in the older classification.

West also publishes a separate series of digests for federal court decisions, containing headnotes reprinted from the *Supreme Court Reporter*, *Federal Reporter*, *Federal Supplement*, *Federal Rules Decisions*, and the reporters for specialized federal courts. The current set is known as the *Federal Practice Digest 4th*. Its volumes are supplemented by annual pocket parts, and the entire set is further updated with bimonthly pamphlets. Earlier cases are covered by four previous sets, the *Federal Digest* (1754–1939), *Modern Federal Practice Digest* (1939–61), *Federal Practice Digest 2d* (1961–75), and *Federal Practice Digest 3d* (1975 to mid–1980s).

The decisions of the Supreme Court of the United States are also covered by a West digest devoted solely to

its decisions, the *United States Supreme Court Digest*. (Note that *Lawyers' Edition* is also accompanied by its own digest, *United States Supreme Court Digest, Lawyers' Edition*, which uses a different classification system.) Other digests for specialized federal courts include *West's Bankruptcy Digest*, *Military Justice Digest*, *Federal Claims Digest*, and *Veterans Appeals Digest*.

All of these regional and jurisdictional digests include Tables of Cases which can be used to find decisions by name. These tables are usually more convenient than the *Decennial Digest* tables since they cover longer time periods and are updated by pocket parts. If the jurisdiction of a case is not known, of course, it may be necessary to consult the tables in the *Decennial* or *General Digests*.

d. *Words and Phrases*

West also reprints some headnote abstracts in a separate multivolume set, *Words and Phrases*. Headnotes are included in *Words and Phrases* if the court is defining or interpreting a legally significant term, and they are arranged alphabetically rather than by key number. *Words and Phrases* can be a very useful tool when the meaning of a specific term is in issue. The current *Words and Phrases* volumes were all published more than 25 years ago, so here it is usually most productive to *begin* research in the pocket part.

The *Words and Phrases* set covers the entire National Reporter System. Shorter Words and Phrases lists also appear in many West digests and in West reporter volumes and advance sheets. Earlier digest Words and Phrases volumes simply list the names and citations for the defining cases, but new editions of these volumes are being published (1999–date) with the text of the head-

notes reprinted. Exhibit 22 shows a page from the Words and Phrases section of the *Federal Practice Digest 4th*, including a headnote from *United States v. Oxx* interpreting the meaning of the term "parachute." (Note in Exhibit 17 that headnotes 2 and 3 of *Oxx* are both followed by references to Words and Phrases as a source for other judicial constructions and definitions.)

§ 4–4. *AMERICAN LAW REPORTS* ANNOTATIONS

At the same time that West was developing its National Reporter System in the late 19th century, other publishers were attempting a different approach to case reporting. These publishers selected "leading cases" for full-text publication, and provided commentaries, or *annotations*, which described other cases with similar facts, holdings, or procedures. Selective publication was not a successful alternative to comprehensive reporting, but the annotations have proved to be valuable case research tools.

Among the early sets of annotated reporters were the "Trinity series" (*American Decisions, American Reports* and *American State Reports*) (1871–1911) and *Lawyers Reports Annotated* (*LRA*) (1888–1918). *LRA*'s successor, *American Law Reports* (*ALR*), began in 1919 and is now published in two current series: *ALR5th* for general and state legal issues, and *ALR Federal* for issues of federal law. A few annotations limited to Supreme Court cases are also published in *United States Supreme Court Reports, Lawyers' Edition*.

Annotations contain a narrative text summarizing the cases on a specific topic and attempting to reconcile conflicting decisions. The coverage of *ALR* is not encyclo-

111 F P D 4th—253   **PARADIGMATIC**

C.D.Cal. 1990. Under California law, "unfair competition," within meaning of primary liability policies' definition of "advertising injury," was ambiguous, thus requiring construction by court, where insurer's definition of "unfair competition" as "palming off," and insureds' suggested definition of unlawful, unfair or fraudulent business practice and unfair, deceptive, untrue or misleading advertising, were both reasonable.—Keating v. National Union Fire Ins. Co. of Pittsburgh, Pa., 754 F.Supp. 1431, reversed 995 F.2d 154.—Insurance 2298.

D.Mass. 1991. "Palming off," within meaning of trademark violation, is selling of good or service of one's own creation under name or mark of another. Lanham Trade-Mark Act, § 43(a), 15 U.S.C.(1982 Ed.) § 1125(a).—Boothroyd Dewhurst, Inc. v. Poli, 783 F.Supp. 670.—Trade Reg 404.

E.D.N.Y. 1992. The gravamen of a common-law unfair competition claim for "palming off" under New York law is that labors and expenditures of plaintiffs have been misappropriated by defendants, and are likely to cause confusion among purchasing public as to origin of product; additionally, there must be some element or showing of "bad faith," and, unlike the requirement of federal law, proof of secondary meaning need not be shown.—Bristol-Myers Squibb Co. v. McNeil-P.P.C., Inc., 786 F.Supp. 182, affirmed in part, vacated in part 973 F.2d 1033.—Trade Reg 404.

S.D.Ohio 1990. "Palming off" occurs when a defendant attempts to bring about consumer confusion by causing consumers to purchase its products under the mistaken belief that they are in fact purchasing plaintiff's goods, and palming off involves directly competing goods.—Worthington Foods, Inc. v. Kellogg Co., 732 F.Supp. 1417.—Trade Reg 404.

PALPABLE DEFECT

E.D.Mich. 1997. "Palpable defect," for purposes of local rule requiring movant seeking reconsideration to demonstrate palpable defect by which court and parties have been misled, is defect that is obvious, clear, unmistakable, manifest, or plain. U.S.Dist.Ct.Rules E.D.Mich., Rule 7.1(h)(3).—Witzke v. Hiller, 972 F.Supp. 426.—Fed Civ Proc 928.

PALPABLE INJURIES

D.D.C. 1987. Deprivation of alleged rights of senator and congressmen to be consulted on compliance with treaty obligations, to participate in internal processes of Congress, and to advance legislative proposals for constituents affecting commitment to Nicaraguan resistance forces and nullification of effectiveness of votes to support national commitment to Nicaraguan resistance were not "palpable injuries," and, thus, senator and congressmen lacked standing to sue President and cabinet members for declaratory judgment that President unconstitutionally abdicated foreign affairs responsibilities by submitting to unconstitutional laws and failed to keep official and political promise to lend full support to resistance fighters. U.S.C.A. Const. Art. 2, §§ 1 et seq., 1, cl. 8, 2, cls. 1, 2; Art. 3, § 1

et seq.—Dornan v. U.S. Secretary of Defense, 676 F.Supp. 6, affirmed 851 F.2d 450, 271 U.S.App.D.C. 195.—Const Law 42.1(1).

PALPABLY UNREASONABLE

C.A.3 (N.J.) 1990. In order for police officer to be held liable for making a determination which was "palpably unreasonable," with respect to the allocation of police personnel, it must be clear when the decision was made, regardless of the consequences, that it was patently unacceptable. N.J.S.A. 59:2–3(d).—Waldorf v. Shuta, 896 F.2d 723.—Mun Corp 747(3).

PAPER

C.D.Cal. 1989. Statute changing prior law by providing that, for purpose of removal on diversity grounds, citizenship of defendants sued under fictitious names shall be disregarded was not a "paper" within statutory provision that, if case is not initially removable, it may be removed within 30 days of service of amended pleading or other paper from which it may be first ascertained that case is one which is or had become removable. 28 U.S.C.A. § 1446(b).—Phillips v. Allstate Ins. Co., 702 F.Supp. 1466.—Rem of C 79(1).

PAPER SIGNED BY THE PARTY

C.A.6 (Mich.) 1999. Garnishee disclosure filed by garnishee bank was "paper signed by the party" under Rule 11. Fed.Rules Civ.Proc.Rule 11(a). 28 U.S.C.A.—Apostolic Pentecostal Church v. Colbert, 169 F.3d 409, rehearing and suggestion for rehearing denied.—Fed Civ Proc 2773.

PAPERS

D.D.C. 1991. Discovery of pleadings from another case does not fall within strictures of criminal discovery rule; pleadings are neither "papers" nor "documents" for purposes of the rule. Fed.Rules Cr.Proc.Rule 16, 18 U.S.C.A.—U.S. v. George, 786 F.Supp. 11.—Crim Law 627.6(3).

PARACHUTE

C.A.10 (Utah) 1997. Parachute used for jumping from buildings, antennae, spans, and earth forms was "parachute" within meaning of regulation prohibiting delivery of persons by parachute in a national park without a permit and not in an emergency, even if parachute had more maneuverability and control than typical parachute, in view of separate regulation defining parachute as device used or intended to be used to retard fall of body or object through the air. 14 C.F.R. § 1.1; 36 C.F.R. § 2.17(a)(3).—U.S. v. Oxx, 127 F.3d 1277, on remand 56 F.Supp.2d 1214.—U S 57.

PARADIGMATIC FIDUCIARY RELATIONSHIP

S.D.N.Y. 1991. Relationship between psychiatrist and patient is a "paradigmatic fiduciary relationship," for purposes of misappropriation theory of securities fraud liability. Securities Exchange Act of 1934, § 10(b), 15 U.S.C.A. § 78j(b).—U.S. v. Willis, 778 F.Supp. 205.—Sec Reg 60.28(4).

pedic, and not every research issue is covered by its annotations. An annotation directly on point, however, can save considerable time for the researcher. It does the initial time-consuming work of finding relevant cases, and also arranges them according to specific fact patterns and holdings. Because they provide a narrative discussion of the cases rather than simply collections of headnotes, annotations are usually easier to use than digests.

Annotations differ significantly from other narrative resources such as treatises and law review articles. Their main purpose is to organize the varied judicial decisions from around the country into a coherent body of law. They generally do not criticize these decisions or analyze legal problems, nor do they attempt to integrate case law into a broader view of society as the better secondary sources do. As the work of the publisher's editorial staffs rather than of leading legal scholars, they are best viewed as research tools rather than as secondary authority which may persuade a tribunal. If they are cited, it is as convenient compilations of prevailing judicial doctrine.

a. Format and Contents

An *ALR* volume contains from ten to twenty annotations, each analyzing decisions on an issue raised in an illustrative recent case, which is printed in full either before the annotation or at the end of the volume. Each annotation begins with a table of contents, a detailed subject index, and a table listing the jurisdictions of the cases discussed. In new volumes since 1992 (the beginning of *ALR5th*), this introductory material has also included a useful Research References section providing leads to encyclopedias, practice aids, digests, and other sources, and including sample electronic search queries and relevant West digest key numbers. Exhibits 23 and

24 show pages from the beginning of an *ALR5th* annotation on the validity of releases exempting the operators of amusement facilities from liability for injuries to patrons. Exhibit 23 shows the table of contents, organizing the annotation's sections according to the reasons why releases have been given or denied effect. Exhibit 24 shows parts of the index, listing specific fact situations and legal issues arising in the cases discussed, and the jurisdictional table, a state-by-state listing of the cases.

As the table of contents in Exhibit 23 indicates, the first two sections of an annotation are "Introduction," describing its scope and listing related *ALR* annotations, and "Summary and Comment," providing a general overview and giving practice pointers. The annotation then summarizes cases on point from throughout the country, arranged according to their facts and holdings. Exhibit 25 shows a page from the annotation discussing two cases in which the Oregon Court of Appeals rejected plaintiffs' arguments that exculpatory releases violated public policy, as well as a California case deciding that parachute jumping is not an ultrahazardous activity requiring the application of strict liability.

The annotation in Exhibits 23–25 was published in 1997, but older annotations also provide references to recent case law through the use of annual supplements. Volumes in *ALR3d*, *ALR4th*, *ALR5th*, and *ALR Federal* are updated through annual pocket parts describing new cases, but *ALR1st* and *ALR2d* use other methods. While these older annotations are not used as often as those in the newer series, many remain current and continue to be updated. *ALR2d* volumes have no pocket parts, so new cases are instead summarized in a separate set of blue *Later Case Service* volumes, which *do* have annual pocket

TABLE OF CONTENTS

Research References
Index
Jurisdictional Table of Cited Statutes and Cases

ARTICLE OUTLINE

Research References

TOTAL CLIENT-SERVICE LIBRARY® REFERENCES

The following references may be of related or collateral interest to a user of this annotation.

Exhibit 23.   Randy J. Sutton, Annotation, *Validity, Construction, and Effect of Agreement Exempting Operator of Amusement Facility from Liability for Personal Injury or Death of Patron,* 54 A.L.R.5TH 513, 514 (1997).

RELEASES—AMUSEMENT PATRONS   54 ALR5th
54 ALR5th 513

Shower, slip and fall while in or exiting, §§ 3[a], 4[a], 5[b]
Signed release, § 3[a]
Signing of agreement by other person on behalf of patron, §§ 5[a], 7
Size of type, §§ 4[c], 5[a], 8
Skiing, §§ 3[a, b], 4[a, b], 5, 6[b]-9
Skydiving, parachuting, and paragliding, §§ 3[a, b], 4[a], 5[b], 6
Sliding, § 9
Slip and fall, §§ 3[a], 4[a, c], 5[b]
Small print, §§ 4[c], 5[a], 8
Snowmobiles, §§ 4[b], 5[b]
Special legal relationship, § 3[a]
Special-use permit, § 5[b]
Sports festival, § 3[b]
Stampede, §§ 4[a], 7
Statutory standards, §§ 5[a], 9
Steam room, §§ 3[a, b]
Strict construction, §§ 3[b], 4[a, b], 5[b]
Strict liability and gross negligence, § 6
Students, §§ 3[a, b], 4, 5[b], 6

Summary and comment, § 2
Swimming pool, fall at or near, §§ 3[a], 5[b]
Taking or retention of ticket, §§ 8, 9
Termination of contract, § 3[a]
Third-party beneficiary contract, § 5[b]
Tobogganing, §§ 4[a], 8
Training of staff, adequacy of, § 3[b]
Type size, §§ 4[c], 5[a], 8
Ultrahazardous activity, § 6[a]
Ultralight aircraft, rental of, § 3[b]
Unconscionability, §§ 3[a], 5
Understandability of release, § 4[c]
Unequal bargaining power, §§ 3[a], 5
Uniform Commercial Code, § 5[a]
Unsigned agreements, § 9
Vapors, inhalation of, § 4[b]
Warn, failure to, §§ 3[b], 6[a]
Weights and weight lifting, §§ 3[c], 4[a]
Whitewater rafting, §§ 3[b], 5[a], 6[a]
Willful and wanton acts, §§ 3[b], 4[c], 6, 7

Jurisdictional Table of Cited Statutes and Cases*

ARIZONA

Sirek v Fairfield Snowbowl (1990, App) 166 Ariz 183, 800 P2d 1291, 72 Ariz Adv Rep 63—§ 4[a]
Valley Nat'l Bank v National Ass'n for Stock Car Auto Racing (1987, App) 153 Ariz 374, 736 P2d 1186—§ 3[a]

CALIFORNIA

Allabach v Santa Clara County Fair Assn. (1996, 6th Dist) 46 Cal App 4th 1007, 54 Cal Rptr 2d 330, 96 CDOS 4662, 96 Daily Journal DAR 7441—§ 3[a]
Allan v Snow Summit, Inc. (1996, 4th Dist) 51 Cal App 4th 1358, 59 Cal Rptr 2d 813, 97 CDOS 13, 97 Daily Journal DAR 9—§§ 3[a], 5[b]

* Statutes, rules, regulations, and constitutional provisions bearing on the subject of the annotation are included in this table only to the extent, and in the form, that they are reflected in the court opinions discussed in this annotation. The reader should consult the appropriate statutory or regulatory compilations to ascertain the current status of relevant statutes, rules, regulations, and constitutional provisions.

For federal cases involving state law, see state headings.

Exhibit 24.   54 A.L.R.5TH at 518.

an additional $300, and because he was under no compulsion to make a parachute jump. Also, the court determined that the transaction had none of the characteristics of one affected by a public interest.

A claim of unequal bargaining power was dismissed in Mann v Wetter (1990) 100 **Or App** 184, 785 P2d 1064, review den 309 Or 645, 789 P2d 1387. In that case, a student died while attending an instructional scuba-diving course. Both the operator of the scuba-diving school and one of its instructors were sued by the deceased's estate. The plaintiff contended that the release signed by the decedent before the accident was ineffective because it was not presented to the decedent until he had already attended some of the classes and had paid his fees in total. Notwithstanding, the court said that these circumstances did not result in unequal bargaining power that would require invalidating the release because the decedent had been free to discontinue the program rather than sign the release.

In Harmon v Mt. Hood Meadows (1997) 146 **Or App** 215, 932 P2d 92, the court held that enforcement of a release against the plaintiff skier in an action for negligence against the defendant ski resort did not offend public policy. The plaintiff executed the release as part of her season-pass application. She was injured while attempting to board a chair lift at the defendant's facility. The court stated that the enforcement of the release provisions to bar the plaintiff's negligence claim would not offend public policy, despite the contention that the provisions relieved the defendant not only from liability for negligence but from "any and all liability," which encompassed conduct beyond mere negligence. The plaintiff's claim was one for mere negligence, the court explained, and thus the provisions were not unenforceable as applied to her even if they might be unenforceable as to the plaintiffs asserting other claims.

§ 6. Gross negligence and strict liability

[a] Release or agreement given effect

In the following cases, the courts held or recognized that exculpatory agreements exempting operators of amusement or recreational activities from liability could be enforceable, as to claims brought by the plaintiffs allegedly based upon gross negligence, willful acts, or strict liability.

The court in Hulsey v Elsinore Parachute Center (1985, 4th Dist) 168 **Cal App 3d** 333, 214 Cal Rptr 194, CCH Prod Liab Rep ¶ 10581, considered a claim by a parachutist that the release he signed in favor of the parachute-jumping school was invalid because parachute jumping is an ultrahazardous activity. The court rejected the plaintiff's contention as to the ultrahazardous nature of parachute jumping, because such an activ-

Exhibit 25. 54 A.L.R.5TH at 564.

parts. Annotations in *ALR1st* are updated through a set called *ALR1st Blue Book of Supplemental Decisions*, which simply lists the citations of relevant new cases.

If later cases substantially change the law on a subject covered by an annotation, a new annotation is written to supplement or to completely supersede the older annotation. The older volume's pocket part or other supplement alerts the researcher to the existence of the newer treatment (another good reason to *always* check the pocket part). Another way to determine whether an annotation has been superseded is to check the "Annotation History Table" in the last volume of the *ALR Index*, which lists all superseding and supplementing annotations.

b.   Finding Annotations

The basic tool for subject access to *ALR* is the six-volume *ALR Index*, which provides coverage of annotations in *ALR2d*, *ALR3d*, *ALR4th*, *ALR5th* and *ALR Federal*, and is kept current by quarterly pocket parts. (The annotations in the first series of *ALR* are indexed in a separate *ALR First Series Quick Index*, and *Lawyers' Edition* annotations are listed in the *Quick Case Table with Annotation References*.) A less comprehensive *ALR Quick Index* covers only *ALR3d*, *ALR4th*, and *ALR5th*, and is published as an annual softcover volume. *ALR Federal* is accompanied by two finding tools: a *Quick Index* limited to its annotations, and a three-volume *Tables* set listing federal cases, statutes, regulations and court rules cited in the annotations. Exhibit 26 shows a page from the *ALR Index*, including references under "Parachutes and Parachuting" to the annotation illustrated and an earlier annotation on liability for a skydiver's injury or death.

ALR INDEX

PALMING OFF—Cont'd
related claim under federal trademark
laws, **62 ALR Fed 428, § 13**
Standing to bring false advertising claim or
unfair competition claim under
§ 43(a)(1) of Lanham Act (15 U.S.C.A.
§ 1125(a)(1)), **124 ALR Fed 189, § 7,
11[b]**

PALM PRINTS
Palm prints as evidence, **28 ALR2d 1115**

PAMPHLETS
Circulars, Brochures, and Pamphlets
(this index)

PANAMA
Pleading and proof of law of foreign
country, **75 ALR3d 177, § 6[c], 9[a, b]**

**PANCREAS AND PANCREATIC
CONDITIONS**
Cancer as compensable under workers'
compensation acts, **19 ALR4th 639,
§ 11**
Excessiveness or adequacy of damages
awarded for injuries to or conditions in
glandular system, **14 ALR4th 539, § 25**
Medical malpractice, loss of chance
causality, **54 ALR4th 10, § 7[d], 8[h]**
Pre-existing conditions
cancer, sufficiency of proof that it
resulted from accident or incident in
suit rather than from pre-existing
condition, **2 ALR3d 384, § 3[a]**
digestive condition, sufficiency of
proof that it resulted from accident
or incident in suit rather than from
pre-existing condition, **2 ALR3d
360, § 7**

PANDERING
Pimping and Pandering (this index)

PANEL CHALLENGE
Counsel's representation of criminal client
regarding right to and incidents of jury
trial, **3 ALR4th 601, § 5**

PANHANDLING
Homeless persons, laws regulating beg-

PANHANDLING—Cont'd
ging, panhandling, or similar activity by
poor or homeless persons, **7 ALR5th
455**

PANIC PEDDLING
Brokers, validity and construction of
antiblockbusting regulations designated
to prevent brokers from inducing sales
of realty because of actual or rumored
entry of racial group in neighborhood,
34 ALR3d 1432

PANTOMIME
Defamation by acts, gestures, pantomime,
or the like, **46 ALR4th 403**

PANTS
Products liability, flammable clothing, **1
ALR4th 251, § 6, 12**

PAPER AND PAPER PRODUCTS
Eminent domain, unity or contiguity of
separate properties sufficient to allow
damages for diminished value of parcel
remaining after taking of other parcel,
59 ALR4th 308, § 52
Taxes, what constitutes manufacturing and
who is a manufacturer under tax laws,
17 ALR3d 7, § 24[b], 48, 49[b], 58

PAPER CARRIERS
Newspaper Carriers (this index)

PAP SMEAR TEST
Malpractice, failure of physician to notify
patient of unfavorable diagnosis or test,
49 ALR3d 501, § 4, 7, 9

PARACHUTES AND PARACHUTING
Injury or death, liability for civilian
skydiver's or parachutist's injury or
death, **95 ALR3d 1280**
Release from liability, validity, construction, and effect of agreement exempting
operator of amusement facility from
liability for personal injury or death of
patron, **54 ALR5th 513, § 3[a, b], 4[a],
5[b], 6**

PARADES
Disguise or mask, validity and construction

Exhibit 26.   5 ALR INDEX 62 (1999).

Remember that each *ALR* annotation includes as section 1[b] a list of other annotations on related topics. If a quick check of the index does not turn up an annotation directly on point but does lead to one on a related issue, the most productive next step may be to turn to that annotation and read through its list of related annotations. This list may lead to analogies or concepts the researcher may not have thought to check in the index. Section 1[b] of the annotation shown in Exhibits 23–25, for example, includes more than two dozen cross-references to annotations on topics such as the liability of owners of skating rinks, health clubs, theaters, and zoos.

Another means of access to annotations is through the *ALR Digest to 3d, 4th, 5th and Federal*, a multivolume set classifying *ALR*'s annotations and cases in a system similar to West's digests, and including references to *American Jurisprudence 2d* and other reference works. There are also older digests covering *ALR1st* and *ALR2d*.

Annotations beginning with *ALR2d* are available on-line through Westlaw and Lexis–Nexis, and beginning with *ALR3d* are also published on CD–ROM. In either version the full texts of the annotations are searchable for particular combinations of terms. Because the descriptions of the facts of the cases include terms that are not relevant to the subject of the annotation, it is often best to limit searches to words in annotation titles or to use a natural language search that ranks documents by relevance.

Many other sources, including some annotated codes and encyclopedias, provide references to relevant *ALR* annotations. Note, for example, the *ALR* references in *Am. Jur. 2d* in Exhibit 1, on page 24. In addition, the two

citators to be discussed in the next section, KeyCite and Shepard's Citations, both list annotations citing cases. Leads to *ALR* annotations are just one of the ways that these services lead from one case to other cases on related topics.

§ 4–5. CITATORS

The body of published American case law is filled with decisions which have long since been overruled or limited to specific facts. Before relying on any case, an attorney must verify its current validity. This process of updating cases has traditionally been performed by checking printed volumes known as *Shepard's Citations*, and as a result it is sometimes known as *Shepardizing*. Today Shepard's information is available electronically as well as in print, and a competing electronic resource named KeyCite provides a similar service.

Whether citators are used electronically or in print, they perform three major functions. They provide parallel citations for the decision and references to other proceedings in the same case, allowing researchers to trace a case's judicial history. They indicate if subsequent cases have overruled, limited, or otherwise diminished a case's precedent, providing the information needed to determine whether it is still good law. They list research leads to later citing cases, as well as periodical articles, attorney general opinions, *ALR* annotations, and other resources, enabling researchers to find related cases and to trace the development of a legal doctrine forward from a known case to the present.

a. KeyCite and Shepard's Citations Online

The two major electronic citator systems, KeyCite and Shepard's Citations, are products of the competing com-

mercial online systems Westlaw and Lexis–Nexis. Both are available as part of subscriptions to these systems, as well as on pay-as-you-go bases through the Internet (<www.keycite.com> and <www.shepards.com>).

On Westlaw and Lexis–Nexis, the citator services are integrated into case display through the use of symbols indicating available information. A Westlaw case display includes a red flag if a case is not good law on some point, a yellow flag if there is some negative history, and a blue "H" to indicate simply that there is some case history information available. Clicking on one of these symbols leads directly to the KeyCite display. Similarly, Lexis–Nexis displays a red stop sign for a case with negative treatment (e.g., it has been reversed or overruled), a yellow caution sign for possible negative treatment, and a blue circle for a case with other citing references. Be aware, however, that "negative" history or treatment is broadly construed by both services. A lower court decision that declines to extend a Supreme Court precedent to an unrelated area is listed as "distinguishing" its holding. This is considered a negative citation, even though it has no impact on the precedential value of the Supreme Court decision.

Both KeyCite and Shepard's distinguish between decisions which may bear a direct impact on a case's validity (KeyCite's "history of the case" section, and "Shepard's for validation") and the full list of citing documents (Key-Cite's "citations" section, and "Shepard's for research"). The first category includes proceedings in the same litigation and any negative citing cases.

While KeyCite and Shepard's both list all documents in the online databases which cite a particular case, the

ways in which they organize these references are different. Shepard's displays citing cases by jurisdiction, beginning with cases from the home jurisdiction of the cited case. KeyCite ranks the citing cases by the extent to which they discuss the cited case, with rankings from four stars (an extended discussion) to one star (mentioned, usually as part of a string citation). KeyCite also indicates those cases that quote directly from the cited case, by adding quotation marks to the display.

Both online citators provide several ways that researchers can focus retrieval. This feature, called *Restrictions* on Shepard's and *Limits* on KeyCite, can be used to see only those references from specific jurisdictions, or those that cite the point of law in particular headnotes. Shepard's can also restrict to cases with particular treatments, e.g. "criticized" or "followed,", and KeyCite can limit by depth of treatment. Shepard's users can also run a search with "focus" terms among the pool of citing documents.

It is also possible to focus on documents discussing a particular point of law, by restricting or limiting retrieval to the headnote from the cited case which states that specific legal principle. Shepard's uses headnotes from both official and National Reporter System versions of cases. These headnote numbers do not necessarily coincide, so be sure to note which reporter you are using. The point of law in *California Reporter* headnote 5, for example, may be the same point summarized in *California Appellate Reports* headnote 4. KeyCite uses only the headnotes from West's National Reporter System, but as a Westlaw component it integrates these headnotes into the

citator process by displaying the text of the headnotes and indicating the number of documents citing the case on each point.

Although their editorial treatment and arrangement differ, KeyCite and Shepard's generally provide references to the same group of citing cases. Both include cases that are designated as unpublished but are available through the online databases, as well as cases published in the official reports, West reporters, and other topical reporters. Occasionally one service includes a reference to an unpublished decision available through one database but not the other, but the differences in case coverage are slight. Both provide accurate coverage and timely notice of new developments.

Coverage of secondary sources in the two services does differ. Both have references to *ALR* annotations and law reviews available online. Shepard's also lists citing references in selected law reviews back as far as 1957, even though the earlier articles are not available online in full text. KeyCite is limited to materials available on Westlaw, but it generally provides more extensive coverage of recent law reviews as well as legal encyclopedias and treatises.

Exhibits 27 and 28 show citator results from the web versions of KeyCite and Shepard's, for *Hulsey v. Elsinore Parachute Center*, one of the cases discussed in the *ALR* annotation shown above in Exhibit 25. The KeyCite result in Exhibit 27 has been limited to three of the cited case's headnotes. Note that a negative case is listed first, and that it quotes from the *Hulsey* opinion. This is followed by other citing cases and secondary sources, including the *ALR* annotation, *Am. Jur. 2d*, and law review articles. The

Shepard's result in Exhibit 28 has been restricted to show only negative cases and to display the cited headnotes in both *Cal. App. 3d* and *Cal. Rptr.* From either of these citator displays, it is possible to click on a citing case or article and link directly to the point in its text where *Hulsey* is cited.

| WL Print/ Download | ▷ Hulsey v. Elsinore Parachute Center, 168 Cal.App.3d 333, 214 Cal.Rptr. 194, Prod.Liab.Rep. (CCH) P 10,581 (Cal.App. 4 Dist., May 16, 1985) (NO. E000643) |

Citations: limited to Headnotes = 5-7
(Showing 14 of 53 documents)

Negative Cases

Distinguished by

1 Baker Pacific Corp. v. Suttles, 269 Cal.Rptr. 709, 714+, 220 Cal.App.3d 1148, 1156+ (Cal.App. 1 Dist. May 25, 1990) (NO. A043155) 〞★ ★ ★ HN: 4,5

Positive Cases
★ ★ ★ **Discussed**

2 Paralift, Inc. v. Superior Court, 29 Cal.Rptr.2d 177, 179+, 23 Cal.App.4th 748, 753+ (Cal.App. 4 Dist. Oct 20, 1993) (NO. D018950) HN: 2,4,6

★ ★ **Cited**

3 Blankenheim v. E. F. Hutton & Co., 266 Cal.Rptr. 593, 598, 217 Cal.App.3d 1463, 1472 (Cal.App. 6 Dist. Feb 15, 1990) (NO. H004920) HN: 4,5

4 Moore v. R.G. Industries, Inc., 789 F.2d 1326, 1328, 4 Fed.R.Serv.3d 1106 (9th Cir.(Cal.) Feb 25, 1986) (NO. 84-2534) HN: 7

Secondary Sources

5 Validity, construction, and effect of agreement exempting operator of amusement facility from liability for personal injury or death of patron, 54 A.L.R.5th 513, §3a+ (1998) HN: 2,4,6

6 Liability for civilian skydiver's or parachutist's injury or death, 95 A.L.R.3d 1280, §3 (1979) HN: 2,4,6,7,8

7 9 Witkin: California Procedure Ch. XIII s 691, APPENDICES. (1997) HN: 6

8 57A Am. Jur. 2d Negligence s 396, GENERALLY; RYLANDS V FLETCHER DOCTRINE HN: 7

9 57A Am. Jur. 2d Negligence s 403, WHAT IS ULTRAHAZARDOUS HN: 7

10 57A Am. Jur. 2d Negligence s 407, PARTICIPANTS IN ULTRAHAZARDOUS ACTIVITIES HN: 7

11 MAKE IT, MARKET IT, AND YOU MAY HAVE TO PAY FOR IT: AN EVALUATION OF GUN MANUFACTURER LIABILITY FOR THE CRIMINAL USE OF UNIQUELY DANGEROUS FIREARMS IN LIGHT OF IN RE 101 CALIFORNIA STREET, 1997 B.Y.U. L. Rev. 131, 167 (1997) HN: 7

12 LEGAL OPINIONS IN CORPORATE TRANSACTIONS: THE OPINION ON AGREEMENTS AND INSTRUMENTS, 12 J. Corp. L. 657, 697 (1987) HN: 5

13 LEGAL OPINIONS IN CORPORATE TRANSACTIONS: THE OPINION ON AGREEMENTS AND INSTRUMENTS, 624 PLI/Corp 291, 333 (1988) HN: 5

14 PREPARING AND INTERPRETING OPINIONS IN FINANCIAL TRANSACTIONS: NINE HARD QUESTIONS, 583 PLI/Corp 293, 447 (1987) HN: 5

© Copyright West Group 2000

Exhibit 27. KeyCite display for *United States v. Oxx,* limited to headnotes 5–7.

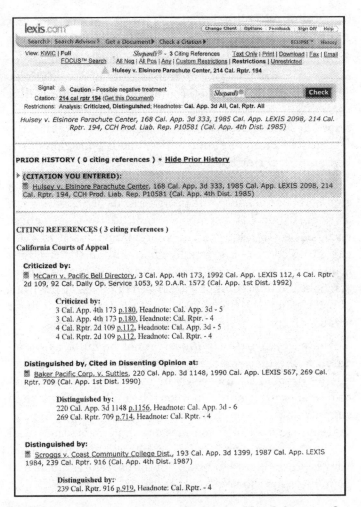

Exhibit 28. Shepard's Citations display for *United States v. Oxx*, restricted to negative treatments.

b. *Shepard's Citations* in Print

While the electronic versions of KeyCite and Shepard's Citations compete for customers, Shepard's is the choice for researchers using print resources to check citations. There is no print counterpart to KeyCite, but print versions of *Shepard's Citations* are published for the Supreme Court, the lower federal courts, every state, the District of Columbia, Puerto Rico, and each region of the National Reporter System.

In order to convey a large amount of information in a small amount of space, the print versions of *Shepard's* use a system of one-letter symbols to indicate the treatment of citing cases. In addition, the abbreviations used to identify citing sources are usually shorter than the citations commonly used in the *Bluebook* and other sources. These symbols and abbreviations are listed in tables at the front of each volume. Exhibit 29 shows a listing of treatment symbols from a recent *Shepard's Citations* volume.

Printed *Shepard's Citations* cannot be quite as up-to-date as the electronic resources, but they are supplemented frequently (biweekly or monthly). Each set contains one or more maroon bound volumes, and supplementary pamphlets of varying colors. To help researchers know which volumes or supplements they need to use, the cover of each supplement includes a list, "What Your Library Should Contain," of the current volumes and pamphlets for the set.

CASE ANALYSIS–ABBREVIATIONS

History of Case

a	(affirmed)	Same case affirmed on appeal.
cc	(Connected case)	Different case from case cited but arising out of same subject matter or intimately connected therewith.
D	(dismissed)	Appeal from or review of same case dismissed.
De	(denied)	Review or rehearing, denied
Gr	(granted)	Review or rehearing granted
m	(modified)	Same case modified on appeal.
r	(reversed)	Same case reversed on appeal.
s	(same case)	Same case as case cited.
S	(superseded)	Substitution for former opinion.
v	(vacated)	Same case vacated.
W	(withdrawn)	Same case withdrawn.
US	cert gran	Certiorari granted by U. S. Supreme Court.
US	cert den	Certiorari denied by U. S. Supreme Court.
US	cert dis	Certiorari dismissed by U. S. Supreme Court.
US	reh den	Rehearing denied by U. S. Supreme Court.
US	reh dis	Rehearing dismissed by U. S. Supreme Court.
US	app pndg	Appeal pending before the U. S. Supreme Court.

Treatment of Case

c	(criticized)	Soundness of decision or reasoning in cited case criticized for reasons given.
d	(distinguished)	Case at bar different either in law or fact from case cited for reasons given.
e	(explained)	Statement of import of decision in cited case. Not merely a restatement of the facts.
f	(followed)	Cited as controlling.
h	(harmonized)	Apparent inconsistency explained and shown not to exist.
j	(dissenting	Citation in dissenting opinion.
L	(limited)	Refusal to extend decision of cited case beyond precise issues involved.
o	(overruled)	Ruling in cited case expressly overruled.
p	(parallel)	Citing case substantially alike or on all fours with cited case in its law or facts.
q	(questioned)	Soundness of decision or reasoning in cited case questioned.

Other

#		Citing references may be of questionable precedential value as review was granted by California Supreme Court or case was ordered not published.

Exhibit 29. SHEPARD'S SOUTHERN REPORTER CITATIONS, at viii (Supp. 1994–99, pt. 1).

Exhibit 30 shows a page from *Shepard's California Reporter Citations*, indicating treatment of *Hulsey v. Elsinore Parachute Center*, 263 Cal. Rptr. 194 (Ct. App. 1985). After the page number and the name and date of the case, the first citation listed is the parallel citation, listed in parentheses. This would be followed by citations of decisions in the same litigation, if any, with symbols to indicate the relationship among the decisions. *Hulsey* has no such listings, but two other cases at pages 153 and 163 were ordered not published (Np).

Next are citations of later citing decisions in California courts, as printed in the *California Reporter*. This lists the exact page on which the Shepardized case is cited, rather than the first page of the citing decision. The *Hulsey* headnote stating the legal principle involved is indicated by small raised numbers to the left of the page numbers of the citing cases. The citations indicate that the point of law in its headnote 4 has been *distinguished* (d), *explained* (e), and *criticized* (c) in later California decisions. Decisions from the state's courts are followed by citations to federal court decisions, arranged by circuit, and to decisions from other states. *Hulsey* has been *followed* (f) by a Ninth Circuit decision, and cited by courts from four other states.

Finally, references to the case in law review articles and *ALR* annotations are noted. The abbreviations used by Shepard's (such as "CFW" for *California Western Law Review* and "SFR" for *University of San Francisco Law Review*) may be unfamiliar, but they are included in the table at the front of each *Shepard's* volume.

References to *Hulsey v. Elsinore Parachute Center* are also listed in *Shepard's California Citations*, under both

CALIFORNIA REPORTER					Vol. 214

—88—
California v
Baird
1985
(1st App.)
(168CA3d237)
f 227CaR[4]660
f 264CaR[8]341
f 720P2d[9]8
Ariz
897P2d654
53Æ1178n
31Æ194s

—93—
California v
Ruhl
1985
(3rd App.)
(168CA3d311)
216CaR913
246CaR[8]394
247CaR[8]324
f 261CaR[9]622
f 261CaR[8]817
d 27CaR2d27
83Æ1032s
3Æ1181s

—99—
California v
Allied Fidelity
Insurance Co.
1985
(2nd App.)
(168CA3d253)
s 207CaR530
s 209CaR592
s 692P2d952
33Æ663s

—105—
California v
Almarez
1985
(2nd App.)
(168CA3d262)
q 215CaR[8]177
c 215CaR[7]504
q 215CaR626
q 215CaR[7]740
q 217CaR731
218CaR[7]496
c 218CaR[7]912
219CaR[7]287
219CaR816
j 219CaR823
219CaR[8]902
219CaR[7]918
j 220CaR473
222CaR311
q 222CaR[8]624
c 223CaR[7]580
230CaR329
234CaR[7]549

240CaR[4]260
246CaR[2]578
252CaR[8]605
45CaR2d[7]176

—109—
Estate of Khan
1985
(2nd App.)
(168CA3d270)
20CaR2d483
e 20CaR2d[7]484
Utah
915P2d507

—113—
National Diver-
sified Services
Inc. v Bern-
stein
1985
(1st App.)
(168CA3d410)
224CaR564
231CaR[8]224
236CaR[6]115
236CaR[3]116
274CaR228
274CaR[8]538
284CaR[8]33
34CaR2d155
59CaR2d[8]781
62CaR2d[8]891
726P2d[8]1299
Mass
514NE1329

—119—
Jahn v Brickey
1985
(4th App.Div.3)
(168CA3d376)
220CaR[8]547
236CaR[8]470
252CaR579
267CaR[8]390
1CaR2d[7]226
35Æ538s
11Æ119n
14Æ380n

—125—
Miller v Supe-
rior Court of
Los Angeles
County
1985
(2nd App.)
(168CA3d376)
225CaR[3]256
226CaR[8]210
28CaR2d[7]527
35CaR2d[8]702
Cir. 9
813F2d258

813F2d[5]259
40HLJ930

—132—
Fox v Alexis
1985
(Supreme Ct.)
(38C3d621)
(699P2d309)
Np09-25-1985
s 197CaR616
214CaR[7]788
f 218CaR671
218CaR672
f 219CaR32
221CaR665
226CaR161
235CaR[3]499
237CaR[8]681
244CaR[7]479
251CaR[8]637
254CaR573
11CaR2d[7]759
20CaR2d120
j 35CaR2d914
42CaR2d429
f 706P2d284
706P2d285
749P2d[7]1334
e 753P2d[5]598
e 753P2d[5]618
23Pcf117
13PLR225

—139—
Thomson v
Call
1985
(Supreme Ct.)
(38C3d633)
(699P2d316)
De07-29-1985
US cert den
474US1057
US cert den
106SC796
s 198CaR320
d 246CaR583
d 246CaR584
254CaR[3]695
273CaR660
273CaR[8]661
48CaR2d681
49CaR2d679
49CaR2d[8]682
f 55CaR2d[7]567
55CaR2d[7]568
55CaR2d[8]571
64CaR2d148
d 64CaR2d150
13PLR234
25SwR305

—153—
California v
Hill
1985
(2nd App.)
(167CA3d175)
Np08-01-1985

—163—
In re Ayres
1985
(4th App.Div.3)
(167CA3d648)
Np08-22-1985
NJ
582A2d1010

—170—
California v
Walmsley
1985
(4th App.Div.1)
(168CA3d636)
221CaR[4]392
221CaR[5]392
c 221CaR[5]393
c 221CaR[8]393
222CaR[7]35
222CaR[3]36
222CaR[8]36
e 222CaR41
d 224CaR[8]16
L 224CaR[3]17
d 225CaR[8]435
244CaR257
249CaR[2]173
249CaR[8]174
265CaR[7]783
273CaR[8]480
273CaR[7]481
275CaR[8]301
278CaR3
286CaR774
f 286CaR775
1CaR2d[8]581
c 1CaR2d[8]582
23CaR2d[8]502
26CaR2d436
44CaR2d[8]506
Conn
540A2d687
Iowa
437NW575
W Va
347SE201
19Æ1251s
15Æ410n

—173—
Northrop Corp.
v Chaparral
Energy Inc.
1985
(2nd App.)
(168CA3d725)

219CaR384

—177—
Heckmann v
Ahmanson
1985
(2nd App.)
(168CA3d119)
219CaR[7]797
244CaR542
251CaR[2]555
j 260CaR779
f 274CaR[18]182
3CaR2d[7]242
j 11CaR2d350
52CaR2d[18]887
j 834P2d1168
Cir. 2
652FS1081
Cir. 6
105BRW[15]413
Cir. 9
834F2d[4]732
936F2d464
109F3d[6]1391
688FS1454
178BRW[22]488
203BRW999
Cir. 10
890FS978
168BRW998
NY
594NYS2d22
594NYS2d27
73CaL1698
77CaL1421
16PLR1034
63SCL75
67SCL329
59ChL1470
88CR331
94CR169
78Geo98
48LCP(3)182
56LCP(3)18
85McL143
136PaL327
67TxL1415
70TxL599

—191—
California v
Bonilla
1985
(2nd App.)
(168CA3d201)
215CaR625
215CaR[7]740
217CaR[7]358
d 218CaR496
220CaR[7]424
221CaR[7]644
36CaR2d[7]388
14Æ227s

—194—
Hulsey v Elsi-
nore Parachute
Center
1985
(4th App.Div.2)
(168CA3d333)
239CaR502
239CaR503
d 239CaR[8]919
242CaR[7]56
242CaR[7]360
e 243CaR[8]425
250CaR[1]303
262CaR732
262CaR733
266CaR598
d 269CaR[4]714
j 269CaR717
274CaR649
j 274CaR653
277CaR[8]896
j 277CaR906
2CaR2d[7]440
c 4CaR2d[4]112
21CaR2d[7]247
21CaR2d[7]248
29CaR2d179
29CaR2d[6]181
29CaR2d[6]182
59CaR2d[7]824
Cir. 9
f 789F2d1328
939FS[1]724
Ariz
736P2d190
Minn
392NW731
SD
514NW703
Wis
432NW631
25CFW261
20SFR228
20SFR725
20WSR215
1991WLR630
95Æ1280s

—205—
Wygant v
Victor Valley
Joint Union
High School
District
1985
(4th App.Div.2)
(168CA3d319)
d 241CaR[1]2
242CaR[3]355
e 242CaR[8]665
242CaR[7]667
j 242CaR668
f 251CaR[1]501
265CaR[1]515
f 269CaR[1]168
Continued

Exhibit 30. SHEPARD'S CALIFORNIA CITATIONS 203 (1997) pt. 3.

California Appellate Reports and *California Reporter* citations. Both state citators and regional citators (including *Shepard's California Reporter Citations*) list citing cases from the same jurisdiction and in federal courts, but citing cases from other states appear only in the regional series.

Supplementary *Shepard's* pamphlets include one feature not found in the bound volumes. Recent citing cases are included before their reporter citations are available, so these are listed by their Lexis citations. Tables in the back of the supplement list these cases and provide names, docket numbers, and dates so that they can be tracked down in print or through court websites.

It may be apparent that the electronic citators have several advantages over the printed *Shepard's Citations*. Citing entries are compiled into one listing, eliminating the need to search through multiple volumes and pamphlets. Because page space is not a concern, case treatments and names of publications are spelled out rather than abbreviated. The researcher can have the computer find specific treatments or headnote numbers, rather than scanning a lengthy list of citations. Finally, hypertext links make it possible to go directly from the online citator to the text of citing cases. The printed version of *Shepard's Citations* can nonetheless be a useful and convenient means to verify the current validity of a decision and to find research leads.

§ 4–6. CONCLUSION

This chapter has introduced both electronic and print resources for case research. Many students tend to rely very heavily on online resources, and only when they leave law school do they learn that computerized research

can be very expensive. Yet financial constraints are only one reason not to rely exclusively on a method that is so dependent on the researcher knowing exactly how to phrase a search request. If the language of a decision does not precisely match the request, it will remain undiscovered unless other research methods are also used. The database systems are most effective as part of a research strategy integrating a number of different approaches.

Often the benefit of an author or editor's work in organizing and analyzing cases is indispensable. Treatises and law review articles analyze the leading cases in a subject area, while digests and annotations sort and index cases by precise facts or issues. A computer can neither decide which cases are most important nor distinguish between holding and dictum. There are times when printed tools can achieve results with greater speed and precision than online research.

No single case-finder is the best for all purposes. Selection of the most useful resource depends upon the nature of the problem at hand. Research involving the interpretation of a statute leads to an annotated code for case-finding, while a problem requiring general background knowledge of a topic could find the researcher beginning with a treatise. Each research problem must be analyzed separately, the available tools evaluated, and the most appropriate approach chosen. Inevitably personal preference plays a part when two or more case-finding tools seem equally useful. Experimentation and the development of skill in using all of these approaches will enable you to make the most effective choices for each problem encountered.

CHAPTER 5

CONSTITUTIONS AND STATUTES

---

§ 5–1. INTRODUCTION

The preceding chapters have focused on case law because of the importance of appellate decisions in the common law system and in American legal education. The judiciary, however, is not the branch of government charged with making laws, and legislative enactments play just as vital a role as decisions in today's legal system. Most appellate court decisions, in fact, involve the application or interpretation of statutes rather than the consideration of common law principles.

This chapter considers both constitutions, which establish the form and limitations of government power, and legislative law. These forms of law are discussed in one chapter because they are often published together, and because research methods are similar. In considering constitutional provisions or statutes, it is important to find not only the relevant text but to find the court decisions that interpret this text and define its terms. The most common research sources for both constitutions and statutes are *annotated codes*, which provide the text of the law in force accompanied by notes of court decisions.

The nature of legal authority assigned to constitutions and legislation is different from that of case law. Statutes have binding or mandatory authority within their own jurisdiction, but in other jurisdictions they have no effect and are not even persuasive authority. One state's laws may influence another state's legislature considering similar legislation, and judicial decisions applying or construing a statute may persuade other courts confronting similar issues, but the statutory language itself carries no authority outside its own jurisdiction.

Determining early in the research process whether constitutional or statutory provisions are involved in a specific problem can save considerable time, as this significantly affects the direction of your research. Introductory commentaries and cases generally provide references to the relevant legislation, and experienced researchers develop a sense of which issues are likely to be governed by constitution or statute, and whether these issues are matters of federal or state law. Substantive criminal law,

for example, is generally defined by the enactments of a state legislature, while defendants' procedural rights are determined by both federal and state constitutional law. As legislatures continue to enact statutes to govern traditional common law areas such as contract and tort, more and more questions involve some statutory research.

§ 5–2.   THE U.S. CONSTITUTION

The United States Constitution is the basic law of the country, defining political relationships, enumerating the rights and liberties of citizens, and creating the framework of national government. Unlike statutes, which are often written in extreme detail and specificity, the Constitution contains concise statements of broad principles. It entered into force in March 1789, and it has only been amended 27 times in more than 200 years. Among the most important of these amendments are the Bill of Rights, guaranteeing personal liberties, and the 14th Amendment, applying these protections to the states.

Although its text has changed little, the Constitution has been applied by the courts to numerous situations which its drafters could not have foreseen. In interpreting constitutional provisions, it is particularly important to examine relevant decisions of the Supreme Court and of the lower federal courts. The language of the Constitution may be less important in legal research than judicial interpretations of constitutional principles.

The text of the Constitution appears in numerous publications ranging from simple pamphlets to standard reference works such as *Black's Law Dictionary*. It is

included in online and CD–ROM collections of federal statutes and is available at dozens of government and private Internet sites.

The Constitution is also printed at the beginning of the *United States Code*, the official publication of federal statutes. More useful in research, however, are the two annotated statutory publications, *United States Code Annotated* (*USCA*) and *United States Code Service* (*USCS*). These publications provide much more than just the text of the Constitution. Each clause is accompanied by abstracts of cases, arranged by subject and thoroughly indexed. Some important provisions have thousands of case abstracts in several hundred subject divisions. The Constitution is so heavily annotated that it occupies 10 volumes in *USCA* and 7 volumes in *USCS*. The annotations are regularly updated in annual pocket parts for each volume and interim pamphlets throughout the year. These exhaustive annotations make the annotated codes key resources in determining how the Constitution's broad principles have been applied to very specific circumstances.

Of the many commentaries on the Constitution, one of the most extensive and authoritative is *The Constitution of the United States of America: Analysis and Interpretation*, published every ten years by the Congressional Research Service of the Library of Congress. This text is a useful starting point for constitutional research, with a thorough analysis of Supreme Court decisions applying each provision of the Constitution. The current version, edited by Johnny H. Killian and George A. Costello, was published in 1996 and covers cases through June 1992.

The volume is updated by a biennial pocket part, but its coverage generally lags a couple of years behind current developments. This edition of the Constitution is available on the Internet at two sites. GPO Access <www. access.gpo.gov/congress/senate/constitution/> provides either text or PDF files (matching the look of the printed pages) and FindLaw <www.findlaw.com/casecode/ constitution/> includes hypertext links to footnotes and to Supreme Court cases discussed. Exhibit 31 shows the beginning of this work's discussion of the Second Amendment, with footnotes citing several scholarly monographs, law review articles, and Supreme Court decisions.

Another helpful background source is Leonard W. Levy et al., eds., *Encyclopedia of the American Constitution* (4 vols. 1986 & supp. 1992), which includes articles on constitutional doctrines as well as on specific court decisions, people, and historical periods. Shorter works providing similar treatment of constitutional issues include Kermit L. Hall, ed., *The Oxford Companion to the Supreme Court* (1992), and Jethro K. Lieberman, *A Practical Companion to the Constitution* (1999). Of numerous scholarly works on the Supreme Court's constitutional jurisprudence, the most extensive is the multivolume Oliver Wendell Holmes Devise *History of the Supreme Court of the United States* (1971–date).

For further historical research, one can turn to the documents prepared by those who drafted, adopted and ratified the Constitution. There was no official record of the debates in the constitutional convention of 1787, but Max Farrand's *The Records of the Federal Convention of 1787* (4 vols. 1937 & supp. 1987) is considered the most authoritative source. The traditional source for ratification debates in the states is Jonathan Elliot, *The Debates*

BEARING ARMS

SECOND AMENDMENT

A well regulated Militia being necessary to the security of a free State, the right of the people to keep and bear Arms shall not be infringed.

In spite of extensive recent discussion and much legislative action with respect to regulation of the purchase, possession, and transportation of firearms, as well as proposals to substantially curtail ownership of firearms, there is no definitive resolution by the courts of just what right the Second Amendment protects. The opposing theories, perhaps oversimplified, are an "individual rights" thesis whereby individuals are protected in ownership, possession, and transportation, and a "states' rights" thesis whereby it is said the purpose of the clause is to protect the States in their authority to maintain formal, organized militia units.[1] Whatever the Amendment may mean, it is a bar only to federal action, not extending to state[2] or private[3] restraints. The Supreme Court has given effect to the dependent clause of the Amendment in the only case in which it has tested a congressional enactment against the constitutional prohibition, seeming to affirm individual protection but only in the context of the maintenance of a militia or other such public force.

In *United States v. Miller*,[4] the Court sustained a statute requiring registration under the National Firearms Act of sawed-off

---

[1] A sampling of the diverse literature in which the same historical, linguistic, and case law background is the basis for strikingly different conclusions is: STAFF OF SUBCOM. ON THE CONSTITUTION, SENATE COMMITTEE ON THE JUDICIARY, 97TH CONGRESS, 2D SESS., THE RIGHT TO KEEP AND BEAR ARMS (Comm. Print 1982); DON B. KATES, HANDGUN PROHIBITION AND THE ORIGINAL MEANING OF THE SECOND AMENDMENT (1984); GUN CONTROL AND THE CONSTITUTION: SOURCES AND EXPLORATIONS ON THE SECOND AMENDMENT (Robert J. Cottrol, ed. 1993); STEPHEN P. HALBROOK, THAT EVERY MAN BE ARMED: THE EVOLUTION OF A CONSTITUTIONAL RIGHT (1984); Symposium, *Gun Control*, 49 LAW & CONTEMP. PROBS. 1 (1986); Sanford Levinson, *The Embarrassing Second Amendment*, 99 YALE L.J. 637 (1989).

[2] Presser v. Illinois, 116 U.S. 252, 265 (1886). *See also* Miller v. Texas, 153 U.S. 535 (1894); Robertson v. Baldwin, 165 U.S. 275, 281–282 (1897). The non-application of the Second Amendment to the States is good law today. Quilici v. Village of Morton Grove, 695 F. 2d 261 (7th Cir. 1982), *cert. denied*, 464 U.S. 863 (1983).

[3] *United States v. Cruikshank*, 92 U.S. 542 (1875).

[4] 307 U.S. 174 (1939). The defendants had been released on the basis of the trial court determination that prosecution would violate the Second Amendment and no briefs or other appearances were filed on their behalf; the Court acted on the basis of the Government's representations.

Exhibit 31. Bearing Arms: Second Amendment, CONSTITUTION OF THE UNITED STATES OF AMERICA: ANALYSIS AND INTERPRETATION 1193 (Johnny H. Killian & George A. Costello eds., 1996).

in the Several State Conventions on the Adoption of the Federal Constitution (2d ed., 5 vols. 1836–45), with a thorough modern treatment, *The Documentary History of the Ratification of the Constitution* (1976–date) still in the process of publication. The Library of Congress provides full-text access to both Farrand's *Records* and Elliot's *Debates* on the Web <lcweb2.loc.gov/ammem/amlaw/>. Philip B. Kurland & Ralph Lerner, eds., *The Founders' Constitution* (5 vols. 1987), and Neil H. Cogan, ed., *The Complete Bill of Rights: The Drafts, Debates, Sources, and Origins* (1997) are useful collections of excerpts from source documents arranged by specific constitutional provision.

§ 5–3. STATE CONSTITUTIONS

Each state in governed by its own constitution, which establishes the structure of government and guarantees fundamental rights. While state constitutions are roughly comparable to their federal counterpart, they tend to be much more detailed and generally are amended far more frequently. Some states have revised and replaced their constitutions several times.

State constitutions can be important sources in cases involving individual rights. While a state cannot deprive citizens of federal constitutional rights, its constitution can guarantee rights beyond those provided under the U.S. Constitution. Just as the U.S. Supreme Court is the arbiter of the scope of protections offered by the federal constitution, the state court of last resort determines the scope of its constitution.

The best source for a state constitution is usually the annotated state code, which provides both the latest text and notes of court decisions interpreting and construing

constitutional provisions. Pamphlet texts are also published in many states, and state constitutions are available through the online databases, as part of many state CD–ROM products, and on the Internet from state government sites. Of several sites providing multistate access to primary sources, the most convenient may be FindLaw's state constitutions listing <www.findlaw.com/11stategov/indexconst.html>.

Current state constitutions are compiled in *Constitutions of the United States: National and State* (7 vols., 2d ed. 1974–date). William F. Swindler, ed., *Sources and Documents of United States Constitutions* (11 vols., 1973–79) also includes superseded state constitutions and other historical documents, with background notes, editorial comments, and a selected bibliography for each state.

For research into a particular state's constitution, one of the best starting places may be a volume in the series *Reference Guides to the State Constitutions of the United States*. This monograph series began with Robert F. Williams, *The New Jersey State Constitution: A Reference Guide* (1990), and now covers more than thirty states. Each volume includes a summary of the state's constitutional history, a detailed section-by-section analysis of the constitution with background information and discussion of judicial interpretations, and a brief bibliographical essay providing references for further research.

Journals and proceedings of state constitutional conventions can provide insight into framers' intent, although the lack of indexing in many older volumes can make for difficult research. These documents are available on microfiche in *State Constitutional Conventions, Commissions, and Amendments*, covering all fifty states

from 1776 through 1988, and listed in a series of bibliographies beginning with Cynthia E. Browne's *State Constitutional Conventions from Independence to the Completion of the Present Union, 1776–1959: A Bibliography* (1973).

§ 5–4. PUBLICATION OF STATUTES

American statutes are published in three forms. The first version of a newly enacted statute is the *slip law*. Each law is issued by itself on a single sheet or as a pamphlet with separate pagination. Neither federal nor state slip laws are widely distributed, and their texts reach the public largely through electronic services and commercial publications.

Next are the *session laws*. The statutes are arranged by date of passage and published in separate volumes for each term of the legislature. Official session laws are generally published only in bound volumes after a session has ended, but commercial *advance session law services* provide the texts of new laws in pamphlet form on a more timely basis. Session law volumes are generally indexed, but these indexes rarely cumulate and subject access to more than one session can be difficult.

In most jurisdictions, the session laws constitute the *positive law* form of legislation, *i.e.*, the authoritative, binding text of the laws. Other forms (such as codes) are only *prima facie* evidence of the statutory language, unless they have been designated as positive law by the legislature.

Although the chronologically arranged session laws contain the official text of legislative enactments, their use as research tools is limited. Researchers usually need

the laws currently in force, rather than the laws passed during a specific legislative term. They also need convenient access to amendments and related legislation. Statutory compilations, known generally as *codes*, collect current statutes of general and permanent application and arrange them by subject. The statutes are grouped into broad subject topics, or *titles*, and within each title they are divided into numbered sections. The parts of a single legislative act may be printed together or may be scattered by subject through several different titles. A detailed index for the entire code provides access to the sections dealing with particular problems or topics.

Many jurisdictions have official code publications containing the text of the statutes in force. If an official edition is published, it is usually the authoritative text and should be cited in briefs and pleadings. However, only some official codes include references to judicial decisions which have applied or construed the statutes. Finding relevant cases is such an important part of statutory research that the most useful sources are commercially published annotated codes which include these notes of decisions. In addition, annotated codes also provide historical comments and cross references to legal encyclopedias and other publications.

Codes, whether annotated or unannotated, must be updated regularly to include the numerous statutory changes which occur every time a legislature meets. An outdated code is virtually useless for current research. Some official codes are updated only by the publication of revised volumes every few years. Most annotated codes, on the other hand, are supplemented by annual pocket parts and quarterly pamphlets.

Printed resources are particularly well suited for statutory research, because code volumes make it easy to find related provisions and to place a section in context. A wide range of electronic resources, however, are available. The official website for almost every jurisdiction provides access to the text of its code. Most of these can be searched by keyword, but very few include notes of court decisions or other research references. More extensive annotated codes are available through the commercial online databases and on CD–ROM.

§ 5–5. FEDERAL STATUTES

The United States Congress meets in two-year terms, consisting of two annual sessions, and enacts several hundred statutes each term. These statutes range from simple designations of commemorative days to complex environmental or tax legislation spanning hundreds of pages. Each act is designated as either a *public law* or a *private law*, and assigned a number indicating the order in which it was passed. Public Law 105–312, for example, is the 312th public law passed during the 105th Congress (1997–98).

Public laws are designed to affect the general public, while private laws are passed to meet special needs of an individual or small group. The distinction between the two is sometimes blurred, as when a special interest group promotes "public" legislation that actually affects very few people. Both types are passed in the same way and both appear in the session laws, but in separate numerical series. Only public laws, however, become part of the statutory code.

a. Slip Laws and Session Laws

The slip law, an individually paginated pamphlet, is the

first official text of a new statute and is available from Congress itself or from the U.S. Government Printing Office. After the end of each session of Congress, the public and private slip laws are cumulated, corrected, and issued in bound volumes as the official *Statutes at Large* for the session. These are cited by volume and page number. Pub. L. 105–312, 112 Stat. 2956 (1998), shown in Exhibit 32, begins on page 2956 of volume 112 of the *Statutes at Large*. Each annual volume, which may actually consist of several separate parts, contains an index.

There is often a frustrating time lag between enactment and distribution of slip laws by the government, and a further delay before *Statutes at Large* volumes are published. Commercial and electronic resources provide the texts of federal enactments much more quickly. Two of the leading printed sources are monthly services accompanying *United States Code Annotated* and *United States Code Service*. These services, West Group's *United States Code Congressional and Administrative News* (*USCCAN*) and Lexis Publishing's *USCS Advance*, both provide the official pagination that will eventually appear in the *Statutes at Large*. Both services also include other materials such as new court rules, presidential documents, and selected administrative regulations. Neither *USCCAN* nor *USCS Advance* includes private laws, which are published only in the official *Statutes at Large*.

USCCAN (but not *USCS Advance*) has two additional features. It reprints selected congressional committee reports (usually considered the most important sources of legislative history, to be discussed in Chapter 6), and it is recompiled into bound volumes at the end of each session. It thus provides a permanent source for federal session

112 STAT. 2956 PUBLIC LAW 105–312—OCT. 30, 1998

Public Law 105–312
105th Congress

An Act

Oct. 30, 1998
[H.R. 2807]

To clarify restrictions under the Migratory Bird Treaty Act on baiting and to facilitate acquisition of migratory bird habitat, and for other purposes.

Be it enacted by the Senate and House of Representatives of the United States of America in Congress assembled,

Migratory Bird
Treaty Reform
Act of 1998.

TITLE I—MIGRATORY BIRD TREATY REFORM

16 USC 710 note.

SEC. 101. SHORT TITLE.

This title may be cited as the "Migratory Bird Treaty Reform Act of 1998".

SEC. 102. ELIMINATING STRICT LIABILITY FOR BAITING.

Section 3 of the Migratory Bird Treaty Act (16 U.S.C. 704) is amended—
(1) by inserting "(a)" after "Sec. 3."; and
(2) by adding at the end the following:
"(b) It shall be unlawful for any person to—
"(1) take any migratory game bird by the aid of baiting, or on or over any baited area, if the person knows or reasonably should know that the area is a baited area; or
"(2) place or direct the placement of bait on or adjacent to an area for the purpose of causing, inducing, or allowing any person to take or attempt to take any migratory game bird by the aid of baiting on or over the baited area.".

SEC. 103. CRIMINAL PENALTIES.

Section 6 of the Migratory Bird Treaty Act (16 U.S.C. 707) is amended—
(1) in subsection (a), by striking "$500" and inserting "$15,000";
(2) by redesignating subsection (c) as subsection (d); and
(3) by inserting after subsection (b) the following:
"(c) Whoever violates section 3(b)(2) shall be fined under title 18, United States Code, imprisoned not more than 1 year, or both.".

Deadline.
16 USC 704 note.

SEC. 104. REPORT.

Not later than 5 years after the date of enactment of this Act, the Secretary of the Interior shall submit to the Committee on Environment and Public Works of the Senate and the Committee on Resources of the House of Representatives a report analyzing the effect of the amendments made by section 2, and the general

Exhibit 32. Migratory Bird Treaty Reform Act of 1998, Pub.L. 105–312, tit. I, 112 Stat. 2956 (1998).

laws back to 1941, although it did not follow the official *Statutes at Large* pagination before 1975.

Other sources may be even more current than *USC-CAN* or *USCS Advance* in printing new legislation. Loose-leaf services in fields such as tax or trade regulation provide very current coverage of congressional action in their subject areas, and are usually supplemented on a weekly basis.

New public laws are also available rapidly online through Westlaw and Lexis–Nexis, with searchable back-files extending to the late 1980s. Beginning with the 104th Congress in 1995, the Government Printing Office's GPO Access provides the text of public laws through the Internet <www.access.gpo.gov/nara/nara005.html>. For current legislation this is one of the quickest and most effective sources, with new laws online within a few days of enactment. For the very latest laws, it may be necessary to check a legislative site such as THOMAS <thomas.loc.gov> for the *enrolled bill*, or the version that was passed by both houses and sent to the President. THOMAS has enrolled bills back to the 101st Congress (1989–90).

Lexis–Nexis has comprehensive retrospective coverage of the *Statutes at Large* back to 1789, but the full text of older laws is not searchable. Statutes can be retrieved by citation, however, and then downloaded as PDF files replicating the original printed pages. The Library of Congress provides similar access to early volumes <lcweb2.loc.gov/ammem/amlaw/>, with coverage planned through 1873.

Although the *Statutes at Large* is not the most convenient source for federal legislation, it maintains a vital

role in legal research. In most instances it is the official statement of the law, and it is a necessary source for determining what specific language Congress enacted at any given time. This is important for lawyers as well as historians. It is often necessary to determine when a particular provision took effect or was repealed, or to reconstruct the precise text in force at a particular time.

b. The *United States Code*

The first official subject compilations of federal legislation were the *Revised Statutes of the United States* of 1873, and its second edition of 1878. The first edition of the *Revised Statutes* was reenacted as positive law in its entirety, expressly repealing the original *Statutes at Large* versions of its contents. It is therefore the authoritative text for most laws enacted before 1873, and is still needed occasionally in modern research.

Although the *Revised Statutes* rapidly became outdated, no other official compilation was prepared for almost fifty years. Finally, in 1926, the first edition of the *United States Code* was published, arranging the laws by subject into fifty titles. The *U.S. Code* is published in a completely revised edition of about 35 volumes every six years, with an annual supplement of one or more bound volumes. These supplements are cumulative, so it is necessary only to consult the main set and its latest supplement. Nearly half of the *U.S. Code* titles have been reenacted as positive law, and for them the code has become the authoritative text. For the others, the *Statutes at Large* is authoritative and the *U.S. Code* is prima facie evidence of the law. A list of all code titles, indicating

which titles have been reenacted, appears in the front of each *U.S. Code* volume and is reproduced here as Exhibit 33.

Unlike citations to the *Statutes at Large* or to cases, citations to the *U.S. Code* refer to title and section rather than to volume and page. For example, 16 U.S.C. § 707 (1994), shown in Exhibit 34, is the citation for section 707 of Title 16 (Conservation). This exhibit from the 1994 *United States Code* shows this provision, governing penalties for violation of the Migratory Bird Treaty Act, prior to its 1988 amendment by Pub. L. No. 105–312, § 103, the session law shown earlier in Exhibit 32.

In addition to the actual text of statutes, the *U.S. Code* also includes historical notes, cross references, and other research aids. Each section is followed by a parenthetical reference to its source in the *Statutes at Large*, including sources for any amendments. This reference leads to the original text, which may be the positive law form, and from there to legislative history documents relating to the law's enactment. In Exhibit 34, note that § 707 was originally enacted in 1918 and had been amended in 1936, 1960, and 1986. The "Amendments" note following the section indicates the precise nature of each of these changes.

Even when discussing statutes currently in force, cases and other documents sometimes refer to provisions by session law citation rather than by code section. It is then necessary to determine where a law is codified, as well as whether it is still in force. One of the simplest ways to do this is to use a *parallel reference table* in two volumes at

---

TITLES OF UNITED STATES CODE

*1. General Provisions.	27. Intoxicating Liquors.
2. The Congress.	*28. Judiciary and Judicial Procedure; and Appendix.
*3. The President.	29. Labor.
*4. Flag and Seal, Seat of Government, and the States.	30. Mineral Lands and Mining.
*5. Government Organization and Employees; and Appendix.	*31. Money and Finance.
†6. [Surety Bonds.]	*32. National Guard.
7. Agriculture.	33. Navigation and Navigable Waters.
8. Aliens and Nationality.	‡34. [Navy.]
*9. Arbitration.	*35. Patents.
*10. Armed Forces; and Appendix.	*36. Patriotic and National Observances, Ceremonies, and Organizations.
*11. Bankruptcy; and Appendix.	*37. Pay and Allowances of the Uniformed Services.
12. Banks and Banking.	*38. Veterans' Benefits; and Appendix.
*13. Census.	*39. Postal Service.
*14. Coast Guard.	40. Public Buildings, Property, and Works; and Appendix.
15. Commerce and Trade.	41. Public Contracts.
16. Conservation.	42. The Public Health and Welfare.
*17. Copyrights.	43. Public Lands.
*18. Crimes and Criminal Procedure; and Appendix.	*44. Public Printing and Documents.
19. Customs Duties.	45. Railroads.
20. Education.	*46. Shipping; and Appendix.
21. Food and Drugs.	47. Telegraphs, Telephones, and Radiotelegraphs.
22. Foreign Relations and Intercourse.	48. Territories and Insular Possessions.
*23. Highways.	*49. Transportation.
24. Hospitals and Asylums.	50. War and National Defense; and Appendix.
25. Indians.	
26. Internal Revenue Code; and Appendix.	

*This title has been enacted as law. However, any Appendix to this title has not been enacted as law.
†This title was enacted as law and has been repealed by the enactment of Title 31.
‡This title has been eliminated by the enactment of Title 10.

Page III

Exhibit 33. Titles of United States Code, 1 UNITED STATES CODE iii (Supp. IV 1998).

the end of the *U.S. Code.* The example shown in Exhibit 35 provides *U.S. Code* references for laws enacted in 1936, including the Act of June 20, 1936, ch. 634, § 2, 49

of any regulation prescribed thereunder shall, when found, be seized and, upon conviction of the offender or upon judgment of a court of the United States that the same were captured, killed, taken, sold or offered for sale, bartered or offered for barter, purchased, shipped, transported, carried, imported, exported, or possessed contrary to the provisions of this subchapter or of any regulation prescribed thereunder, shall be forfeited to the United States and disposed of by the Secretary of the Interior in such manner as he deems appropriate.

(July 3, 1918, ch. 128, § 5, 40 Stat. 756; 1939 Reorg. Plan No. II, § 4(f), eff. July 1, 1939, 4 F.R. 2731, 53 Stat. 1433; Oct. 17, 1968, Pub. L. 90–578, title IV, § 402(b)(2), 82 Stat. 1118; Nov. 8, 1978, Pub. L. 95–616, § 3(h)(1), 92 Stat. 3111; Dec. 1, 1990, Pub. L. 101–650, title III, § 321, 104 Stat. 5117.)

AMENDMENTS

1978—Pub. L. 95–616 made provisions respecting seizures and judgment of court applicable to birds, or parts, nests, or eggs sold or offered for sale, bartered or offered for barter, purchased, imported and exported and substituted "any regulation prescribed thereunder" in two places for "any regulations made pursuant thereto" and "any regulation made pursuant thereto" and provision for disposition of the birds, etc., by Secretary of the Interior in such manner as he deems appropriate for prior provision for such disposition as directed by court having jurisdiction.

CHANGE OF NAME

"United States magistrate judges" substituted for "United States magistrates" in text pursuant to section 321 of Pub. L. 101–650, set out as a note under section 631 of Title 28, Judiciary and Judicial Procedure. Previously, "United States magistrates" substituted in text for "United States commissioners" pursuant to Pub. L. 90–578. See chapter 43 (§ 631 et seq.) of Title 28.

TRANSFER OF FUNCTIONS

Enforcement functions of Secretary or other official in Department of the Interior related to compliance with protection of certain birds under this subchapter with respect to pre-construction, construction, and initial operation of transportation system for Canadian and Alaskan natural gas transferred to Federal Inspector, Office of Federal Inspector for Alaska Natural Gas Transportation System, until first anniversary of date of initial operation of Alaska Natural Gas Transportation System, see Reorg. Plan No. 1 of 1979, §§ 102(e), 203(a), 44 F.R. 33663, 33666, 93 Stat. 1373, 1376, effective July 1, 1979, set out in the Appendix to Title 5, Government Organization and Employees. Office of Federal Inspector for the Alaska Natural Gas Transportation System abolished and functions and authority vested in Inspector transferred to Secretary of Energy by section 3012(b) of Pub. L. 102–486, set out as an Abolition of Office of Federal Inspector note under section 719e of Title 15, Commerce and Trade.

Transfer of functions of Secretary of Agriculture to Secretary of the Interior by Reorg. Plan No. II of 1939, see Transfer of Functions note set out under section 701 of this title.

§ 707. Violations and penalties; forfeitures

(a) Except as otherwise provided in this section, any person, association, partnership, or corporation who shall violate any provisions of said conventions or of this subchapter, or who shall violate or fail to comply with any regula-

tion made pursuant to this subchapter shall be deemed guilty of a misdemeanor and upon conviction thereof shall be fined not more than $500 or be imprisoned not more than six months, or both.

(b) Whoever, in violation of this subchapter, shall knowingly—

(1) take by any manner whatsoever any migratory bird with intent to sell, offer to sell, barter or offer to barter such bird, or

(2) sell, offer for sale, barter or offer to barter, any migratory bird shall be guilty of a felony and shall be fined not more than $2,000 or imprisoned not more than two years, or both.

(c) All guns, traps, nets and other equipment, vessels, vehicles, and other means of transportation used by any person when engaged in pursuing, hunting, taking, trapping, ensnaring, capturing, killing, or attempting to take, capture, or kill any migratory bird in violation of this subchapter with the intent to offer for sale, or sell, or offer for barter, or barter such bird in violation of this subchapter shall be forfeited to the United States and may be seized and held pending the prosecution of any person arrested for violating this subchapter and upon conviction for such violation, such forfeiture shall be adjudicated as a penalty in addition to any other provided for violation of this subchapter. Such forfeited property shall be disposed of and accounted for by, and under the authority of, the Secretary of the Interior.

(July 3, 1918, ch. 128, § 6, 40 Stat. 756; June 20, 1936, ch. 634, § 2, 49 Stat. 1556; Sept. 8, 1960, Pub. L. 86–732, 74 Stat. 866; Nov. 10, 1986, Pub. L. 99–645, title V, § 501, 100 Stat. 3590.)

AMENDMENTS

1986—Subsec. (b). Pub. L. 99–645 substituted "shall knowingly" for "shall" in introductory provisions.

1960—Pub. L. 86–732 designated existing provisions as subsec. (a), inserted "Except as otherwise provided in this section", and added subsecs. (b) and (c).

1936—Act June 20, 1936, substituted "conventions" for "convention".

EFFECTIVE DATE OF 1936 AMENDMENT

Section effective June 30, 1937, see section 1 of act June 20, 1936, set out as a note under section 703 of this title.

TRANSFER OF FUNCTIONS

For transfer of certain enforcement functions of Secretary or other official in Department of the Interior under this subchapter to Federal Inspector, Office of Federal Inspector for the Alaska Natural Gas Transportation System, and subsequent transfer to Secretary of Energy, see Transfer of Functions note set out under section 706 of this title.

SECTION REFERRED TO IN OTHER SECTIONS

This section is referred to in sections 718g, 4406 of this title; title 43 section 1474c.

§ 708. State or Territorial laws or regulations

Nothing in this subchapter shall be construed to prevent the several States and Territories from making or enforcing laws or regulations not inconsistent with the provisions of said conventions or of this subchapter, or from making

Exhibit 34. 16 U.S.C. § 707 (1994).

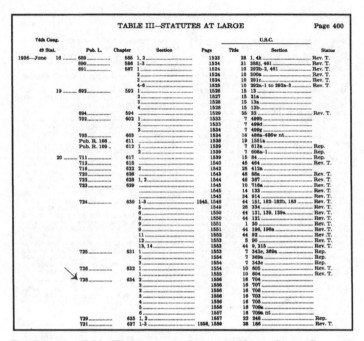

Exhibit 35. Table III–Statutes at Large, 27 UNITED STATES CODE 103, 400 (1994).

Stat. 1556, which amended 16 U.S.C. § 707. Note that it is possible to work from the year (1936), the term of Congress (74th), or *Statutes at Large* volume (49); and that some sections listed in this exhibit have been repealed (Rep.) or transferred when code titles were revised (Rev. T.). Other parallel reference tables provide access from the former numbering of revised titles to current section numbers, and from the *Revised Statutes* to the *U.S. Code*.

Another table, "Acts Cited by Popular Name," can be used to find an act if its citation is not known. This table

```
┌──────────────────────────────────────────────────────────────────────────────┐
│ Page 937                 ACTS CITED BY POPULAR NAME                            │
│                                                                                │
│ Migrant Health Act—Continued          Dec. 22, 1971, Pub. L. 92–214, §§ 1, 2, 85 Stat. │
│   Aug. 1, 1977, Pub. L. 95–83, title III, § 303,     777                       │
│     91 Stat. 388                       Feb. 17, 1976, Pub. L. 94–215, § 3, 90 Stat. │
│   Nov. 10, 1978, Pub. L. 95–626, title I,     189                              │
│     §§ 102(a), 103(a)–(g)(1)(B), (2), (h), (i), 92     Apr. 21, 1976, Pub. L. 94–273, § 34, 90 Stat. │
│     Stat. 3551–3555                         380                                 │
│   July 10, 1979, Pub. L. 96–32, § 6(a), 93 Stat.     Oct. 20, 1978, Pub. L. 95–552, § 1, 92 Stat. │
│     83                                      2071                                │
│   Aug. 13, 1981, Pub. L. 97–35, title IX, § 930,     Nov. 8, 1978, Pub. L. 95–616, § 3(i), 92 Stat. │
│     95 Stat. 569                            3112                                │
│   Dec. 21, 1982, Pub. L. 97–375, title I,     Oct. 14, 1982, Pub. L. 97–307, 96 Stat. 1450 │
│     § 107(b), 96 Stat. 1820            July  18, 1984, Pub. L. 98–369, title X, │
│   Apr. 24, 1986, Pub. L. 99–280, §§ 6, 7, 100     § 1077(a), (b)(3), 98 Stat. 1054, 1055 │
│     Stat. 400, 401                     Nov. 7, 1986, Pub. L. 99–625, § 3, 100 Stat. │
│   Aug. 10, 1988, Pub. L. 100–386, § 2, 102 Stat.     3502                      │
│     919                                Nov. 10, 1986, Pub. L. 99–645, title II, § 202, │
│ Migration and Refugee Assistance Act of 1962     100 Stat. 3586                │
│   Pub. L. 87–510, June 28, 1962, 76 Stat. 121     Nov. 14, 1988, Pub. L. 100–653, title III, │
│     (Title 22, § 2601 et seq.)              § 302, 102 Stat. 3827              │
│   Pub. L. 88–634, title II, § 201, Oct. 7, 1964, 78   Migratory Bird Treaty Act │
│     Stat. 1021                         July 3, 1918, ch. 128, 40 Stat. 755 (Title 16, │
│   Pub. L. 94–141, title V, § 501(a), Nov. 29,     § 703 et seq.)              │
│     1975, 89 Stat. 771                 June 20, 1936, ch. 634, §§ 1–5, 49 Stat. 1555, │
│   Pub. L. 96–212, title III, § 312(b), Mar. 17,     1556                       │
│     1980, 94 Stat. 116                 Sept. 8, 1960, Pub. L. 86–732, 74 Stat. 866 │
│   Pub. L. 96–465, title II, § 2206(a)(10), Oct.   Dec. 5, 1969, Pub. L. 91–135, § 10, 83 Stat. │
│     17, 1980, 94 Stat. 2162                 282                                │
│   Pub. L. 99–93, title I, §§ 111, 112(a), 113,   June 1, 1974, Pub. L. 93–300, § 1, 88 Stat. 190 │
│     Aug. 16, 1985, 99 Stat. 410, 411   Nov. 8, 1978, Pub. L. 95–616, § 3(h), 92 Stat. │
│   Pub. L. 101–246, title VII, Feb. 16, 1990, 104     3111                      │
│     Stat. 74                           Nov. 10, 1986, Pub. L. 99–645, title V, § 501, │
│   Pub. L. 103–236, title I, § 164(b), title IV,     100 Stat. 3590             │
│     § 430(a), Apr. 30, 1994, 108 Stat. 411, 459   Dec. 13, 1989, Pub. L. 101–233, § 15, 103 Stat. │
│ Migratory Bird Conservation Act             1977                               │
│   Feb. 18, 1929, ch. 257, 45 Stat. 1222 (Title   Mike Mansfield Fellowship Act │
│     16, § 715 et seq.)                 Pub. L. 103–236, title II, pt. C, §§ 251–257, │
│   June 15, 1935, ch. 261, title III, § 301, 49     Apr. 30, 1994, 108 Stat. 428–432 (Title 22, │
│     Stat. 381                               § 6101 et seq.)                    │
└──────────────────────────────────────────────────────────────────────────────┘
```

Exhibit 36. Acts Cited by Popular Name, 26 UNITED STATES CODE 639, 937 (1994).

lists laws alphabetically under either short titles assigned by Congress or names by which they have become commonly known, and provides citations to the laws in both the *Statutes at Large* and the *U.S. Code*. Exhibit 36 shows a page from this table in the 1994 *U.S. Code*, with several session law references under the heading "Migratory Bird Treaty Act." It would rarely be necessary to check all these references, because the first entry also provides the *U.S. Code* citation for the act.

Without a reference to a specific statute, the place to begin research in the *U.S. Code* is its general index. This basic tool for finding federal statutes by subject consists of several volumes, and it is updated in each annual

supplement. Exhibit 37 shows a page from the index providing references to a variety of provisions under the heading "Migratory Birds," including a reference to § 707 under the subheading "Fines, penalties and forfeitures." Statutory indexes are often full of cross-references (such as the "generally, this index" entries in this exhibit) and long lists of subheadings and sub-subheadings. Indexes can be unwieldy and confusing, but they remain essential resources in statutory research. Statutes are often easier to find through indexes than through full-text keyword searches, which may yield too many irrelevant results.

There are several electronic sources for the *United States Code*, including the Internet, the online systems, and CD–ROM. The Government Printing Office publishes an annual CD–ROM edition of the code, incorporating the supplement and including the popular name table and general index. The code is also available on the Internet from Cornell Law School's Legal Information Institute <www.law.cornell.edu/uscode>, GPO Access <www. access.gpo.gov/congress/cong013.html>, and the House of Representatives Office of the Law Revision Counsel <uscode.house.gov/>. These versions offer flexible search approaches, but they are no more up-to-date than the most recent printed edition. It is necessary to note the date of *either* print or electronic sources consulted and then check the session laws or online databases for recent legislation.

MIGRATORY BIRD REFUGES AND SANCTUARIES—Continued

Flumes on bird sanctuaries, appropriations for construction, 16 § 715k

Gifts of land for use as sanctuaries, 16 § 715d

Hunting and conservation stamp tax, migratory waterfowl, moneys from sale of stamps, acquisition, areas for, 16 § 718d

Jurisdiction of State over areas acquired, 16 § 715g

Location of areas for refuge, appropriation for, 16 § 715k

Migratory birds, defined, 16 § 715j

Military reservations not subject to use as sanctuaries, 16 § 715d

Power sites, use for bird sanctuaries, 16 § 715o

Purchase or rental of approved areas, 16 § 715d

Reservations,
  As defeating acquisition of, 16 § 715e
  Protected, 16 § 715k

Rights of way over lands acquired as sanctuaries, existence of as affecting right to acquire, 16 § 715e

Selection of areas for purchase or rental and fixing prices thereof, 16 § 715a

Spillways on bird sanctuaries, appropriations for construction of, 16 § 715k

State game laws, applicability to bird refuges, 16 § 715h

Survey of suitable areas for refuges, 16 § 715k

Take, defined, migratory bird conservation, 16 § 715n

Upper Mississippi River Wild Life and Fish Refuge, generally, this index

Washington State, acquisition of lands, 16 § 666e

Wetlands and Wetlands Resources, generally, this index

Wyandotte National Wildlife Refuge, generally, this index

MIGRATORY BIRD TREATY ACT

Text of Act, 16 § 703 et seq.

Migratory Birds, generally, this index

Short title, 16 § 710

MIGRATORY BIRDS

Administration, areas of lands, etc., to conserve and protect under treaty obligations, 16 § 715i

Antarctic Conservation, generally, this index

Appropriations, 16 §§ 709a, 715k

Expenses of Migratory Bird Commission, 16 § 715q

Junior Duck Stamp Conservation and Design Program, 16 § 719c

Arrest,
  Eagles, provisions applicable to, 16 § 668b
  Violation of laws relating to, 16 § 706

Bald Eagle, generally, this index

Bear River Migratory Bird Refuge, 16 § 690 et seq.

Breeding and sale for food supply, 16 § 711

California, areas in for management of migratory waterfowl, 16 § 695 et seq.

Capturing, prohibition against, 16 § 703

Central Valley project, California, reauthorization, etc., 16 § 695d et seq.

Cheyenne Bottoms Migratory Bird Refuge, 16 § 691 et seq.

Circulars, posters, etc., appropriations for in cooperation with local authorities in wild life conservation, 16 § 715k

Coastal Barrier Resources, generally, this index

Commission. Migratory Bird Conservation Commission, generally, this index

Conservation, Junior Duck Stamp Conservation and Design Program, establishment, report, etc., 16 § 719 et seq.

Conservation Act, applicable to wildlife management areas in California, 16 § 695b

Conservation Commission. Migratory Bird Conservation Commission, generally, this index

Conservation fund,
  Hunting and conservation stamp tax, migratory waterfowl. Waterfowl, this index
  Migratory waterfowl, preservation of wetlands, etc. Waterfowl, this index
  National Wildlife Refuge System,
    Deposit of sums received for granting right-of-way, easement, etc., 16 § 668dd
    Payments into, proceeds of transferred or disposed lands, 16 § 668dd

Conventions,
  Between U.S., Great Britain, Japan, and Union of Soviet Socialist Republics, definition of migratory birds, 16 § 715j
  Between U.S. and Great Britain, violation of, 16 § 703
  Between U.S. and the Union of Soviet Socialist Republics, 16 § 703
  Implementing regulations, 16 § 712

Cooperation of State in enforcement of law relating to, 16 § 715p

Crop damage, prevention of damage by migratory waterfowl by grain made available by CCC, 7 § 442 et seq.

Defined, protection, 16 § 715j

Department of Interior, preservation, distribution, introduction and restoration of, 16 § 701

Determination as to when and how birds may be taken, killed or possessed, 16 § 704

Effective dates of 1958 amendments, 16 § 718b note

Eggs,
  Forfeiture of eggs taken in violation of law, 16 § 706
  Taking, etc., unlawful, 16 § 703

Endangered Species, this index

Expenditures, 16 § 715k-1
  Necessary to enforce law relating to, 16 § 715k

Exportation, rules and regulations by Secretary of Interior, 16 § 704

Farms, breeding on for food supply, 16 § 711

Federal Inspector for Alaska Natural Gas Transportation System, transfer of enforcement functions from Secretary of Interior, etc., to, 5 App., Reorg. Plan No. 1 of 1979

Fines, penalties and forfeitures,
  Guns, traps, nets and other equipment, when used in violation, 16 § 707
  Taking of birds' nests or eggs, 16 § 706
  Use to implement North American wetlands conservation provisions, 43 § 1474c
  Violation of law relating to, 16 § 707

Food supply, breeding and sale for, 16 § 711

Great Lakes fish and wildlife restoration. Great Lakes Fisheries, generally, this index

Exhibit 37. General Index, 32 UNITED STATES CODE 1077 (1994).

c. Annotated Codes

The *United States Code* has the text of federal laws, but two major shortcomings limit its value to legal researchers. It is not updated on a very timely basis, and there is no information about court decisions applying or interpreting code sections. These court decisions are so important that most researchers turn instead of one of two commercially published, annotated editions of the code, *United States Code Annotated* (*USCA*), published by West Group, or *United States Code Service* (*USCS*), published by Lexis Publishing. Beyond the text of the law and notes of court decisions, they also provide references to legislative history, administrative regulations, and various secondary sources. These features have made the annotated codes the most widely used sources of federal statutes.

Exhibits 38 through 40 show the same section of Title 18 that was shown in Exhibit 34, as published in *USCA* and *USCS*. Exhibit 38 shows the text of section 707 in *USCA*, followed by a "Historical Note" on amendments in 1936 and 1960 and references to *West's Federal Forms* and the *Code of Federal Regulations*. Exhibit 39 shows the following *USCA* page, containing references to West's key number system and *Corpus Juris Secundum*, as well as an index to the notes of decisions and the first few case abstracts. Exhibit 40 shows the text of the section in *USCS*, with historical notes similar to those in *USCA*. The next page in *USCS* (not shown) provides cross-references and summaries of interpretive notes and decisions.

Either annotated code will serve admirably for most research purposes, but for extensive analysis of a particular statute it maybe necessary to check both *USCA* and *USCS*. Each code provides selective annotations of court

quires that protected birds be forfeited to the United States upon conviction of the offender, and as even if defendant was not convicted under the indictment, if the birds were found to be "possessed contrary to the provisions this subchapter" they would be forfeited to the United States. U.S. v. Drake, C.A.Colo. 1981, 655 F.2d 1025.

§ 707. Violations and penalties; forfeitures

(a) Except as otherwise provided in this section, any person, association, partnership, or corporation who shall violate any provisions of said conventions or of this subchapter, or who shall violate or fail to comply with any regulation made pursuant to this subchapter shall be deemed guilty of a misdemeanor and upon conviction thereof shall be fined not more than $500 or be imprisoned not more than six months, or both.

(b) Whoever, in violation of this subchapter, shall—

(1) take by any manner whatsoever any migratory bird with intent to sell, offer to sell, barter or offer to barter such bird, or

(2) sell, offer for sale, barter or offer to barter, any migratory bird shall be guilty of a felony and shall be fined not more than $2,000 or imprisoned not more than two years, or both.

(c) All guns, traps, nets and other equipment, vessels, vehicles, and other means of transportation used by any person when engaged in pursuing, hunting, taking, trapping, ensnaring, capturing, killing, or attempting to take, capture, or kill any migratory bird in violation of this subchapter with the intent to offer for sale, or sell, or offer for barter, or barter such bird in violation of this subchapter shall be forfeited to the United States and may be seized and held pending the prosecution of any person arrested for violating this subchapter and upon conviction for such violation, such forfeiture shall be adjudicated as a penalty in addition to any other provided for violation of this subchapter. Such forfeited property shall be disposed of and accounted for by, and under the authority of, the Secretary of the Interior.

(July 3, 1918, c. 128, § 6, 40 Stat. 756; June 20, 1936, c. 634, § 2, 49 Stat. 1556; Sept. 8, 1960, Pub.L. 86–732, 74 Stat. 866.)

Historical Note

1960 Amendment. Pub.L. 86–732 designated existing provisions as subsec. (a), inserted "Except as otherwise provided in this section" therein, and added subsecs. (b) and (c).

1936 Amendment. Act June 20, 1936 substituted "conventions" for "convention".

Effective Date of 1936 Amendment. Amendment by Act June 20, 1936 effective June 30, 1937, see section 1 of Act June 20, 1936, set out as an Effective Date of 1936 Amendment note under section 703 of this title.

Legislative History. For legislative history and purpose of Pub.L. 86–732, see 1960 U.S. Code Cong. and Adm.News, p. 3459.

West's Federal Forms

Sentence and fine, see § 7531 et seq.

Code of Federal Regulations

Seizure and forfeiture procedures, 50 CFR 12.1 et seq.

Exhibit 38. 16 U.S.C.A. § 707 (West 1985).

Library References

Game ⊜8, 10.
C.J.S. Game §§ 16, 17.

Notes of Decisions

1. Constitutionality

Felony penalty provision of subsec. (b) of this section for offense of selling or offering for sale any migratory bird violates due process of law, since provision does not specify intent as element of the offense, and penalty of maximum sentence of two years' imprisonment or $2,000 fine or both is a severe penalty, irreparably damaging a person's reputation. U.S. v. St. Pierre, D.C.S.D.1983, 578 F.Supp. 1424.

2. Purpose

Subsec. (b) of this section providing that anyone who sells or offers for sale any migratory bird shall be guilty of a felony, was intended to provide more severe penalty for market hunters who commercialize the de-struction of migratory birds, and congressional purpose and intent to protect migratory birds applies not only to those who slaughter and sell whole migratory birds, but also to those who kill such birds and sell the bird parts. U.S. v. St. Pierre, D.C.S.D.1983, 578 F.Supp. 1424.

3. Law governing

The more severe criminal sanctions possible under the Bald and Golden Eagles Protection Act, section 668 et seq. of this title, and the differences in the scheme of regulation indicate that the law applicable to that Act is not necessarily directly applicable to this subchapter. U.S. v. Corbin Farm Service, D.C. Cal.1978, 444 F.Supp. 510, affirmed 578 F.2d 259.

4. Jurisdiction

Assertion that if defendants had complied with migratory game bird-tagging regulation as regulation was interpreted by United States magistrate it would have required defendants to incriminate themselves was not jurisdictional and could not be raised for first time on appeal to district court from judgments of conviction. U.S. v. Mielke, D.C.Okl.1973, 367 F.Supp. 518, affirmed 488 F.2d 15.

5. Indictment or information—Generally

Indictment charging violation of this subchapter by hunting birds over baited field was not unconstitutional as violation of due process clause of U.S.C.A. Const.Amend. 5 where hunting was generally prohibited and lawful right to hunt was granted only where permission had been granted by Secretary of Agriculture [now Secretary of the Interior]. U.S. v. Griffin, D.C.Ga.1935, 12 F.Supp. 135.

6. —— Consolidation

Under circumstances, consolidation of four informations charging defendant with illegal possession or sale of wild ducks was not abuse of discretion. U.S. v. Stocker, C.A.Ill. 1960, 273 F.2d 754, 75 A.L.R.2d 703, certiorari denied 80 S.Ct. 879, 362 U.S. 963, 4 L.Ed.2d 878.

7. —— Dismissal

Although undercover agents of Fish and Wildlife Service violated district court rules and policies of the Justice Department with regard to the issuing of press releases and pretrial publicity following arrest of defend-

Exhibit 39.   16 U.S.C.A. § 707 (West 1985), continued.

16 USCS § 706, n 2   CONSERVATION

no power to make warrantless search on probable cause under Migratory Bird Treaty Act (16 USCS §§ 703–711). United States v FMC Corp. (1977, WD NY) 428 F Supp 615.

Fish and Wildlife Service agent who was on privately owned duck hunting club property per-

forming routine checks for valid hunting licenses was not required by 16 USCS § 706 to have search warrant before performing license checks, since, under Fourth Amendment, no search warrant was necessary. United States v Wylder (1984, DC Or) 590 F Supp 926.

§ 707. Violations and penalties; forfeitures

(a) Except as otherwise provided in this section, any person, association, partnership, or corporation who shall violate any provisions of said conventions or of this Act, or who shall violate or fail to comply with any regulation made pursuant to this Act shall be deemed guilty of a misdemeanor and upon conviction thereof shall be fined not more than $500 or be imprisoned not more than six months, or both.

(b) Whoever, in violation of this Act, shall knowingly—

(1) take by any manner whatsoever any migratory bird with intent to sell, offer to sell, barter or offer to barter such bird, or

(2) sell, offer for sale, barter or offer to barter, any migratory bird shall be guilty of a felony and shall be fined not more than $2,000 or imprisoned not more than two years, or both.

(c) All guns, traps, nets and other equipment, vessels, vehicles, and other means of transportation used by any person when engaged in pursuing, hunting, taking, ensnaring, trapping, capturing, killing, or attempting to take, capture, or kill any migratory bird in violation of this Act with the intent to offer for sale, or sell, or offer for barter, or barter such bird in violation of this Act shall be forfeited to the United States and may be seized and held pending the prosecution of any person arrested for violating this Act and upon conviction for such violation, such forfeiture shall be adjudicated as a penalty in addition to any other provided for violation of this Act. Such forfeited property shall be disposed of and accounted for by, and under the authority of, the Secretary of the Interior.

(July 3, 1918, ch 128, § 6, 40 Stat. 756; June 20, 1936, ch 634, § 2, 49 Stat. 1556; Sept. 8, 1960, P.L. 86-732, 74 Stat. 866; Nov. 10, 1986, P. L. 99-645, Title V, § 501, 100 Stat. 3590.)

HISTORY; ANCILLARY LAWS AND DIRECTIVES

References in text:

"This Act", referred to in this section, is Act July 3, 1918, ch 128, 40 Stat. 755, which is classified generally as 16 USCS §§ 703 et seq. For full classification of this Act, consult USCS Tables volumes.

The phrase "said conventions" in subsec. (a) means those named in 16 USCS § 703.

Amendments:

1936. Act June 20, 1936 (effective 6/30/37, as provided by § 1 of such Act, which appears as 16 USCS § 703 note), substituted "conventions" for "convention".

1960 Act Sept. 8, 1960, designated existing provisions as subsec. (a), and

Exhibit 40.   16 U.S.C.S. § 707 (Law, Co-op. 1994).

decisions, and some cases may be found in one but not in the other. *USCA*'s annotations are generally the more extensive of the two, but numerous cases appear only in *USCS*.

It is also worth noting that not every code section is followed by notes of decisions. Not every single section of the *U.S. Code* has been the subject of judicial interpretation. Some sections are uncontroversial and have not led to litigation, while others may be too new for any reported cases. The absence of annotations means that a section must be interpreted without the assistance of court decisions directly on point.

There are small discrepancies in statutory language between the versions of the code. The official *U.S. Code* and *USCA* both make minor technical changes in integrating *Statutes at Large* provisions into the code format, while *USCS* preserves the original language as published in the *Statutes at Large*. In subsections (a) and (b) of § 707, for example, the *U.S. Code* and *USCA* refer to the migratory bird protection laws as "this subchapter," but *USCS* uses the term "this Act" as it appeared in the original 1918 legislation.

The unofficial editions are far more current than the official *U.S. Code*, with supplementation by annual pocket parts, quarterly pamphlets, and revised volumes as necessary. When using a *USCA* or *USCS* volume, *always* check its pocket part for recent amendments and notes of new decisions. Exhibit 41 shows these two features in the pocket part for *USCS*, showing the 1998 amendment to § 707 and a reference to a 1997 Court of Appeals decision discussing the meaning of the word "knowingly" in this section.

MIGRATORY BIRDS **16 USCS § 715f**

inducing, or allowing any person to take or attempt to take any migratory game bird by the aid of baiting on or over the baited area.
(As amended Oct. 30, 1998, P. L. 105-312, Title I, § 102, 112 Stat. 2956.)

HISTORY; ANCILLARY LAWS AND DIRECTIVES

Amendments:
1998. Act Oct. 30, 1998 designated the existing provisions as subsec. (a); and added subsec. (b).

Other provisions:
Report on effect of Oct. 30, 1998 amendments. Act Oct. 30, 1998, P. L. 105-312, Title I, § 104, 112 Stat. 2956, provides: "Not later than 5 years after the date of enactment of this Act, the Secretary of the Interior shall submit to the Committee on Environment and Public Works of the Senate and the Committee on Resources of the House of Representatives a report analyzing the effect of the amendments made by section 2 [102] [amending this section], and the general practice of baiting, on migratory bird conservation and law enforcement efforts under the Migratory Bird Treaty Act (16 U.S.C. 701 et seq.).".

CODE OF FEDERAL REGULATIONS

Add:
50 CFR Part 14.

§ 707. Violations and penalties; forfeitures

(a) Except as otherwise provided in this section, any person, association, partnership, or corporation who shall violate any provisions of said conventions or of this Act, or who shall violate or fail to comply with any regulation made pursuant to this Act shall be deemed guilty of a misdemeanor and upon conviction thereof shall be fined not more than $15,000 or be imprisoned not more than six months, or both.

(b) [Unchanged]

(c) Whoever violates section 3(b)(2) [16 USCS § 704(b)(2)] shall be fined under title 18, United States Code, imprisoned not more than 1 year, or both.

(d) All guns, traps, nets and other equipment, vessels, vehicles, and other means of transportation used by any person when engaged in pursuing, hunting, taking, trapping, ensnaring, capturing, killing, or attempting to take, capture, or kill any migratory bird in violation of this Act with the intent to offer for sale, or sell, or offer for barter, or barter such bird in violation of this Act shall be forfeited to the United States and may be seized and held pending the prosecution of any person arrested for violating this Act and upon conviction for such violation, such forfeiture shall be adjudicated as a penalty in addition to any other provided for violation of this Act. Such forfeited property shall be disposed of and accounted for by, and under the authority of, the Secretary of the Interior.
(As amended Oct. 30, 1998, P. L. 105-312, Title I, § 103, 112 Stat. 2956.)

HISTORY; ANCILLARY LAWS AND DIRECTIVES

Amendments:
1998. Act Oct. 30, 1998, in subsec. (a), substituted "$15,000" for "$500"; redesignated subsec. (c) as subsec. (d); and added new subsec. (c).

INTERPRETIVE NOTES AND DECISIONS

3. Elements of offense
word "knowingly" in 16 USCS § 707 applies to putative offender's actions and jury instructions that defendant need not know his actions were unlawful was correct. United States v Pitrone (1997, CA1 Mass) 115 F3d 1.

§ 710. Partial invalidity

HISTORY; ANCILLARY LAWS AND DIRECTIVES

Short title:
Act Oct. 30, 1998, P. L. 105-312, Title I, § 101, 112 Stat. 2956, provides: "This title [amending 16 USCS §§ 704 and 707 and appearing in part as 16 USCS § 704 note] may be cited as the 'Migratory Bird Treaty Reform Act of 1998'.".

MIGRATORY BIRD CONSERVATION

§ 715f. Consent of State to conveyance

No deed or instrument of conveyance in fee shall be accepted by the Secretary of Agriculture [Secretary of the Interior] under this Act unless the State in which the area lies shall have consented by law to the acquisition by the United States of lands in that State.
(As amended Oct. 31, 1994, P. L. 103-434, Title XIII, 108 Stat. 4565.)

15

Exhibit 41. 16 U.S.C.S. § 707 (Lexis Supp. 1999).

The annotated codes also include extensive indexes, parallel reference tables, and popular name tables similar to those in the *U.S. Code*. Like the code sections, these features are updated in the annual supplements and interim pamphlets.

Both annotated editions of the code are available in CD–ROM and online (*USCA* on Westlaw and *USCS* on Lexis–Nexis). Westlaw has the code in both unannotated (USC) and annotated (USCA) forms, allowing the researcher to decide whether or not to include the extensive case annotations in a search. In some instances searching keywords in the annotations may retrieve far too many documents, but at other times the wording of the annotations may lead to sections that might not appear relevant at first glance. The online code databases are updated to include laws from the current session of Congress; a note at the beginning of each section indicates the latest public law to be included in code coverage. Westlaw brings section further up to date by including an "update" feature for amendments that have not yet been incorporated.

One advantage of using a code section in a printed book is the ability to survey neighboring sections to get a sense of its context. Westlaw and Lexis–Nexis provide browsing capabilities, but it is necessary to select "documents in sequence" or "book browse" to move between sections.

Looseleaf services provide another source for current, annotated statutes in some subject fields. Most services include federal statutes affecting their fields, accompanied by abstracts of judicial and administrative decisions, relevant administrative regulations, and explanatory

text. Major tax services such as the CCH *Standard Federal Tax Reports* are basically heavily annotated editions of the Internal Revenue Code (26 U.S.C.).

d. KeyCite and Shepard's Citations

While *USCA* and *USCS* provide notice of statutory amendments and citing cases, more extensive research leads can be found by using KeyCite or Shepard's Citations. Westlaw's KeyCite is available only electronically, while Shepard's information can be found in the printed *Shepard's Federal Statute Citations* or online through Lexis–Nexis. A major advantage of KeyCite and Shepard's is that they are much more up-to-date than the annotations in the codes. The latest decisions can be found in the citators months before case annotations are written and published.

KeyCite's coverage of statutes includes the cases noted in *USCA*'s annotations, but expands on these by listing other citing cases and articles. The cases from the annotations are listed under the index headings used in *USCA*, but KeyCite does not include the annotation abstracts. For these cases, KeyCite is less useful than the USCA database unless a researcher wishes to limit retrieval to particular jurisdictions or dates. The other cases and articles are simply listed by jurisdiction in reverse chronological order as "additional citations," with no indexing, but they represent references that cannot be found through the annotated code. The older "additional citations" cases listed may be somewhat marginal, but this is also where the most recent court decisions can be found. KeyCite also provides references to pending legislation and to any law review articles and other secondary sources available through Westlaw.

Shepard's, online or in print, lists citing sources under the exact provision or provisions cited. A case citing a specific subsection is listed under that subsection, while one citing a range of sections is listed under an entry for the entire range. It may therefore be necessary to scan a number of entries to find relevant citations. Shepard's has separate listings, for example, for "16 U.S.C. § 707" and for subsections such as "16 U.S.C. § 707(a)" and "16 U.S.C. § 707 (b)(2)." Still other documents citing the entire Migratory Bird Treaty Act are listed under "16 U.S.C. §§ 703 et seq." or "16 U.S.C. 703 to 712." This approach is ideal for research needing to focus in on a very specific subsection, but it makes it more difficult to get a comprehensive listing of all relevant documents. Shepard's coverage of law reviews, both in print and online, is far less extensive than KeyCite's.

Shepard's also covers other forms of legislative material besides the current *United States Code*. Other sections of *Shepard's Federal Statute Citations* cover citations to the U.S. Constitution and acts in the *Statutes at Large* which have not been incorporated into the code. On the other hand, citations appearing in state cases and law reviews are *not* included in *Shepard's Federal Statute Citations*. It is necessary to check other publications for these references. State court decisions citing federal laws are listed in Shepard's individual state citators, and citing articles in several law reviews are listed in *Shepard's Federal Law Citations in Selected Law Reviews*. The electronic version of Shepard's cumulates these various citing sources into one listing.

Both citators provide notice of legislative changes as well as judicial citations. KeyCite does this by including the statutory notes from *USCA*, while Shepard's includes

Statutes at Large references with symbols indicating the nature of the change. This information had been dropped from coverage after the 1996 *Shepard's Federal Statute Citations* volumes, but coverage was resumed in the 1998–99 supplements.

§ 5–6. STATE STATUTES

State statutes appear in many of the same forms as their federal counterparts, with slip laws, session laws, codes, and annotated codes. Current session laws and codes are available from government Internet sites, and annotated codes are published both online and on CD–ROM.

a. Slip Law and Session Laws

Slip laws are issued in many of the states, but they are rarely distributed very widely in paper. On the other hand, almost every state legislature now provides Internet access to recently enacted laws. In most instances, however, these are available as bills, not as session laws, and are mixed in with bills that are still pending or that did not become law. Two easy ways to find legislative websites are to start with the state homepage (<www.state.___.us>, using the state's postal abbreviation), or to check a site with multistate links such as Washburn University's StateLaw <www.washlaw.edu/uslaw/statelaw.html> .

Every state has a session law publication similar to the *U.S. Statutes at Large*, containing the laws enacted at each sitting of its legislature, usually with an index for each volume or session. The names of these publications vary from state to state (*e.g.*, *Acts of Alabama*, *Statutes of California*, *Laws of Delaware*). In most states the session laws are the authoritative positive law text of the stat-

utes, and they may be needed to examine legislative changes or to reconstruct the statute in force at a particular date.

Commercially published session law services for most states contain laws from a current legislative session, very much as *USCCAN* and *USCS Advance* do for congressional enactments, and the online systems provide the texts of new legislation from every state, with retrospective files going back to at least 1991.

b. Codes

All states have subject compilations of their statutes similar to the *U.S. Code*. Some states publish unannotated official codes, but most researchers rely on commercially published collections annotated with notes of relevant court decisions and other references. The authority of unofficial codes varies from state to state, but they are usually accepted as at least *prima facie* evidence of the statutory law.

Annotated state codes are edited and supplemented in much the same way as federal statutes, although there are variations from state to state. Some codes are more thorough and comprehensive than others. Most codes are published by either West Group or Lexis Publishing, and some states have competing codes from both publishers. Supplementation is generally by annual pocket parts, updated in many states by quarterly interim pamphlets. A few state codes are published in binders or in annual softcover editions, rather than as bound volumes with pocket parts.

The outline and arrangement of code material varies from state to state. While most codes are divided into

titles and sections, in a format similar to the *U.S. Code*, several states have individual codes designated by name rather than title number (e.g., commercial code, penal code, tax code). Exhibit 42 shows a section of the California Fish and Game Code, as published in *West's Annotated California Codes*. Note that it provides not only the text of the statute, but historical notes tracing its development, references to regulations and encyclopedias, and an annotation of a California Attorney General opinion.

State codes usually provide references to the original session laws in parenthetical notes following each section, as shown in Exhibit 42, and some include notes indicating the changes made by each amendment. Most also include tables with cross references from session law citations and earlier codifications to the current code. Each state code has a substantial general index of one or more volumes.

At least one annotated code from every state is in each ABA-approved law school library. The *Bluebook* (16th ed. 1996) provides a listing by state of the names and citations of current official and commercially published codes. State legal research guides (listed in Appendix B on page 392) provide information about earlier codes and statutory revisions, official and unofficial editions, and statutory indexes for individual states.

Almost every state provides access to its code through a government website. The official status of these codes varies, and the statutes are rarely accompanied by very extensive notes. Most codes can be accessed through browsing the table of contents or searching by keyword. Several convenient compilations of links are available,

NONGAME BIRDS   **§ 3806**
Pt. 2   Note 1

§ 3806. License for feeding migratory game birds

In order to aid in relieving widespread waterfowl depredation of agricultural crops, the department may issue licenses under regulations which the commission may prescribe to permit the feeding of migratory game birds. The commission may prescribe an annual fee for the license.

(Stats.1957, c. 456, p. 1379, § 3806. Amended by Stats.1985, c. 1463, § 18; Stats.1986, c. 1368, § 15.)

Legislative Counsel Notes

No substantive change except "department" for "commission" in issuance of licenses. (See § 13.3 of Fish and Game Code of 1933, as amended.)

Historical and Statutory Notes

Operative effect of legislation by Stats.1985, c. 1463, see Historical and Statutory Notes under Fish and Game Code § 331.

Section 29 of Stats.1985, c. 1463, provides:

"Sections 1 to 28, inclusive, of this act shall become operative only if Assembly Bill 2436 of the 1985–86 Regular Session of the Legislature is enacted. This section shall become operative only if both this bill and Assembly Bill 2436 are passed by the Legislature on or before September 13, 1985."

A former § 1204, enacted in 1933, as part of the codification, amended by Stats.1933, c. 726, p. 1790, repealed in 1945, was derived from Pen.C. § 626½, added by Stats.1927, c. 750, p. 1419, § 1; and from Penal Code § 626d, added by Stats.1901, c. 274, p. 820, § 5, amended by Stats.1905, c. 287, p. 256, § 3; Stats.1907, c. 420, p. 761, § 3; Stats.1911, c. 404, p. 811, § 3; Stats.1915, c. 672, p. 1319, § 1; Stats.1919, c. 345, p. 719, § 3; Stats.1919, c. 361, p. 757, § 1. The former section provided a duck season and provided for bag and possession limits.

Similar to § 1204 of the Fish and Game Code of 1933, added by Stats.1951, c. 180, p. 433, § 1, amended by Stats.1953, c. 168, p. 1082, § 1.

Code of Regulations References

Feeding of migratory waterfowl, see 14 Cal. Code of Regs. § 508.

Library References

Game ☞5.
WESTLAW Topic No. 187.
C.J.S. Game § 15.

Legal Jurisprudences

Cal Jur 3d Fish and Game § 34.

United States Code Annotated

Hunting conservation stamp tax, see 16 U.S.C.A. § 718 et seq.
Migratory bird conservation act, see 16 U.S.C.A. § 715 et seq.
Migratory bird treaty act, see 16 U.S.C.A. § 703 et seq.
Protection of migratory game and insectivorous birds, see 16 U.S.C.A. § 701.
State laws or regulations consistent with migratory bird treaty act, see 16 U.S.C.A. § 708.

Notes of Decisions

In general   1

1. In general

Violation of regulations (14 Cal.Adm.Code 508) regarding licensing of persons for feeding of migratory waterfowl is misdemeanor for which criminal complaint may be filed against licensee for having knowledge of and aiding and abetting acts or omissions of his employees; department can refuse issuance of feeding license to licensee with license suspended or revoked during preceding year only if fish and game commission enacts regulations allowing department to do so. 58 Ops.Atty.Gen. 311, 5–16–75.

17

Exhibit 42. CAL. FISH & GAME CODE § 3806 (West 1998).

including StateLaw <www.washlaw.edu/uslaw/statelaw.
html> and FindLaw's list of state codes <www.findlaw.
com/11stategov/indexcode.html>.

Lexis–Nexis and Westlaw provide access to codes from
all fifty states, as well as the District of Columbia, Puerto
Rico, and the Virgin Islands. Most of the state code
databases include the case notes and other references
from the annotated codes. This broadens the search base
from the bare statutory language, but it may make it
more difficult to weed out sections that are only margin-
ally relevant. Westlaw users can choose between annotated and unannotated versions of codes; Lexis–Nexis
users can use a *text* or *unanno* segment search to limit
queries to the statutory language. Both systems also add
notices to recently amended statutes to check slip laws
that have not yet been incorporated into the code
database.

Codes from every state are also available on CD–ROM.
Some CD–ROM publications include both statutes and
cases, while others contain simply the annotated code.
Both keyword searching and code indexes are generally
available.

c. KeyCite and Shepard's Citations

State code sections can also be checked in KeyCite or
Shepard's Citations, which may retrieve cases and articles not mentioned in the annotated code. KeyCite
generally provides more references to secondary sources,
but its coverage is limited to current code provisions.
Shepard's also provides coverage of state constitutions
and session laws, as well as earlier versions of code
provisions. Shepard's generally lists statutes as cited, so

it may be necessary to check references under both a current code section and its predecessors to find relevant material.

Each printed state Shepard's citator includes a "Table of Acts by Popular Names or Short Titles," providing the code citations of listed acts. Statutes from all jurisdictions are covered, in one alphabetical listing, in *Shepard's Acts and Cases by Popular Names: Federal and State*. This set is most useful when the title but not the state of an act is known, or when similar acts from several states are sought.

d. Multistate Research Sources

Most state statutory research situations require finding the law in one particular state, and that state's code is the primary research tool. Sometimes, however, it is necessary to compare statutory provisions among states or to survey legislation throughout the country. Multistate surveys of state laws can be a frustrating and time-consuming process, since each state code may use different terminology for similar issues. It is possible, and sometimes necessary, to begin with each state code's index, but several other resources can assist in this research.

Topical looseleaf services often collect state laws in their subject areas, making it easy to compare state provisions in areas such as taxation or employment law. More general coverage is provided by the *Martindale-Hubbell Law Digest*, an annual two-volume publication summarizing state law on a variety of subjects. A companion publication to the *Martindale-Hubbell Law Directory*, the digest is arranged by state and covers more than 100 legal topics. It provides citations to both code sections

and court decisions. The *Digest* is available through Lexis–Nexis, but it isn't included with the free Internet version of Martindale–Hubbell.

Another source comparing state laws is Richard A. Leiter, *National Survey of State Laws* (2d ed. 1997). This book is arranged by topic rather than by state, with tables summarizing state laws in 43 areas and providing citations to codes. Numerous other resources summarize state laws on specific topics, but many of them omit the code references that are essential for verifying and updating their information.

Collections and lists of state statutes are described in a valuable series of bibliographies called *Subject Compilations of State Laws* (1981–date). This set does not itself summarize or contain references to state codes, but it lists sources which provide this information. These include books, compendia, and law review articles, which often have footnotes with extensive listings of state code citations. Exhibit 43 shows an excerpt from this publication, with an entry under the heading "Fetuses" for the *Dickinson Law Review* comment shown in Exhibit 4 on page 37. Note that the entry in Exhibit 43 includes a reference to footnotes 30 and 31, which list 17 states regulating fetal homicide.

Westlaw and Lexis–Nexis offer databases combining all available state codes or all state session laws. These databases can be invaluable, although it is important to remember that any single search may not retrieve all relevant laws. Different legislatures may use different terminology for similar laws.

In some subject areas the Internet provides convenient multistate access to code provisions. One of the most

---

Fetuses

Cloning Human Beings: Report and Recommendations of the National Bioethics Advisory Commission. Rockville, MD: U.S. National Bioethics Advisory Commission, 1997. 110 pp. & apps. QH442.2.U56 1997. 174'.957. PrEx1.19:B52C62. 97-172800.

P. 89, fn. 6. Citations only. Cites to codes. Covers the ten states that have laws "regulating research and/or experimentation on conceptus, embryos, fetuses, or unborn children that use broad enough language to include early stage conceptus." Includes Florida, Louisiana, Maine, Massachusetts, Michigan, Minnesota, New Hampshire, North Dakota, Pennsylvania, and Rhode Island.

Note: Available on the Internet. URL: [www.bioethics.gov/pubs/cloning1/cloning.pdf].

Leventhal, Cari L. "The Crimes Against the Unborn Child Act: Recognizing Potential Human Life in Pennsylvania Criminal Law." *Dickinson Law Review* 103 (1998):173-97.

P. 177, fns. 30 and 31. Summaries. Cites to codes and cases. Covers the seventeen states that "prohibit the killing of a fetus outside the domain of legal abortion."

Exhibit 43. Entries from Cheryl Rae Nyberg, SUBJECT COMPILATIONS OF STATE LAWS, 1998–1999: AN ANNOTATED BIBLIOGRAPHY (2000).

comprehensive sites is Cornell Legal Information Institute's topical index to state statutes on the Internet <www.law.cornell.edu/topics/state_statutes.html>, with links in several dozen broad categories. Sites tracking more specific issues are listed in recent *Subject Compilations of State Laws* volumes; as with printed sources, it is important that these are regularly updated and that they provide the code citations necessary for further research.

e. Uniform Laws

Most multistate research requires finding a wide variety of legislation covering a particular topic. In a growing number of areas, however, states have adopted virtually identical acts. This can dramatically reduce the confusion caused by conflicting state statutes. The National Conference of Commissioners on Uniform State Laws (NCCUSL), created in 1892 to prepare legislation which would decrease unnecessary conflicts, has drafted more

than 200 laws. Almost 150 of these are in force in at least one state, and some (such as the Uniform Commercial Code or Uniform Child Custody Jurisdiction Act) have been enacted in virtually every jurisdiction.

Uniform Laws Annotated, published by West Group (and available online from Westlaw), contains every uniform law approved by the NCCUSL, lists of adopting states, Commissioners' notes, and annotations to court decisions from any adopting jurisdiction. These annotations allow researchers in one state to study the case law developed in other states with the same uniform law. A case from another state is not binding authority, but its interpretation of similar language may be quite persuasive. The set is supplemented annually by pocket parts and by a pamphlet entitled *Directory of Uniform Acts and Codes; Tables—Index*, which lists the acts alphabetically and includes a table of jurisdictions indicating the acts adopted in each state.

The text of a uniform law can also be found, of course, in the statutory code of each adopting state, accompanied by annotations from that state's courts. The state code contains the law as actually adopted and in force, rather than the text as proposed by the Commissioners. The NCCUSL version is merely a proposal, but the state code version is the law.

The NCCUSL's uniform laws, as well as drafts of its current projects, are available on the Internet <www.law.upenn.edu/bll/ulc/ulc_frame.htm>. Cornell's Legal Information Institute provides "Uniform Law Locators" <www.law.cornell.edu/states/index.html>, which list links to official sites where the text as adopted in particular states can be found.

The NCCUSL is not the only organization drafting legislation for consideration by state legislatures. The American Law Institute has produced the Model Penal Code and other model acts; the American Bar Association has promulgated and revised the Model Business Corporation Act; and the Council of State Governments publishes an annual volume of *Suggested State Legislation*.

§ 5–7. CONCLUSION

In some ways statutory research is easier than case research, because the major resources are more accessible and more regularly updated. In many situations a good annotated code provides most of the necessary research leads. This convenience is undercut, however, by the opacity of statutory language. Judicial prose can be a model of clarity when compared to the texts of many federal and state statutes.

In researching statutory or constitutional law, the resources discussed in this chapter are only a first step. Besides finding a relevant provision and making sure that it remains in force, it is usually necessary to read judicial decisions applying or construing its language. Administrative regulations may provide more specific requirements, and attorney general opinions on the meaning of the provision may also be available. A further understanding may be gained from treatises or law review articles.

Finally, ambiguities and vagueness in statutes often lead to difficulties in interpretation. Some statutory ambiguities stem from poor draftsmanship, but many are the inevitable result of negotiation and compromise in the legislative process. Lawyers frequently study legislative

documents in attempting to determine the meaning of the statutory text. This research in legislative history is the focus of the next chapter.

CHAPTER 6

LEGISLATIVE INFORMATION

---

§ 6–1. INTRODUCTION

The ambiguities so common in the language of statutes require lawyers and scholars to locate legislative documents from which they can learn the intended purpose of an act or the meaning of particular statutory language. Researchers also need to investigate the current progress of a proposed law under consideration by the legislature. These processes—determining the meaning or intent of an enacted law, and ascertaining the status of a pending bill—comprise legislative history research.

Legislative history is an area in which there is a strong dichotomy between federal and state research. Federal

legislative history is a well-developed area with numerous sources, while state legislative history research can be quite frustrating. It is also an area in which the Internet has made a significant contribution to the dissemination of information. Federal and state government websites make it quite easy to learn about the status of pending legislation and to obtain documents relating to recently passed acts. Research into the background of older laws, however, still requires access to printed sources.

§ 6–2. FEDERAL LEGISLATIVE HISTORY SOURCES

An understanding of the legislative process is essential for research in legislative history. Numerous background sources are available for understanding Congress and its work. One of the most extensive reference works is Donald C. Bacon, Roger H. Davidson & Morton Keller, eds., *Encyclopedia of the United States Congress* (4 vols. 1995), which provides a broad historical and political science perspective on the institution. In Congressional Quarterly's *Guide to Congress* (2 vols., 5th ed. 2000), Part III, Congressional Procedures, is particularly useful in understanding committee and floor action.

Two shorter official documents prepared by the House and Senate parliamentarians, *How Our Laws Are Made* and *Enactment of a Law*, are available from THOMAS <thomas.loc.gov>, under the heading "The Legislative Process." The Library of Congress provides links to these documents, as well as to several other guides and glossaries of congressional terminology <lcweb.loc.gov/global/legislative/legproc.html>.

Each stage in the enactment of a federal law may result in a significant legislative history document. The follow-

ing are the most important steps in the legislative process and their related documents:

Action	Document
Preliminary inquiry	Hearings on the general subject of the proposed legislation
Executive recommendation	Presidential message proposing an administration bill
Introduction of bill and referral to committee	Slip bill as introduced
Hearings on bill	Transcript of testimony and exhibits
Approval by committee	Committee report, including committee's version of bill
Legislative debates	*Congressional Record*, sometimes including texts of bill in amended forms
Passage by first house	Final House or Senate version of the proposed legislation
Other house	Generally same procedure and documents as above
Referral to conference committee (if texts passed by houses differ)	Conference committee version of bill; conference committee report
Passage by one or both houses of revised bill	Enrolled bill sent to President
Approval by President	Presidential signing statement; slip law (also *USCCAN* and *USCS Advance* pamphlets); subsequently published in *Statutes at Large* and classified by subject in the *U.S. Code*

Of the many types of documents issued by Congress, a few are particularly important for legislative history research. *Bills* are the major source for the texts of pending or unenacted legislation. *Committee reports* analyze and describe bills and are usually considered the most authoritative sources of congressional intent. *Floor debates* may contain a sponsor's interpretation of a bill or the only explanation of last-minute amendments. In addition, *hearings* can provide useful background on the purpose of an act.

a. Bills

The texts of bills are needed by researchers interested in pending or failed legislation, and may also help in interpreting an enacted law. Variations among the bills and amendments that led to a law can aid in determining the intended meaning of the act. Each deletion or addition made during the legislative process implies a deliberate choice of language by the legislators.

Bills are individually numbered in separate series for each house, and retain their identifying numbers through both sessions of a Congress. Pending bills lapse at the end of the two-year term, and they must be reintroduced the following term if they are to be considered.

Some public laws arise from *joint resolutions* rather than bills. These usually, but not always, deal with matters of a limited or temporary nature. Joint resolutions and bills differ in form but have the same legal effect. Two other forms of resolution are less important because they do not have the force of law: *concurrent resolutions* expressing the opinion of both houses of Congress, and *simple resolutions* concerning the procedures of just one house.

An individual bill or resolution can be obtained from its sponsor, the clerk of the House or Senate, or a congressional committee to which it was referred. Bills are received by many large law libraries in slip form or on microfiche, and they are available electronically from several sources. The Library of Congress's THOMAS system <thomas.loc.gov> has the text of bills since 1989, and the Government Printing Office's GPO Access <www.access.gpo.gov/congress/> begins coverage in 1993 with PDF files replicating the printed bills. Texts of bills are also available online from commercial electronic services, including Lexis–Nexis and Congressional Quarterly's *CQ. com On Congress* <oncongress.cq.com>.

Exhibit 44 shows the bill H.R. 2202 as introduced in the House of Representatives, printed from the GPO Access website. This bill, as amended, became the National Bone Marrow Registry Reauthorization Act of 1998, Pub. L. 105–196, 112 Stat. 631.

b. Committee Reports

Reports are generally considered the most important source of legislative history. They are issued by the committees of each house on bills reported out of committee (*i.e.*, sent to the whole house for consideration) and by conference committees of the two houses to reconcile differences between House and Senate versions of a bill. (Committees also issue reports on various investigations, studies and hearings not related to pending legislation.) Reports usually include the text of the bill, describe its contents and purposes, and give reasons for the committee's recommendations, sometimes with minority views. One of the most useful portions of a committee report is

I

105TH CONGRESS
1ST SESSION

H. R. 2202

To amend the Public Health Service Act to revise and extend the bone marrow donor program, and for other purposes.

IN THE HOUSE OF REPRESENTATIVES

JULY 17, 1997

Mr. YOUNG of Florida (for himself, Mr. BLILEY, Mr. SAXTON, Mr. STOKES, Mr. HOYER, Mr. HALL of Ohio, Mr. McDADE, Mr. SHAW, Mr. WATTS of Oklahoma, Mr. WAXMAN, Mr. HEFLEY, Mr. MOAKLEY, Mr. DELLUMS, Mr. HILLEARY, Mr. BORSKI, Ms. GRANGER, Mr. HORN, Mr. COBURN, Mr. HASTINGS of Florida, Mr. THOMPSON, Mr. PICKETT, Mr. MASCARA, Mr. PETERSON of Minnesota, Mr. THORNBERRY, Mr. GORDON, Mr. BLUNT, Mr. McNULTY, Mr. PASTOR, Mr. MORAN of Virginia, Ms. ROS-LEHTINEN, Mrs. MINK of Hawaii, Ms. EDDIE BERNICE JOHNSON of Texas, Ms. DUNN, Mr. FALEOMAVAEGA, Mr. CONDIT, Mr. DUNCAN, Mr. GREENWOOD, Mr. GUTIERREZ, Mr. SHIMKUS, Mr. CLAY, Mr. BOB SCHAFFER of Colorado, Mr. BOEHLERT, Mr. DEFAZIO, Mr. QUINN, Ms. NORTON, Mr. CALVERT, Mr. WISE, Ms. PELOSI, Mr. FRELINGHUYSEN, Mr. FROST, Mrs. LOWEY, Mr. BARTON of Texas, Ms. DELAURO, Mr. LATHAM, Mr. FOLEY, Mr. SPENCE, Mr. CANADY of Florida, Mr. HINCHEY, Ms. KILPATRICK, Mr. BOYD, Ms. SLAUGHTER, Mr. BONILLA, Mr. ABERCROMBIE, Mrs. THURMAN, and Mr. PORTER) introduced the following bill; which was referred to the Committee on Commerce

---

A BILL

To amend the Public Health Service Act to revise and extend the bone marrow donor program, and for other purposes.

1   *Be it enacted by the Senate and House of Representa-*

2   *tives of the United States of America in Congress assembled,*

Exhibit 44.   H.R. 2202, 105th Cong. (1997).

usually the section-by-section analysis of the bill, explaining the purpose and meaning of each provision.

Committee reports are published in numbered series which indicate house, Congress, and report number, with conference committee reports included in the series of House reports. Exhibit 45 shows the first page of H.R. Rep. No. 105–538 (1998), reporting the House Committee on Commerce's views on H.R. 2202. Note at the bottom of the page that the committee is amending the bill by deleting everything after the enacting clause ("Be it enacted . . .") and substituting its own language. This is not an uncommon form of amendment, but it is one that can make it difficult to track changes between versions of a bill.

Committee reports are issued by the Government Printing Office, and are sometimes available from the committee or from the House or Senate clerk. All the reports for a session are published, along with House and Senate Documents, in the bound official compilation called the *Serial Set*. GPO Access and THOMAS coverage begins in 1995, and the commercial databases have all committee reports beginning in 1990 as well as selected earlier coverage. Selected reports are also reprinted in *United States Code Congressional and Administrative News* (*USCCAN*).

Reports are the final product of committee deliberation. The process by which committees reach consensus is through *markup sessions*, but the proceedings of these sessions are only rarely published. News agencies specializing in Capitol Hill matters, however, frequently publish

105TH CONGRESS *2d Session*	HOUSE OF REPRESENTATIVES	REPORT 105–538

NATIONAL BONE MARROW REGISTRY REAUTHORIZATION ACT OF 1998

————

MAY 18, 1998.—Committed to the Committee of the Whole House on the State of the Union and ordered to be printed

————

Mr. BLILEY, from the Committee on Commerce,
submitted the following

REPORT

[To accompany H.R. 2202]

[Including cost estimate of the Congressional Budget Office]

The Committee on Commerce, to whom was referred the bill (H.R. 2202) to amend the Public Health Service Act to revise and extend the bone marrow donor program, and for other purposes, having considered the same, reports favorably thereon with an amendment and recommends that the bill as amended do pass.

CONTENTS

The amendment is as follows:
Strike out all after the enacting clause and insert in lieu thereof the following:

59–006

Exhibit 45.   H.R. Rep. No. 538 (1998).

news stories on markup sessions, available through on-line services such as Lexis–Nexis and *CQ.com On Congress*.

c. Debates

Debates in the House and Senate are generally not as influential as committee reports as sources of legislative intent. While reports represent the considered opinion of those legislators who have studied the bill most closely, floor statements are often political hyperbole and may not even represent the views of legislators supporting the bill. The most influential floor statements are those from a bill's sponsor or its floor managers (the committee members responsible for steering the bill through consideration). These may even explain aspects of a bill not discussed in a committee report or correct a report's erroneous statements.

In a few instances, floor debates are the best available legislative history source. Bills are often amended on the floor, sometimes with language that was not considered in committee and thus was not discussed in a committee report. If so, the record of floor debate may be the only explanation available of the purpose and meaning of the amendment.

The source for debates is the *Congressional Record*, a nearly verbatim transcript published each day that either house is in session. It is subject to revision only by members of Congress who wish to amend their own remarks. In addition, the *Record* includes extensions of floor remarks, exhibits from legislators, communications on pending legislation, and other material senators and

representatives wish to have printed. Each daily issue has separately paginated sections for Senate and House proceedings.

The *Congressional Record* never contains hearings and only rarely includes committee reports—although it does include the text of conference committee reports. Bills are sometimes read into the *Record*, particularly if they have been amended on the floor or in conference committee. The *Congressional Record's* primary role, however, is as a report of debates and actions taken. An excerpt from the *Record*, showing House consideration of H.R. 2202, is shown in Exhibit 46. The illustrated page includes part of the text of the bill as reported from committee, and remarks by the Republican and Democratic floor managers (Michael Bilirakis and Sherrod Brown).

Each *Congressional Record* issue contains a Daily Digest summarizing the day's activities. The digest provides news of bills introduced, reports filed, and measures debated or passed, and lists committee meetings held. *Record* page references for floor activity are included, making the Daily Digest a good starting place if only the date of congressional action is known.

An index to the *Record*, by subject, name of legislator, and title of legislation, is published every two weeks. The index includes a "History of Bills and Resolutions" table, which lists references for all bills acted on during the two-week period. If a bill is listed, however, the history is a cumulative record of all activity from its introduction.

The *Congressional Record* can be searched electronically through several online sources. Coverage begins in 1989 on THOMAS, and in 1994 on GPO Access (which

(3) The number of such patients for whom the Registry began a preliminary search but for whom the full search process was not completed, and the reasons underlying such circumstances.

(4) The extent to which the plan required in section 2(b)(2) of this Act (relating to the relationship between the Registry and donor centers) has been implemented.

(5) The extent to which the Registry, donor centers, donor registries, collection centers, transplant centers, and other appropriate entities have been complying with the standards, criteria, and procedures under subsection (a) of such section 379 (as redesignated by section 2(c) of this Act).

(b) REPORT.—A report describing the findings of the study under subsection (a) shall be submitted to the Congress not later than October 1, 2001. The report may not be submitted before January 1, 2001.

SEC. 6. COMPLIANCE WITH NEW REQUIREMENTS FOR OFFICE OF PATIENT ADVOCACY.

With respect to requirements for the office of patient advocacy under section 379(d) of the Public Health Service Act, the Secretary of Health and Human Services shall ensure that, not later than 180 days after the effective date of this Act, such office is in compliance with all requirements (established pursuant to the amendment made by section 2(d)) that are additional to the requirements that under section 379 of such Act were in effect with respect to patient advocacy on the day before the date of the enactment of this Act.

SEC. 7. EFFECTIVE DATE.

This Act takes effect October 1, 1998, or upon the date of the enactment of this Act, whichever occurs later.

The SPEAKER pro tempore. Pursuant to the rule, the gentleman from Florida (Mr. BILIRAKIS) and the gentleman from Ohio (Mr. BROWN) each will control 20 minutes.

The Chair recognizes the gentleman from Florida (Mr. BILIRAKIS).

GENERAL LEAVE

Mr. BILIRAKIS. Mr. Speaker, I ask unanimous consent that all Members may have 5 legislative days within which to revise and extend their remarks on H.R. 2202 and to insert extraneous material on the bill.

The SPEAKER pro tempore. Is there objection to the request of the gentleman from Florida?

There was no objection.

(Mr. BILIRAKIS asked and was given permission to revise and extend his remarks.)

Mr. BILIRAKIS. Mr. Speaker, I yield myself such time as I may consume.

Mr. Speaker, I am delighted this afternoon, truly delighted, to ask my colleagues in the House to support H.R. 2202, the National Bone Marrow Registry Reauthorization Act of 1998. I would like to acknowledge the hard work of Mr. Marc Wheat of the Majority staff, Mr. John Ford of the Minority staff, and other staffers from Mr. YOUNG's office and staffers in the Senate in the process of working out this legislation.

I know that many of my colleagues in the House have heard from individuals whose lives were saved by this program, but many Members may not know that this legislation has been championed by a man whose own daughter was saved by the program. Coincidentally, if that is a proper word, he decided to go forward with this program quite a few years ago, and it was after he decided to go through with this program and put it into effect that his daughter was saved by the program.

□ 1545

That, of course, I am referring to my friend and colleague, the gentleman from Florida (Mr. BILL YOUNG).

The gentleman from Florida (Mr. YOUNG) secured the original appropriation which established this important program in early 1987 through a grant to the Department of the Navy. In this Congress he has worked tirelessly to secure reauthorization of the program, and I was pleased to support his effort as a cosponsor of H.R. 2202.

In 1997 the National Marrow Donor Program was responsible for facilitating 1,280 unrelated marrow transplants, men and women who never met each other but knew that through the simple procedure of marrow donation a life would be saved.

There are approximately 5,000 to 7,000 Americans who could benefit from potentially lifesaving unrelated donor transplants, and yet for many, matches cannot be found yet. But thanks to the great work of the men and women in this program, over 3 million Americans have volunteered to be listed confidentially in a registry of the national marrow donor program.

Through innovative cooperation with programs in other countries, including Germany, France, Israel, South Africa, Greece, among others, patients can search for their tissue type through a worldwide network of 37 registries in 29 countries. Through this network the National Marrow Donor Program has direct access to over 4 million volunteer donors worldwide.

The language in the bill under consideration today is identical to an amendment approved by voice vote in the Subcommittee on Health and Environment which I chair. My substitute amendment represented a consensus position developed through long negotiations between the majority and minority of the Committee on Commerce and the Committee on Labor and Human Resources in the other body, the Department of Health and Human Resources, the Food and Drug Administration, the National Institutes of Health, the National Bone Marrow Donor Program itself, and many associations and interested parties who want to see this authorization pass this year.

Mr. Speaker, I want to again express my great appreciation on behalf of all of us, and on behalf of the many people out there who have benefited from this program and who will continue to benefit, and to the gentleman from Florida (Mr. YOUNG) for his efforts to secure this reauthorization.

Mr. Speaker, I urge all of my colleagues to join me in expressing their strong support for passage of this important legislation.

Mr. Speaker, I reserve the balance of my time.

Mr. BROWN of Ohio. Mr. Speaker, I yield myself such time as I may consume.

Mr. Speaker, I rise in support of the legislation we are considering today to reauthorize the National Bone Marrow Donor Registry Program. This program has given thousands of patients suffering from diseases like leukemia a second chance at life.

I would like to recognize the work of my chairman, the gentleman from Florida (Mr. MIKE BILIRAKIS) and the sponsor of this legislation, the gentleman from Florida (Mr. BILL YOUNG), in moving this important bill to the floor.

I extend a special thanks to the gentlewoman from Southern California (Ms. JUANITA MILLENDER-McDONALD), who has worked tirelessly to include provisions in the bill to help meet the needs of minority and mixed-race patients. For patients who suffer from terminal diseases, such as cancer and blood and immune system disorders, the transplantation of bone marrow offers their only hope for a cure.

In 1987, with a small grant to the Department of the Navy, the National Marrow Donor Program was established to help facilitate bone marrow matches between patients and donors and maintain a registry of individuals willing to donate marrow. I am pleased that since its inception 12 years ago NMDP has facilitated over 6,500 marrow transplants between unrelated patients and donors around the world. Further, the annual number of transplants has increased by 53 percent between 1994 and 1997, since NMDP was transferred to Health Resources Services Administration.

I am pleased the legislation we are considering today builds upon this success by fully funding current and new innovative educational campaigns to increase the number of willing donors which will obviously, in turn, increase the number of successful transplantations. Working with patients and physicians, NMDP and its partners can improve outreach and increase awareness of the importance of marrow donation. This work is especially important if we are going to continue to increase the number of minorities, such as African Americans and Latinos, who are successfully matched with willing donors.

Mr. Speaker, we can all take pride in the accomplishments of this lifesaving program. I am hopeful we can work together to ensure that more sick patients have access to these lifesaving therapies by passing this legislation today.

Mr. Speaker, I reserve the balance of my time.

Mr. BILIRAKIS. Mr. Speaker, I gladly yield such time as he may consume to the gentleman from Florida (Mr. BILL YOUNG), my friend, neighbor, and colleague.

(Mr. YOUNG of Florida asked and was given permission to revise and extend his remarks.)

Mr. YOUNG of Florida. Mr. Speaker, I thank the gentleman for yielding me the time.

Exhibit 46.   144 CONG. REC. H3427 (daily ed. May 19, 1998).

also has the index and "History of Bills and Resolutions" tables back to 1983). THOMAS's version has links from the index and Daily Digest to *Record* pages and to bill texts, while GPO Access has the *Record* in PDF format as well as cumulative versions of the index and "History of Bills and Resolutions." Westlaw and Lexis–Nexis coverage extends back to 1985.

Several years after the session, a bound edition of more than 20 volumes is published. This edition renumbers the separately paginated Senate and House sections into one sequence, and it includes a cumulative index, a compilation of the Daily Digest, and a cumulative "History of Bills and Resolutions" table listing all bills introduced during the session and summarizing their legislative history.

The predecessors of the *Congressional Record*, which began in 1873, are: the *Annals of Congress* (1789–1824); the *Register of Debates* (1824–37); and the *Congressional Globe* (1833–73). *House* and *Senate Journals* are also published, but unlike the *Congressional Record*, they do not include the verbatim debates. The journals merely record the proceedings, indicate whether there was debate, and report the resulting action and votes taken. The *House Journal* is more voluminous and includes the texts of bills and amendments considered; both journals also include "History of Bills and Resolutions" tables.

d. Hearings and Other Congressional Publications

Senate and House committees hold hearings on proposed legislation and on other subjects under congressional investigation such as nominations or impeachments. Government officials, scholars, and interested parties read prepared statements and answer questions from committee members. The transcripts of most hearings are published, accompanied by material submit-

ted by interested individual and groups such as statements, article reprints, or statistical material.

The purpose of a hearing is to determine the need for new legislation or to bring before Congress information relevant to its preparation and enactment. Hearings provide useful background information, but they are not generally considered persuasive sources of legislative history on the meaning of an enacted bill. Because they focus more on the views of interested parties rather than those of the lawmakers themselves, their importance as evidence of legislative intent is limited.

Hearings are generally identified by the title which appears on the cover, the bill number, the name of the subcommittee and committee, the term of Congress, and the year. Exhibit 47 shows the front page of *The Gift of Life: Increasing Bone Marrow Donation and Transplantation: Joint Hearing Before the Subcomm. on Public Health and Safety of the Senate Comm. on Labor and Human Resources and the Subcomm. on Health and Environment of the House Comm. on Commerce*, 105th Cong. (1998).

A search for relevant hearings should not be limited to the session in which a particular law is enacted, because hearings may extend over more than one session and be issued in several parts and volumes. Hearings are not held for all bills, however, and not all hearings are published.

Hearings are available from the particular committee and are issued by the Government Printing Office. Some hearings beginning in 1997 are available through GPO Access and THOMAS, and witnesses' statements are usually available from the online databases well before

S. HRG. 105–582

THE GIFT OF LIFE: INCREASING BONE MARROW DONATION AND TRANSPLANTATION

JOINT HEARING

BEFORE THE

SUBCOMMITTEE ON PUBLIC HEALTH AND SAFETY

OF THE

COMMITTEE ON LABOR AND HUMAN RESOURCES
UNITED STATES SENATE

AND THE

SUBCOMMITTEE ON HEALTH AND ENVIRONMENT

OF THE

COMMITTEE ON COMMERCE
HOUSE OF REPRESENTATIVES

ONE HUNDRED FIFTH CONGRESS

SECOND SESSION

ON

AUTHORIZING FUNDS FOR THE NATIONAL MARROW DONOR PROGRAM
(H.R. 2202)

APRIL 23, 1998

Committee on Commerce Serial No. 105–100

Printed for the use of the Committee on Labor and Human Resources

U.S. GOVERNMENT PRINTING OFFICE

48–029 CC   WASHINGTON : 1998

For sale by the U.S. Government Printing Office
Superintendent of Documents, Congressional Sales Office, Washington, DC 20402
ISBN 0-16-057412-9

Exhibit 47. *The Gift of Life: Increasing Bone Marrow Donation and Transplantation: Joint Hearing Before the Subcomm. on Public Health and Safety of the Senate Comm. on Labor and Human Resources and the Subcomm. on Health and Environment of the House Comm. on Commerce, 105th Cong. (1998).*

the full transcripts are published. Most committees now provide Internet access to material from their hearings, including prepared statements of legislators and witnesses.

Congress also produces a variety of other publications which are less frequently consulted in legislative history research. These publications can, however, be important sources of related information.

Committee prints contain a variety of material prepared specifically for the use of a committee, ranging from studies by the committee staff or outside experts to compilations of earlier legislative history documents. Some prints contain statements by committee members on a pending bill. Others can be useful analyses of laws under the jurisdiction of a committee, such as the House's biennial *Green Book: Background Material and Data on Major Programs Within the Jurisdiction of the Committee on Ways and Means*. Committee prints are distributed by the Government Printing Office, but they are not as widely available online as reports or hearings. Selective coverage through Lexis–Nexis begins in 1994, and GPO Access has a limited number of prints beginning in 1997.

Only occasionally useful as sources of legislative history, *House and Senate documents* include reports of some congressional investigations not found in the regular committee reports, special studies or exhibits prepared for Congress, presidential messages, and communications from executive departments or agencies. They are published in a numbered series for each house, and appear in the official *Serial Set*. Some presidential documents, including messages accompanying proposed legislation and statements issued when signing or vetoing bills, also

appear in the *Congressional Record* and the *Weekly Compilation of Presidential Documents*.

The Senate issues two series of publications in the process of treaty ratification. *Treaty documents* contain the texts of treaties before the Senate for its advice and consent, and *Senate executive reports* from the Foreign Relations Committee contain its recommendations on pending treaties. These publications are discussed more fully in Chapter 11. Other Senate committees also issue executive reports, containing their recommendations on presidential nominations to the executive and judicial branches.

§ 6–3. CONGRESSIONAL RESEARCH RESOURCES

While researchers are interested in Congress for numerous reasons, this discussion focuses on tools useful for two basic legal research tasks: investigating the meaning of an enacted law, and tracking the status of pending legislation. A number of approaches can be used for these purposes. For recently enacted laws and pending legislation, electronic resources provide current and thorough coverage. For older bills, the choices dwindle to a few tools that have been published for many years or that provide retrospective coverage.

The *bill number* is usually the key to finding congressional documents or tracing legislative action. It appears on an enacted law both in its slip form and in the *Statutes at Large*. In chapter 5, note in Exhibit 32 on page 138 that the bill number (H.R. 2807) is included in brackets in the left margin. Bill numbers have been included in *Statutes at Large* since 1903; earlier numbers can be found in Eugene Nabors, *Legislative Reference Checklist* (1982).

```
LEGISLATIVE HISTORY—H.R. 2202:
HOUSE REPORTS: No. 105–538 (Comm. on Commerce).
CONGRESSIONAL RECORD, Vol. 144 (1998):
     May 19, considered and passed House.
     June 24, considered and passed Senate.
                              O
```

Exhibit 48.   Legislative History, Pub.L. 105–196, 112 Stat. 631, 637 (1998).

Bill numbers do not appear, unfortunately, in the *United States Code* or in either of its annotated editions.

Bill numbers lead easily to printed or electronic status tables, which indicate actions taken and provide references to relevant documents. Many status tables include a short summary of each bill. These tables can be used both for pending bill searches and for retrospective research on enacted laws.

A quick head start in legislative history research can come from the Public Law itself. At the end of each Public Law, in either slip law or *Statutes at Large*, there appears a brief legislative history summary with citations of committee reports, dates of consideration and passage in each house, and references to presidential statements. The summary for the National Bone Marrow Registry Reauthorization Act of 1998 is shown in Exhibit 48. Note that it provides references to the House report and *Congressional Record* debate shown in earlier exhibits, but no references to hearings. Summaries have appeared at the end of each law passed since 1975, and *Statutes at Large* volumes from 1963 to 1974 include separate "Guide to Legislative History" tables.

a.   THOMAS and Other Congressional Websites

For current legislation or laws enacted since 1973, one of the easiest places to begin research is with Congress itself. THOMAS <thomas.loc.gov> is the website developed by the Library of Congress to make legislative information freely available to the public. The scope of THOMAS has grown considerably since its introduction in 1995, and it now provides access to a wide range of information and documents.

THOMAS provides numerous search options. In addition to bill or public law number, legislation can be found by keyword, subject, date, or sponsor. Legislative history summaries are available for laws enacted since 1973, but summaries for older laws lack some of the features for more recent legislation. Links to the text of legislation, for example, are available beginning in 1989, and *Congressional Record* page references and links have been added beginning in 1993. The first page of the THOMAS summary for H.R. 2202 is shown in Exhibit 49. Note in particular the "Floor Actions" status section, tracing the bill's course and providing links to the *Congressional Record* and to the text of House report.

THOMAS has the text of many congressional documents, but it also includes links to the Government Printing Office's GPO Access <www.access.gpo.gov/congress/>, which provides these documents as PDF files. GPO Access is the more comprehensive source for documents, but it is a less user-friendly and informative site than THOMAS. Its search functions are more limited, and there are no links between its congressional documents.

THOMAS and GPO Access are the major comprehensive websites for congressional information. In addition,

---

Bill Summary & Status for the 105th Congress

Item 1 of 1

PREVIOUS:ALL | NEXT:ALL
NEW SEARCH | HOME | HELP

H.R.2202
Public Law: 105-196 (07/16/98)
SPONSOR: Rep Young, C. (introduced 07/17/97)

Jump to: Titles, Status, Committees, Amendments, Cosponsors, Summary

---

TITLE(S):

- SHORT TITLE(S) AS INTRODUCED:
  National Marrow Donor Program Reauthorization Act of 1997

- SHORT TITLE(S) AS REPORTED TO HOUSE:
  National Bone Marrow Registry Reauthorization Act of 1998

- SHORT TITLE(S) AS PASSED HOUSE:
  National Bone Marrow Registry Reauthorization Act of 1998

- SHORT TITLE(S) AS PASSED SENATE:
  National Bone Marrow Registry Reauthorization Act of 1998

- SHORT TITLE(S) AS ENACTED:
  National Bone Marrow Registry Reauthorization Act of 1998

- OFFICIAL TITLE AS INTRODUCED:
  A bill to amend the Public Health Service Act to revise and extend the bone marrow donor
  program, and for other purposes.

STATUS: Floor Actions
07/16/98 Public Law 105-196 (7/20/98 CR D795)
07/08/98 Measure presented to President (7/14/98 CR H5487)
07/07/98 Enrolled Measure signed in Senate (CR S7574)
06/30/98 Enrolled Measure signed in House (7/14/98 CR H5415)
06/24/98 Measure passed Senate (CR S7037)
06/24/98 Measure considered in Senate (CR S7037)
06/24/98 Called up by unanimous consent discharging Senate Committee on Labor and Human
Resources (CR S7037)
05/20/98 Referred to Senate Committee on Labor and Human Resources (CR S5217)
05/19/98 Measure passed House, amended (CR H3429)
05/19/98 Measure considered in House (CR H3425-3429)
05/19/98 Measure called up under motion to suspend rules and pass in House (CR H3425)
05/18/98 Reported to House from the Committee on Commerce with amendment, H. Rept. 105-538 (CR
H3366)

Exhibit 49. Bill Summary & Status, H.R. 2202, <thomas.loc.gov>.

each chamber maintains a website (<www.senate.gov> and <www.house.gov>) with information on its procedures as well as links to pages for individual members and committees. Most committee homepages have summaries of major pending legislation, background information, hearing statements, and schedules of upcoming meetings.

Numerous other government and commercial websites have congressional information. The Library of Congress provides links to many of these sites <lcweb.loc.gov/global/legislative/congress.html>, including an annotated list of "Congressional Mega Sites" and links for information on committees, schedules, and floor proceedings.

b.   Congressional Information Service (CIS)

Despite its official-sounding name, Congressional Information Service (CIS) is not an government office but a commercial enterprise (and now a branch of Lexis–Nexis). CIS provides the most extensive indexing available of congressional information, covering virtually all congressional publications since 1789 except the *Congressional Record* and its predecessors. CIS publishes its information in several formats: printed indexes, online through Lexis–Nexis, on CD–ROM as *Congressional Masterfile*, and on the Web as Congressional Universe <web.lexis-nexis.com/cis/>.

CIS first began indexing congressional materials in 1970, and its coverage is divided into two basic time periods. For the period before 1970, it publishes several retrospective indexes covering the Serial Set, executive documents and reports, hearings, and committee prints. These printed indexes are cumulated on CD–ROM as *Congressional Masterfile I.* Access is generally by keyword searching, but specific fields such as bill numbers can be

searched and retrieval can be limited to specific years in order to focus on particular legislation. CIS coverage before 1970 is not available on the Internet or through Lexis–Nexis.

For the period since 1970, CIS coverage is a bit more sophisticated. Abstracts and extensive subject indexes cover all congressional publications except the *Congressional Record*. These abstracts and indexes are available in monthly pamphlets (*CIS/Index*) with annual cumulations (*CIS/Annual*), on CD–ROM, through Lexis–Nexis, or on the Web.

In the printed *CIS/Index*, reports, hearings, prints, and documents are indexed by subject, title, and bill number; the indexes provide references to abstracts summarizing the contents of these documents. Exhibit 50 shows the CIS abstract for the hearing shown in Exhibit 47 on page 181, indicating the names and affiliations of the witnesses and the focus of their testimony. The number beginning with "Y4.L11/4" after the Senate Hearing number in the abstract is the Superintendent of Documents classification, which is used in most libraries for locating government publications. The "S541–40" in the heading for the abstract is the CIS accession number for the publication, and is the number used to find this hearing in CIS's microfiche collection of documents. To experienced researchers, both "Y4.L11/4" and "S541" identify this hearing as a publication of the Senate Committee on Labor and Human Resources.

Since 1984, *CIS/Annual* has included *Legislative Histories* volumes providing references for each public law to bills, hearings, reports, debates, presidential documents and any other legislative actions. Rather than limiting

S541–40   GIFT OF LIFE: INCREASING BONE MARROW DONATION AND TRANSPLANTATION.
Apr. 23, 1998. 105-2.
v+62 p.   GPO $3.25
S/N 552-070-22818-7.
CIS/MF/3
•Item 1043-A; 1043-B.
S. Hrg. 105-582.
°Y4.L11/4:S.HRG.105-582.

Joint hearing before the *Subcom on Public Health and Safety* and the House Commerce Committee *Subcom on Health and Environment* to examine activities of HHS National Marrow Donor Program (NMDP), in connection with NMDP authorization.

Supplementary material (p. 44-62) includes witnesses' written statements, submitted statements, and correspondence.

S541–40.1: Apr. 23, 1998. p. 9-13.

Witness: **YOUNG, C. W. Bill,** (Rep, R-Fla)

Statement and Discussion: Merits of continued funding for NMDP.

S541–40.2: Apr. 23, 1998. p. 13-23.

Witnesses: **FOX, Claude E., III,** Acting Administrator, Health Resources and Services Administration.
ZUMWALT, Elmo R., Jr., Chairman, Public Policy Committee, NMDP.
HOWE, Craig W. (Dr.), CEO, NMDP.

Statements and Discussion: Benefits of NMDP; efforts to improve NMDP registry, including expansion of potential minority donors.

S541–40.3: Apr. 23, 1998. p. 24-35.

Witnesses: **WEDGE, Robert, Jr.,** leukemia patient.
HERNANDEZ, Angel, parent of leukemia patient.
CALLENDER, Clive O. (Dr.), Principal Investigator, National Minority Organ Tissue Transplant Education Program.

Statements and Discussion: Importance of bone marrow donation programs; perspectives on need to add minorities to NMDP registry.

S541–40.4: Apr. 23, 1998. p. 35-43.

Witnesses: **LENFANT, Claude J. (Dr.),** Director, National Heart, Lung, and Blood Institute.
SNYDER, Edward L. (Dr.), President, American Association of Blood Banks.

Statements and Discussion: Support for NMDP; perspectives on use of blood stem cell transplants as alternative to marrow transplants.

Exhibit 50.   CIS/ANNUAL 1998: ABSTRACTS OF CONGRESSIONAL PUBLICATIONS 554 (1999).

coverage to a single term of Congress, they include references to earlier hearings and other documents on related bills from *prior* Congressional sessions. These are probably the most complete and descriptive summaries of the legislative history of federal enactments. Exhibit 51 shows the CIS legislative history of the National Bone Marrow Registry Reauthorization Act of 1998. Note that this summary includes not only the report, debate and hearing shown in this chapter's exhibits, but similar consideration in the 104th Congress in 1995–96. These earlier documents may be quite relevant in interpreting the bill that was eventually passed in 1998.

From 1970 to 1983, CIS included legislative histories of enacted laws in its *Abstracts* volumes. These are nearly as extensive as the later histories, but they are less convenient to use because they simply list the CIS numbers for the reports, hearings and other materials. It is necessary to turn to the abstracts for more information. These summaries, nonetheless, are among the most thorough sources available for their period.

The Congressional Universe website provides all the information in *CIS/Index*, with several enhancements including keyword searching and links from legislative histories to the documents described. Other features include bill-tracking; full-text access to bills, reports, the *Congressional Record*, and other congressional documents beginning in the 1980s; transcripts of hearing testimony; and information on committees and legislators.

c. *USCCAN*

U.S. Code Congressional and Administrative News (*USCCAN*) was mentioned in Chapter 5 as a source of the

---

Public Law 105-196   **112 Stat. 631**

National Bone Marrow Registry Reauthorization Act of 1998

July 16, 1998

Public Law

1.1 Public Law 105-196, approved July 16, 1998. (H.R. 2202)

(CIS98:PL105-196   7 p.)

"To amend the Public Health Service Act to revise and extend the bone marrow donor program, and for other purposes."
Amends the Public Health Service Act to revise and authorize FY99-FY2003 appropriations for HHS bone marrow transplant programs, including activities of the National Bone Marrow Donor Registry.

P.L. 105-196 Reports

104th Congress

2.1 S. Rpt. 104-256 on S. 1324, "Organ and Bone Marrow Transplant Program Reauthorization Act of 1995," Apr. 22, 1996.

(CIS96:S543-1   56 p.)
(Y1.1/5:104-256.)

Recommends passage, with an amendment in the nature of a substitute, of S. 1324, the Organ and Bone Marrow Transplant Program Reauthorization Act of 1995, to amend the Public Health Service Act in the following titles:
Title I, the Solid-Organ Transplantation Program Act of 1995, to authorize FY97-FY2001 appropriations for HHS organ transplant programs established under the National Organ Transplant Act of 1984, including grants and cooperative agreements with public and nonprofit organizations to increase organ donations.
Title II, the Bone Marrow Transplantation Program Reauthorization Act of 1995, to authorize FY97-FY99 appropriations for and revise HHS bone marrow transplant programs, including activities of the National Bone Marrow Donor Registry.

105th Congress

2.2 H. Rpt. 105-538 on H.R. 2202, "National Bone Marrow Registry Reauthorization Act of 1998," May 18, 1998.

(CIS98:H273-7   19 p.)
(Y1.1/8:105-538.)

Recommends passage, with an amendment in the nature of a substitute, of H.R. 2202, the National Bone Marrow Registry Reauthorization Act of 1998, to amend the Public Health Service Act to authorize FY99-FY2003 appropriations for HHS bone marrow transplant programs, including activities of the National Bone Marrow Donor Registry.

105th Congress, 2nd Session

H.R. 2202 is related to 104th Congress S. 1324.

P.L. 105-196 Debate

142 Congressional Record
104th Congress, 2nd Session - 1996

4.1 Sept. 9, Senate consideration and passage of S. 1324, p. S10080.

144 Congressional Record
105th Congress, 2nd Session - 1998

4.2 May 19, House consideration and passage of H.R. 2202, p. H3425.

4.3 June 24, Senate consideration and passage of H.R. 2202, p. S7037.

P.L. 105-196 Hearings

104th Congress

5.1 "Reauthorization of the National Organ Transplant Act," hearings before the Senate Labor and Human Resources Committee, July 20, 1995.

(CIS95:S541-69   iv+118 p.)
(Y4.L11/4:S.HRG.104-169.)

105th Congress

5.2 "Gift of Life: Increasing Bone Marrow Donation and Transplantation," hearings before the Subcommittee on Public Health and Safety, Senate Labor and Human Resources Committee and the Subcommittee on Health and Environment, House Commerce Committee, Apr. 23, 1998.

(CIS98:S541-40   v+62 p.)
(Y4.L11/4:S.HRG.105-582.)

CIS/INDEX Legislative Histories   77

Exhibit 51. National Bone Marrow Registry Reauthorization Act of 1998, CIS/ANNUAL 1998: LEGISLATIVE HISTORIES OF U.S. PUBLIC LAWS 77 (1999).

texts of enacted laws. For most acts it also reprints one or more committee reports, making it a convenient compilation for basic legislative research. The scope of coverage varies, but *USCCAN* generally prints either a House or Senate report and the conference committee report, if one was issued. It also provides references to some of the committee reports it does not reprint, and to the dates of consideration in the *Congressional Record*.

The public laws and committee reports are published in separate "Laws" and "Legislative History" sections of *USCCAN*. Each section prints material in order by public law number, and cross-references are provided between the laws and reports. Exhibit 52 shows the beginning of the House report on the National Bone Marrow Registry Reauthorization Act of 1998, as set out in *USCCAN*. Note that the report is preceded by references to steps in the passage of the legislation, including dates of consideration and passage in each house. The report is reprinted in full, except for the portion printing the text of the act.

Both the monthly advance sheets of *USCCAN* and the annual bound volumes also include tables with basic legislative history information. For each public law, these tables list the date approved, *Statutes at Large* citation, bill and report numbers, committees, and dates of passage. Each monthly issue also includes a table of "Major Bills Pending," arranged by subject and showing the progress of current legislation.

USCCAN provides only selective coverage of committee reports, and further research is often required. But it does offer a handy starting point and is easily accessible in

NATIONAL BONE MARROW
REGISTRY REAUTHORIZATION ACT OF 1998

PUBLIC LAW 105–196, see page 112 Stat. 631

DATES OF CONSIDERATION AND PASSAGE

House: May 19, 1998

Senate: May 20, June 24,1998

Cong. Record Vol. 144 (1998)

**House Report (Labor and Human Resources Committee)
No. 105–538, May 18, 1998
[To accompany H. R. 2202]**

The House Report is set out below .

HOUSE REPORT NO. 105–538

[page 1]

* * * * * * * * *

The Committee on Commerce, to whom was referred the bill (H.R. 2202) to amend the Public Health Service Act to revise and extend the bone marrow donor program, and for other purposes, having considered the same, reports favorably thereon with an amendment and recommends that the bill as amended do pass.

* * * * * * * * * *

[page 6]

PURPOSE AND SUMMARY

H.R. 2202, the National Bone Marrow Registry Reauthorization Act of 1998, amends Section 379 of the Public Health Service Act (42 U.S.C. 274k) to reauthorize the National Bone Marrow Donor Registry.

BACKGROUND AND NEED FOR LEGISLATION

More than 30,000 children and adults in the U.S. are diagnosed each year with leukemia, aplastic anemia, or other life-threatening diseases. For many, the only hope for survival is a marrow transplant.

273

Exhibit 52. H.R. Rep. No. 538 (1998), *reprinted in* 1998 U.S.C.C.A.N. 273.

most law libraries. For a researcher looking for general background or a section-by-section analysis, *USCCAN* may be all that is needed.

d. *Congressional Index* and Other Commercial Sources

CCH's *Congressional Index* is issued in two looseleaf volumes for each Congress, with weekly updates. Its extensive coverage of pending legislation includes an index of bills by subject and author, a digest of each bill, and a status table of actions taken on each bill (but not the documents themselves). This status table contains references to hearings, a feature lacking in many other legislative research aids. Although similar services are also provided by THOMAS and other electronic sources, *Congressional Index* remains one of the most convenient and current printed sources of congressional information.

Often several bills are introduced on related topics, and it can be difficult to tell from electronic sources which of these bills (if any) is being acted upon. In such cases, using a printed index and status table may be a quicker way to compare bills than a series of electronic queries. Exhibit 53 shows an excerpt from the status table section of *Congressional Index*, with information on the progress of H.R. 2202 from introduction to passage and enactment. The key stages, including hearings, are indicated in a standard, rather telegraphic format. Unlike the CIS legislative history, there are no references to a related bill in an earlier term of Congress.

Congressional Index does not contain the texts of bills or reports, but it does provide a wide range of other information on Congress, including lists of members and committee assignments; an index of enactments and

```
                    ★ 2202
Introduced ......................... 7/17/97
Ref to H Commerce Com ............. 7/17/97
Hrgs by Health Subcom .............. 4/23/98
Hrgs by Labor Com ................. 4/23/98
Hrgs by Public Health Subcom ........ 4/23/98
Approved w/amdts by Health Subcom . . 5/12/98
Ordered reptd w/amdts by Commerce Com
    ............................... 5/14/98
Reptd w/amdts, H Rept 105-538, by Commerce
    Com ........................... 5/18/98
Passed as amended under suspension of rules by
    2/3 vote (Voice) ................. 5/19/98
Ref to S Labor Com ................. 5/20/98
Labor Com discharged ............... 6/24/98
Passed by S (Voice)................. 6/24/98
Sent to President ................... 7/8/98
Signed by President ................. 7/16/98
Public Law 105-196 (112 Stat 631) ..... 7/16/98
```

Exhibit 53.   1997–1998 Cong. Index (CCH) 35,042 (Dec. 9, 1998).

vetoes; lists of pending treaties, reorganization plans, and nominations; a table of voting records; and a weekly newsletter on developments in Congress. *Congressional Index* began publication in 1938, and the older volumes can be valuable sources of information on bills predating the coverage of electronic bill-tracking services.

Congressional Quarterly (CQ) is a news service and publisher of several sources of information on congressional activity. Its most widely read publication is *CQ Weekly* (formerly *Congressional Quarterly Weekly Report*), which provides background information on pending legislation and news of current developments. (Another publication, *CQ Daily Monitor*, is more frequently updated but less widely available.) *CQ Weekly* contains tables of House and Senate votes, a status table for major legislation, and a legislative history table for new public

laws. CQ Library <library.cq.com> provides a subscription-based Web version of *CQ Weekly* and free access to a detailed index, which is updated weekly. An annual *Congressional Quarterly Almanac* cumulates much of the information in the Weekly Report into a useful summary of the congressional session. The 1998 consideration of H.R. 2202 received little attention from *CQ Weekly*, but Exhibit 54 shows a page from a 1995 issue discussing action by the Senate Labor and Human Resources Committee on an earlier version of the bill.

CQ also has a subscription Internet service, *CQ.com On Congress* <oncongress.cq.com>, which provides bill-tracking information and the text of documents. CQ's services in this area are similar to those provided by Westlaw and Lexis–Nexis: all three have databases providing up-to-date information on the progress of a bill through Congress; the texts of bills, committee reports, and the *Congressional Record*; and a wide range of other information on Congress and its members.

Numerous other newspapers and magazines also focus on developments in Washington. In addition to general news sources, specialized publications include *National Journal* (weekly) and *Roll Call* (twice weekly). National Journal also publishes a *CongressDaily* newsletter, and all three of these publications are available through both Westlaw and Lexis–Nexis.

e.   Printed Congressional Status Tables

As noted earlier, the *Congressional Record* includes status tables which can be useful for both current and retrospective research. A "History of Bills and Resolutions" table is published in the biweekly index and cumulated for each session in the bound index volume. It

HEALTH

Panel OKs Bill To Strengthen Organ Donor Programs

The Senate Labor and Human Resources Committee approved a bill (S 1324) to strengthen programs that match organ and bone marrow donors with people suffering from such illnesses as heart disease or leukemia.

The measure, S 1324, would reauthorize federal oversight of the nation's organ and bone marrow transplant programs. It was sponsored by Chairwoman Nancy Landon Kassebaum, R-Kan., and approved by voice vote Nov. 8.

Under the proposal, the Solid Organ Transplant program would be reauthorized for five years. The program could receive nearly $2 million in fiscal 1997; $1.1 million in 1998; and $250,000 annually in 1999 through 2001.

The bill would also renew the Bone Marrow Transplantation program for three years. The initiative would be authorized at $13.5 million in fiscal

By Robert Marshall Wells

BOXSCORE
Bill: S 1324 — Organ donor programs.
Latest action: The Senate Labor and Human Resources Committee approved the measure Nov. 8.
Next likely action: Senate floor consideration.
Background: The bill seeks to strengthen organ procurement organizations and increase donor registration.

1997; $12.2 million in 1998, and unspecified sums in 1999.

Edward M. Kennedy of Massachusetts, the Labor panel's ranking Democrat, and an original cosponsor of the bill, said the measure is needed to bridge a gap between the number of potential donors and those in need of organs and bone marrow.

Through better communication and reporting techniques, the bill would aim to strengthen the network of organ procurement organizations and increase donor registration through public education programs and other activities developed at the local level.

The bill also would allow the Department of Health and Human Services to impose a new "data management fee" to be paid by transplant centers and organ procurement firms.

Money collected from the new fee would be used to ensure that the financial stability of existing national donor and patient registries would be sustained well into the future.

The measure could reach the Senate floor before the end of the year, but House consideration is unlikely until 1996. ∎

CORRECTION

Immigration overhaul. Weekly Report, p. 3305, photo caption. Texas Rep. John Bryant is a Democrat. ∎

SECTION NOTES

Older Americans Act Markup Postponed

Rep. Randy "Duke" Cunningham, R-Calif., postponed an Economic and Educational Opportunities subcommittee markup Nov. 9 on legislation to reauthorize the 1965 Older Americans Act after Democrats complained about how fast the panel was asked to consider the bill.

They also expressed frustration that too many committee members were involved in other issues — such as budget and appropriations measures — to concentrate on the bill.

Cunningham, chairman of the Early Childhood, Youth and Families Subcommittee, agreed to allow the panel to continue its markup of the measure (HR 2570) on Nov. 16.

The bill aims to streamline federal programs that feed, transport and employ poor senior citizens.

Among the better-known programs are "Meals on Wheels" and the Senior Community Service Employment Pro-

gram, which subsidizes part-time community service jobs for unemployed, low-income seniors. The current three-year authorization expires in September 1996. *(1992 Almanac, p. 466)*

As proposed by Cunningham, the legislation would consolidate 23 programs into nine and eliminate funding for grants to national organizations under the Senior Community Service Employment Program.

Under the measure, the act would be reauthorized for five years. Funding would be authorized at $1.4 billion in fiscal 1997, and at unspecified sums through fiscal 2001.

Committee Removes Hurdle On Flag Burning Vote

Majority Leader Bob Dole, R-Kan., has promised a Senate vote by the end of the year on a constitutional amendment to ban flag desecration, and the Judiciary Committee took a step Nov. 9 to smooth the way toward clearing the measure.

The House passed the resolution (H J Res 79) on June 28, and the Senate Judiciary Committee approved an identical resolution (S J Res 31) on July 20. The measure seeks a constitutional amendment to allow Congress and the states to pass laws banning physical desecration of the U.S. flag. *(Weekly Report, pp. 2195, 1933)*

Proposed constitutional amendments require a two-thirds majority — 67 votes if all senators vote — to pass.

The panel approved by voice vote H J Res 79, so that the full Senate can use it as a legislative vehicle when it takes up flag burning. If the Senate passes H J Res 79 without amendment, it could be sent on to the states for ratification, avoiding other procedural steps.

Supporters as well as opponents say that when the measure does go to the floor, the vote will be close.

If the resolution passes, it must still be ratified by three-fourths, or 38, of the states.

Exhibit 54. Robert Marshall Wells, *Panel OKs Bill To Strengthen Organ Donor Programs,* 53 Cong. Q. Weekly Rep. 3464 (1995).

includes a brief summary of each bill, the committee investigating the proposed legislation, and any actions taken to date, including amendments and passage. This is one of the best sources of page references to debates within the *Record*, and includes report and public law numbers. It does not, however, include any references to hearings.

The biweekly table lists only those bills and resolutions acted upon within the preceding two week period, so it may be necessary to consult more than one index to find references to a particular bill. If a bill is listed, however, the information is cumulative from date of introduction. (Unlike the printed table, the online version through GPO Access <www.access.gpo.gov/su_docs/aces/aaces190. html> cumulates all entries from the beginning of the session.) An entry from this table for H.R. 2202, after it had been signed into law, is shown in Exhibit 55. Note that it provides detailed *Congressional Record* page references, including several additions of cosponsors, but no mention of the hearing shown in Exhibit 47 or of actions on any related bills.

The final cumulative table is not issued for several years after the end of a session. It is published after the bound edition of the *Record* and uses the final pagination instead of the separate "S" and "H" pages in the daily edition. While this table is less complete than commercial sources such as *CIS/Index* or *Congressional Index*, it remains one of the best sources available for older laws. These tables have been published annually since the 1867 volume of the *Congressional Globe*, long before the earliest coverage of most commercial publications.

H.R. 2202—A bill to amend the Public Health Service
Act to revise and extend the bone marrow donor
program, and for other purposes; to the Committee
on Commerce.

Cosponsors added, H64 [27JA], H386 [5FE], H851
[4MR], H1550 [25MR], H1854 [31MR], H2236
[22AP], H3014 [7MY], H3247 [13MY], H3312
[14MY]

Reported with amendment (H. Rept. 105–538), H3366
[18MY]

Rules suspended. Passed House amended, H3425
[19MY]

Text, H3425 [19MY]

Message from the House, S5217 [20MY], S7574 [7JY]

*Received in the Senate and referred to the Committee
on Labor and Human Resources,* S5217 [20MY]

Passed Senate, S7037 [24JN]

Message from the Senate, H5299 [25JN]

Examined and signed in the Senate, S7574 [7JY]

Examined and signed in the House, H5415, H5487
[14JY]

Presented to the President (July 8, 1998), H5487 [14JY]

Approved [Public Law 105–196] (signed July 16, 1998)

Exhibit 55.   History of Bills and Resolutions, CONG. RECORD INDEX, July
20 to Aug. 7, 1998, at H.B. 20.

Both houses and most committees issue calendars of
pending business for the use of their members. Perhaps
the most valuable of these is *Calendars of the United
States House of Representatives and History of Legislation,* which is issued daily. Each issue is cumulative and
includes all bills in either House or Senate that have been
reported out of committee. Committee calendars are also
excellent sources of information on upcoming hearings.
Current House and Senate calendars are available on the
Internet through GPO Access <www.access.gpo.gov/
congress/cong003.html> and <.../cong004.html>.

f. Compiled Legislative Histories

Gathering a complete legislative history can be a very time-consuming process, as the necessary documents are scattered among many publications and may be difficult to obtain. For some major enactments, however, convenient access is provided by publications which reprint the important bills, debates, committee reports, and hearings. These compiled histories can save the considerable time and trouble involved in finding relevant references and documents. They are published both by government agencies (particularly the Congressional Research Service of the Library of Congress) and by commercial publishers. . Online compiled legislative histories, including bills and committee reports, are available on Lexis–Nexis for major acts in areas such as bankruptcy, tax, and environmental law.

The basic tool for identifying and locating published compiled legislative histories is Nancy P. Johnson's *Sources of Compiled Legislative Histories* (1979–date). Arranged chronologically by Congress and Public Law number, it provides a checklist of all available compiled legislative histories from 1789 through 1996, and includes an index by name of act. It covers not only compilations which reprint the legislative history documents in full, but law review articles and other sources that list and discuss relevant documents but do not reprint them. Compilations issued by the government are listed and indexed in Bernard D. Reams, Jr., *Federal Legislative Histories: An Annotated Bibliography and Index to Officially Published Sources* (1994)

g. Directories

One of the fastest and simplest ways to find information on pending legislation is to call a congressional staff

member responsible for drafting or monitoring the bill. The best sources for detailed information on staff members are two competing commercial directories, *Congressional Staff Directory* (three times per year) and *Congressional Yellow Book* (quarterly). Internet versions of both directories are updated weekly but are available to subscribers only.

The *Official Congressional Directory* (biennial) is not as detailed as the commercial directories, but it does provides information about individuals, offices and the organizational structure of Congress. This directory is available through GPO Access <www.access.gpo.gov/congress/cong016.html>; the Internet version, unlike its print counterpart, is modified during the term to reflect changes. Two useful sources for background information on members of Congress, both published biennially, are *The Almanac of American Politics* and *Politics in America: Members of Congress in Washington and at Home*.

§ 6–4. STATE LEGISLATIVE INFORMATION

Legislative history on the state level is a research area of sharp contrasts. Information on current legislation is widely available on the Internet, but documents that might aid in the interpretation of enacted laws can be difficult or impossible to find.

First the good news: most state legislatures do excellent jobs of providing Internet access to current status information and to the text of pending bills. The better websites have several means of searching for bills, and some offer e-mail notification services when particular bills are acted upon.

These legislative websites can be found from state homepages (<www.state.___.us, using the state's postal abbreviation), or from one of the many general starting points. MultiState Associates, Inc.'s "State Legislative Presence on the Internet" page <www.multistate.com/weblist.htm> has links to each state legislature, an indication whether the state provides free access to the full text of bills and to status information, and comments on each site.

A useful feature found on many legislative websites is an introductory guide to the state's lawmaking procedures. State legislatures generally follow the federal paradigm, but there can be significant differences from state to state and an important first step in studying legislative action in a particular state is to learn about its procedures. Guides and other resources, such as charts showing how bills become law, can save considerable time and confusion.

The commercial databases also provide text and status information for pending legislation. Both Westlaw and Lexis–Nexis have databases for each state, as well as multistate databases useful for monitoring developments in legislatures throughout the country.

Researchers needing to interpret enacted statutes face a more difficult task. Bills from older sessions can be hard to locate. Almost every state has a legislative journal, but very few of these actually include transcripts of the debates. Only a few states publish committee reports, and even fewer publish hearings.

The materials that are available vary widely from state to state. Often they are not published in either print or

electronic form, but are only available at the state capitol. Some states have "bill jackets" with legislative information, and some have microform records or tape recordings of sessions. In many instances, contemporary newspaper accounts may be the best available source of information about a sponsor's intent or proceedings.

Many states have official agencies responsible for recommending and drafting new legislation. These groups, including law revision commissions, judicial councils, and legislative councils, often publish annual or topical reports summarizing their work. For recommendations enacted into law, these reports may be valuable legislative history documentation.

Lynn Hellebust's *State Legislative Sourcebook: A Resource Guide to Legislative Information in the Fifty States* (annual) is a useful source for identifying the resources available for each state. It provides information on the legislative processes and include references to available published and online sources. References include a "best initial contact" for each state, as well as information on websites, introductory guides, bill status telephone numbers, bill tracking services, and legislative documents such as session laws and summaries of legislation.

Other resources provide leads to finding available information in a specific state, although most of these predate widespread Internet access. The National Conference of State Legislatures has published a disk entitled *Legislative Intent Research: A 50–State Guide* (1996); and Jose R. Torres & Steve Windsor, "State Legislative Histories: A Select, Annotated Bibliography," 85 L. Libr. J. 545 (1993), summarizes books, pamphlets and articles avail-

able for each state at the time. In addition, most of the state legal research guides listed in Appendix B, on page 392, include discussion of legislative history resources.

Directory information on state legislatures, including organization, members, committees, and staffs, is contained in official state manuals (sometimes called *Bluebooks* or *Redbooks*), published annually or biennially by most states. A list of these directories, *State Reference Publications*, is published annually. The directory for a specific state is likely to provide the most detailed information, but several multistate directories are also published. General state government directories such as *State Yellow Book* and *State Staff Directory* include extensive coverage of the legislative branches, with information on both individual members and committees. The Council of State Governments publishes an annual *CSG State Directory* in three parts; legislatures are covered in *Directory I: Elective Officials* and *Directory II: Legislative Leadership, Committees and Staff*.

§ 6–5. CONCLUSION

Legislative history is sometimes viewed as an arcane and complex field, rather than as a basic legal research process. A grasp of the major resources, however, is necessary for any lawyer. Legislative materials are essential tools both in interpreting statutes and in monitoring current legal developments.

The electronic resources available from the online databases and from the government itself have made information on pending legislation easily accessible, while research into the history of enacted laws remains a more refined skill. For federal statutes, a review of material reprinted in *USCCAN* may be sufficient to determine

whether a further inquiry in legislative resources in necessary; from there a fuller picture may be obtained from *CIS/Index* or other tools. For state statutes, the materials available vary dramatically between jurisdictions.

Legislative history materials can be useful in statutory research, but they are just one of several important resources in understanding statutes. The court decisions found through annotated codes and other means may provide authoritative interpretations, and even secondary sources may be persuasive in determining the scope and meaning of an act. As will be discussed in the next chapter, many statutes are also supplemented by more detailed regulations and decisions from administrative agencies.

CHAPTER 7

ADMINISTRATIVE LAW

---

§ 7–1. INTRODUCTION

The executive is one of the three coordinate branches of government, but traditionally its lawmaking role has been limited to orders and regulations needed to carry out the legislature's mandates. With the rise of government bureaucracy, however, the rules created by executive agencies are often the legal sources with the most immediate and pervasive impact.

Administrative law takes several forms, as agencies can act somewhat like legislatures and somewhat like courts. They may promulgate binding regulations governing areas of their expertise, or they may decide matters involving particular litigants on a case-by-case basis. Approaches vary from agency to agency.

Although executive agencies have existed in this country since its creation, the real growth of administrative law began in the late 1800s as the government sought to deal with increasingly complex problems of society and economy. In the 1930s, Congress created new regulatory agencies such as the Federal Communications Commission and the Securities and Exchange Commission to carry out its New Deal legislation. A third boom in administrative law occurred around 1970, as additional agencies such as the Environmental Protection Agency and the Consumer Product Safety Commission were created to address growing environmental and health concerns. Administrative regulations and decisions have continued to proliferate to this day.

Most of this chapter focuses on federal administrative law, but state agencies can play just as important a role in many areas of activity. States also delegate lawmaking responsibilities to counties and cities, which enact ordinances and have their own local agencies. While federal administrative law is relatively easy to research, state and local sources may be quite difficult to locate and even harder to update.

§ 7–2. BACKGROUND REFERENCE MATERIALS

In researching administrative law, it is important to determine what agency has jurisdiction and to develop a preliminary understanding of its structure and functions. In some situations the relevant agency is obvious, but in

others it may require background analysis or a close reading of statutory and judicial sources to determine an agency's role.

A useful source for finding federal agencies is *Washington Information Directory* (annual), which is organized by subject and provides descriptions and access information for federal agencies as well as congressional committees and nongovernmental organizations. The topic "Government Information," for example, lists several agencies including the National Archives and Records Administration; Library of Congress offices; congressional committees with jurisdiction in the area; and interest groups such as the American Society of Access Professionals.

Once a relevant agency has been identified, a valuable next step is to consult the *United States Government Manual*. This annual directory of the federal government, available in print and on the Internet <www.access.gpo. gov/nara/nara001.html>, provides descriptive listings of each executive department and more than 50 independent agencies and commissions. It includes references to statutes under which the agencies operate and explains their functions and major operating units. Organizational charts are provided for most major agencies, and sources of information (including publications, telephone numbers, and websites) are listed. The *Government Manual* is one of the most important reference books of the federal government, and can often save a researcher considerable time by providing quick answers to questions which might otherwise require extensive research. Exhibit 56 shows the first page of its entry for the National Archive and Records Administration (NARA). Note that mail, telephone, and Internet access information are provided,

as well as the names of key officers and a description of the agency's mission and major activities.

The *United States Government Manual* provides an even-handed treatment of the entire federal government. More extensive discussion of major regulatory agencies available in the commercially published *Federal Regulatory Directory* (9th ed. 1999), and historical background on specific agencies and on the administration generally can be found in George T. Kurian, ed., *A Historical Guide to the U.S. Government* (1998).

While the *Government Manual* and the *Federal Regulatory Directory* provide the names of major agency officials, neither volume is updated very frequently and neither provides an extensive listing of other staffers. Several directories provide more detailed information about specific personnel, including telephone numbers and e-mail addresses. Three with comparable coverage are *Carroll's Federal Directory* (bimonthly), *Federal Staff Directory* (three times a year) and *Federal Yellow Book* (quarterly). These directories are available in a variety of formats, including CD–ROMs and subscription websites, and each is accompanied by a companion volume covering regional offices outside the Washington, D.C. area.

One of the most convenient sources of information on an agency is its website. Here, depending on the agency, it is usually possible to find introductory overviews, speeches, policy documents, directories, and other useful resources. The *Government Manual* provides Internet addresses, and several lists of government websites can be found on the Internet. Two of the most exhaustive are Chicago–Kent College of Law's Federal Web Locator

NATIONAL ARCHIVES AND RECORDS ADMINISTRATION

8601 Adelphi Road, College Park, Maryland 20740–6001
Phone, 301–713–6800. Internet, http://www.nara.gov/.

Archivist of the United States	JOHN W. CARLIN
Deputy Archivist of the United States	LEWIS J. BELLARDO
Executive Director, National Historical Publications and Records Commission	ANN CLIFFORD NEWHALL
Director of the Federal Register	RAYMOND A. MOSLEY
Assistant Archivist for Regional Records Services	RICHARD L. CLAYPOOLE
Assistant Archivist for Presidential Libraries	DAVID F. PETERSON
Assistant Archivist for Records Services— Washington, DC	MICHAEL J. KURTZ
Assistant Archivist for Human Resources and Information Services	L. REYNOLDS CAHOON
Assistant Archivist for Administrative Services	ADRIENNE C. THOMAS
General Counsel	GARY M. STERN
Inspector General	KELLY A. SISARIO
Director, Information Security Oversight Office	STEVEN GARFINKEL

[For the National Archives and Records Administration statement of organization, see the *Federal Register* of June 25, 1985, 50 FR 26278]

The National Archives and Records Administration (NARA) ensures, for citizens and Federal officials, ready access to essential evidence that documents the rights of American citizens, the actions of Federal officials, and the national experience. It establishes policies and procedures for managing U.S. Government records and assists Federal agencies in documenting their activities, administering records management programs, scheduling records, and retiring noncurrent records. NARA accessions, arranges, describes, preserves, and provides access to the essential documentation of the three branches of Government; manages the Presidential Libraries system; and publishes the laws, regulations, and Presidential and other public documents. It also assists the Information Security Oversight Office, which manages Federal classification and declassification policies, and the National Historical Publications and Records Commission, which makes grants nationwide to help nonprofit organizations identify, preserve, and provide access to materials that document American history.

The National Archives and Records Administration is the successor agency to the National Archives Establishment, which was created in 1934 and subsequently incorporated into the General Services Administration as the National Archives and Records Service in 1949. NARA was established as an independent agency in the executive branch of the Government by act of October 19, 1984 (44 U.S.C. 2101 *et seq.*), effective April 1, 1985.

Activities

Archival Program The National Archives and Records Administration maintains the historically valuable records of the U.S. Government dating from the Revolutionary War era to the recent past; arranges and preserves records and prepares finding aids to facilitate their use; makes records available for use in research rooms in its facilities; answers written and oral

Exhibit 56. National Archives and Records Administration, THE UNITED STATES GOVERNMENT MANUAL 1999/2000, at 590 (1999).

<www.infoctr.edu/fwl/> and Louisiana State University's U.S. Federal Government Agencies Directory <www.lib.lsu.edu/gov/fedgovall.html>.

§ 7–3. FEDERAL REGULATIONS

The basic mechanism by which most agencies govern their areas of expertise is the *regulation*, a detailed administrative order similar in form to a statute. Regulations are also known as *rules*; these terms are used interchangeably in administrative law. The publication of regulations follows a standard procedure: they are first issued chronologically in a daily gazette, the *Federal Register*; and then the rules in force are arranged by subject in the *Code of Federal Regulations*. These two publications are the central resources in federal administrative law research.

a. *Federal Register*

As more and more executive and administrative orders and regulations were promulgated in the early New Deal period, locating regulations and determining which were in effect became increasingly difficult. There was no requirement that regulations be published or centrally filed, and two cases reached the U.S. Supreme Court before it was discovered that the administrative orders on which they were based were no longer in effect. This embarrassment, and the resulting criticism, led Congress in 1935 to establish a daily publication of executive and administrative promulgations. The *Federal Register* began publication on March 14, 1936 as a chronological source for administrative documents, similar to a session law text.

To have general legal effect, executive orders and administrative regulations must be published in the *Federal*

Register. A regulation which is not published in the *Register* is not binding unless one can be shown to have had *actual* and *timely* notice of the regulation. Since this is quite difficult to prove, the requirement effectively deters nonpublication.

In 1946 the Administrative Procedure Act expanded the scope of the *Federal Register* considerably by creating a rulemaking system requiring the publication of proposed regulations for public comment. Agencies now do much more than print the text of new rules in the *Register*; they provide explanatory preambles explaining the need for the regulatory changes and responding to comments on proposed rules.

These preambles make the *Federal Register* more than a simple "session regulation" text, because the explanatory information never appears in a codified form. Exhibit 57 shows a final rule of the National Archives and Records Administration as published in the *Federal Register*, including an explanation that the agency is amending its regulation to reflect a 1998 U.S. Court of Appeals decision.

Each daily *Federal Register* begins with a table of contents and a list noting the *Code of Federal Regulations* citations of new or proposed regulations in the issue. The table of contents is organized alphabetically by agency, so researchers can easily monitor a particular agency's activity. A portion of the table of contents for the issue containing the regulation in Exhibit 57 is shown in Exhibit 58, indicating this final rule as well as some proposed rules and several notices from other agencies. Exhibit 59 shows part of the list of *CFR* parts affected in

and September 30, 1999. During the process of the electrical modifications it was discovered that deterioration to the structural steel at the bridge had occurred. As a result, the bridge owner has requested a second deviation to replace the deteriorated structural steel.

Thirty days notice to the Coast Guard for approval of the maintenance repairs was not given by the bridge owner because this work involves vital, unscheduled maintenance that must be performed without undue delay. The Coast Guard has approved Amtrak's request because the work was determined to be necessary for public safety and the continued operation of the bridge.

This deviation to the operating regulations allows the bridge owner to require a two-hour advance notice for bridge openings for the Amtrak Bridge, mile 3.0, across the Thames River in New London, Connecticut. The deviation will be in effect from Sunday through Thursday, 10 p.m. to 12 a.m. and 1 a.m. to 4:30 a.m., October 17, 1999, through November 11, 1999. Requests for bridge openings can be made by calling (860) 395–2355 or on marine radio channel 13 VHF/FM. Mariners requiring an emergency opening are advised to call Amtrak's Chief Dispatcher at (617) 345–7569. Vessels that can pass under the bridge without an opening may do so at all times.

In accordance with 33 CFR 117.35(c), this work will be performed with all due speed in order to return the bridge to normal operation as soon as possible. This deviation from the operating regulations is authorized under 33 CFR 117.35.

Dated: October 14, 1999.

Robert F. Duncan,

Captain, U.S. Coast Guard, Acting Commander, First Coast Guard District.

[FR Doc. 99–27553 Filed 10–20–99; 8:45 am]

BILLING CODE 4910–15–M

NATIONAL ARCHIVES AND RECORDS ADMINISTRATION

36 CFR Part 1275

RIN 3095–AA91

Nixon Presidential Materials

AGENCY: National Archives and Records Administration (NARA).

ACTION: Final rule.

SUMMARY: This rule amends regulations on preservation and processing of and access to the Presidential historical materials of Richard M. Nixon in

---

NARA's custody to reflect the 1998 decision of the U.S. Court of Appeals that the private or personal segments of the original tape recordings must be returned to the Nixon estate. The amended rule affects NARA and the Nixon estate. Other members of the public are not affected because no public access to the private and personal segments of the tapes has ever been permitted.

EFFECTIVE DATE: November 22, 1999.

FOR FURTHER INFORMATION CONTACT: Nancy Allard at telephone number 301–713–7360, ext. 226, or fax number 301–713–7270.

SUPPLEMENTARY INFORMATION: NARA published a notice of proposed rulemaking on July 14, 1999 (64 FR 37922). One comment supporting the proposed rule was received from a member of the public. Accordingly, we are adopting the proposed rule without change.

This rule is not a significant regulatory action for the purposes of Executive Order 12866 and has not been reviewed by the Office of Management and Budget. It is not a major rule as defined in the Congressional Review Act. As required by the Regulatory Flexibility Act, I certify that this rule will not have a significant impact on a substantial number small entities because it applies only to NARA and the estate of former President Nixon.

List of Subjects in 36 CFR Part 1275

Archives and records.

For the reasons set forth in the preamble, NARA amends part 1275 of title 36, Code of Federal Regulations, as follows:

PART 1275—PRESERVATION AND PROTECTION OF AND ACCESS TO THE PRESIDENTIAL HISTORICAL MATERIALS OF THE NIXON ADMINISTRATION

1. The authority citation for part 1275 continues to read as follows:

Authority: Sec. 102(a) of the National Archives and Records Administration Act of 1984, Pub. L. 98–497; 44 U.S.C. 2104; and secs. 103 and 104 of the Presidential Recordings and Materials Preservation Act 88 Stat. 1695; 44 U.S.C. 2111 note.

2. Revise paragraph (a) of § 1275.48 to read as follows:

§ 1275.48   Transfer of materials.

(a) The Archivist will transfer sole custody and use of those materials determined to be private or personal, or to be neither related to abuses of governmental power nor otherwise of general historical significance, to former President Nixon's estate, or, when

---

appropriate and after notifying the Nixon estate, to the former staff member having primary proprietary or commemorative interest in the materials. Such materials to be transferred include all segments of the original tape recordings that have been or will be identified as private or personal.

* * * * *

3. Revise paragraph (e) of § 1275.64 to read as follows:

§ 1275.64   Reproduction of tape recordings of Presidential conversations.

* * * * *

(e) The Archivist shall produce and maintain a master preservation copy of the original tape recordings for preservation purposes. The Archivist shall ensure that the master preservation copy, like the portions of the original tape recordings retained by the Archivist, does not contain those segments of the tape recordings which have been identified as private or personal and which have been transferred to the Nixon estate in accordance with § 1275.48.

Dated: October 14, 1999.

John W. Carlin,

Archivist of the United States.

[FR Doc. 99–27374 Filed 10–20–99; 8:45 am]

BILLING CODE 7515–01–P

ENVIRONMENTAL PROTECTION AGENCY

40 CFR Part 180

[OPP–300934; FRL–6386–1]

RIN 2070–AB78

Metolachlor; Extension of Tolerance for Emergency Exemptions

AGENCY: Environmental Protection Agency (EPA).

ACTION: Final rule.

SUMMARY: This regulation extends time-limited tolerances for the combined residues of the herbicide metolachlor and its metabolites in or on spinach at 0.3 part per million (ppm) for an additional 19½-month period and grass forage at 10 ppm and grass hay at 0.2 ppm for an additional 2-year period. These tolerances will expire and be revoked on December 31, 2001. This action is in response to EPA's granting of emergency exemptions under section 18 of the Federal Insecticide, Fungicide, and Rodenticide Act authorizing use of the pesticide on spinach and grass grown for seed. Section 408(l)(6) of the Federal Food, Drug, and Cosmetic Act

---

Exhibit 57.   Nixon Presidential Materials, 64 Fed. Reg. 56,678 (1999) (to be codified at 36 C.F.R. pt. 1275).

Federal Register/Vol. 64, No. 203/Thursday, October 21, 1999/Contents V

Exhibit 58. Contents, FEDERAL REGISTER, Oct. 21, 1999, at v.

CFR PARTS AFFECTED IN THIS ISSUE

A cumulative list of the parts affected this month can be found in the Reader Aids section at the end of this issue.

Exhibit 59. CFR Parts Affected in This Issue, FEDERAL REGISTER, Oct. 21, 1999, at vii.

the same *Federal Register* issue, with a reference to the new rule governing Nixon presidential materials.

Several readers' aids are provided in the back of each issue, including telephone numbers for information and assistance, a listing of *Federal Register* pages and dates for the month, and a list of new public laws. The most important of these readers' aids is a cumulative list of *CFR* parts affected since the beginning of the month. This list, which looks like a longer version of the one shown in Exhibit 59, is one of the basic tools for determining the current status of federal regulations.

An index to the *Federal Register*, arranged by agency rather than by subject, is published monthly. Each index cumulates references since the beginning of the year. For more detailed indexing, including access by subject, it is necessary to turn to the commercially published *CIS Federal Register Index*, which is issued weekly with bound semiannual volumes.

Recent *Federal Register* issues, back to volume 59 (1994), are available on the Internet from GPO Access <www.access.gpo.gov/su_docs/aces/aces140.html>. Regulations can be found by browsing the daily tables of contents or through keyword searches. A search can be limited to particular sections of the *Register* (e.g. final rules and regulations, proposed rules, notices) or specific dates, and results are ranked for relevance. Documents can then be viewed either as simple text or as PDF files replicating the printed page. The *Federal Register* is also available online through Westlaw and Lexis–Nexis; coverage begins in the summer of 1980, with new issues online within a day of publication.

Most large law libraries have complete runs of the *Federal Register* back to 1936 in microform. The *Register* has permanent reference value because it contains mate-

rial which never appears in the *Code of Federal Regulations*. Not only does it provide the agency preambles explaining regulatory actions, but it may also be the only available source for temporary changes occurring between annual *CFR* revisions. Researching the histories of administrative agency regulations would be impossible without access to the *Federal Register*.

The Federal Register: What It Is and How to Use It (rev. ed. 1992) provides a detailed explanation of the publication of federal regulations. This pamphlet's discussion of print resources is still useful, although it lacks coverage of GPO Access and other means of electronic access.

b. *Code of Federal Regulations*

As with statutes, chronological publication of regulations is insufficient to provide reasonable access. Researchers also need subject access to regulations in force, regardless of when they were first promulgated. In 1937 the Federal Register Act was amended to create the *Code of Federal Regulations*, with provisions for indexing and supplementation. The first *CFR* was published in 1938. The set now consists of over 200 paperback volumes, which are revised and reissued each year.

The regulations in the *CFR* are collected from the *Federal Register* and arranged in a subject scheme of fifty titles, similar to that of the *U.S. Code*. The titles are divided into chapters, each containing the regulations of a specific agency. The back of every *CFR* volume contains an alphabetical list of federal agencies indicating the title and chapter of each agency's regulations.

CFR chapters are divided into parts, each of which covers a particular topic. Finally parts are divided into sections, the basic unit of the *CFR*. Exhibits 60 and 61

show sample pages of the *CFR* from Title 36 (Parks, Forests, and Public Property), Chapter XII (National Archives and Records Administration), Part 1275 (Preservation and Protection of and Access to the Presidential Historical Materials of the Nixon Administration). A citation to the *CFR* provides the title, part, section, and year of publication: 36 C.F.R. § 1275.64 (1999). (Note that the section is a distinct number, not a decimal; § 1275.64 is not between § 1275.6 and § 1275.7.)

At the beginning of each *CFR* part is an *authority note* showing the statutory authority under which the regulations have been issued. After this note, or at the end of each section, is a *source note* providing the citation and date of the *Federal Register* in which the regulation was last published in full. This reference is the key to finding background information and comments explaining the regulations. In Exhibit 60, note that the regulations are issued under the authority of several statutes, including the Presidential Recordings and Materials Preservation Act; and that the source for Part 1275 generally is 51 Fed. Reg. 7230, Feb. 28, 1986.

CFR volumes are updated and replaced on a rotating cycle throughout the year. The revisions of the various titles are issued on a quarterly basis: Titles 1–16 with regulations in force as of January 1; titles 17–27 as of April 1; titles 28–41 as of July 1; and titles 42–50 as of October 1. The *CFR* pages shown in Exhibits 60 and 61 are current as of July 1, 1999, before the amendments shown in the *Federal Register* in Exhibit 57.

The *CFR* includes an annually revised *Index and Finding Aids* volume providing access by agency name and subject. This index is far less thorough than most statu-

SUBCHAPTER F—NIXON PRESIDENTIAL MATERIALS

PART 1275—PRESERVATION AND PROTECTION OF AND ACCESS TO THE PRESIDENTIAL HISTORICAL MATERIALS OF THE NIXON ADMINISTRATION

AUTHORITY: Sec. 102(a) of the National Archives and Records Administration Act of 1984, Pub. L. 98–497; 44 U.S.C. 2104; and secs. 103 and 104 of the Presidential Recordings and Materials Preservation Act 88 Stat. 1695; 44 U.S.C. 2111 note.

SOURCE: 51 FR 7230, Feb. 28, 1986, unless otherwise noted.

§1275.1　Scope of part.

This part sets forth policies and procedures concerning the preservation and protection of and access to the tape recordings, papers, documents, memorandums, transcripts, and other objects and materials which constitute the Presidential historical materials of Richard M. Nixon, covering the period beginning January 20, 1969, and ending August 9, 1974.

Subpart A—General Provisions

§1275.10　Purpose.

This part 1275 implements the provisions of title I of the Presidential Recordings and Materials Preservation Act (Pub. L. 93–526; 88 Stat. 1695). It prescribes policies and procedures by which the National Archives and Records Administration will preserve, protect, and provide access to the Presidential historical materials of the Nixon Administration.

§1275.12　Application.

This part 1275 applies to all of the Presidential historical materials of the Nixon Administration in the custody of the Archivist of the United States pursuant to the provisions of title I of the Presidential Recordings and Materials Preservation Act (Pub. L. 93–526; 88 Stat. 1695).

Exhibit 60.　Nixon Presidential Materials, 36 C.F.R. pt. 1275 (1999).

§1275.58 Deletion of restricted portions.

The Archivist will provide a requester any reasonably segregable portions of otherwise restricted materials after the deletion of the portions which are restricted under this §1275.50 or §1275.52.

§1275.60 Requests for declassification.

Challenges to the classification and requests for the declassification of national security classified materials shall be governed by the provisions of 36 CFR part 1254 of this chapter, as that may be amended from time to time.

§1275.62 Reference room locations, hours, and rules.

The Archivist shall, from time to time, separately prescribe the precise location or locations where the materials shall be available for public reference, and the hours of operation and rules governing the conduct of researchers using such facilities. This information may be obtained by writing to: Office of Presidential Libraries (NL), The National Archives, Washington, DC 20408.

§1275.64 Reproduction of tape recordings of Presidential conversations.

(a) To ensure the preservation of original tape recordings of conversations which were recorded or caused to be recorded by any officer or employee of the Federal Government and which:

(1) Involve former President Richard M. Nixon or other individuals who, at the time of the conversation, were employed by the Federal Government; and

(2) Were recorded in the White House or in the office of the President in the Executive Office Buildings located in Washington, DC; Camp David, MD; Key Biscayne, FL; or San Clemente, CA; and

(3) Were recorded during the period beginning January 20, 1969, and ending August 9, 1974, the Archivist will produce duplicate copies of such tape recordings in his custody for public and official reference use. The original tape recordings shall not be available for public access.

(b) Since the original tape recordings may contain information which is sub-

ject to restriction in accordance with §1275.50 or §1275.52, the archivists shall review the tapes and delete restricted portions from copies for public and official reference use.

(c) Researchers may listen to reference copies of the tape recordings described in paragraph (a) of this section in a National Archives building in the Washington, DC area and at other reference locations established by the Archivist in accordance with §1275.62.

(d) The reproduction for members of the public of the reference copies of the available tape recordings described in paragraph (a) of this section will be permitted as follows: Copies of tape recordings will be made available following the public release of the last of the tape segments contemplated in §1275.42(a). If the releases contemplated in §1275.42(a) are not completed by December 31, 1999, NARA will, beginning January 1, 2000, allow members of the public to obtain copies only of the abuses of governmental power tapes, together with any other tapes publicly released as of the effective date of the Settlement Agreement. If the releases contemplated in §1275.42(a) are not completed by December 31, 2002, NARA will, beginning January 1, 2003, allow members of the public to obtain copies of all tapes that have been made available to the public by that date and tapes that subsequently become available as they are released. Such copying will be controlled by NARA or its designated contractor. The fees for the reproduction of the tape recordings under this section shall be those prescribed in the schedule set forth in part 1258 of this chapter or pertinent successor regulation, as that schedule is amended from time to time.

(e) The Archivist shall produce and maintain a master preservation copy of the original tape recordings for preservation purposes.

[51 FR 7230, Feb. 28, 1986, as amended at 61 FR 17846, Apr. 23, 1996]

§1275.66 Reproduction and authentication of other materials.

(a) Copying of materials other than tape recordings described in §1275.64 may be done by NARA, by a contractor designated by NARA, or by researchers using self-service copiers. Such self-

Exhibit 61. 36 C.F.R. §§ 1275.58 to 1275.66 (1999).

tory indexes, and it lists parts rather than specific sections. It has no entries under "Nixon" and only a cross-reference under "Presidential records," but Exhibit 62 shows a page under "Archives and records" with a reference to 36 C.F.R. Part 1275. Much more detailed subject access is provided in the commercially published, multivolume *Index to the Code of Federal Regulations*.

The *CFR* is available in several electronic formats. The most widely available is the Internet version at GPO Access <www.access.gpo.gov/nara/cfr/>. This version replicates the paper edition and is updated on the same basis. Sections can be retrieved by citation, and either individual titles or the entire *CFR* can be searched. As with the *Federal Register*, documents can be viewed and printed as PDF files.

More current versions of the *CFR* are available online from Westlaw and Lexis–Nexis. Instead of being revised just once a year, these files are updated on an ongoing basis to reflect changes published in the *Federal Register*. Of the two, Lexis–Nexis usually incorporates changes a bit more quickly, generally two or three weeks after they appear in the *Register*. Westlaw's *CFR* may not seem quite as current, but it includes "This document has been amended" notices linking affected sections to *Federal Register* documents the same day they are published.

To determine what regulations were in force at a particular time, older editions of the *CFR* are sometimes needed. GPO Access coverage starts with selected 1996 volumes, and it is retaining older editions as new versions are added. The online databases provide more extensive historical access, with older editions of the *CFR* back to

CFR Index **Armed forces**

National Archives and Records Administration
- Audiovisual records management, 36 CFR 1232
- Creation and maintenance of Federal records, 36 CFR 1222
- Declassification of and public access to National security information, 36 CFR 1260
- Disposition of Federal records, 36 CFR 1228
- Electronic records management, 36 CFR 1234
- Exhibits, 36 CFR 1284
- Federal records, general, 36 CFR 1220
- Fees, 36 CFR 1258
- Location of records and hours of use, 36 CFR 1253
- Micrographics records management, 36 CFR 1230
- National Historical Publications and Records Commission, 36 CFR 1206
- Nixon Presidential Administration, historical materials, preservation and protection of and access to, 36 CFR 1275
- Presidential Records Act, implementation, 36 CFR 1270
- Program assistance, 36 CFR 1238
- Public use of records, donated historical materials, and facilities; general, 36 CFR 1252
- Records and donated historical materials, availability, 36 CFR 1254
- Restrictions on use of records, 36 CFR 1256
- Vital records management, 36 CFR 1236

National Historical Publications and Records Commission, 36 CFR 1206

Naturalization records, certifications, 8 CFR 343c

Naval Discharge Review Board, 32 CFR 724

Navy Department, reporting births and deaths in cooperation with other agencies, 32 CFR 735

Nixon Presidential Administration, historical materials, preservation and protection of and access to, 36 CFR 1275

Postal Service
- Protection of information, 39 CFR 267
- Record retention and disposition, 39 CFR 263
- Records and information management, 39 CFR 261
  - Definitions, 39 CFR 262
- Vital records protection, 39 CFR 264

Prisoners, access to records, 28 CFR 513

Surface Transportation Board, railroads and maritime carriers, documents recordation, 49 CFR 1177

Veterans Affairs Department, general provisions, 38 CFR 1

Arctic Research Commission

Nondiscrimination on basis of disability in federally conducted programs or activities, 45 CFR 2301

Armed forces

See also Specific military departments; Armed forces reserves; Conscientious objectors; Military academies; Military law; Military personnel; Selective service system

Air installations compatible use zones, 32 CFR 256

American National Red Cross and United Service Organizations, Inc. assignment of employees to duty with military services, 32 CFR 253

Armed services military club and package stores, 32 CFR 261

Banking offices on Defense Department installations, procedures governing, 32 CFR 230

Chaplains for the military services, 32 CFR 65

Civil authorities aid
- Employment of troops, 32 CFR 501
- Relief assistance, 32 CFR 502

Civil disturbances, employment of military resources in event of, 32 CFR 215

Community relations program policy, 32 CFR 238

Credit unions on DOD installations, procedures governing, 32 CFR 231a

Defense acquisition regulatory system, 32 CFR 160

Defense contracts
- Commercial activities program, 32 CFR 169
- Commercial activities program procedures, 32 CFR 169a
- Competitive information certificate and profit reduction clause, 32 CFR 173

71

Exhibit 62. CFR Index, CFR INDEX AND FINDING AIDS 1, 71 (1999).

the early 1980s. Most large law libraries have microform collections of older *CFR*s back to the original 1938 edition.

c. Finding and Updating Regulations

Regulatory research involves several distinct steps. The first is finding regulations, by using an index or through leads in an annotated code or other source. Once a relevant regulation is found, it must be updated to determine whether any changes have occurred since the most recent *CFR* version. Finally, it is necessary to check for any judicial decisions applying the regulation or adjudicating its validity.

There are several methods of finding federal regulations, including agency websites and directories as well as references in cases, texts, and articles. In addition to the official and commercial indexes for the *Federal Register* and the *Code of Federal Regulations*, and online access through the database systems, numerous other sources provide references to relevant regulations.

Leads from statutes to regulations can be found in several ways. Both annotated editions of the United States Code contain cross-references to regulations in the notes following specific sections. In addition, the *Index and Finding Aids* volume of the *Code of Federal Regulations* contains a "Parallel Table of Authorities and Rules," allowing a researcher with a statute or presidential document to find regulations enacted under its authority.

Administrative regulations on selected subjects, such as taxation, labor relations, and securities, also appear in commercially published looseleaf services. Most services are thoroughly indexed and frequently supplemented, usually on a weekly basis. For that reason and also because regulations are integrated with related primary

sources and interpretive material, researchers often turn to looseleaf services, if available, for convenient and current access to administrative regulations.

Finding relevant regulations, however, is only the first step of research. Next it is necessary to verify that those regulations remain current. For users of Westlaw, Lexis–Nexis, or looseleaf services, this is a relatively simple task because the versions of *CFR* available through these sources are regularly updated. For others, it is necessary to update a regulation from the most recent annual *CFR* edition. The key tool for this purpose is a monthly pamphlet accompanying the *CFR* entitled *LSA: List of CFR Sections Affected* (also available through GPO Access <www.access.gpo.gov/nara/lsa/aboutlsa.html>).

LSA lists *Federal Register* pages of any new rules affecting *CFR* sections, and indicates the nature of the change with notes such as "amended," "removed," or "revised." *LSA* also includes references to proposed rules, listed separately by part rather than by specific section. Exhibit 63 shows a page from the October 1999 *LSA*, indicating that several sections of 36 *CFR* had been revised, removed, or added since the July 1, 1999 revision. This pamphlet includes references to the final rule shown in Exhibit 57 and to 64 Fed. Reg. 37922, the July 14, 1999 issue in which this rule was proposed.

Each *LSA* issue cumulates all changes since the latest *CFR* edition, so the scope of coverage varies between titles depending on the date of revision. Unless the latest *CFR* volume is more than a year old, it is not necessary to examine more than the most recent monthly issue. *LSA* brings a search for current regulations up to date within a month or so. The very latest changes not yet covered in

690.7 (c) redesignated as (d); new
  (c) added 58295

Proposed Rules:

75 54254
600—699 (Ch. VI) 46628
600...38272
614...57288
668.............38272, 38504, 41752, 43024, 43582
673...42206
674..41232, 42206
675...42206
676...42206
682...............................42176, 43024, 43428
685...43428
690...42206
694...39109

TITLE 35—PANAMA CANAL

**No amendments to 35 CFR have been
published in the** FEDERAL REGISTER
since July 1, 1999.

TITLE 36—PARKS, FORESTS, AND
PUBLIC PROPERTY

**Chapter I—National Park Service,
Department of the Interior (Parts
1—199)**

13 Authority citation revised 56463
13.65 (a) added; (b)(5) and (6) re-
  moved.......................................56463

**Chapter II—Forest Service, De-
partment of Agriculture (Parts
200—299)**

242.24 Revised 35780
242.25 Added; eff. 7-1-99 through
  6-30-00.....................................35788
242.24 (a) introductory text and
  (1) correctly revised 35823
251.56 (a)(1)(ii)(G) note added..........48960
251.80—251.102 (Subpart C) Au-
  thority citation revised............37846
251.84 Existing text designated
  as (a); (b) added 37846
251.90 (c) revised 37846
251.91 (a) revised 37846
251.92 (a)(8) added; (c) revised 37846
251.93 (b) revised 37846
251.94 (b) revised 37846
251.103 Added 37846

**Chapter XII—National Archives
and Records Administration
(Parts 1200—1299)**

1254.20 Regulation at 64 FR 19901
  confirmed 48961
1275.48 (a) revised............................56678
1275.64 (e) revised...........................56678

Proposed Rules:

13 41854
51 47336
217 ....54074, 56293
219 ....54074, 56293
242...49278
300—399 (Ch. II) 58368
327...38854
1010....................................39951, 51488
1191..................................37326, 42056
1211 58568
1228 50028
1275 37922

TITLE 37—PATENTS, TRADE-
MARKS, AND COPYRIGHTS

**Chapter I—Patent and Trademark
Office, Department of Commerce (Parts 1—199)**

1.1 (a)(2) revised..............................48917
1.4 (a)(2) amended; (d)(1) intro-
  ductory text and (ii) revised;
  (d)(1)(iii) added 48917
1.5 (c) revised.................................48917
1.6 (a)(1) revised; (a)(4) added..........48917
1.23 Revised 48917
2.1 Revised.....................................48917
2.6 Introductory text, (a)(6) and
  (14) revised; (a)(20) and (21)
  added.......................................48917
2.17 (c) and (d) added.......................48918
2.20 Revised 48918
2.21 Revised 48918
2.31 Removed 48918
2.32 Revised 48918
2.33 Revised 48918
2.34 Revised 48919
2.35 Redesignated as 2.37; new
  2.35 added 48920
2.37 Removed; new 2.37 redesig-
  nated from 2.35 48920
2.38 (a) revised 48920
2.39 Removed 48920
2.45 Revised 48920

Exhibit 63.   LSA: LIST OF CFR SECTIONS AFFECTED, Oct. 1999, at 93.

LSA can then be found by using the cumulative List of CFR Parts Affected in the latest *Federal Register* issue. The last issue in each month not yet covered by *LSA* needs to be checked. These lists in the *Register* thus serve as a daily supplement to the *CFR* and *LSA*.

Because regulations change so frequently, it is not uncommon to hit a dead end when trying to track down a *CFR* reference from a case or article. The cited regulations may have been repealed or moved to another *CFR* location. Tables to help trace what has happened to regulations are published in the back of each *CFR* volume, indicating all sections that have been repealed, transferred, or otherwise changed since 1986. Earlier changes from 1949 to 1985 are listed in a separate series of *List of CFR Sections Affected* volumes for the entire *CFR*.

No matter what format of *CFR* is used, it contains no annotations of court decisions like *United States Code Annotated* or *United States Code Service*. Yet a court may invalidate a regulation or provide an important interpretation of key provisions. As they do with cases and statutes, Shepard's Citations and KeyCite provide references to court decisions citing regulations.

In print, *Shepard's Code of Federal Regulations Citations* provides citations to court decisions and selected law review articles which have cited or discussed sections of the *Code of Federal Regulations*. Shepard's indicates the year of the *CFR* edition cited (with an asterisk), or the year of the citing reference if no *CFR* edition is specified (with a delta). As in Shepard's statutory citators, alphabetical symbols indicate significant impact of court decisions on cited regulations. Exhibit 64 shows a page from

this citator, listing decisions under regulations in Titles 36 and 37 of *CFR*. Note that various sections in Part 1275 have been cited in court decisions in 843 F.2d and 978 F.2d, while other citing references include Supreme Court cases, an *ALR* annotation, and law review articles. Note also that in 1974 an earlier version of 37 C.F.R. § 1.14(b) was found constitutional (C).

The electronic versions of Shepard's mirror its printed counterpart, with the same scope of coverage and descriptive notes. KeyCite provides a simple list of case citations, without annotations, but its coverage of citations in law reviews and other secondary sources is considerably more extensive than Shepard's.

To summarize research approaches using printed sources, a complete search for a current regulation involves these steps:

(a) Find a relevant *Code of Federal Regulations* section, by consulting the subject index in the *Index and Finding Aids* volume or through references in an annotated code or other source.

(b) Locate the regulation in the current annual edition of its *CFR* title, noting the date of the latest revision.

(c) Check the latest monthly pamphlet of *LSA* to determine if changes in the section have occurred since the last revision.

(d) Use the cumulative List of CFR Parts Affected in the most recent issue of the *Federal Register*. This list updates the *LSA* pamphlet by indicating any changes made within the current month. Depending on the

CODE OF FEDERAL REGULATIONS			TITLE 37
§ 1275.30 Cir. DC 978F2d1285△1992	Cir. Fed. 722F2d1572△1983 728F2d1439△1984 CCPA 680F2d156△1982 ClCt 25ClC96*1990	617FS1394△1985 Cir. 9 287F2d846△1961 577F2d616*1977 Cir. DC 465F2d610*1972 745FS2△1990 88FRD52△1953	**§ 1.32** Cir. 4 718FS1284△1989 Cir. Fed. 772F2d1568△1985 15F3d1051*1992
§ 1275.42(b) Cir. DC 843F2d1476*1987 978F2d1286△1992	**§ 1.6** Cir. 6 666FS1068△1987	Cir. DC 773F2d1219△1985 870F2d1572△1989 Calif 143CaR42△1978	**§ 1.33(a)** Cir. DC 748FS902△1990 Cir. Fed. 772F2d1568△1985
§ 1275.44 Cir. DC 978F2d1272*1992	**§ 1.7** Cir. 3 136FS622△1955 Cir. DC 671F2d536△1982	Ky 624SW833△1981	**§ 1.33(b)** Cir. Fed. 819F2d1123△1987
§ 1275.44(a) Cir. DC 843F2d1476*1987 978F2d1286△1992	**§ 1.8** Cir. 6 666FS1069*1977 Cir. DC 696FS698△1988	**§ 1.14(a)** 395US672*1967 23LE623*1967 89SC1911*1967 Cir. 4 502F2d127△1974	**§ 1.34(b)** Cir. DC 748FS902△1990
§ 1275.44(c) Cir. DC 843F2d1479*1987	CCPA 588F2d1341△1978	Cir. 9 577F2d613*1977 244FS543△1965	**§ 1.36** Cir. 10 811FS568△1992
§ 1275.46(b) Cir. DC 843F2d1476*1987	**§ 1.8(a)** Cir. 6 666FS1069*1977	Cir. DC 606F2d1218*1978	**§ 1.41** Cir. 7 640FS1140△1986 Cir. Fed. 772F2d1568△1985
→ **§ 1275.48** Cir. DC 978F2d1272*1992	CCPA 588F2d1341△1978	**§ 1.14(b)** 416US485△1974 40LE327△1974 94SC1888△1974	**§ 1.45** Cir. 4 444F2d408△1971 CCPA 572F2d861△1978 591F2d697△1979
§ 1275.50(a) Cir. DC 843F2d1476*1987	**§ 1.9(c)** 72VaL727*1985	Cir. 3 543FS538△1982 Cir. 4 → C502F2d127△1974 357FS1330△1973	
§ 1275.52(b) Cir. DC 843F2d1476*1987 978F2d1272*1992	**§ 1.11** 395US669*1967 23LE622*1967 89SC1910*1967 Cir. 7 489FS553*1979 Cir. DC 465F2d610*1972 606F2d1218*1978	Cir. 9 577F2d613*1977 Cir. DC 606F2d1218*1978	**§ 1.45(b)** Cir. 3 352FS1375△1972 Cir. Fed. 754F2d358△1985 CCPA 530F2d1393△1976 591F2d697△1979
§ 1280.6 30MJ267△1990		**§ 1.14(e)** Cir. DC 720FS194△1990	
TITLE 37 Cir. Fed. 849F2d1425△1988	**§ 1.11(a)** Cir. 2 145FRD631△1993	**§ 1.20(b)** Cir. 6 625FS1430△1986	**§ 1.45(c)** CCPA 503F2d563△1974
§ 1.1 et seq. Cir. 1 487FS1108*1979 Cir. 7 582FS1014△1984 Cir. 9 577F2d612*1977 779F2d525△1985	**§ 1.11(b)** Cir. 4 704F2d1321*1982 Cir. 7 663F2d731*1980 Cir. DC 745FS1△1990 Cir. Fed. 751F2d1221△1984	**§ 1.20(c)** 72VaL760*1985	**§ 1.46** Cir. Fed. 772F2d1568△1985
§§ 1.1 to 1.352 24ÆRF634n		**§ 1.22** Cir. Fed. 777F2d1567△1985	**§ 1.47** 119FRD116△1988 Cir. 4 444F2d408△1971 Cir. Fed. 796F2d447△1986 CCPA 515F2d1170△1975
§ 1.1 Cir. 2 469FS814△1979	**§ 1.11(d)** Cir. Fed. 897F2d514*1989	**§ 1.23** Cir. Fed. 777F2d1563△1985	
§ 1.2 373US389△1963 10LE435△1963 83SC1328△1963 Cir. 3 558FS772△1981 Cir. 8 538F2d193*1961 Cir. 9 545FS509*1961 Cir. DC 464F2d752*1971	**§ 1.13** 395US669*1967 23LE622*1967 89SC1910*1967	**§ 1.26(c)** 758F2d596△1985 771F2d481△1985 72VaL761*1985	**§ 1.47(a)** CCPA 517F2d1371△1975
	§ 1.14 Cir. 2 145FRD633△1993 Cir. 3 543FS538△1982 Cir. 5 722FS328△1989 Cir. 7 405F2d102△1968	**§ 1.31** 373US384△1963 10LE432△1963 83SC1325△1963 Cir. 1 653F2d707△1981 Cir. 2 235FS13△1964 34StnL77△1981	**§ 1.47(b)** Cir. 5 537F2d191△1976 Cir. DC 464F2d748*1971 377FS1285△1974

403

Exhibit 64. 2 SHEPARD'S CODE OF FEDERAL REGULATIONS CITATIONS 403 (1994).

dates covered in the most recent *LSA*, it may be necessary to check the last *Federal Register* in the preceding month as well.

(e) Locate changes found in steps (c) and (d) by consulting the daily issues of the *Federal Register*.

(f) Check the regulation in *Shepard's Code of Federal Regulations Citations* to obtain citations to decisions interpreting it.

Some of these steps, of course, can be avoided by using electronic resources or a looseleaf service, if available. Whatever approach is used, it is necessary to verify that the regulation is current and to find court decisions that may affect its scope or validity.

One final note: Many agencies supplement regulations in the *Federal Register* and *CFR* with manuals and policy statements. These documents are generally for guidance only, without the same force of law as regulations, but they can still provide greater detail or clarify ambiguous regulations with illustrative examples. Supplementary materials such as these are often not published in printed form, but many are available through agency websites. The amount of information and ease of access vary considerably from agency to agency.

§ 7–4. ADMINISTRATIVE DECISIONS AND RULINGS

Besides promulgating regulations of general application, administrative agencies also have quasi-judicial functions in which they hold hearings and issue decisions involving specific parties. The procedures and precedential value of these decisions vary between agencies, as do means of publication and ease of access.

About fifteen regulatory commissions and other agencies publish decisions in a form similar to official reports of court decisions. These reports are usually published first in advance sheets or slip decisions and eventually cumulated into bound volumes. Depending on the agency, the volumes may include indexes, digests and tables. However, because most of these aids are noncumulative, applying only to the decisions in one volume, they are of limited utility.

Commercial looseleaf services and topical reporters are a major source of administrative decisions in their subject fields. A wide range of Securities and Exchange Commission decisions and releases, for example, are printed in CCH's *Federal Securities Law Reports*. These services, which will be discussed in Chapter 9, usually appear more promptly and contain better indexing than the official reports, and they combine these administrative decisions with other sources such as related statutes, regulations, and court decisions.

A growing number of administrative decisions are available on the Internet, but as yet there is little consistency in how agencies provide access to these documents. One of the most extensive and current listings of decisions on the Web is available from the University of Virginia Law Library <www.law.virginia.edu/Library/govadm. htm>. Lexis–Nexis and Westlaw include decisions of several dozen agencies in topical databases. Online coverage includes many administrative decisions that are not published in either official reports or looseleaf services, and generally extends much earlier than official websites.

One genre of administrative decisions, Attorney General opinions, deserves special mention. As the federal government's law firm, the Department of Justice provides legal advice to the President and other departments. Traditionally these opinions were signed by the U.S. Attorney General and published in a series entitled *Opinions of the Attorneys General of the United States*; in recent years, however, this function has been delegated to the Office of Legal Counsel (OLC), which has published *Opinions of the Office of Legal Counsel* since 1977. Opinions of both the Attorney General and OLC are also available online through the database systems, and OLC opinions are on the Internet <www.usdoj.gov/olc/mem_ops.htm> from 1993 to date.

A researcher specializing in a particular area must be familiar with decisions of relevant agencies. For nonspecialists, the easiest way to learn of administrative decisions is through the annotations in *United States Code Service*. *USCS* includes notes of decisions from more than fifty commissions and board. Sections of the Packers and Stockyards Act in 7 U.S.C.S., for example, are accompanied by notes of administrative proceedings in *Agriculture Decisions* as well as court cases. *United States Code Annotated* does not include references to administrative decisions except opinions of the Attorney General and Office of Legal Counsel.

Shepard's covers the decisions of federal agencies in *Shepard's United States Administrative Citations*, which lists citations to the decisions and orders of more than a dozen major administrative tribunals, and in several of its topical citators. These citators provide citations to agency decisions in court cases and law review articles as

well as in later agency decisions. Decisions of the Federal Energy Regulatory Commission, for example, can be Shepardized in *Shepard's Federal Energy Law Citations*. Other topical citators containing coverage of administrative decisions include *Federal Labor Law Citations*, *Federal Tax Citations*, *Immigration and Naturalization Citations*, and *Occupational Safety and Health Citations*.

§ 7–5. PRESIDENTIAL LAWMAKING

In addition to supervising the executive departments and agencies, the President of the United States also has several lawmaking roles. He sends legislative proposals to Congress, approves or vetoes bills which have passed both houses, and issues a range of legally binding documents in his own right.

A number of reference sources provide background information on the presidency. These address numerous political and historical aspects of the institution and the men who have been president. The most extensive is Leonard W. Levy & Louis Fisher, eds., *Encyclopedia of the American Presidency* (4 vols., 1994), with more than 1,000 articles, including discussion of presidential powers, relations with Congress, and key legislation. Michael Nelson, ed., *Guide to the Presidency* (2 vols., 2d. ed. 1996) is another major reference work, arranged topically rather than alphabetically. Part III, "Powers of the Presidency," discusses the president's various roles and actions; and Part VI, "The Chief Executive and the Federal Government," analyzes relations with Congress, the Supreme Court, and the federal bureaucracy.

The major legal documents issued by the president are *executive orders* and *proclamations*. While the distinction

between the two can be blurred, executive orders usually involve an exercise of presidential authority related to government business while proclamations are announcements of policy or of matters requiring public notice. Proclamations are often ceremonial or commemorative, but some take important legal actions such as implementing trade agreements or declaring treaties to be in force.

Executive orders and proclamations are numbered in separate series and published in the *Federal Register*. A variety of other presidential documents are also printed in the *Federal Register* but not included in either of these numbered series. Presidential determinations, issued pursuant to particular statutory mandates, are also issued in a numbered series, and other unnumbered documents include various memoranda and notices. Many, but not all, of these documents deal with foreign affairs issues. Exhibit 65 shows a presidential memorandum ordering that regulations and other documents be written clearly, as printed in the *Federal Register*.

Presidential documents in the *Federal Register* are indexed in its monthly and annual indexes, as well as the more extensive commercial *CIS Federal Register Index* (1984–date) and *CIS Index to Presidential Executive Orders and Proclamations* (covering 1787–1983).

Presidential documents from the *Federal Register* are reprinted in a number of locations, including the monthly pamphlets of *USCS Advance* (*USCCAN* generally includes only executive orders and proclamations) and an annual compilation of title 3 of the *Code of Federal Regulations*. This compilation includes a subject index and several tables which list the year's presidential documents, indicate older executive orders and proclama-

31885

Federal Register
Vol. 63, No. 111
Wednesday, June 10, 1998

Presidential Documents

Title 3—

The President

Memorandum of June 1, 1998

Plain Language in Government Writing

Memorandum for the Heads of Executive Departments and Agencies

The Vice President and I have made reinventing the Federal Government a top priority of my Administration. We are determined to make the Government more responsive, accessible, and understandable in its communications with the public.

The Federal Government's writing must be in plain language. By using plain language, we send a clear message about what the Government is doing, what it requires, and what services it offers. Plain language saves the Government and the private sector time, effort, and money.

Plain language requirements vary from one document to another, depending on the intended audience. Plain language documents have logical organization, easy-to-read design features, and use:

- common, everyday words, except for necessary technical terms;
- "you" and other pronouns;
- the active voice; and
- short sentences.

To ensure the use of plain language, I direct you to do the following:

- By October 1, 1998, use plain language in all new documents, other than regulations, that explain how to obtain a benefit or service or how to comply with a requirement you administer or enforce. For example, these documents may include letters, forms, notices, and instructions. By January 1, 2002, all such documents created prior to October 1, 1998, must also be in plain language.

- By January 1, 1999, use plain language in all proposed and final rulemaking documents published in the **Federal Register**, unless you proposed the rule before that date. You should consider rewriting existing regulations in plain language when you have the opportunity and resources to do so.

The National Partnership for Reinventing Government will issue guidance to help you comply with these directives and to explain more fully the elements of plain language. You should also use customer feedback and common sense to guide your plain language efforts.

I ask the independent agencies to comply with these directives.

This memorandum does not confer any right or benefit enforceable by law against the United States or its representatives. The Director of the Office

Exhibit 65.   Memorandum of June 1, 1998, 64 Fed. Reg. 31,885 (1998).

tions affected during the year, and list statutes cited as authority for presidential documents.

Proclamations, but not executive orders, are printed in the annual *Statutes at Large* volumes. Major orders and proclamations are also reprinted after relevant statutory provisions in the *U.S. Code*, *USCA*, and *USCS*; tables in

each version of the code list presidential documents by number and indicate where they can be found. *Reorganization plans*, an older form of presidential action no longer in use, were published in the *Federal Register*, *CFR*, and *Statutes at Large*, and many are reprinted in all three versions of the *U.S. Code*.

Several other presidential documents do not appear in the *Federal Register*. Messages to Congress, explaining proposed legislation or vetoes, reporting on the state of the nation, and serving other functions, are published in the *Congressional Record*, in the *House* and *Senate Journals*, and as House and Senate Documents. Signing statements are often issued when approving legislation, and may provide the president's interpretation of a statute. Although their value as legislative history is disputed, since 1986 these statements have been reprinted with the committee reports in *USCCAN*.

Most of these various presidential documents, including those published in the *Federal Register*, appear in the official *Weekly Compilation of Presidential Documents*, along with speeches, transcripts of news conferences, and other material. The *Weekly Compilation* is accompanied by cumulative semiannual and annual indexes.

Public Papers of the Presidents is an official Federal Register publication cumulating the contents of the *Weekly Compilation of Presidential Documents*. Series of annual volumes have been published for Herbert Hoover and for all presidents after Franklin D. Roosevelt, and cumulated indexes for the papers of each administration have also been published. Papers of Roosevelt and most of the earlier presidents are generally available in commercially published editions.

On the Internet, the *Weekly Compilation of Presidential Documents* since 1993 is available from GPO Access <www.access.gpo.gov/nara/nara003.html>, as are *Public Papers* volumes beginning with 1996. A wide range of documents since 1993 can also be found in the White House's Virtual Library <www.whitehouse.gov/library/>. Westlaw has executive orders since 1936 and other presidential documents since 1984, and Lexis–Nexis has all presidential documents since 1981.

Coverage of proclamations, executive orders, and reorganization plans is included in *Shepard's Code of Federal Regulations Citations*. The presidential documents are listed by number, with references to citing court decisions and law review articles.

§ 7–6. STATE ADMINISTRATIVE LAW

Like the federal government, the states have experienced a dramatic increase in the number and activity of their administrative agencies. In many states, however, publication of agency rules and decisions is far less systematic than it is on the federal level.

Nearly all states publish official manuals paralleling the *United States Government Manual* and providing quick access to information about government agencies and officials. These directories vary in quality; some describe state agency functions and publications, while others are simply government phone directories. They're listed in *State Reference Publications* (annual), which also has information about Internet sites, general reference works, statistical abstracts, and other sources.

In addition, a number of directories provide multistate access to officials' names and numbers. These include

Carroll's State Directory (three times a year), *State Staff Directory* (three times a year), and *State Yellow Book* (quarterly). The Council of State Governments' *CSG State Directory, Directory III: Administrative Officials* (annual) lists officials by function, rather than by state, and may be the most convenient source for someone needing to contact similar officials in several states. While not a directory, CSG's biennial *Book of the States* provides in one volume basic information on government operations in each of the fifty states.

Of several websites providing links to state government information on the Internet, two of the most thorough are Chicago–Kent College of Law's State Web Locator <www.infoctr.edu/swl/> and Piper Resources' State and Local Government on the Net <www.piperinfo.com/state/states.html>. Both include not only general links but extensive listings of executive departments and agencies.

a. Regulations

Almost every state issues a subject compilation of its administrative regulations, and most supplement these with weekly, biweekly or monthly registers. While the states generally follow the paradigm established by the *CFR* and *Federal Register*, few state administrative codes and registers are as organized and accessible as their federal counterparts. Some simply compile a variety of material submitted by individual agencies, and some have incomplete coverage. Indexing is often inadequate, sometimes even nonexistent.

The *Bluebook* identifies administrative codes and registers in its list of basic primary sources for each state, and the National Association of Secretaries of State (NASS) publishes an annual *State and Federal Survey*

with summary information about each publication. Two sources for more detailed information are *BNA's Directory of State Administrative Codes and Registers: A State-by-State Listing* (2d ed. 1995) and *Guide to the Administrative Regulations of the States & Territories* (2 vols., annual).

Although fewer states provide Internet access to regulations than to statutes, a majority of administrative codes and a growing number of registers are now available. One of the easiest ways to find available sites is through the National Association of Secretaries of State's "Administrative Codes and Registers" list of links <www. nass.org/acr/acrdir.htm>. Westlaw and Lexis–Nexis do not have comprehensive coverage, but each has administrative codes from at least half of the states. They also have regulations from all fifty states in a few specialized areas such as environmental law, insurance, and taxation.

Some of the administrative codes and registers include executive orders or similar legal pronouncements from governors. The NASS *State and Federal Survey* and *BNA's Directory of State Administrative Codes and Registers* both indicate which sources include gubernatorial documents. Several governors include the text of executive orders on their websites, which can be accessed through state government homepages or by links from the National Governors Association <www.nga.org/subtocgov. htm>.

For those states without comprehensive compilations or registers, a researcher must apply to the Secretary of State or to the particular agency for a copy of a specific

regulation. Contact information and procedures are explained in BNA's *Directory of State Administrative Codes and Registers*.

b. Decisions and rulings

Decisions of some state agencies, especially those dealing with banking, insurance, public utilities, taxation, and workers' compensation, may be published in official form in chronological series. A few looseleaf services and topical reporters also include state administrative decisions, and a growing number of state agency decisions are included in the online databases or on agency websites.

The opinions of state attorneys general, issued in response to questions from government officials, can have considerable significance in legal research. Although attorney general opinions are advisory in nature and do not have binding authority, they are given considerable weight by the courts in interpreting statutes and regulations. Most states publish attorney general opinions in slip form and bound volumes, although in some states there is a long time lag between an opinion's issuance and its publication. Each volume generally has an index, but these rarely cumulate. Many attorneys general have recent opinions on their websites, which can be found through links at the National Association of Attorneys General website <www.naag.org/about/ag. html>. State attorney general opinions are also available online in Lexis–Nexis and Westlaw, with coverage in most states beginning in 1977. Some attorney general opinions are included in the annotations in state codes, but this coverage is quite incomplete.

§ 7–7. LOCAL LAW

Cities and counties are administrative units of the states, with lawmaking powers determined by state con-

stitution or by legislative delegation of authority. They create a variety of legal documents which can be important in legal research. *Charters* are the basic laws creating the structure of local government, and *ordinances* are local enactments governing specific issues. In addition many localities have administrative agencies which issue rules or decisions.

Unfortunately local law sources can often be quite difficult to locate. Most large cities and counties publish collections of their charters and ordinances, with some attempt at regular supplementation, and in recent years there has been a significant improvement in the publication of municipal ordinances of smaller jurisdictions by specialized legal publishers. For many cities and counties, however, there is still no accessible, up-to-date compilation, and individual ordinances must be obtained from the local clerk's office.

A growing number of local laws are available on the Internet. The Seattle Public Library <www.spl.org/govpubs/municode.html> and the Municipal Code Corporation <www.municode.com/database.html> have the two most extensive sets of links to collections of local ordinances. Each provides access to several hundred codes from almost every state.

Ordinance Law Annotations (15 vols., 1969–date), a subject digest of judicial decisions involving local ordinances, provides brief abstracts of decisions under alphabetically arranged subject headings divided into specific subtopics. A case table accompanying this set lists court decisions on local law issues, by state and locality.

On the municipal and local level, administrative decisions are almost never published, and regulations, if published, are rarely kept up to date. When a specific regulation is known to exist, it must be obtained by request from a town clerk or particular agency. It is difficult, however, to determine the existence of local regulations since they are not available to the public in a compiled or current text, and are rarely indexed in official files.

Because so little local law information is published, direct contact by telephone or e-mail may be essential. Information on local governments throughout the country can be found in several directories, published by the same companies that issue federal and state government directories. These include *Carroll's Municipal Directory*, *Carroll's County Directory*, *Municipal Staff Directory*, and *Municipal Yellow Book* (all semiannual).

§ 7–8. CONCLUSION

From its early days as one of the most bibliographically inaccessible areas of law, federal administrative law has developed a highly sophisticated research framework. This development stemmed from several publishing innovations, including the looseleaf services, the improvements brought by the Federal Register System, and improved access through the online databases and the Internet. Access to state administrative law is less advanced but is improving steadily.

It is important to remember that administrative agency actions are governed by statutes and reviewable by the courts. Administrative procedure acts and judicial decisions have established many important procedural safe-

guards of agency rulemaking and adjudication. Administrative law research is rarely limited to the specialized publications discussed in this chapter.

CHAPTER 8

COURT RULES AND PRACTICE

---

§ 8–1. INTRODUCTION

This chapter covers a number of resources dealing with court proceedings. Some of these, such as the rules governing trial procedures and lawyer conduct, have the force of law. Others, such as briefs and docket sheets, contain background information on decided cases or pending lawsuits. A third group, the directories and formbooks, provide practical assistance for lawyers who need to contact courts, draft documents, or transact other legal business.

These are materials with which any litigator should be familiar, but their value extends to other legal research situations as well. All lawyers, of course, must follow rules of professional conduct, and sources such as briefs and model jury instructions can provide important information about substantive legal issues.

§ 8–2. COURT RULES

Rules for the regulation of court proceedings have the force of law, but they generally cannot supersede or conflict with statutes. Most jurisdictions have sets of rules governing trial and appellate procedure, as well as rules for specialized tribunals or particular actions such as admiralty or habeas corpus. These rules are created in a variety of ways. Some are enacted by statute, but most are promulgated by the courts themselves or by conferences of judges. Exhibit 66 shows rules from the United States Court of Appeals for the Eighth Circuit governing several matters, including law students' participation in court proceedings.

a. Federal Rules

Under the Rules Enabling Act, 28 U.S.C. § 2072, federal courts have the power to adopt rules governing their procedures as long as they do not "abridge, enlarge, or modify any substantive right." Individual federal courts have had rules since the beginning of the judicial system, but the modern era of rules of national scope began with the adoption of the Federal Rules of Civil Procedure in 1938. These rules were prepared by a judicial advisory committee and approved by the Supreme Court, as were subsequent sets of rules governing criminal procedure (1946) and appellate procedure (1968). The Federal Rules of Evidence were originally drafted by judges, but they were enacted by Congress in 1975 due to their possible impact on substantive rights.

Federal court rules are available in a variety of pamphlets and reference publications, as well as online from both Westlaw and Lexis–Nexis. All of the major sets of rules are printed in the *U.S. Code*, accompanied by

RULE 45A: Clerk.

Clerk to furnish copies. — When an opinion is filed, the clerk will mail a copy to counsel for each of the parties. Additional copies of an opinion will be available from the clerk for $5.00 each. Annual subscriptions to all published opinions of the court will be available at a rate set by the court.

Cross references.
FRAP 45.

RULE 46A: Admitting, suspending, and disciplining attorneys.

Applicants for admission must pay an admission fee of $40.00, for deposit in the Attorney Admission Fee Fund. An attorney who is appointed to represent a party proceeding in forma pauperis may appear in the case without being admitted to the bar of this court.

Cross references.
FRAP 46; 8th Cir. R. 47H.

RULE 46B: Student practice.

Any law student acting under a supervising attorney may appear and participate in proceedings in this court.

(a) *Eligibility.* — To be eligible to appear and participate, a law student must:

(1) be a student in good standing in a law school approved by the American Bar Association;

(2) have completed legal studies equivalent to three semesters;

(3) file with the clerk of court:

(i) a certificate from the dean of the law school or a faculty member stating the student is of good moral character, satisfies the requirements listed above, and is qualified to serve as a legal intern;

(ii) a certificate stating the student has read and agrees to abide by the rules of the court, all applicable codes of professional responsibility, and other relevant federal practice rules;

(iii) a notice of appearance prescribed by the court and signed by the supervising attorney and the client in each case in which the student is participating or appearing as a law student intern; and

(4) be introduced to the court by an attorney admitted to practice in this court.

(b) *Restrictions.* — No law student admitted under these rules may:

(1) request or receive compensation from the client;

(2) appear in court without the supervising attorney; or

(3) file any documents or papers with the court that have not been read, approved, and signed by the supervising attorney and cosigned by the student.

This restriction does not prevent the supervising attorney, law school, public defender, or government from paying compensation to the law student, or an agency from charging for its services.

(c) *Supervising attorneys.* — A person acting as a supervising attorney under this rule must be admitted to practice in this court and must:

(1) assume responsibility for the conduct of the student;

Exhibit 66. 8th Cir. R. 45A–46B, *reprinted in* Nebraska Rules of Court Annotated 589 (Lexis 2000).

Advisory Committee comments. *USCA* and *USCS* also include annotations of cases in which the rules have been applied or construed, as well as other research aids such as references to treatises, law review articles, and legal encyclopedias. These annotations can be quite extensive; the Federal Rules of Civil Procedure, for example, occupy ten volumes in *USCA*.

A somewhat less overwhelming source of annotated federal rules is the *United States Supreme Court Digest, Lawyers' Edition*. Volume 17 to 22 of this set include the text of all of the major rules series, as well as rules for specialized federal courts, accompanied by advisory committee comments and annotations of Supreme Court cases. While it's annotations are not comprehensive, this may be a useful starting point for someone seeking significant judicial interpretations of the rules.

The most scholarly sources for the federal rules are the treatises on federal procedure, Wright & Miller's *Federal Practice and Procedure* (58 vols., 1969–date) and *Moore's Federal Practice* (31 vols., 3d ed. 1997–date). These works are organized rule-by-rule, providing the texts and official comments accompanied by historical background, discussion, and extensive analysis of the cases. Both analyze the civil, criminal, and appellate rules; Wright & Miller also cover the Federal Rules of Evidence. These treatises are among the secondary authorities most often cited by the federal courts.

Rules of the Supreme Court are also included in the *U.S. Code*, *USCA*, and *USCS*; and of individual Courts of Appeals in the annotated codes. Lower federal court rules from the entire country are published in a five-volume looseleaf set, *Federal Local Court Rules*, and local U.S.

District Court rules are usually available in court rules pamphlets published for individual states. The rules shown in Exhibit 66, for example, are from an annual publication called *Nebraska Rules of Court Annotated*, containing both state and federal rules. Local court rules are generally available on Westlaw and Lexis–Nexis, although rules for federal district courts are included not with other federal materials but in databases covering state court rules.

Most court rules are available at free Internet sites, but without the helpful commentary and annotations found in the treatises or annotated codes. The Federal Rules of Civil Procedure, Federal Rules of Evidence, and Supreme Court Rules are available as hypertext publications from Cornell's Legal Information Institute <www.law.cornell. edu/rules/>, and the University of Kansas provides the Federal Rules of Criminal Procedure <www.law.ukans. edu/research/frcrimI.htm>. Local rules are increasingly available on individual courts' websites, and some sites also include answers to frequently asked questions about filing requirements and trial procedures. Links to local pages are maintained by the Administrative Office of the U.S. Courts <www.uscourts.gov/links.html>.

Lawyers can learn of changes in procedural rules by monitoring the advance sheets for any of West's federal court reports. In addition, amendments to the major federal rules are printed by Congress as House Documents and are reproduced in the official *U.S. Reports*, *Lawyers' Edition*, *USCCAN* and *USCS Advance*.

KeyCite and Shepard's coverage of court rules is similar to that for statutes. KeyCite begins with the annotations from *USCA*, but expands this to include additional cases

and secondary sources. Shepard's can be accessed online or in *Shepard's Federal Statute Citations*, and covers local rules as well as the major national sets. The printed version provides references to rule amendments and to citations in federal court decisions and *ALR* annotations. Citing law review articles are listed separately in *Shepard's Federal Law Citations in Selected Law Reviews*, and state cases citing federal rules are listed in the individual Shepard's state citators. These references are cumulated in the online version of Shepard's.

The Federal Sentencing Guidelines are not court rules, but they occupy a similarly anomalous position in the hierarchy of legal authorities. They were originally promulgated in 1987 by the U.S. Sentencing Commission, which was created by Congress as an independent agency within the judicial branch. The sentencing guidelines are not published with the official *U.S. Code*, but the commission publishes a biennial *Guidelines Manual* in print and on the Internet <www.ussc.gov/guidelin.htm>. Both *USCA* and *USCS* include annotated versions accompanied by notes of court decisions and other references. Like the court rules, the sentencing guidelines are also available from the online databases and are covered in *Shepard's Federal Statute Citations*.

Wright & Miller and *Moore's Federal Practice* do not cover sentencing guidelines, but shorter works such as Roger W. Haines, Jr., et al., *Federal Sentencing Guidelines Handbook: Text and Analysis* (annual); Thomas W. Hutchison et al., *Federal Sentencing Law and Practice* (annual); and Gerald S. McFadden et al., *Federal Sentencing Manual* (2 vols., 1989–date) provide similar treatment, combining the text of the guidelines with commentary and analysis of cases.

b. State Rules

There are significant differences in rules and procedures from state to state, although these distinctions are gradually decreasing as more and more states have adopted provisions modeled on the federal rules. Some states have court procedures governed by statutory codes rather than rules, and there are even some common law rules established on a case-by-case basis.

The rules governing proceedings in state courts are usually included in the annotated state codes, accompanied by notes of relevant cases, as well as on Westlaw and Lexis–Nexis. Most states also have annual paperback volumes providing convenient access to rules and procedural statutes. Many of these publications are unannotated, but some contain useful case annotations and comments by scholars or drafting committees.

More elaborate practice sets in many jurisdictions include all of these features, as well as legal forms for each rule and section. Like Wright & Miller or *Moore's Federal Practice*, the best of these provide a scholarly commentary on the procedures and extensive analysis of relevant case law.

Most state court websites, even those without opinions, provide convenient access to rules and other procedural information. Two leading sources for finding both trial and appellate state courts on the Web are the National Center for State Courts <ncsc.dni.us/court/sites/courts. htm> and Courts.net <www.courts.net/>.

The online citators have only partial coverage of state court rules, but Shepard's printed state citators note rule changes and citations in federal and state court decisions, selected law reviews, *ALR* annotations, and (in some

states) attorney general opinions. The text of new amendments to rules can be found in the advance sheets to most court reports, including the West regional reporters.

§ 8–3. LEGAL ETHICS

Courts are responsible in most jurisdictions for governing the professional activities of lawyers, although in some states power is delegated to bar associations or oversight boards. The materials in this area are found in a distinct body of literature consisting of codified rules of conduct, advisory ethics opinions, and disciplinary decisions.

While rules vary from state to state, most jurisdictions have adopted some form of the Model Rules of Professional Conduct, promulgated by the American Bar Association in 1983. A few states still have rules based on the ABA's older Model Code of Professional Responsibility (1969). The rules in force are usually included in the volumes containing a state's court rules, although they can sometimes be difficult to find. Only a few of these sources are annotated with notes of decisions under the rules. The *National Reporter on Legal Ethics and Professional Responsibility* (1982–date), a looseleaf service, reprints the unannotated rules for every state as well as the District of Columbia and Puerto Rico.

Annotated Model Rules of Professional Conduct (4th ed. 1999) provides the text of the ABA rules with comments, legal background, and notes of decisions from various jurisdictions. Although it contains the ABA's rules rather than those adopted in any specific state, this is a useful source for comparative analysis and commentary. The annotated rules are available online from Westlaw;

Lexis–Nexis has the Model Rules with official comments but no background notes and annotations.

The leading modern treatise on legal ethics is Geoffrey C. Hazard, Jr. & W. William Hodes, *The Law of Lawyering: A Handbook on the Model Rules of Professional Conduct* (2 vols., 2d ed. 1990–date). The American Law Institute's *Restatement of the Law: The Law Governing Lawyers* has not even been published yet in its official final version but is already influential.

Ethics opinions, generally prepared in response to inquiries from attorneys, are issued by the courts, the American Bar Association, and state and local bar associations. Court decisions and ABA opinions are available on Westlaw and Lexis–Nexis, but very few state bar opinions are online. Some can be found in the *National Reporter on Legal Ethics and Professional Responsibility*, and most state bars have publications either summarizing ethics opinions or reprinting them in full text.

The *ABA/BNA Lawyers' Manual on Professional Conduct* (1984–date) is often a good place to begin research. This looseleaf service includes an extensive commentary with background and practical tips, as well as news of developments and abstracts of new decisions. It is available both in print and on Westlaw.

Most state bars and disciplinary agencies have websites providing information about procedures for filing complaints and resolving problems with lawyers, and some of these include the text of rules and ethics opinions. The American Legal Ethics Library <www.law.cornell.edu/ethics/> and Legalethics.com <www.legalethics.com> have extensive collections of links to sites in this field.

§ 8–4. RECORDS AND BRIEFS

The materials submitted by the parties in cases before appellate courts are often available for research use. The record consists of a transcript of proceedings in the lower court, including the trial testimony, pleadings, motions, and judgments. Briefs are the written arguments and authorities cited by the attorneys for the parties on appeal. These documents enable researchers to study in detail the arguments and facts of significant cases decided by appellate courts.

Records and briefs are usually filed by the report citation or docket number of the case in which they were submitted. Except for Supreme Court briefs available online, there is little direct subject or keyword access to these documents. A researcher interested in a particular decision, however, can pursue these additional sources of information on the case.

The records and briefs of the Supreme Court of the United States go to several libraries around the country, while many more libraries subscribe to microform editions. Filings since 1979 are available online through Lexis–Nexis, and Westlaw coverage begins in 1990. Many cases have a substantial number of briefs, with filings by several amici curiae supporting one side or the other. For example, *Oncale v. Sundowner Offshore Services, Inc.*, the case shown in Exhibits 8 through 10 in Chapter 3, had eight amicus briefs filed on behalf of some thirty interest groups.

Transcripts of Supreme Court oral arguments are also available in various formats. Microform collections begin

with the 1953 term, and online coverage starts in 1989 (Lexis–Nexis) or 1990 (Westlaw). Both briefs and argument transcripts for hundreds of major cases, dating back to the 19th century, are reprinted in *Landmark Briefs and Arguments of the Supreme Court of the United States: Constitutional Law* (1975–date). Cases through the 1973 term are covered in the first 80 volumes of this set, and about a dozen new cases are added each year.

Records and briefs of the U.S. Courts of Appeals and state appellate courts have a more limited distribution, but they can often be found in local law libraries within the circuit or state. For a few courts, they are also available in microform. In many cases, however, it may be necessary to contact the court or a judicial records center to obtain copies.

§ 8–5.   OTHER CASE INFORMATION

Appellate cases generally follow a standard path and produce a written record consisting of the parties' briefs, the lower court record, and the court's opinion (which may or may not be published in the reporters or available online). The documentation of other trial court litigation, on the other hand, may be harder to identify and find. Some cases result in judges' opinions, such as a decision granting a motion for summary judgment, but many matters are decided without a written opinion. A case may be resolved by jury verdict, summary disposition, or settlement agreement. Some cases go to trial without any written submissions on points of law; others produce dozens of memoranda or briefs submitted to support or oppose motions before, during and after trial. For infor-

mation on trial court proceedings, it may be necessary to rely on news reports, to contact the attorneys, or to get documents directly from the court.

Documents submitted in a case are kept on file at the courthouse or a records center. Many courts are developing electronic systems in which pleadings and other documents are submitted and retained online, but paper remains the most prevalent form for case documents. The first step in obtaining documents is usually to determine the case number, or docket number. This may be mentioned in an appellate decision or secondary source, but it may be necessary to ask the court clerk to consult an index by party name. Each case has a docket sheet listing the proceedings and documents filed; these were traditionally on paper but most are now maintained electronically. The docket sheet provides the information needed to obtain documents. Some courts accept requests electronically or by telephone, while for others it is necessary to apply by mail or in person.

In many instances, access to docket sheet information for pending cases is available electronically. The federal courts' fee-based information system, known as PACER (Public Access to Court Electronic Records), is in the process of moving to the Web, but most courts still require direct dial-in access. Each court maintains its own records and database, but the system has a central registration process and a national index of cases by party name. Information about the PACER program is available on the Internet <pacer.psc.uscourts.gov/>.

Commercial subscription services, such as CourtLink <www.courtlink.com> and CaseStream <www.case-stream.com>, also monitor activity in federal district

courts, and some state courts, and provide more convenient access to this information. CourtLink dockets are also available by subscription through Westlaw, and Case-Stream through Lexis–Nexis.

While docket information for some state courts is available online, for others it may be more difficult to obtain. Most states have electronic docket systems, but means of access vary. The best bet is to contact the individual court and determine availability and procedures.

Access methods for both federal and state courts are explained in *The Sourcebook to Public Record Information: The Comprehensive Guide to County, State, & Federal Public Records Sources* (1999). This book also explains about access to other public records, such as property and licensing information. Much of this data is available through subscription based commercial services, including Westlaw and Lexis–Nexis. A few services, such as KnowX <www.knowx.com>, permit free searching but charge for documents retrieved.

§ 8–6. DIRECTORIES OF COURTS AND JUDGES

Court directories serve a number of purposes. They provide contact information for clerks' offices, and some include biographical data on judges. This can be useful information for litigants appearing before a particular judge or panel; in law schools, the heaviest users of court directories are often students seeking clerkships after graduation.

Federal courts and judges are covered in a number of directories. An official *United States Court Directory* (semiannual) provides names, addresses and telephone numbers. *Judicial Staff Directory* (annual) and *Judicial*

Yellow Book (semiannual) include basic biographical information for judges, as well as extensive listings of court personnel such as clerks and staff attorneys. Like other volumes in the Staff Directories and Yellow Books series, these are available electronically as well as in print. A two-volume looseleaf publication, *Almanac of the Federal Judiciary*, is the most thorough source for biographical information, including noteworthy rulings, media coverage, and lawyers' evaluations of the judge's ability and temperament. The *Almanac* is available through Westlaw, but without the candid lawyers' evaluations.

Several directories cover both federal and state courts. *BNA's Directory of State and Federal Courts, Judges, and Clerks* (biennial) provides addresses and telephone numbers, and includes a list of Internet sites and a personal name index. *The American Bench* (biennial) is the most comprehensive biographical source, covering almost every judge in the United States. It includes an Alphabetical Name Index indicating the jurisdictions for all judges listed. Two other directories with less comprehensive coverage of state courts are *Judicial Yellow Book*, which includes state appellate courts but not trial courts; and *WANT's Federal–State Court Directory* (annual), which has just one page per state listing a few key officials. More thorough coverage is provided by WANT's *Directory of State Court Clerks & County Courthouses* (annual), and through its subscription website <www.courts.com>. Both WANT directories and the BNA directory include charts explaining the structure of each court's judicial system.

Westlaw's version of West Legal Directory includes contact information for courts and biographical entries for federal and state judges. This information does not

appear to be available in the Internet version of West Legal Directory <www.lawoffice.com>.

Sometimes information is needed not for a current judge but for a judge involved in an older case being studied or sitting on a particular court. If only the last name at the head of an opinion is known, the first step may be to determine a judge's full name. This can be found in tables in the front of most reporter volumes. *Federal Reporter*, for example, has since 1882 listed the sitting federal judges, with footnotes indicating any changes since the previous volume. Similar listings appear in each of West's regional reporters and in most official state reports. Biographical information on most appellate judges can be found in standard sources such as *American National Biography* (24 vols., 1999) or *Who Was Who in America* (14 vols., 1943–date). The Federal Judicial Center's "Jugdes of the United States Courts" <air. fjc.gov/history/judges_ frm.html> contains breif entries for all federal judges since 1789.

§ 8–7. FORMBOOKS AND JURY INSTRUCTIONS

In the course of legal practice, many basic transactions and court filings occur with regularity. Rather than re-draft these documents each time the need arises, attorneys frequently work from sample versions of standard legal documents and instruments. Model forms are available from a variety of printed and electronic sources. Some sets are annotated with discussion of the underlying laws, checklists of steps in completing the forms, and citations to cases in which the forms were in issue.

Several multivolume compilations of forms, with extensive indexing, notes and cross-references, are published.

Some of these are comprehensive national works containing both procedural forms, such as complaints and motions, and transactional forms, such as contracts and wills. Most, however, are limited to particular jurisdictions or particular types of forms.

Two of the major form sets are published as adjuncts to *American Jurisprudence 2d* and are linked to that encyclopedia by frequent cross-references. *American Jurisprudence Legal Forms 2d* (58 vols., 1971–date) provides forms of instruments such as contracts, leases, and wills, and *American Jurisprudence Pleading and Practice Forms* (rev. ed., 70 vols., 1966–date) focuses on litigation and other practice before courts and administrative agencies. Both sets are divided into several hundred topical chapters mirroring the organization of *Am. Jur. 2d*.

Others comprehensive sets include Jacob Rabkin & Mark H. Johnson, *Current Legal Forms, with Tax Analysis* (34 vols., 1948–date) and *West's Legal Forms* (39 vols., 2d ed. 1981–date). Unlike the *Am. Jur.* sets, these are arranged by broad practice area such as estate planning or real estate. They may be better for understanding a wider range of related issues, but perhaps less useful for finding forms on very fact-specific topics.

Three major sets devoted to forms used in federal practice are *Bender's Federal Practice Forms* (20 vols., 1951–date), *Federal Procedural Forms, Lawyers' Edition* (37 vols., 1975–date) and *West's Federal Forms* (21 vols., 1952–date). Each of these has a different structure. *Bender's Federal Practice Forms* is arranged by rule. *Federal Procedural Forms, Lawyers' Edition* is a compan-

ion to West Group's encyclopedic *Federal Procedure, Lawyers' Edition*, and is organized similarly, with several dozen subject chapters. *West's Federal Forms* is arranged instead by court, with separate volumes covering forms needed in the Supreme Court, Courts of Appeals, District Courts, Bankruptcy Courts, and specialized national courts such as the Court of Federal Claims. Exhibit 67 shows a page from *Federal Procedural Forms*, including part of a background explanation, footnote references to the *U.S. Code* and *Federal Procedure*, and the beginning of a sample complaint alleging discriminatory deprivation of civil rights.

Sets of forms, varying in complexity and volume, are also published for most states and for particular subject areas. In addition, manuals of practice for virtually every state contain sample forms, and compilations of statutory forms are often issued in conjunction with state codes.

Several sets of forms are available on CD–ROM, streamlining the drafting process by eliminating the need to retype each new form. These CD–ROM publications include both *Am. Jur.* form sets, *Bender's Federal Practice Forms*, *Federal Procedural Forms*, *Michie's Forms on Disc*, and *West's Legal Forms*. In addition, most law firms have electronic libraries of forms and pleadings for in-house use.

A more limited range of forms is available from free Internet sites. These collections are not as thorough as the commercial collections, but they may be satisfactory for simple transactions. FindLaw <www.findlaw.com/16forms/index.html> has links to more than 100 sites, including general collections, specialized resources, and

program upon a finding of failure to comply with any requirement imposed pursuant to § 1682, then any aggrieved person or entity (including any state or political subdivision thereof and any agency of either) may obtain judicial review of the action in accordance with the procedures relating generally to judicial review of administrative actions.[68] Such an action is not committed to unreviewable agency discretion within the meaning of the Administrative Procedure Act.[69]

C. PROCEDURAL FORMS

1. COMPLAINTS

**§ 10:387.   Complaint—By female athletes—Denied participation in tennis program—For declaratory and
injunctive relief [20 USC § 1681; 28 USC § 1343;
42 USC § 1983; 45 CFR § 86.41; FRCP 8(a), 57,
65]**

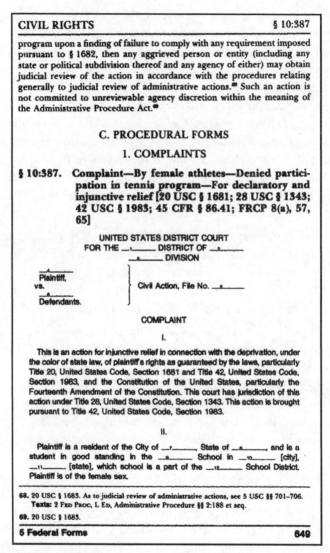

UNITED STATES DISTRICT COURT
FOR THE ___1___ DISTRICT OF ___2___
___3___ DIVISION

Plaintiff,
vs.
___5___
Defendants.

Civil Action, File No. ___6___

COMPLAINT

I.

This is an action for injunctive relief in connection with the deprivation, under the color of state law, of plaintiff's rights as guaranteed by the laws, particularly Title 20, United States Code, Section 1681 and Title 42, United States Code, Section 1983, and the Constitution of the United States, particularly the Fourteenth Amendment of the Constitution. This court has jurisdiction of this action under Title 28, United States Code, Section 1343. This action is brought pursuant to Title 42, United States Code, Section 1983.

II.

Plaintiff is a resident of the City of ___7___, State of ___8___, and is a student in good standing in the ___9___ School in ___10___ [city], ___11___ [state], which school is a part of the ___12___ School District. Plaintiff is of the female sex.

---

68. 20 USC § 1683. As to judicial review of administrative actions, see 5 USC §§ 701–706.
Texts: 2 Fed Proc, L Ed, Administrative Procedure §§ 2:188 et seq.

69. 20 USC § 1683.

Exhibit 67.   Civil Rights § 10:387, 5 Federal Procedural Forms, Lawyers' Edition 649 (1996).

government agencies. The Internet Legal Resource Guide <www.ilrg.com/forms.html> also provides links to sources for forms, with a basic archive of about 100 forms in a dozen practice areas.

Most jurisdictions have published sets of *model* or *pattern jury instructions* designed for judges to explain the applicable law to jurors before they weigh the evidence and reach their decision. Model jury instructions can be useful as forms, and they also provide a concise summary of a jurisdiction's ruling law on the issues covered. Some of these sets of instructions are published by state court systems, and others by bar associations. Still others are unofficial but highly respected, such as Edward J. Devitt et al., *Federal Jury Practice and Instructions* (4th/5th eds., 4 vols. 1987–date), which is available on Westlaw as well as in print. The subject heading used by the Library of Congress and in most online catalogs for these sets is "Instructions to juries—[State]."

Michie's Jury Instructions, available on CD and through Lexis–Nexis, contains more than 5,000 model instructions from several print products, for both federal and state jurisdictions. Instructions for a few individual states are also available online.

§ 8–8. CONCLUSION

Court rules have taken a back seat in this text to more wide-ranging sources such as judicial decisions and statutes, but they have the force of law and can be vital in determining procedural rights. Some rules, such as those establishing the principles of legal ethics, must be known and followed by every practicing attorney. Most of the materials discussed in this chapter may primarily be of

use in litigation, but overall they are essential in dealing with many aspects of the judicial system.

CHAPTER 9

TOPICAL RESEARCH SOURCES

§ 9–1. INTRODUCTION

The resources many lawyers turn to most often are not the general codes, digests, and indexes we have discussed thus far, but instead tools narrowly designed for use in specialized areas of law. Topical looseleaf and electronic services make lawyers' work easier by compiling related statutes, cases, and regulations in one location along with explanations and necessary forms. These resources and others also provide the current awareness lawyers need to respond to and anticipate new legal developments, such as recently decided cases or proposed regulations. These are essential tools for specialists, but others can make profitable use of them as well.

§ 9–2. LOOSELEAF SERVICES

The looseleaf service, one of the unique inventions of legal bibliography, is a frequently supplemented tool which focuses on a specific subject area and contains

primary legal sources, finding aids, and secondary material. The best looseleaf services provide seamless access to a diverse collection of documents as well as prompt notice of developments in the courts, legislatures, and agencies. A looseleaf service provides *comprehensive* and *current* access to a particular field of law.

The first looseleaf services were issued just before World War I to facilitate research in the new federal income tax law. Other services developed in public law areas where government regulation was the central focus of legal development, such as labor law, antitrust, and securities. Services are now also published in such varied areas as criminal law, environmental protection, health care, and housing.

There are several ways to determine whether a service is published in a particular area of interest. References to looseleaf services may appear in law review articles and cases, and lawyers or professors specializing in a field can provide helpful advice. *Legal Looseleafs in Print* is an annual directory of looseleaf publications, including (but not limited to) regularly supplemented services. At the end of this volume, Appendix C provides a selected list of looseleaf and electronic services in fields of major interest.

There are two basic types of looseleaf services, *cumulating* and *interfiling*. In a cumulating service, new updating material is usually filed as a unit at the end of the set. This material *supplements* the existing compilation and does not replace pages already filed. Cumulating services are useful in areas where it is necessary to monitor new information from a variety of sources. *The United States Law Week*, published by the Bureau of National Affairs (BNA), is representative of the genre.

Other cumulating BNA services, such as *Antitrust & Trade Regulation Report*, *Criminal Law Reporter*, *Family Law Reporter*, and *Securities Regulation & Law Report,* serve as excellent current awareness tools in their fields.

Interfiling services, on the other hand, are updated by replacing superseded material with revised pages. New pages are inserted where appropriate within the service, rather than simply added at the end. Page numbering is designed to facilitate accurate filing and can be rather convoluted; page 10,001 may be followed, for example, by pages 10,001–1 and 10,001–2. For researchers to find specific references, many interfiling services assign *paragraph numbers* to each section of material. A "paragraph" in this sense can vary in length from a few sentences to several pages. Each code section, for example, may be assigned one paragraph number, no matter what its length. It retains this number no matter how many new pages are added to the service. Paragraph numbers, not page numbers, are generally used in indexes and cross-references.

Interfiling services are well suited to areas in which it is essential to integrate recent legal developments with a large body of primary sources such as statutes or regulations. CCH (formerly Commerce Clearing House) publishes a wide variety of interfiling services, such as *Federal Securities Law Reports*, *Standard Federal Tax Reports*, and *Trade Regulation Reports*.

Some services have the attributes of both cumulating and interfiling services, with current awareness newsletters and regularly updated compilations of primary sources. Whether cumulating or interfiling, or both, a looseleaf service must be frequently supplemented if it is

to be a trustworthy resource. Most of the major services are updated weekly or biweekly. Many treatises are also published in looseleaf binders, but they are not looseleaf *services* if they are only updated once or twice a year.

Looseleaf services cover a wide range of subjects, and no two services are exactly alike. The methods of access and organization vary according to the nature of the primary sources, the characteristics of the legal field, and the editorial approach. In areas where one major statute dominates the legal order, the service may be arranged by statutory sections or divisions. Most taxation services, for example, are structured according to the sections of the Internal Revenue Code. If several statutes are significant, the service can be divided into areas by the relevant statutes. Labor law services, for example, offer separate treatment of the Labor Management Relations Act, Title VII of the Civil Rights Act of 1964, and the Fair Labor Standards Act. In other fields where common law or judicial rules predominate, or where there is a mixture of case and statutory law (such as family law, trusts and estates, or corporations), the service may follow a logical arrangement by subject.

Despite differences in organization, looseleaf services share several common features. They present *all* relevant primary authority in one place, regardless of its original form of publication. This may include decisions of federal and state courts; statutes, both federal and state; and regulations, decisions, and other documents from administrative agencies in the field. Even though much of this material is available elsewhere in the law library, it could be quite time-consuming to gather the various sources when beginning each research project.

Looseleaf services also summarize and analyze these primary sources. Some contain detailed analytical notes by topic, which function like case digests in explaining and providing access to the primary sources. Exhibits 68 and 69 show examples from CCH's *Standard Federal Tax Reports*, a typical interfiling service. Exhibit 68 reprints the statute and Internal Revenue Service regulations governing the exclusion from gross income of the rental value of parsonages. Exhibit 69 contains parts of the publisher's explanation of these provisions and annotations of court and administrative decisions. The statute is also found in the *U.S. Code*, regulations in the *CFR*, and case notes in annotated codes; but the looseleaf service brings these materials together along with an explanatory overview and news of new developments.

Looseleaf and topical reporters often have cases that are not published in the West system, including a number of federal trial court decisions as well as rulings of state and federal administrative agencies. These decisions and rulings are generally published first in weekly looseleaf inserts. Some services then publish permanent bound volumes of decisions, while others issue transfer binders for storage of older material.

In addition to publishing court and administrative decisions, looseleaf services also provide systems for digesting and indexing these decisions. To the extent that the cases are also published in West's National Reporter System, this coverage may overlap with West's key-number digest system. A specialized system, however, can respond more quickly to developments in a particular area, and may offer a more sophisticated analysis of topics within its expertise. The West system, for example, has just one key number for sexual harassment, but

[¶ 6850]   **RENTAL VALUE OF PARSONAGES**

'86 Code

Sec. 107 [1986 Code]. In the case of a minister of the gospel, gross income does not include—

(1) the rental value of a home furnished to him as part of his compensation; or

(2) the rental allowance paid to him as part of his compensation, to the extent used by him to rent or provide a home.

.20 A Committee Report on 1954 Code Sec. 107 as originally enacted was reproduced at 571 CCH ¶ 1101.10.

● *Regulations*

[¶ 6851] § 1.107-1. **Rental value of parsonages.**—(a) In the case of a minister of the gospel, gross income does not include (1) the rental value of a home, including utilities, furnished to him as a part of his compensation, or (2) the rental allowance paid to him as part of his compensation to the extent such allowance is used by him to rent or otherwise provide a home. In order to qualify for the exclusion, the home or rental allowance must be provided as remuneration for services which are ordinarily the duties of a minister of the gospel. In general, the rules provided in § 1.1402(c)-5 will be applicable to such determination. Examples of specific services the performance of which will be considered duties of a minister for purposes of section 107 include the performance of sacerdotal functions, the conduct of religious worship, the administration and maintenance of religious organizations and their integral agencies, and the performance of teaching and administrative duties at theological seminaries. Also, the service performed by a qualified minister as an employee of the United States (other than as a chaplain in the Armed Forces, whose service is considered to be that of a commissioned officer in his capacity as such, and not as a minister in the exercise of his ministry), or a State, Territory, or possession of the United States, or a political subdivision of any of the foregoing, or the District of Columbia, is in the exercise of his ministry provided the service performed includes such services as are ordinarily the duties of a minister.

(b) For purposes of section 107, the term "home" means a dwelling place (including furnishings) and the appurtenances thereto, such as a garage. The term "rental allowance" means an amount paid to a minister to rent or otherwise provide a home if such amount is designated as rental allowance pursuant to official action taken prior to January 1, 1958, by the employing church or other qualified organization, or if such amount is designated as rental allowance pursuant to official action taken in advance of such payment by the employing church or other qualified organization when paid after December 31, 1957. The designation of an amount as rental allowance may be evidenced in an employment contract, in minutes of or in a resolution by a church or other qualified organization or in its budget, or in any other appropriate instrument evidencing such official action. The designation referred to in this paragraph is a sufficient designation if it permits a payment or a part thereof to be identified as a payment of rental allowance as distinguished from salary or other remuneration.

(c) A rental allowance must be included in the minister's gross income in the taxable year in which it is received, to the extent that such allowance is not used by him during such taxable year to rent or otherwise provide a home. Circumstances under which a rental allowance will be deemed to have been used to rent or provide a home will include cases in which the allowance is expended (1) for rent of a home, (2) for purchase of a home, and (3) for expenses directly related to providing a home. Expenses for food and servants are not considered for this purpose to be directly related to providing a home. Where the minister rents, purchases, or owns a farm or other business property in addition to a home, the portion of the rental allowance expended in connection with the farm or business property shall not be excluded from his gross income. [Reg. § 1.107-1.]

Exhibit 68.   I.R.C. § 107, [1999] 2 Stand. Fed. Tax Rep. (CCH) ¶ 6850.

RENTAL VALUE OF PARSONAGES— § 107 [¶ 6850] **19,759**

Parsonages and Rental Allowances Furnished to Ministers of the Gospel

● ● *CCH Explanation*

dwelling but include the cost of utilities (Rev. Rul. 71-280, at ¶ 6852.07). Moreover, a minister may generally use the allowance to purchase a house and furniture in his own name without having the allowance taxed to him (Reg. § 1.107-1(c) and Rev. Rul. 71-280, at ¶ 6852.07). All ministers must treat unexpended amounts as fully taxable (*J.L. Swaggart*, Dec. 41,394(M), at ¶ 6852.70).

Ministers who receive tax-free housing allowances are permitted to deduct mortgage interest and property taxes on their homes (Code Sec. 265(a)(6) (see ¶ 14,054.0236) and Rev. Rul. 87-32, at ¶ 6852.10). Ministers may file an amended return if mortgage interest or property taxes were not claimed in a prior year and claiming them would result in lower tax liability; however, no provision was made to allow taxpayers to file amended returns for tax years that are otherwise closed.

Retired ministers also may exclude the rental value of a residence furnished by a church and a rental allowance paid by a church as part of compensation for past services (Rev. Rul. 63-156, at ¶ 6852.27). Retired ministers also may exclude that portion of pension payments that is designated as a rental allowance by the religious denomination's national governing body having complete control over the retirement fund (Rev. Rul. 62-117, at ¶ 6852.07). However, amounts paid by a church to the widow of a retired minister are not excludable as a rental allowance (Rev. Rul. 72-249, at ¶ 6852.31).

Any exclusion that is allowed is limited to the regular tax on income. For purposes of computing the self-employment tax (when applicable), the Code Sec. 107 exclusions are disregarded (see ¶ 32,578.068).—CCH.

● ● ● *Annotations by Topic*

Advance rulings	.023	Sacerdotal functions	.28
Designation required	.07	Services performed away from home.	
Expenses paid	.10	Surviving spouse	.31
Minister of the gospel defined:		Minister's parsonage and rental allowance	.33
Charitable activities	.16	Other compensation	.34
Educational activities	.18	Pension plans	.35
Hospital services	.17	Property donated by minister	.37
Jewish faith	.19	Reasonable allowance	.40
Ministerial functions	.21	Rental to third party	.50
Nursing home services	.23	Unexpended funds	.70
Ordained	.25	Prior law:	
Prison chaplain	.26	Obsolete rulings	.95
Retired minister	.27	Peculiar to 1939 Code	.92

.023 Advance rulings.—The IRS will not issue advance rulings or determination letters as to whether amounts distributed to a retired minister from a pension or annuity plan should be excludable from the minister's gross income as a parsonage allowance.

Rev. Proc. 98-3, I.R.B. 1998-3, 100.

.07 Designation required.—The employing church's retroactive designation of a "rental allowance" for taxpayer-minister was not timely under Reg. § 1.107-1(b). The timing requirement in the regulation is valid.

D.E. Ling, DC Minn., 62-1 USTC ¶ 9143, 200 FSupp 282.

A self-employed evangelistic minister was not invidiously discriminated against by the requirement within Reg. § 1.107-1(b) that relates to a designation of a parsonage allowance by an employing church or other qualified organization.

M.A. Warnke, DC Ky., 86-2 USTC ¶ 9570, 641 FSupp 1083.

An individual who was paid a salary but was not furnished with a parsonage could not exclude an amount as allowance for rent and utilities because there was no designation of a rental allowance in the amount of salary paid to him.

R.R. Eden, 41 TC 605, Dec. 26,637.

Standard Federal Tax Reports   **Reg. § 1.107-1(c)**   **¶ 6852.07**

Exhibit 69. Parsonages and Rental Allowances Furnished to Ministers of the Gospel: CCH Explanation, [1999] 2 Stand. Fed. Tax Rep. (CCH) ¶ 6852.01.

BNA's digests for *Fair Employment Practices* have more than twenty distinct subdivisions, including classifications for specific issues such as union liability, constructive discharge, and same-sex harassment.

The cases in most topical reporters can be updated using KeyCite or Shepard's Citations. In print, several specialized citators include coverage of these reporters. *Shepard's Environmental Law Citations*, for example, covers decisions published in BNA's *Environment Cases* and the Environmental Law Institute's *Environmental Law Reporter*, and *Shepard's Labor Law Citations* provides coverage of several reporters including CCH's *Employment Practices Decisions* and BNA's *Fair Employment Practice Cases*.

One of the most valuable functions of a looseleaf service is that it provides coverage of proposed legislation, pending litigation, and other developments in the area covered. Approaches vary from service to service. *Fair Employment Practices* includes a biweekly *Summary of Latest Developments* newsletter. *Standard Federal Tax Reports* has several current awareness approaches, including weekly "CCH Comments" articles, a *Taxes on Parade* newsletter, and extra issues providing the text of important new documents such as pending bills and committee reports.

Detailed, regularly updated indexes provide fast and convenient access to looseleaf services. A typical service includes several kinds of indexes. The general or *topical index* provides detailed subject access. In many services, an additional index known as a "Current Topical Index" or "Latest Additions to Topical Index" covers new material between the periodic recompilations of the main index.

Cumulating services such as BNA's *Antitrust & Trade Regulation Report* or *Family Law Reporter* generally have just one index, which is updated every two or three months. Exhibit 70 shows a page from the topical index for *Standard Federal Tax Reports*, with several references under "Clergy" to the material shown in Exhibits 68 and 69. Note that the index includes very detailed references to specific annotations.

Finding lists provide direct references to particular statutes, regulations, or cases by their citations. These can be particularly useful in searching for numerically designated agency materials, such as IRS rulings or SEC releases. Some of these lists also serve as citator services, providing information on the current validity of materials listed.

Note that Exhibits 68 and 69 have both page numbers at the top (19,757 and 19,759) and paragraph numbers at the bottom (¶ 6851 and ¶ 6852.07). It is easy to be misled by the page numbers, but remember that they are used only for filing purposes and that the paragraph numbers are the points of reference to the material cited in the index and finding lists.

Another device used in some services is the *cumulative index*. This is not a subject index but a tool providing cross-references from the main body of the service to current material. Under listings by paragraph number, cumulative indexes update each topic with leads to new materials which have not yet been incorporated into the main discussion. Exhibit 71 shows a page from the Cumulative Index in *Standard Federal Tax Reports*, including references under code section 107 (¶ 6852) to two Revenue Procedures and a Tax Court decision.

38 9-16-99 **Topical Index** **10,337**

References are to paragraph (¶) numbers.

CLERGY—continued
. educational activities 6852.18
. educational expenses 8632.203
. foreign earned income 32,599.30
. hospital services 6852.17
. interest paid
. . mortgage . . 9402.045; 9402.48; 14,054.0236
. investment tax credit 4580.92
. Jewish cantor 6852.01; 6852.19
. meals and lodging 7222.73; 8523.2748
. minister of the gospel, defined
. . charitable activities 6852.16
. . educational activities 6852.18
. . hospital services 6852.17
. . Jewish cantor 6852.01; 6852.19
. . ministerial functions 6852.01; 6852.21
. . nonreligious activities 6852.01
. . nursing home services 6852.23
. . ordination 6852.25
. . prison chaplain 6852.26
. . retired minister 6852.27
. . sacerdotal function 6852.28
. . services performed away from home
.... 6852.29
. . surviving spouse 6852.31
. . traveling evangelist 6852.01
. Ministerial functions 6852.01; 6852.21
. missionaries, gross income 5504.4897
. nonprofit activities 12,177.1457
. nonreligious activities 6852.01
. nursing home services 6852.23
. ordination 6852.25
. parsonage rental allowance
. . advance rulings 6852.023
. . cash payments 6852.01
. . expenses, deductibility 14,054.40
. . mortgage interest, deductibility
.... 14,054.0236
. . real property taxes, deductibility
.... 14,054.0236
. . unexpended funds 6852.70
↘ . parsonage rental value ...... 6850—6852.53
. . designation required 6852.07
. . effect of rental allowance on deductions
for residence 14,054.0236; 14,054.05
. . expenses paid 6852.10
. . interest and taxes, deductibility . 6852.01—
6852.06
. . minister of the gospel, defined . . 6852.16—
6852.31
. . other compensation 6852.34
. . pension plan benefits 17,508.122
. . pension plans 6852.35
. . property donated by minister 6852.37
. . questions and answers 6852.33
. . reasonable allowance 6852.40
. . rental to third party 6852.50
. prison chaplain 6852.26
. retired minister 6852.27
. retirement benefits not subject to
self-employment tax . . . 32,560; 32,578.068
. sacerdotal function 6852.28
. self-employed ministers, retirement plans
.... 18,330; 18,347.117
. . church plans 19,150; 19,157A.045
. self-employment tax—see Self-employment
tax: ministers or members of religious
orders
. services performed away from home
.... 6852.29
. survivors of
. . election as to social security coverage
.... 32,560
. . parsonage rental value 6852.31
. taxes paid 9502.49
. trade or business
. . self-employment tax 32,585
. traveling evangelist 6852.01

CLERGY—continued
. traveling expenses 8550.08
. 2% floor on itemized deductions . . . 6064.25
. withholding of tax on wages . 33,502; 33,522;
33,533.05; 33,533.25

Clerical errors on returns, abatement of assessment 37,545; 37,549.01

Clerical help, investors 12,523.0134

Clerk of Courts
cash receipts of more than $10,000,
information returns 36,200; 36,202;
36,203.05

***Clifford* rule trusts**—see also Grantor trusts
.... 24,683.01—24,683.05
. interest paid 9104.322
. tax planning, individuals 670.11

Climate control system, investment tax credit
.... 4580.516

Clinic
association taxable as corporation
.... 43,084.57
. low-income taxpayers 42,816M.01

Closed banks—see Banks and banking:
insolvent banks

Closed tax cases, reopening 43,352.08

Closed transactions, losses . 9805.01; 9902.2455

Closely connected persons, entertainment expenses 14,408A.025

Closely held corporations—see Corporations:
closely held

CLOSING AGREEMENTS . . . 41,080—41,090.70;
43,282.0138; 43,364—43,368
. Accelerated Issue Resolution (AIR)
.... 43,368.015
. annulment 41,080
. approval 41,080; 41,081; 43,364
. . Acting Secretary of Treasury . . . 41,090.11
. authority to enter 41,080; 41,090.028
. authorization 41,080
. basis 41,090.13
. carryovers 41,090.16
. consideration 41,090.17
. deficiency dividend credit, personal holding
companies 23,290
. deficiency notice coupled with . . . 37,549.21
. defined contribution plans, restorative
payments 41,090.50
. detrimental reliance 41,090.19
. dissolved corporation 41,090.21
. district courts 41,605.0186
. earnings and profits 15,612.695
. effect .... 43,368; 43,368.01—43,368.05
. error in revenue agent's report . . . 41,090.40
. estates 41,090.24
. estoppel 41,090.26
. examination of books 41,090.15
. false statements in connection with,
penalties 41,333.01
. finality ..... 41,080; 41,090.014; 41,090.279—
41,090.326
. Form 4549 .... 41,090.0275
. forms prescribed . . . 41,090.016; 41,090.0275;
43,364
. fraud 41,080; 41,090.014; 41,090.336
. interest on overpayment, recovery
.... 41,090.66
. letter for IRS agent distinguished . 41,090.19
. lump-sum settlement 41,090.66
. misrepresentation of fact 41,090.40
. mistakes 41,090.014

Standard Federal Tax Reports **CLO**

Exhibit 70. Topical Index, [1999 Index] Stand. Fed. Tax Rep. (CCH) 10,201, 10,337.

43 10-21-99 **Cumulative Index to 1999 Developments** **75,321**

(For Reports 1-42)

(See also Cumulative Index at page 75,251.)

From Compilation Paragraph No.			To New Development Paragraph No.
	.968	*Brewer* aff'd, CA-9 (unpub. op.)—Settlement proceeds paid to taxpayer's attorney as legal fees not excludable from income	50,276
	.968	Brown aff'd, CA-6 (unpub. op.)—Back pay award includible in gross income	50,544
	.968	*Dewey* aff'd, CA-10 (unpub. op.)—ADEA settlement proceeds includible in income	50,275
	.971	*Ball* aff'd, CA-5—Separation payments included in gross income	50,195
	.971	Gerbec aff'd, rev'd and rem'd, CA-6—Portions of ERISA settlement representing compensation for personal injuries excludable from income	50,194
		Code Sec. 105—Amounts received under accident and health plans	
6702	.01	Rebate program for employee out-of-pocket medical expenses not includible—Comment	48,725B
	.01	VEBA health insurance benefits for domestic partners includible in employee's gross income—Letter Ruling	47,276
	.21	*Hernandez* aff'd, CA-9 (unpub. op.)—Disability benefits includible in income	50,305
	.22	Rev. Procs. 98-3 and 96-56 superseded—Rev. Proc.	46,250
	.245	*Kees*, TCM—Former employee's disability benefits includible in income	47,877
	.37	*Chernik*, TCM—No exclusion for disability benefits attributable to contributions by employer	48,183
	.45	*Chernik*, TCM—Benefits calculated with reference to salary and years of service, not to type of injury	48,183
	.45	*Hernandez* aff'd, CA-9 (unpub. op.)—Disability benefits includible in income	50,305
	.48	*Hernandez* aff'd, CA-9 (unpub. op.)—Disability benefits includible in income	50,305
	.48	*Kees*, TCM—Former employee's disability benefits includible in income	47,877
	.48	*Stolte*, TCM—Disability payments received by physically impaired surgeon excludable from gross income	48,132
	.50	*Stolte*, TCM—Disability payments received by physically impaired surgeon excludable from gross income	48,132
	.52	*Chernik*, TCM—No exclusion for disability benefits attributable to contributions by employer	48,183
	.54	*Hernandez* aff'd, CA-9 (unpub. op.)—Disability benefits includible in income	50,305
	.72	Rev. Procs. 98-3 and 96-56 superseded—Rev. Proc.	46,250
6709	.18	Rev. Proc. 98-3 amplified—Rev. Proc.	46,057
6712	.20	Rev. Proc. 98-3 amplified—Rev. Proc.	46,057
		Code Sec. 106—Contributions by employer to accident and health plans	
6803	.01	VEBA health insurance benefits for domestic partners includible in employee's gross income—Letter Ruling	47,276
	.193	Employer contributions were benefits; excludable from employees' gross income—Letter Ruling	47,461
		Code Sec. 107—Rental value of parsonages	
6852	.023	Rev. Proc. 98-3 amplified—Rev. Proc.	46,057
	.023	Rev. Procs. 98-3 and 96-56 superseded—Rev. Proc.	46,250
	.07	*Logie*, TCM—Undesignated parsonage allowance not excludible or deductible	47,691
		Code Sec. 108—Income from discharge of indebtedness	
7010	.012	Stock issued in cancellation of indebtedness was not contribution to capital—Letter Ruling	47,302
	.014	*Eberle*, TCM—Shareholder could not increase stock basis by S corporation's COD income	48,151
	.014	*Nelson* aff'd, CA-10—S corporation's excludable debt discharge income did not increase shareholders' basis in stock	50,646
	.014	S shareholder's basis not increased by exempt DOI income—Comment	48,732B
	.014	Winn (here *Gitlitz*) aff'd, CA-10—S corporation's excludable debt discharge income did not increse shareholders' basis in stock	50,645
	.0275	IRS fails to properly compute DOI income on mortgage default—Comment	48,727A
	.0275	*Johnson*, TCM—Retired teacher taxable on debt discharge income from foreclosure of residence	48,010
	.037	*Brickman*, TCM—Taxpayers had to reduce NOL by debt discharge income excused for insolvency	47,644
	.037	FMV of assets exempt from creditor's claims includible in determining insolvency—Letter Ruling	47,456
	.037	IRS determines insolvency by including assets exempt from creditors—Comment	48,740A
	.037	*Merkel* aff'd, CA-9—Insolvency exclusion did not apply to debt discharge income	50,848
	.056	*Preslar* rev'd and rem'd, CA-10—Taxpayer realized income on discharge of undisputed debt	50,258
	.056	Tenth Circuit narrows disputed debt exception to COD income—Comment	48,716A
	.063	*Preslar* rev'd and rem'd, CA-10—Taxpayer realized income on third-party lender's discharge of debt	50,258
	.063	Tenth Circuit narrows disputed debt exception to COD income—Comment	48,716A
	.083	*Conviser*, TCM—Shareholder could not increase basis in stock by COD income realized by S corporation	47,884
	.083	*Cronin*, TCM (¶47,858)—S corporation owner could not increase stock basis by COD income realized by insolvent entity. Taxpayer on appeal to CA-7.	
	.083	*Eberle*, TCM—Shareholder could not increase stock basis by S corporation's COD income	48,151
	.083	*Farley*, DC Pa.—Shareholders of insolvent S corporations could not increase stock basis by COD income	50,370
	.083	Gaudiano, TCM (¶47,713)—Shareholders could not increase stock bases by S corporation's excluded COD income. Taxpayer on appeal to CA-6.	

99(19) CCH—Standard Federal Tax Reports **¶7010**

Exhibit 71. Cumulative Index to 1999 Developments for Reports 1–42, [1999] 19 Stand. Fed. Tax Rep. (CCH) 75,301, 75,321 (Oct. 21, 1999).

Detailed instructions, often entitled "How to Use This Reporter" or "About This Publication," are frequently provided at the beginning of the first volume of a looseleaf service. A particular service may include features that appear confusing at first but are very useful to the experienced researcher. These instructions are often neglected by researchers, but a few moments of orientation can save considerable time and frustration.

Because looseleaf services differ depending on the subject matter and the publisher's approach, it is difficult to generalize about the best research procedures. The following steps, however, are applicable to most services:

1. Determine whether a looseleaf service is available for the subject.

2. Obtain an adequate working orientation by perusing the instructions at the front of the service.

3. Use the service's indexes to locate the specific material needed for the problem. Most often this means beginning in the topical index by subject. A finding list can be used if you already have a reference to a specific relevant document (such as an order, regulation, or ruling).

4. Study the texts of the relevant primary sources, as well as the service's editorial explanations and commentary.

5. Follow research leads suggested by cross-references to cases and other documents.

6. Update your research results by checking the cumulative or "latest additions" indexes for recent materials, and by using a citator if available.

§ 9–3. TOPICAL ELECTRONIC RESOURCES

Looseleaf services remain the preferred research tools of many specialists, and they are the topical resources most likely to be available to public law library patrons. An increasing number of lawyers and other researchers, however, rely on electronic services to perform similar functions. Like looseleaf services, topical CD or Internet systems provide both explanatory or analytical material and the texts of primary sources under discussion. Key-word searching provides more flexibility than looseleaf indexes, and hypertext links allow researchers to move conveniently back and forth between different types of documents. Some of the information available through these services is only issued electronically, but many online services have counterparts in print. The *Fair Employment Practices* and *Standard Federal Tax Reports* services discussed in the preceding section, for example, are also available in both CD and Internet versions.

CD services eliminate the need for laborious filing of replacement pages, but new discs are generally not issued as frequently as looseleaf supplements. CD users must usually finish updating their research through the online systems or other means. Internet-based services, on the other hand, can be constantly updated without need for new discs or other supplementation. Exhibit 72 shows part of the same explanation already seen in Exhibit 69, as retrieved from the CCH Internet Tax Research Net-Work <tax.cch.com>. The text is the same in both sources, but this version includes underlined links to code sections, revenue rulings, and other documents.

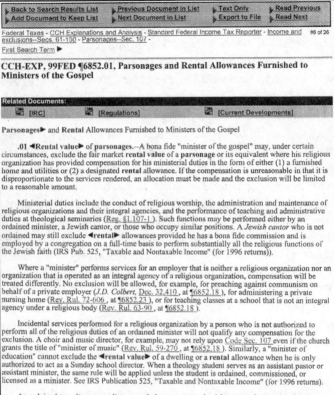

Back to Search Results List   Previous Document in List   Text Only   Read Previous
Add Document to Keep List   Next Document in List   Export to File   Read Next

Federal Taxes - CCH Explanations and Analysis - Standard Federal Income Tax Reporter - Income and   #6 of 26
exclusions--Secs. 61-150 - Parsonages--Sec. 107 -
First Search Term ▶

CCH-EXP, 99FED ¶6852.01, Parsonages and Rental Allowances Furnished to Ministers of the Gospel

Related Documents:

    [IRC]   [Regulations]   [Current Developments]

Parsonages▶ and Rental Allowances Furnished to Ministers of the Gospel

.01 ◀Rental value▶ of parsonages.--A bona fide "minister of the gospel" may, under certain circumstances, exclude the fair market rental value of a parsonage or its equivalent where his religious organization has provided compensation for his ministerial duties in the form of either (1) a furnished home and utilities or (2) a designated rental allowance. If the compensation is unreasonable in that it is disproportionate to the services rendered, an allocation must be made and the exclusion will be limited to a reasonable amount.

Ministerial duties include the conduct of religious worship, the administration and maintenance of religious organizations and their integral agencies, and the performance of teaching and administrative duties at theological seminaries (Reg. §1.107-1). Such functions may be performed either by an ordained minister, a Jewish cantor, or those who occupy similar positions. A Jewish cantor who is not ordained may still exclude ◀rental▶ allowances provided he has a bona fide commission and is employed by a congregation on a full-time basis to perform substantially all the religious functions of the Jewish faith (IRS Pub. 525, "Taxable and Nontaxable Income" (for 1996 returns)).

Where a "minister" performs services for an employer that is neither a religious organization nor an organization that is operated as an integral agency of a religious organization, compensation will be treated differently. No exclusion will be allowed, for example, for preaching against communism on behalf of a private employer (J.D. Colbert, Dec. 32,410, at ¶6852.18), for administering a private nursing home (Rev. Rul. 72-606, at ¶6852.23), or for teaching classes at a school that is not an integral agency under a religious body (Rev. Rul. 63-90, at ¶6852.18).

Incidental services performed for a religious organization by a person who is not authorized to perform all of the religious duties of an ordained minister will not qualify any compensation for the exclusion. A choir and music director, for example, may not rely upon Code Sec. 107 even if the church grants the title of "minister of music" (Rev. Rul. 59-270, at ¶6852.18). Similarly, a "minister of education" cannot exclude the ◀rental value▶ of a dwelling or a rental allowance when he is only authorized to act as a Sunday school director. When a theology student serves as an assistant pastor or assistant minister, the same rule will be applied unless the student is ordained, commissioned, or licensed as a minister. See IRS Publication 525, "Taxable and Nontaxable Income" (for 1996 returns).

An ordained traveling evangelist can exclude amounts received from out-of-town churches that are designated as ◀rental▶ allowances, provided the amounts are actually used to maintain his permanent home (Rev. Rul. 64-326, at ¶6852.29). However, if a minister purchases a house in his own name and rents it out while traveling, the portion of the rental allowance for the portion of the year in which the residence was rented to others is not excludable (Rev. Rul. 72-588, at ¶6852.50).

Cash payments are excludable only when they are officially designated as a ◀rental▶ allowance by the employer before they are paid. When they are allowed as an exclusion, they are not limited to the

Exhibit 72. CCH–EXP, 99FED ¶6852.01, Parsonages and Rental Allowances Furnished to Ministers of the Gospel, CCH Internet Tax Research Network <tax.cch.com>.

The annual *Directory of Law–Related CD–ROMs* provides an extensive listing of more than 1,500 electronic services. The directory's focus is CDs, but it also indicates which services listed are available on the Internet. Appendix C in this volume, listing major services, includes coverage of both CD and Internet services.

The online databases have numerous topical electronic libraries which combine cases, statutes, regulations, and other sources in specialized databases or libraries. They also provide access to many of the major looseleaf services. Most of BNA's weekly services, for example, are available through both Westlaw and Lexis–Nexis, as is the *Environmental Law Reporter*. The listing in Appendix C indicates a service's availability through the major database systems.

§ 9–4. CURRENT AWARENESS SOURCES

It is essential that lawyers be aware of activity in their areas of expertise, not just new court decisions but also legislative and regulatory changes. Several approaches are available to keep on top of current developments, recent scholarly literature, and new issues.

a. Legal Newsletters and Newspapers

Looseleaf services are often excellent sources of information about current developments in particular fields. Many include newsletters summarizing developments; the *Fair Employment Practices* and *Standard Federal Tax Reports* newsletters noted in § 9–2 are just two examples.

A large number of separate current awareness newsletters are also published for this express purpose. Some are available free, but many of these newsletters are quite

expensive. Weekly newsletters may cost $1000 or more per year. Some newsletters are delivered by fax or e-mail rather than print. Because specialized newsletters often have a limited circulation, they may be difficult for nonsubscribers to locate in academic or public law libraries. But they may nonetheless be the best available sources for learning about newly developing areas of law. One reason for this is that newsletters are often the forum through which practitioners in a very specialized area share information. They may, for example, print photocopies of trial court decisions that will never be published in the regular court reports.

Among the leading newsletter publishers are several companies that make their products available through Westlaw and Lexis–Nexis. In addition to its looseleaf services, BNA publishes more than two dozen daily newsletters in areas such as environmental law, labor law, and taxation. Some of these are available in print, but others are published only in electronic versions. Andrews Publications and Mealeys Publications both publish several newsletters covering current areas of litigation such as latex allergies and reinsurance coverage. These are available either through the online databases or directly from the publishers.

In addition, a growing number of law firms produce newsletters for their clients and other readers. These may serve as marketing tools for their firms, but many also provide useful information about developing areas of law. Firm newsletters are often available through law firm websites.

The leading source for identifying available newsletters is the annual *Legal Newsletters in Print*. This directory

describes more than 2,200 newsletters, with information about subscription prices and Internet access. A subject index provides topical access to its listings. Newsletter Access <www.newsletteraccess.com> lists fewer legal newsletters but is available on the Internet.

News on developments in the law is also available from a number of daily and weekly legal newspapers. These vary considerably in coverage. Some serve simply as vehicles for local court calendars and legal announcements, but others include new court decisions and articles on developing legal topics. Westlaw and Lexis–Nexis both provide access to several daily newspapers, including the *Chicago Daily Law Bulletin* and the *New York Law Journal*. They also have two national weekly newspapers, the *National Law Journal* and *Legal Times*, as well as numerous other local and regional legal newspapers.

Most legal newspapers now have Internet sites as well; one of the leading sources is Law News Network <www.law.com>, with stories from the *National Law Journal* and its affiliated regional newspapers. FindLaw <www.findlaw.com/15reference/legalnews.html> lists several other news sources and has its own page of Reuters wire service stories on legal topics, arranged by subject.

b.   Tables of Contents Services

Specialists need to know about scholarly as well as legal developments. A new article directly on a topic of concern may be published in any of the hundreds of law reviews and other legal journals published in this country. Some lawyers scan new issues of journals in their area of expertise, but more systematic ways of surveying the vast majority of journal literature are also available.

The principal publication providing information about new journal issues is *Current Index to Legal Periodicals*, published weekly by the University of Washington's Marian Gould Gallagher Law Library. This index covers nearly 500 law reviews, indexing articles under about 100 subject headings and listing each issue's table of contents. The index can be searched online through Westlaw, and subscribers can receive customized weekly e-mail limited to particular subjects and journal titles. Further information is available on the Web <lib.law.washington.edu/cilp/cilp.html>.

The Tarlton Law Library at the University of Texas also provides table of contents access to more than 750 law-related journals, free on the Web and updated daily <tarlton.law.utexas.edu/tallons/content_search.html>. The Texas site does not index articles by subject, but keyword searching is available.

Some specialists can rely on services such as the Social Science Research Network (SSRN) <www.ssrn.com> to learn of new scholarly work in their area. This network serves as a forum for scholars in various disciplines, including law, to share recent articles and works-in-progress. New abstracts are delivered to subscribers by e-mail, and a searchable Internet archive includes several thousand downloadable full-text documents.

c. Mailing Lists

One of the most effective ways to keep on top of developments in a particular area, or to seek assistance with difficult research issues, is to subscribe to an e-mail list in the area. Some lists are used for dissemination of information by organizations or government agencies, while others are designed for specialists, professors, and

others with an interest in an area to share news and ideas. Posing questions to a list often yields results that would otherwise elude most researchers. Chances are that some list subscriber may be able to help with a thorny legal issue or can identify a source for an obscure document. Older messages to a list, if available in a searchable Internet archive, may form a valuable repository of information in the area.

Hundreds of mailing lists on legal topics are maintained. The most extensive guide to these sources, covering more than 1,200 law-related lists, is Lyonette Louis–Jacques's Law Lists <www.lib.uchicago.edu/cgi-bin/law-lists>. This searchable database provides information about the scope of each list, instructions for subscribing, and links to archives on the Web.

Nonlegal lists can also provide relevant information, of course, so more general directories such as the Directory of Scholarly and Professional E–Conferences <www.n2h2.com/KOVACS/> or Topica <www.topica.com> may also be useful.

Several government agencies have mailing lists with e-mail notification of new developments. These include several dozen EPA lists <www.epa.gov/epahome/list.serv.htm>, the FCC Daily Digest <www.fcc.gov/Daily_Releases/Daily_Digest/>, and the IRS Digital Dispatch <www.irs.ustreas.gov/prod/help/newmail/maillist.html>. Agency websites in other areas may provide information about similar lists in other areas.

§ 9–5. SPECIALIZED INDEXES AND GUIDES

Law journals were introduced in Chapter 2, but that discussion focused on academic law reviews and the

general *Index to Legal Periodicals and Books* and *Legal Resource Index*. More specialized publications and indexes are also available.

Besides the numerous topical law reviews edited by students at almost every law school, specialized journals are issued by bar associations and commercial publishers. Articles in these journals tend to be shorter and more practical than those found in academic law reviews, often focusing on current developments of interest to practicing lawyers. Among the most respected of the specialized bar journals are several published by sections of the American Bar Association.

A useful source for identifying publications in a particular specialty is Anderson's Directory of Law Reviews and Scholarly Legal Publications <www.andersonpublishing. com/lawschool/directory/>, which lists 600 journals by subject. It provides separate listing of student-edited journals and non-student-edited peer review and trade journals.

While the major periodical indexes provide extensive coverage, several specialized indexes are also available. Taxation has two major indexes: CCH's *Federal Tax Articles* (1969–date, monthly), with abstracts of journal articles arranged by Internal Revenue Code section; and *Index to Federal Tax Articles* (1975–date, quarterly), a subject/author index with retrospective coverage back to 1913. *Environmental Law Reporter* includes a monthly "Journal Literature" feature listing new law review articles by subject. *Criminal Justice Periodicals Index* was

published in print form from 1975 to 1998, but is now available only online through such suppliers as Dialog, ProQuest, or Westlaw.

For research in legal history, the predecessor to the *Index to Legal Periodicals*, entitled *Index to Legal Periodical Literature* (6 vols., 1888–1939), may be of use. This index covers articles as far back as 1770, and is sometimes called the Jones–Chipman index after the names of its editors. Another useful source for legal historians is Kermit Hall, *A Comprehensive Bibliography of American Constitutional and Legal History* (7 vols., 1984–91), which lists books and articles dealing with legal history and published since 1896.

A general research guide such as this *Nutshell* cannot examine the idiosyncracies of specialized areas of law, but guides to specific topics are available. Many guides (sometimes called "pathfinders") have been published in legal bibliography journals such as *Law Library Journal* and *Legal Reference Services Quarterly*, and a subject listing of specialized guides on the Internet is available from the University of Akron Law Library <www.uakron.edu/law/richert/index1.html>.

Tax research is the focus of several published works, including Gail Levin Richmond, *Federal Tax Research: Guide to Materials and Techniques* (5th ed., 1997), and Barbara H. Karlin, *Tax Research* (2000). Leah Chanin, ed., *Specialized Legal Research* (1987–date), covers more than a dozen topics, with chapters on admiralty, banking law, copyright, customs, environmental law, government contracts, immigration, income tax, labor and employment law, military and veterans law, patents and trade-

marks, securities regulation, and the Uniform Commercial Code. The volume also includes a bibliography of other specialized legal research sources.

§ 9–6. CONCLUSION

Looseleaf and electronic services, current awareness tools, and other specialized materials are some of the most important resources in the arsenal of practicing lawyers. Unlike more general sources such as court reports and codes, these materials are not published in one convenient and standardized format. Learning what resources are available in a particular area may require some preliminary research into indexes and directories, and it may take some time to master these specialized resources. But they can lead directly to more effective research and help you anticipate legal developments.

CHAPTER 10

REFERENCE RESOURCES

---

§ 10–1.   INTRODUCTION

This brief chapter serves two purposes. First, it looks at legal resources designed to provide answers to relatively simple questions. These are not sources for lengthy legal analysis but for telephone numbers, addresses, facts, and statistics. Knowing how to find this information quickly can save valuable time for other aspects of legal research.

The chapter also introduces more general reference sources for interdisciplinary research. Many law students focus so intently on legal literature that they neglect information from other disciplines. General sources, however, can provide essential background information, and scholarship in the sciences and social sciences can provide valuable perspectives in analyzing legal issues.

Some reference resources have been discussed in earlier chapters. Dictionaries and related research aids were covered in Chapter 1, at pages 10-13, and multistate surveys and almanacs such as the *Martindale-Hubbell Law Digest* were discussed in Chapter 5, at pages 162-164.

285

There remain, however, other reference materials with which lawyers need to be familiar.

§ 10–2. LEGAL DIRECTORIES

Chapters 6 through 8 discussed directories covering federal and state governments, including legislatures, administrative agencies, and courts. The law does not live by government alone, however, and directories of lawyers and legal organizations can also be valuable sources of information. Legal directories provide background information on other lawyers and can help in establishing contacts within the profession. Organizations interested in particular issues may provide networking opportunities or insights unavailable in any printed or electronic sources.

Numerous directories provide contact and biographical information for lawyers. Most focus on individual states or particular specialties, but two comprehensive directories of the legal profession are available. They are published by divisions of the parent companies of Lexis–Nexis and Westlaw, and each covers close to a million lawyers. Neither, however, includes every single lawyer in the country.

The more established source, and the only one available in print format, is the *Martindale-Hubbell Law Directory*. Eighteen volumes of this annual publication contain listings of lawyers and law firms, arranged by state and city. At the beginning of each volume are blue pages containing "Practice Profiles," with a one-line entry for each lawyer indicating date of birth, date of admission to practice, college, law school, and address or affiliation. "Professional Biographies" provide fuller descriptions of those lawyers and firms who purchase space beyond the

simple alphabetical listings. The set is accompanied by alphabetical and areas of practice indexes. Lawyers in corporate law departments are listed geographically and have fuller listings in a separate *Martindale-Hubbell Corporate Law Directory*; selected lawyers in other countries are covered by *Martindale-Hubbell International Law Directory*, which has its own alphabetical and practice indexes.

One useful feature of *Martindale-Hubbell* is its rating system, which evaluates U.S. lawyers based on interviews with their peers. Legal ability ratings range from A (Very High to Preeminent) to C (Good to High), and these are published only if accompanied by an ethical standards rating of V (Very High). Ratings are not provided for all lawyers listed in the directory.

The *Martindale-Hubbell Law Directory* is available on CD–ROM, online through Lexis–Nexis, and on the Internet as the Martindale–Hubbell Lawyer Locator <www.martindale.com/locator/>. A related site designed for clients and the public, lawyers.com <www.lawyers.com>, is limited to lawyers and firms with paid listings. Neither Internet site, unfortunately, includes lawyer ratings.

The other comprehensive directory of attorneys, West Legal Directory (WLD), is published only electronically on CD–ROM, through Westlaw, and on the Internet <www.lawoffice.com>. Like *Martindale-Hubbell*, WLD has both simple free listings and more extensive paid entries. Coverage in the two sources is comparable, although only WLD includes telephone numbers in its basic listings.

Several other national directories of lawyers and law firms are available, although none is as comprehensive as *Martindale-Hubbell* or WLD. *Who's Who in American*

Law (biennial) is a useful source of biographical information on prominent attorneys and legal scholars, and the *Law Firms Yellow Book* (semiannual) provides information on the management and recruiting personnel of major law firms. Two annual publications specifically designed for job-seeking law students are the National Association for Law Placement's *Directory of Legal Employers* (also available on Lexis–Nexis), with basic data on firms and their attorneys, and *The Insider's Guide to Law Firms*, with narrative entries on large law firms in major cities.

Law firm websites usually include information about the firms' attorneys and their practices. Internet addresses are available from *Martindale-Hubbell*, WLD, and several web-based directories. Nearly 100 local, national, and international directories are available through FindLaw <www.findlaw.com/14firms/>, which also has its own listings alphabetically, by location, and by practice area.

Other directories focus on attorneys working outside law firms. *Directory of Corporate Counsel* (2 vols., annual) is similar in scope to the *Martindale-Hubbell Corporate Law Directory*, with biographical information on lawyers working for corporations and nonprofit organizations. Directories of public interest and government law offices include *Directory of Legal Aid and Defender Offices in the United States* and *National Directory of Prosecuting Attorneys* (both biennial).

Interest groups, professional organizations, and trade associations can be invaluable sources of information in

their areas of concern. Links to legal organization websites, including state bar associations, are available
from several websites including FindLawand Martindale–Hubbell <www.
martindale.com/profession/barassoc/us.cfm>. Broader
coverage of legal and nonlegal organizations is provided
by the *Encyclopedia of Associations* (3 vols., annual),
with contact information for more than 20,000 national
organizations. Exhibit 73 shows entries for just two of
the listed organizations of attorneys. Note that the
entries include website addresses, if available, and information on the organizations' publications and
meetings. The *Encyclopedia of Associations* is also available online through both Westlaw and Lexis–Nexis, and
on CD–ROM and the Internet <www.galegroup.com> as
Associations Unlimited. Another directory, *National
Trade and Professional Associations of the United States*
(annual), is less extensive than the *Encyclopedia of
Associations* but just as useful for finding addresses and
telephone numbers of business-related organizations.

While most directories are somewhat specialized, a few
try to provide answers to a wider range of inquiries. *Law
and Legal Information Directory* (biennial) is a large
volume covering legal organizations and bar associations
as well as other resources such as law libraries, lawyer
referral services, and a variety of federal and state
government agencies. A handier desktop work by Arlene
L. Eis, *The Legal Researcher's Desk Reference* (biennial),
has an impressive array of directory information including government offices, courts, and bar associations, and

---

Attorneys   ★4893★

★4891★   NATIONAL ASSOCIATION OF RETAIL COLLECTION ATTORNEYS (NARCA)
1515 N. Warson, Ste. 109
St. Louis, MO 63132
Marti Revor, Exec. Officer
TF: (800)633-6069
FX: (314)428-6190
E-mail: narca@primary.net
Website: http://www.narca.com
Founded: 1993. **Members:** 600. **Membership Dues:** large law firms, $325 (annual) ● small law firms, $250 (annual). **Staff:** 2. **Budget:** $200,000. **State Groups:** 5. **Languages:** English. Collection law firms. Works to assist consumer collection law firms and creditors. Establishes performance standards; lobbies for creditors' rights legislation; offers electronic forwarding of claims (NARCA-NET); provides collection support; conducts educational programs. **Telecommunication Services:** phone referral service.
Publications: *NARCA Newsletter*, quarterly. Advertising: accepted ● Membership Directory, annual. Circulation: 6,500.
Conventions/Meetings: convention (exhibits) - 3/year.

★4892★   NATIONAL ASSOCIATION OF WOMEN LAWYERS (NAWL)
750 N. Lake Shore Dr.
Chicago, IL 60611
Peggy L. Golden, Exec.Dir.
PH: (312)988-6186
Founded: 1911. **Members:** 1,200. **Staff:** 1. **Languages:** English. Membership is open to any person who is a member in good standing of the bar of any state or U.S. territory, any non-U.S. legal professional (attorney or judge), any prospective attorney currently attending law school, and any state or local bar or law school association with compatible objectives. **Awards:** Outstanding Law Student Program. Frequency: annual. Type: recognition ● Outstanding Member. Frequency: annual. Type: recognition ● Service Award. Frequency: annual. Type: recognition ● Toch Award. Frequency: annual. Type: recognition. **Affiliated With:** American Bar Association; International Bar Association; International Federation of Women Lawyers. **Absorbed:** Women Lawyers Club.
Publications: *Presidents Newsletter*, quarterly. For members only. Advertising: not accepted ● *Women Lawyer's Journal*, quarterly. Magazine. Publishes articles addressing current issues in domestic and foreign law. Price: $16.00/year. ISSN: 0473-7468. Advertising: accepted.
Conventions/Meetings: annual conference ● annual Midyear Conference ● annual regional meeting.

Exhibit 73.   Section 3: Legal, Governmental, Public Administration, and Military Organizations, 1 ENCYCLOPEDIA OF ASSOCIATIONS 525, 533 (35th ed. 1999).

also includes other resources such as state court organization charts and lists of Internet sites.

§ 10–3. STATISTICS

Lawyers need demographic and statistical information for many purposes, from preparing to cross-examine an expert witness to supporting a discrimination claim. Statistics are published in a variety of sources, some focused on legal matters and some more general.

Statistics on the legal system include data on courts, lawyers, and the criminal justice system. Information on court caseloads can be found in the Administrative Office of the U.S. Courts's annual *Judicial Business of the United States Courts* (also available online <www.uscourts.gov/publications.html>), and the National Center for State Courts' annual *State Court Caseload Statistics*. The composition of the U.S. legal profession is analyzed in *The Lawyer Statistical Report*, published periodically by the American Bar Foundation; the most recent report, published in 1999, covers the profession as of 1995.

Criminal statistics are more widely available, from both federal and state governments. Each year the U.S. Department of Justice publishes two major sources in print and on the Internet. The Federal Bureau of Investigation issues *Uniform Crime Reports* (also known as *Crime in the United States*) <www.fbi.gov/ucr.htm>, focusing on criminal activities, and the Bureau of Justice Statistics issues *Sourcebook of Criminal Justice Statistics* <www.ojp.usdoj.gov/bjs/>, providing a broader survey of the social and economic impacts of crime.

No. 333. First Professional Degrees Earned in Selected Professions: 1970 to 1996

[First professional degrees include degrees which require at least 6 years of college work for completion (including at least 2 years of preprofessional training). See Appendix III]

Type of degree and sex of recipient	1970	1975	1980	1985	1990	1992	1993	1994	1995	1996
Medicine (M.D.):										
Institutions conferring degrees.....	86	104	112	120	124	120	122	121	119	119
Degrees conferred, total.........	8,314	12,447	14,902	16,041	15,075	15,243	15,531	15,368	15,537	15,341
Percent to women...........	8.4	13.1	23.4	30.4	34.2	35.7	37.7	37.9	38.8	40.9
Dentistry (D.D.S. or D.M.D.):										
Institutions conferring degrees.....	48	52	58	59	57	52	55	53	53	53
Degrees conferred, total.........	3,718	4,773	5,258	5,339	4,100	3,593	3,605	3,787	3,897	3,697
Percent to women...........	0.9	3.1	13.3	20.7	30.9	32.3	33.9	38.5	36.4	35.8
Law (LL.B. or J.D.):										
Institutions conferring degrees.....	145	154	179	181	182	177	184	185	183	183
Degrees conferred, total.........	14,916	29,296	35,647	37,491	36,485	38,848	40,302	40,044	39,349	39,828
Percent to women...........	5.4	15.1	30.2	38.5	42.2	42.7	42.5	43.0	42.6	43.5
Theological (B.D., M.Div., M.H.L.):										
Institutions conferring degrees.....	(NA)	(NA)	(NA)	(NA)	(NA)	(NA)	(NA)	186	192	184
Degrees conferred, total.........	5,298	5,095	7,115	7,221	5,851	5,251	5,447	5,967	5,978	5,879
Percent to women...........	2.3	6.8	13.8	18.5	24.8	23.3	24.8	24.8	25.7	25.2

NA Not available.

Source: U.S. National Center for Education Statistics, *Digest of Education Statistics,* annual.

Exhibit 74. First Professional Degree Earned in Selected Professions: 1970 to 1996, U.S. BUREAU OF THE CENSUS, STATISTICAL ABSTRACT OF THE UNITED STATES 206 tbl. 333 (119th ed. 1999).

The *Statistical Abstract of the United States*, published annually by the Bureau of the Census in print, on CD–ROM, and on the Internet <www.census.gov/statab/www/>, is a general reference source with which any legal researcher should be familiar. It covers a wide range of economic and demographic statistics, and is particularly useful because it gives source information for each table. It thus serves as a convenient lead to agencies and publications with more extensive coverage of specific areas. Exhibit 74 shows a table from the *Statistical Abstract*, providing annual statistics on law school degrees conferred. Note that the table includes a source reference to *Digest of Education Statistics*, where more detailed information may be available. Another source for federal statistics is the Federal Interagency Council on Statistical Policy's FedStats website <www.fedstats.gov>, with links to numerous government statistical sources.

Yearbooks and annual reports of trade associations, labor unions, financial institutions, public interest groups, and government agencies generally contain statistical data relating to their work and interests. Access to these sources can be obtained through the CIS publications *American Statistics Index* (1973–date, covering U.S. government sources) and *Statistical Reference Index* (1980–date, covering state government and private sources). These are available on CD–ROM as *Statistical Masterfile* and on the Web as *CIS Statistical Universe*.

§ 10–4. NEWS AND BUSINESS INFORMATION

Any practicing lawyer must keep abreast of developments in business, politics, and society. Legal newspapers, discussed in Chapter 9, focus on law-related developments, but for a broader picture it is necessary to monitor more general sources such as the major newspapers or news websites. In addition to providing current awareness, news stories can also be rich sources for factual research or background information.

Two of the most convenient news sources for law students are Westlaw and Lexis–Nexis. Westlaw provides access to hundreds of newspapers, as well as wire services and business publications, by arrangement with Dow Jones Interactive and DIALOG; and Lexis–Nexis has a NEWS library with the text of newspapers, magazines, trade journals, newsletters, and wire services. The two systems have considerable overlap in coverage, with the major exceptions being the *Wall Street Journal* (Westlaw only) and the *New York Times* (retrospective coverage on Lexis–Nexis only). Other electronic sources of news abound, including websites for these newspa-

pers (<www.nyt.com> and <interactive.wsj.com>) and the Dow Jones Interactive website <www.djinteractive.com>.

Business developments are a major focus of research in news sources. Company information is also available through a number of other print and electronic directories and databases. The leading provider of data on both public and private businesses is Dun & Bradstreet, which publishes several directories as well as in-depth profiles of individual companies. D & B material is available through Westlaw and on the Web <www.dnb.com>, and Companies Online <www.companiesonline.com> provides free access to some D & B information. Other sources for company information include Hoover's Online <www.hoovers.com> and 1Jump <www.1jump.com>.

Publicly traded companies must submit a wide range of financial information to the Securities and Exchange Commission, much of which is available through the SEC's EDGAR (Electronic Data Gathering Analysis and Retrieval) system. EDGAR resources are available directly from the SEC <www.sec.gov/edgarhp.htm> and through several commercial services including Westlaw and Lexis–Nexis. Free Internet sites with enhanced EDGAR access include 10K Wizard <www.tenkwizard.com> and FreeEdgar <www.freeedgar.com>. Disclosure, the company that processes SEC filings, has extensive financial information on its Global Access website <www.disclosure.com/dga/>, and can also provide copies of materials not available online.

§ 10–5. INTERDISCIPLINARY RESEARCH

Legal research is rarely confined to the insular world of cases, statutes, and law review articles. It is important for researchers to be able to find information in a wide variety of disciplines.

Periodical indexes. Several indexes to nonlegal periodical literature can provide valuable leads. Some of these are specialized indexes in other disciplines, while others provide comprehensive coverage of a wide range of sources (including legal journals).

One of the simplest places to begin looking for material in nonlegal sources is *Index to Periodical Articles Related to Law* (1958–date, 6 vols. with quarterly updates). This index focuses on articles with legal content but excludes those covered in the standard legal periodical indexes. It covers popular magazines as well as scholarly journals.

Indexes from other disciplines such as *ABI/INFORM* (business and economics), *PAIS International* (public policy), or *PsycINFO* (psychology and related disciplines) may provide background information or interdisciplinary perspectives. A few indexes are available free on the Internet, such as the National Library of Medicine's *PubMed* and *Internet Grateful Med* versions of *MEDLINE*, the comprehensive index of biomedical journals <www.nlm.nih.gov/databases/freemedl.html>. Most, however, are accessible by subscription only. A number of indexes are available through Westlaw, and researchers with access to university libraries usually have access to many more, either in print, on CD, or through subscription websites.

The Institute for Scientific Information (ISI) publishes several citation indexes which function like Shepard's in other academic disciplines. They can be used to find articles citing a particular author or source, or to search for articles by author or keyword. The most useful for legal research may be *Social Sciences Citation Index* (covering 1966–date), which includes extensive coverage of legal journals. Others are *Science Citation Index* (1955–date) and *Arts & Humanities Citation Index* (1976–date). These are available on CD and online through several databases, including Westlaw, as *Scisearch*, *Social Scisearch*, and *Arts & Humanities Search*. ISI also publishes *Current Contents*, a weekly service providing the tables of contents of new scholarly journal issues, available in print or electronically; the *Social & Behavioral Sciences* edition includes numerous law-related titles.

One of the most extensive indexes is *ProQuest Direct* <www.umi.com/proquest/>, which covers more than 6,000 journals. Some articles are represented only by citations or abstracts, but many are available in full text or as scanned images of the original printed versions. *UnCoverWeb* <uncweb.carl.org> provides even more comprehensive coverage of current journal literature, with tables of contents information for nearly 18,000 journals. Searching is free, and articles available for electronic or fax delivery for a fee. Two subscription web services providing access to older journal articles are *Periodical Contents Index* (PCI) <pci.chadwyck.com>, covering several thousand journals back as far as 1770, and JSTOR <www.

jstor.org>, with full-text retrospective coverage of more than 100 major scholarly journals.

Online catalogs. A vast world of information lies beyond the online catalog of the local law library. Two of the best ways to tap into this world are through the huge bibliographic databases of the Online Computer Library Center (OCLC) <www.oclc.org> and the Research Libraries Group (RLG) <www.rlg.org>. For researchers at member institutions, these databases are available on the Internet as WorldCat and RLIN, respectively. OCLC's FirstSearch and RLG's Eureka websites provide access to this information and other sources such as periodical indexes and current awareness tools.

One of the most extensive of individual library catalogs is that of the Library of Congress <catalog.loc.gov>, with access to LC's 12 million records as well as a gateway for searching more than 200 other online catalogs. Even more catalogs are accessible through webCATS <www. lights.com/webcats/>, which lists links to libraries geographically or by type (including law and other specialties).

Other reference sources. Most disciplines have an extensive literature of encyclopedias, dictionaries, bibliographies, research guides, directories, indexes, and other sources that can be of value in a research project. The standard, comprehensive source for identifying available reference materials is the American Library Association's *Guide to Reference Books* (11th ed. 1996). The *Guide* describes basic resources in hundreds of disciplines, pro-

viding just enough background to help the legal researcher know where to look.

§ 10–6. CONCLUSION

This chapter's introductory survey has presented just a small sampling of the many resources available for answering reference questions and for expanding research into other disciplines. Bibliographies such as the *Guide to Reference Books* can provide further leads, and reference librarians can suggest other sources and research approaches.

CHAPTER 11

INTERNATIONAL LAW

---

§ 11–1. INTRODUCTION

Public international law is the body of law which governs relations among nations. Although its primary historical functions have been the preservation of peace and regulation of war, international law now governs an ever broader range of transnational activities. It regulates matters from copyright protection to the rights of refugees, and agreements such as the Convention on Contracts for the International Sale of Goods (CISG) have made international law an inherent aspect of commercial activity. *Private* international law (or conflict of laws)

determines where, and by whose law, controversies involving more than one jurisdiction are resolved, as well as how foreign judgments are enforced.

A modern legal practice often requires knowledge of international law. Lawyers representing an American firm investing in another country, for example, must be aware of treaties between the two nations as well as the investment and trade laws of both the United States and the other country. They may also need to examine jurisdictional issues in resolving disputes or in determining the application of one country's rules in the other's courts. This chapter focuses on international law, while research in the law of foreign countries is the subject of Chapter 12.

The classic statement of the sources of international law doctrine is found in Article 38 of the Statute of the International Court of Justice. *Treaties* and *international custom* are generally considered the two most important sources. If a treaty is relevant to a problem involving its signatories, it is the primary legal authority. International custom consists of the actual conduct of nations, when that conduct is consistent with the rule of law. Custom is not found in a clearly defined collection of sources, but is established instead by evidence of state practices. Other sources include *judicial decisions* and *scholarly writings*, although these are subsidiary to treaties and international custom. Judicial decisions are not considered binding precedents in subsequent disputes, but they are evidence of international practice and can aid in treaty interpretation and in the definition of customary law.

The Internet has had a dramatic impact on international legal research. International law sources have

traditionally been difficult to identify and locate, but many are now widely available through the websites of the United Nations and other international organizations. This chapter discusses some specific resources available on the Internet, but it also provides general addresses that can serve as useful starting points for further research.

International law has its own terminology, and a dictionary may be an essential research tool. Two leading works are Clive Parry et al., *Parry and Grant Encyclopaedic Dictionary of International Law* (1986), and James R. Fox, *Dictionary of International and Comparative Law* (2d ed. 1997). More specialized works, such as H. Victor Condé, *A Handbook of International Human Rights Terminology* (1999), are also available.

§ 11–2. INTERNATIONAL ORGANIZATIONS

While national governments are the major parties in international law, the field cannot be studied without understanding the vital role of intergovernmental organizations. Worldwide and regional organizations establish norms, promote multilateral conventions, and provide mechanisms for the peaceful resolution of conflicts. Several have established adjudicatory bodies by whose decisions nations agree to be bound. Even when not acting as lawmaking bodies, international organizations compile and publish many of the most important research sources in international law.

a.   United Nations

The United Nations has greatly influenced the development of international law, by providing an organizational forum and a center for the preparation and promo-

tion of legislation and conventions. Its six principal organs are the General Assembly, Security Council, Economic and Social Council, Trusteeship Council, Secretariat, and International Court of Justice (ICJ). This section provides a general introduction to the UN; its treaty work and the ICJ will be discussed in greater detail in §§ 11–3 and 11–4.

The United Nations website <www.un.org> provides a wealth of information on the organization, including news, descriptive overviews of its activities, and access to numerous documents. The best printed source for basic information on the UN's structure and membership is *United Nations Handbook*, published annually by the New Zealand Ministry of External Relations and Trade. More in-depth reference works include Rüdiger Wolfrum, ed., *United Nations: Law, Policies, and Practice* (2 vols., 1995), with alphabetically arranged chapters on specific issues and entities; and Oscar Schachter & Christopher C. Joyner, eds., *United Nations Legal Order* (2 vols., 1995), an American Society of International Law work with about two dozen chapters providing U.S. perspectives of UN activities in areas such as human rights and environmental law.

The *Yearbook of the United Nations* is one of the best starting points for historical research on UN activities. Although coverage is delayed several years, this publication summarizes major developments, reprints major documents, and provides references to other sources. Each volume includes a thorough index.

Among the most important documents for UN research are the *General Assembly Official Records* (GAOR). The records of the meetings of the assembly and its commit-

tees are accompanied by *Annexes* containing the more important documents produced during the session, and by *Supplements* containing annual reports submitted to the General Assembly by the Secretary–General, the Security Council, the International Court of Justice, and various committees. The final supplement each year compiles all the resolutions passed by the General Assembly during the session.

Resolutions are also reprinted in the *Yearbook of the United Nations* and are available on the Internet. The United Nations Optical Disk System <www.ods.un.org> is a subscription website with the full text of resolutions from the General Assembly, Security Council, and Economic and Social Council since 1946, as well as other documents beginning in 1992. Free (but more limited) sources for resolutions include UN websites for General Assembly resolutions since 1981 <gopher.un.org/11/ga/recs/> and Security Council resolutions since 1974 <www.un.org/Docs/sc.htm>.

Early General Assembly and Security Council resolutions were reprinted in separate series of *United Nations Resolutions* (35 vols., 1973–92), edited by Dusan J. Djonovich, but these only cover through 1986 and 1979 respectively. For subject access and somewhat more current coverage, Dietrich Rauschning et al., eds., *Key Resolutions of the United Nations General Assembly, 1946–1996* (1997), and Karel C. Wellens, ed., *Resolutions and Statements of the United Nations Security Council (1946–1992): A Thematic Guide* (2d ed. 1993), are helpful.

The UN produces a broad range of other publications, including several specialized yearbooks, statistical compilations, and conference proceedings. Despite the impor-

tance of these publications, identifying and finding them is not always easy. The United Nations has successively used several different indexing systems. The current system, *United Nations Documents Index*, began publication in 1998, but it has several predecessors: *UNDOC* (1979–96), *UNDEX* (1974–78), and an earlier *United Nations Documents Index* (1950–73). *UNBIS Plus on CD–ROM*, updated quarterly, combines several print indexes in a keyword-searchable format, as well as the full text of resolutions. The commercial *Readex CD–ROM Index to United Nations Documents and Publications* (available by subscription on the Web as *Access UN* <www.newsbank.com>) covers back to 1966 and should eventually have comprehensive retrospective coverage.

Much of the work of the United Nations in particular subject fields is conducted by related international organizations, such as the Food and Agriculture Organization, the World Health Organization, and UNESCO. These organizations are referred to by the UN Charter as "specialized agencies" and submit their reports to the Economic and Social Council, which forwards them to the General Assembly. Several of these agencies have extensive law-related activities which produce documentation useful to the legal researcher. The United Nations System website locator <www.unsystem.org> provides access to sites for more than eighty specialized organizations.

Hans von Mangoldt & Volker Rittberger, eds., *The United Nations System and Its Predecessors* (2 vols., 1997), contains numerous documents on the UN and related agencies, including charters, constitutions, and selected resolutions. *United Nations Documentation: Research Guide* <www.un.org/Depts/dhl/resguide/> provides a concise introduction to available resources, with a basic

overview of major sources and more in-depth coverage of some topics such as human rights and international law; and several more extensive guides are published, including Peter I. Hajnal, ed., *International Information: Documents, Publications, and Electronic Information of International Governmental Organizations* (2d ed. 1997).

b. World Trade Organization

The World Trade Organization <www.wto.org>, the successor to the General Agreement on Tariffs and Trade (GATT), was established in 1995 as the principle international body administering trade agreements among member states. The WTO acts as a forum for trade negotiations, seeks to resolve trade disputes, and oversees national trade policies. It is governed by a Ministerial Conference, which meets every two years, while most operations are handled by its General Council.

The basic documents governing WTO operations are reprinted in *The Results of the Uruguay Round of Multilateral Trade Negotiations: The Legal Texts* (1994) and are available on the Internet <www.wto.org/wto/legal/legal. htm>. The WTO's *Annual Report* (1996–date) contains one volume of commentary on the organization's work and one of trade statistics. The WTO Secretariat has published *Guide to the Uruguay Round Agreements* (1999), designed to make the WTO rules easier to understand; and Joseph F. Dennin, ed., *Law and Practice of the World Trade Organization* (5 vols., 1995–date) is a major collection of treaties, dispute resolution decisions, and commentary.

WTO panel decisions and appellate body reports are available in several commercial series, including the looseleaf *International Trade Law Reports* (1996–date),

the bound *WTO Dispute Settlement Decisions: Bernan's Annotated Reporter* (1998–date), and Westlaw and Lexis–Nexis. Dispute resolution pages on the WTO website <www.wto.org/wto/dispute/dispute.htm> include these decisions as well as information about rules and procedures.

c.   European Union and Other Regional Organizations

For American lawyers, the European Union <europa. eu.int> is probably the most frequently encountered of the world's many regional organizations. The EU was established in 1993 by the Maastricht Treaty, as the more ambitious successor to the European Communities (European Atomic Energy Community, European Coal and Steel Community, and European Economic Community). As economic and social developments lead to increasing European integration, the EU can be seen more as a supranational government than as a regional organization.

The major institutions of the EU are the European Parliament, a large elected body exercising mostly advisory powers; the Council, the major decision-making body consisting of one minister from each member country; the Commission, a permanent executive body responsible for implementing the organizing treaties and managing the Union; and the European Court of Justice (which will be discussed in § 11–4 with other regional courts).

The *Official Journal of the European Communities* consists of two series, *Legislation* (L) and *Information and Notices* (C), with European Parliament debates published as an annex. Indexes are issued monthly, and the semiannual *Directory of Community Legislation in Force*

provides subject access to treaties, regulations, directives and other legislative actions. The monthly *Bulletin of the European Union* reviews activities and reprints selected documents, and the annual *General Report on the Activities of the European Union* provides an overview of developments.

Several introductory reference works are available. Desmond Dinan, ed., *Encyclopedia of the European Union* (1998) is an alphabetically arranged overview of major topics and institutions, with bibliographies after most articles providing further leads. Other useful one-volume works include D. Lasok & K.P.E. Lasok, *Law and Institutions of the European Union* (6th ed. 1994), and P.S.R.F. Mathijsen, *A Guide to European Union Law* (7th ed. 1999). *European Current Law* (1992–date, monthly) provides information on legal developments in the EU and throughout Europe, and *European Access* (1980–date, bimonthly) is a current awareness guide to new publications by and about the EU.

CCH's *European Union Law Reporter* is one of the most useful starting points for American lawyers, because of its familiar looseleaf format, broad scope, and frequent supplementation. In addition to its primary emphasis on the European Union, it also provides limited coverage of other regional organizations and summarizes the domestic legislation of European countries on a variety of subjects.

Two works providing detailed analysis of the treaties creating the European Union are Dennis Campbell, ed., *The Law of the European Community: A Commentary on the EEC Treaty* (6 vols., 1976–date), and Neville March Hunnings, ed., *Encyclopedia of European Union Law:*

Constitutional Texts (5 vols., 1996–date). An older companion to the latter work, *Encyclopedia of European Community Law: Secondary Legislation* (11 vols., 1973–date) includes coverage of such matters as employment law, intellectual property, and competition law.

Eur–Lex <europa.eu.int/eur-lex/en/index.html> is a free website with access to basic EU treaties, the *Directory of Community Legislation in Force*, and recent legislation and cases. A more extensive legal site, CELEX, is available on a subscription basis <europa.eu.int/celex> or through Lexis–Nexis. Coverage includes treaties, secondary legislation, preparatory documents, and national provisions implementing EU directives. An extensive set of links to numerous other EU Internet resources is maintained by the University of California Library <lib.berkeley.edu/GSSI/eu.html>.

Other important regional organizations include the Organization of American States (OAS) <www.oas.org>, often considered the oldest regional organization; and the Council of Europe <www.coe.fr>, the major advocate of democracy and the rule of law in Europe. Both of these organizations draft and promote multilateral treaties among their member states, and work to protect human rights in their member countries. Their activities in these areas will be discussed in the following sections. G. Pope Atkins, *Encyclopedia of the Inter–American System* (1997) provides a one-volume overview of the OAS and other Western Hemisphere organizations.

Information on major intergovernmental organizations is included as Part One of the *Europa World Year Book* (2 vols., annual), which also provides extensive background

information and statistics on the nations of the world. The *Yearbook of International Organizations* (3 vols., biennial) contains descriptions and directory information for thousands of international groups and associations, with indexes by name, country and subject; and U.S.-based organizations interested in international issues are listed by subject in Congressional Quarterly's *International Information Directory* (biennial).

§ 11–3. TREATIES

Treaties are formal agreements between countries, and have legal significance for both domestic and international purposes. Treaties between two governments are called *bilateral*; those entered into by more than two governments are called *multilateral*. The initial signatures to a treaty establish that its text is authentic and definitive, but nations are not bound until they approve the treaty through ratification, accession, or some other procedure. Parties may include reservations excluding certain provisions, or declarations providing their own interpretations of treaty terms. Treaties usually indicate the point at which they enter into force, often (in the case of multilateral conventions) when a specified number of nations have indicated their ratification or accession.

Under Article VI of the Constitution providing that treaties are part of the supreme law of the land, they have the same legal effect and status as federal statutes. Treaties and statutes can supersede each other as the controlling law within the United States, but a treaty no longer valid as the law of the land may still be binding between the U.S. and another country. Treaties of the United States are negotiated and drafted by the executive

branch but require approval by two-thirds of the Senate. Most treaty sources also cover executive agreements, which are made with other countries by the President without Senate consent.

Treaty research generally involves the following steps: (1) finding its text in an authoritative source; (2) determining whether it is in force and with what parties and reservations; and (3) interpreting its provisions, with the aid of such resources as commentaries, judicial decisions, and legislative history.

a. Sources

Treaties are published in a variety of forms—official and unofficial, national and international, current and retrospective. The *Bluebook* generally specifies citation of bilateral treaties to an official U.S. source (usually *UST*), and of multilateral treaties to an official international source as well (usually the *United Nations Treaty Series*). Not all treaties, however, appear in these standard sources, and it may also be necessary to check journals, commercially published compilations, and electronic sources for the texts of some agreements.

U.S. sources. Until 1949, treaties were published in the *Statutes at Large* for each session of Congress. These have been compiled into a definitive, official compilation, *Bevans' Treaties and Other International Agreements of the United States of America 1776–1949* (13 vols., 1968–75). This set contains four volumes of multilateral treaties (arranged chronologically), eight volumes of bilateral treaties (arranged alphabetically by country), and indexes by country and subject.

Beginning in 1950, *United States Treaties and Other International Agreements* (*UST*) has been the official,

permanent form of publication for all treaties and executive agreements to which the United States is a party. *UST* volumes are published after a long delay, currently more than fifteen years. Exhibit 75 shows the first page of a treaty between the United States and Iraq, as published in *UST*.

Treaties and agreements are issued first in a slip format in the preliminary series, *Treaties and Other International Acts Series (TIAS)*. Slip treaties are consecutively numbered and issued in separately paginated pamphlets, containing the treaty text in English and in the languages of the other parties. *TIAS* publication is more current than *UST*, but still involves a time lag of several years.

Because of the long delays in the publication of *TIAS* and *UST*, several commercial services are important sources for current access to treaties. *Hein's UST Current Service* (1990–date), on microfiche, and *Consolidated Treaties & International Agreements: Current Document Service, United States* (1990–date), in print, both provide copies of new treaties and agreements, with indexing by country and subject. The American Society of International Law's bimonthly *International Legal Materials* (1962–date) contains the texts of treaties of major significance and sometimes provides drafts before final agreement.

Treaties in *ILM* are available on both Westlaw and Lexis–Nexis, and the Westlaw database USTREATIES provides more comprehensive access to treaties beginning in 1979. The most extensive electronic collection, *TIARA (Treaties & International Agreements Researchers' Archive),* has more than 11,000 treaties from 1783 to date,

IRAQ

Cultural Relations

Agreement signed at Baghdad January 23, 1961;
Entered into force August 13, 1963.

CULTURAL AGREEMENT BETWEEN THE UNITED STATES OF AMERICA AND THE REPUBLIC OF IRAQ

The Government of the United States of America and the Government of the Republic of Iraq:

In consideration of the bonds of friendship and understanding existing between the peoples of the United States of America and of the Republic of Iraq;

In view of the expressed desire of both Governments for an agreement which would encourage and further stimulate the present cultural exchange between the two countries;

Inspired by the determination to increase mutual understanding between the peoples of the United States of America and the Republic of Iraq;

Agree as follows:

Article I

Each Government shall encourage the extension within its own territory of a better knowledge of the history, civilization, institutions, literature and other cultural accomplishments of the people of the other country by such means as promoting and facilitating the exchange of books, periodicals and other publications; the exchange of musical, dramatic, dance and athletic groups and performers; the exchange of fine art and other exhibitions; the exchange of radio and television programs, films, phonograph records and tapes; and by the establishment of university courses and chairs and language instruction.

Article II

The two Governments shall promote and facilitate the interchange between the United States of America and the Republic of Iraq of prominent citizens, professors, teachers, technicians, students and other qualified individuals from all walks of life.

TIAS 5411   (1168)

Exhibit 75. Cultural Agreement between the United States of America and the Republic of Iraq, Jan. 23, 1961, U.S.–Iraq, 14 U.S.T. 1168.

and is available on CD–ROM, through the online databases, and by subscription on the Internet <www.oceanalaw.com> as *U.S. Treaties Researcher*.

General sources. The most comprehensive source for modern treaties is the *United Nations Treaty Series* (*UNTS*), containing nearly 2,000 volumes. Since 1946 this series has published all treaties registered with the United Nations by member nations (including the U.S.) in their original languages, as well as in English and French translations. Exhibit 76 shows the first page of the 1984 Convention against Torture and Other Cruel, Inhuman or Degrading Treatment or Punishment, as published in *UNTS*. Note that footnote 1 identifies the twenty ratifications that caused the convention to enter into force in 1987.

On the Internet, the United Nations Treaty Collection <untreaty.un.org/> has the text of more than 30,000 treaties, searchable by name, subject, date, or parties. Access to this website is available on a subscription basis. Free sources for the texts of major multilateral treaties and conventions include the Multilaterals Project at the Fletcher School of Law and Diplomacy <fletcher.tufts.edu/multilaterals.html> and the University of Minnesota Human Rights Library <www1.umn.edu/humanrts/>.

Treaties predating the creation of the United Nations can be found in two older series. The *League of Nations Treaty Series* (*LNTS*) (205 vols., 1920–46) is similar in scope to the *UNTS*, and a retrospective treaty collection, *Consolidated Treaty Series* (*CTS*) (243 vols., 1969–86) contains all treaties between nation states from 1648 to 1918. *CTS* prints treaties in the language of one of the

CONVENTION[1] AGAINST TORTURE AND OTHER CRUEL, INHUMAN OR DEGRADING TREATMENT OR PUNISHMENT

The States Parties to this Convention,

Considering that, in accordance with the principles proclaimed in the Charter of the United Nations, recognition of the equal and inalienable rights of all members of the human family is the foundation of freedom, justice and peace in the world,

Recognizing that those rights derive from the inherent dignity of the human person,

Considering the obligation of States under the Charter, in particular Article 55, to promote universal respect for, and observance of, human rights and fundamental freedoms,

Having regard to article 5 of the Universal Declaration of Human Rights[2] and article 7 of the International Covenant on Civil and Political Rights,[3] both of which provide that no one shall be subjected to torture or to cruel, inhuman or degrading treatment or punishment,

Having regard also to the Declaration on the Protection of All Persons from Being Subjected to Torture and Other Cruel, Inhuman or Degrading Treatment or Punishment, adopted by the General Assembly on 9 December 1975,[4]

Desiring to make more effective the struggle against torture and other cruel, inhuman or degrading treatment or punishment throughout the world,

Have agreed as follows:

PART I

Article 1. 1. For the purposes of this Convention, the term "torture" means any act by which severe pain or suffering, whether physical or mental, is intentionally inflicted on a person for such purposes as obtaining from him or a third person informa-

---

[1] Came into force on 26 June 1987, i.e., the thirtieth day after the date of the deposit with the Secretary-General of the United Nations of the twentieth instrument of ratification or accession, in accordance with article 27 (1), including the provisions of articles 21 and 22 concerning the competence of the Committee against Torture, more than five States* having declared that they recognize the competence of the Committee, in accordance with articles 21 and 22:

State	Date of deposit of the instrument of ratification or accession (a)		State	Date of deposit of the instrument of ratification or accession (a)	
Afghanistan**	1 April	1987	Norway*	9 July	1986
Argentina*	24 September	1986	Philippines	18 June	1986 a
Belize	17 March	1986 a	Senegal	21 August	1986
Bulgaria**	16 December	1986	Sweden*	8 January	1986
Byelorussian Soviet Socialist			Switzerland*	2 December	1986
Republic**	13 March	1987	Uganda	3 November	1986 a
Cameroon	19 December	1986 a	Ukrainian Soviet Socialist		
Denmark*	27 May	1987	Republic**	24 February	1987
Egypt	25 June	1986 a	Union of Soviet Socialist		
France* **	18 February	1986	Republics**	3 March	1987
Hungary**	15 April	1987	Uruguay	24 October	1986
Mexico	23 January	1986			

* See p. 204 of this volume for the texts of the declarations recognizing the competence of the Committee against Torture, in accordance with articles 21 and 22.

** See p. 207 of this volume for the texts of the reservations made upon ratification.

[2] United Nations, *Official Records of the General Assembly, Third Session,* Part I, p. 71.

[3] United Nations, *Treaty Series,* vol. 999, p. 171; vol. 1057, p. 407 (rectification of Spanish authentic text); vol. 1059, p. 451 (corrigendum to vol. 999).

[4] United Nations, *Official Records of the General Assembly, Thirtieth Session,* Supplement No. 34 (A/10034), p. 91.

Exhibit 76. Convention against Torture and Other Cruel, Inhuman or Degrading Treatment or Punishment, Dec. 10, 1984, 1465 U.N.T.S. 85.

signatories, usually accompanied by an English or French translation. Although there is no subject index, the set includes a chronological list and an index to parties.

The most important regional compilations for American lawyers are those published by the OAS and the Council of Europe. The *Organization of American States Treaty Series* (1957–date) and its predecessor, the *Pan American Union Treaty Series* (1934–56), contain multilateral treaties of Western Hemisphere countries, including the United States. Treaties among European states are published individually in the *European Treaty Series* (1950–date) and cumulated in the bound volumes of *European Conventions and Agreements* (1971–date). New European agreements often appear in the annual *European Yearbook*, which also reports on the activities of more than a dozen regional organizations.

Both the OAS <www.oas.org/en/prog/juridico/english/treaties.html> and the Council of Europe <conventions.coe.int> provide Internet access to major treaties. The Hague Conference on Private International Law <www.hcch.net/e/conventions/> has the text of several dozen conventions it has drafted on issues such as international civil procedure and recognition of judgments; some of these are available only in French, but sources for English translations are listed.

National treaty series include *United Kingdom Treaty Series* (1892–date); *Canada Treaty Series/Recueil des Traités* (1928–date); and *Recueil des Traités et Accords de la France* (1958–date). Many foreign countries publish current treaties in their official gazettes and on government websites, and new treaties are often printed in international law yearbooks and journals.

b.   Indexes and Guides

Treaties are generally published chronologically rather than by subject, so finding tools or indexes are needed to identify agreements on a particular topic. Many of these same resources also provide information on treaty status.

Treaties in Force, an annual publication of the Department of State, is the official index to current United States treaties and agreements. It provides citations to all of the major treaty publications, including *Bevans*, *UST*, and the *League of Nations* and *United Nations Treaty Series*. The first section of *Treaties in Force* lists bilateral treaties by country and, under each country, by subject; and the second section lists multilateral treaties by subject. Exhibit 77 shows portions of each section, covering the bilateral and multilateral agreements seen in Exhibits 75 and 76.

A commercially published *Guide to the United States Treaties in Force*, edited by Igor I. Kavass and Adolf Sprudzs, is also issued annually and provides several additional means of access to current treaties, including subject and country indexes to both bilateral and multilateral treaties.

Treaties in Force is available on the Web <www.state.gov/www/global/legal_affairs/legal_adviser.html>, but the online version is not updated between annual editions. Information on recent treaty developments can be found in "Treaty Actions," a monthly feature in *US Department of State Dispatch*, an official weekly magazine which replaced the monthly *Department of State Bulletin* in 1990. The *Treaties in Force* website includes links to the "Treaty Actions" information, and the full *Dispatch* is also

change of notes at Tehran July 27, 1960; entered into force July 27, 1960.
11 UST 2163; TIAS 4581; 393 UNTS 338.

VISAS

Agreement relating to the reciprocal waiver of passport visa fees for nonimmigrants. Exchange of notes at Tehran March 27 and April 20 and 21, 1926; entered into force April 21, 1926; operative May 15, 1926.
8 Bevans 1260.

Agreement relating to the reciprocal issuance of multiple-entry nonimmigrant visas. Exchange of letters at Tehran December 13 and 16, 1976; entered into force December 16, 1976; effective January 1, 1977.
28 UST 8161; TIAS 8751.

IRAQ

CLAIMS

Agreement concerning claims resulting from attack on the U.S.S. *Stark*. Exchange of notes at Baghdad March 27 and 28, 1989; entered into force March 28, 1989.
TIAS 12030.

COMMERCE (See also ECONOMIC AND TECHNICAL COOPERATION)

Treaty of commerce and navigation. Signed at Baghdad December 3, 1938; entered into force June 19, 1940.
54 Stat. 1790; TS 960; 9 Bevans 7; 203 LNTS 107.

CULTURAL RELATIONS

Cultural agreement. Signed at Baghdad January 23, 1961; entered into force August 13, 1963.
14 UST 1168; TIAS 5411; 488 UNTS 163.

CUSTOMS

Agreement relating to the privilege, on a reciprocal basis, of free entry to all articles imported for the personal use of consular officers. Exchange of notes at Washington March 14, May 15, June 19, and August 8, 1951; entered into force August 8, 1951.
5 UST 657; TIAS 2956; 229 UNTS 185.

TIMBER (Cont'd)

United Kingdom
United States

NOTES:
[1] With declaration(s).
[2] For the Kingdom in Europe.

TONNAGE MEASUREMENT

(See under MARITIME MATTERS)

TORTURE

Convention against torture and other cruel, inhuman or degrading treatment or punishment. Done at New York December 10, 1984; entered into force June 26, 1987; for the United States November 20, 1994.
TIAS
Parties:
Afghanistan [1]
Albania
Algeria
Antigua & Barbuda
Argentina
Armenia
Australia
Austria [2]
Azerbaijan
Bahrain [1]
Belarus [1][2]
Belize
Benin
Bosnia-Herzegovina
Brazil
Bulgaria [1]
Burundi
Cambodia
Cameroon
Canada
Cape Verde
Chad
Chile
China [1][3]
Colombia
Congo, Dem. Rep.
Costa Rica
Cote d'Ivoire
Croatia
Cuba
Cyprus
Czech Rep. [2]
Czechoslovakia
Denmark [2]
Ecuador [1]
Egypt
El Salvador
Estonia
Ethiopia
Finland
Former Yugoslav Republic of Macedonia
France [1][2]
Georgia

Exhibit 77. U.S. DEP'T OF STATE, TREATIES IN FORCE: A LIST OF TREATIES AND OTHER INTERNATIONAL AGREEMENTS OF THE UNITED STATES IN FORCE ON JANUARY 1, 1999, at 140, 466 (1999).

available on the Internet <www.state.gov/www/publications/dispatch/index.html>, as well as through Westlaw and Lexis–Nexis.

The major collections and series of U.S. treaties and international agreements are indexed in Igor I. Kavass, ed., *United States Treaty Index: 1776–1990 Consolidation* (13 vols., 1991–98). This work includes a numerical guide to treaties and agreements, and indexes by date, country, and subject. The consolidated index is updated semiannually by the *Current Treaty Index*, and cumulative electronic access to both publications is available through *Hein's United States Treaty Index on CD–ROM*.

The *United Nations Treaty Series* is the major international source for treaties, but it has no cumulative official index. Initially, indexes were published for every 100 volumes of *UNTS*; more recent indexes cover 50 volumes apiece and are published after a time lag of several years. A commercial publication, *United Nations Treaty Indexing Service*, consists of a paper *Current United Nations Treaty Index* covering recently published treaties, and an electronic *United Nations Master Treaty Index on CD–ROM*, which is in the process of providing complete retrospective coverage.

The leading index for finding multilateral conventions is Christian L. Wiktor, *Multilateral Treaty Calendar, 1648–1995* (1998). This lists more than 6,000 agreements chronologically, identifies sources in more than 100 publications, and provides information on treaty status. The *Multilateral Treaty Calendar* entry for the Torture Convention in Exhibit 76 is shown in Exhibit 78. Note that it lists more than a dozen sources for the text of the treaty,

including the *UNTS* and several journals, but that it does not list the nations that are parties to the agreement.

The source for determining the status of, and identifying the parties to, major conventions is the annual *Multilateral Treaties Deposited with the Secretary–General*, published by the United Nations. This listing of nearly 500 treaties is arranged by subject, and provides citations, information on status, a list of parties with dates of signature and ratification, and the text of any reservations imposed by individual parties. Coverage is limited to treaties concluded under UN auspices or for which the Secretary–General acts as depository, so it excludes such major agreements as the Geneva Conventions of 1949 or the Convention on International Trade in Endangered Species (CITES). Exhibit 79 shows the first page of the entry for the Torture Convention as of 30 April, 1999, with more than 100 countries now parties to the convention. Individual countries' declarations, reservations, and objections are noted on following pages after the list of parties. An Internet version of this work, available through the U.N. Treaty Collection website <untreaty.un. org> is updated more frequently than the print version.

M.J. Bowman & D.J. Harris, *Multilateral Treaties: Index and Current Status* (1984 with periodic supplements), also provides information on sources and lists parties, but it is not updated as regularly as the UN publication. It covers more than 1,000 agreements, including some predating or not deposited with the UN. The *World Treaty Index*, compiled by Peter H. Rohn (5 vols., 2d ed. 1983–84) is growing increasingly dated, but it provides comprehensive coverage of some 44,000 bilateral and multilateral treaties from 1900 to 1980, indexing

---

1264   MULTILATERAL TREATY CALENDAR

> FEBRUARY 28, 1975; includes internal agreements (2) on the implementing measures and procedures, and on the financing and administration of Community aid; protocol No. 8 concerns products within the province of the European Coal and Steel Community; see also protocol consequent on the accession of Spain and Portugal to the EEC of DECEMBER 9, 1987; superseded by convention of DECEMBER 15, 1989 (Lomé IV).

December 10, 1984   **Human Rights**

Convention against torture and other cruel, inhuman or degrading treatment or punishment. *Convention contre la torture et autres peines ou traitements cruels, inhumains ou dégradants.*

> Adopted at New York (U.N.) December 10, 1984
> Printed text: 1465 UNTS 85, 113 (E), 123 (F); US Treaty Doc. 100-20; BTS 107(1991), Cm. 1775; CTS 1987/36; ATS 1989/21; SDIA 32:11 (1984); JORF 1987:13268; RTAF 1987/68; 73 VBD A900; UNJY 1984:135; 23 ILM 1027 (draft); 24 ILM 535; 4 DJI 29; 115 JDI 189; 92 RGDIP 226
> Depository: United Nations
> Entered into force: June 26, 1987
> Status: 93 parties (UN Status, Dec. 1995, p. 184; US TIF, Jan. 1995, p. 433)
> Note: Adopted by the U.N. General Assembly on December 10, 1984 (Res. 39/46), and opened for signature on February 4, 1985; refers to U.N. Charter of JUNE 26, 1945, Universal Declaration of Human Rights of DECEMBER 10, 1948, and U.N. declaration on the protection of all persons from being subjected to torture, etc., of DECEMBER 9, 1975; establishes a Committee Against Torture (Comité contre la torture); see also amendments to articles 17 (7), and 18 (5), adopted on SEPTEMBER 8, 1992, and European convention for the prevention of torture of NOVEMBER 26, 1987. For information on the Committee, see Yrbk. Int. Org., 1995/96, vol. 1, pp. 271-272.

December 11, 1984   **Economic Cooperation**

Agreement on economic cooperation. *Accord de coopération économique.*

> Concluded between: Belgo-Luxembourg Economic Union, and Mexico
> Signed at Mexico City December 11, 1984
> Printed text: 1446 UNTS 47, 51 (F), 57 (E)
> Entered into force: February 3, 1986

December 14, 1984   **Trade and Commerce**

Convention on Central American tariffs and customs procedures. *Convention relative au régime tarifaire et douanier de l'Amérique centrale.*

> Concluded at Guatemala City December 14, 1984
> Cited in: UN Stat. 1994:373
> Depository: OCAS
> Entered into force: September 18, 1985
> Note: See also related protocol of JANUARY 9, 1992, convention on Central American legislation relating to customs duties of goods of JUNE 7, 1985, second protocol of NOVEMBER 5, 1994, and third protocol of DECEMBER 12, 1995 (UN Stat. 1997:33).

December 17, 1984   **Seabeds**

[Agreement on the preservation of the confidentiality of data of applications related to seabed areas]. *Accord sur la préservation du caractère confidentiel des données relatives aux sites faisant l'objet d'une demande dans les grands fonds marins.*

> Concluded between: France, India, Japan, and Soviet Union
> Done at Geneva December 17, 1984
> Printed text: JORF 1985:4658; RTAF 1985/37; 4 DJI 492
> Entered into force: December 17, 1984
> Note: See also agreement of DECEMBER 5, 1986.

Exhibit 78. CHRISTIAN L. WIKTOR, MULTILATERAL TREATY CALENDAR, 1648–1995, at 1264 (1998).

IV.9: Torture and other cruel, inhuman or degrading treatment or punishment

9. CONVENTION AGAINST TORTURE AND OTHER CRUEL, INHUMAN OR DEGRADING TREATMENT OR PUNISHMENT

Adopted by the General Assembly of the United Nations on 10 December 1984

ENTRY INTO FORCE: 26 June 1987, in accordance with article 27 (1).[1]
REGISTRATION: 26 June 1987, No. 24841.
TEXT: United Nations, *Treaty Series*, vol. 1465, p. 85.
STATUS: Signatories: 66. Parties: 114.

Note: The Convention, of which the Arabic, Chinese, English, French, Russian and Spanish texts are equally authentic, was adopted by resolution 39/46[2] of 10 December 1984 at the thirty-ninth session of the General Assembly of the United Nations. The Convention is open for signature by all States, in accordance with its article 25.

Participant	Signature	Ratification, accession (a), succession (d)	Participant	Signature	Ratification, accession (a), succession (d)
Afghanistan	4 Feb 1985	1 Apr 1987	Guatemala		5 Jan 1990 a
Albania		11 May 1994 a	Guinea	30 May 1986	10 Oct 1989
Algeria	26 Nov 1985	12 Sep 1989	Guyana	25 Jan 1988	19 May 1988
Antigua and Barbuda		19 Jul 1993 a	Honduras		5 Dec 1996 a
Argentina	4 Feb 1985	24 Sep 1986	Hungary	28 Nov 1986	15 Apr 1987
Armenia		13 Sep 1993 a	Iceland	4 Feb 1985	23 Oct 1996
Australia	10 Dec 1985	8 Aug 1989	India	14 Oct 1997	
Austria	14 Mar 1985	29 Jul 1987	Indonesia	23 Oct 1985	28 Oct 1998
Azerbaijan		16 Aug 1996 a	Ireland	28 Sep 1992	
Bahrain		6 Mar 1998 a	Israel	22 Oct 1986	3 Oct 1991
Bangladesh		5 Oct 1998 a	Italy	4 Feb 1985	12 Jan 1989
Belarus	19 Dec 1985	13 Mar 1987	Jordan		13 Nov 1991 a
Belgium	4 Feb 1985		Kazakhstan		26 Aug 1998 a
Belize		17 Mar 1986 a	Kenya		21 Feb 1997 a
Benin		12 Mar 1992 a	Kuwait		8 Mar 1996 a
Bolivia	4 Feb 1985	12 Avr 1999	Kyrgyzstan		5 Sep 1997 a
Bosnia and Herzegovina		1 Sep 1993 d	Latvia		14 Apr 1992 a
Brazil	23 Sep 1985	28 Sep 1989	Libyan Arab		
Bulgaria	10 Jun 1986	16 Dec 1986	Jamahiriya		16 May 1989 a
Burkina Faso		4 Jan 1999 a	Liechtenstein	27 Jun 1985	2 Nov 1990
Burundi		18 Feb 1993 a	Lithuania		1 Feb 1996 a
Cameroon		19 Dec 1986 a	Luxembourg	22 Feb 1985	29 Sep 1987
Cambodia		15 Oct 1992 a	Malawi		11 Jun 1996 a
Canada	23 Aug 1985	24 Jun 1987	Mali		26 Feb 1999 a
Cape Verde		4 Jun 1992 a	Malta		13 Sep 1990 a
Chad		9 Jun 1995 a	Mauritius		9 Dec 1992 a
Chile	23 Sep 1987	30 Sep 1988	Mexico	18 Mar 1985	23 Jan 1986
China[3]	12 Dec 1986	4 Oct 1988	Monaco		6 Dec 1991 a
Colombia	10 Apr 1985	8 Dec 1987	Morocco	8 Jan 1986	21 Jun 1993
Costa Rica	4 Feb 1985	11 Nov 1993	Namibia		28 Nov 1994 a
Côte d'Ivoire		18 Dec 1995 a	Nepal		14 May 1991 a
Croatia		12 Oct 1992 d	Netherlands[7]	4 Feb 1985	21 Dec 1988
Cuba	27 Jan 1986	17 May 1995	New Zealand	14 Jan 1986	10 Dec 1989
Cyprus	9 Oct 1985	18 Jul 1991	Nicaragua	15 Apr 1985	
Czech Republic[4]		22 Feb 1993 d	Niger		5 Oct 1998 a
Democratic Republic			Nigeria	28 Jul 1988	
of the Congo		18 Mar 1996 a	Norway	4 Feb 1985	9 Jul 1986
Denmark	4 Feb 1985	27 May 1987	Panama	22 Feb 1985	24 Aug 1987
Dominican Republic	4 Feb 1985		Paraguay	23 Oct 1989	12 Mar 1990
Ecuador	4 Feb 1985	30 Mar 1988	Peru	29 May 1985	7 Jul 1988
Egypt		25 Jun 1986 a	Philippines		18 Jun 1986 a
El Salvador		17 Jun 1996 a	Poland	13 Jan 1986	26 Jul 1989
Estonia		21 Oct 1991 a	Portugal	4 Feb 1985	9 Feb 1989
Ethiopia		14 Mar 1994 a	Republic of Korea		9 Jan 1995 a
Finland	4 Feb 1985	30 Aug 1989	Republic of		
France	4 Feb 1985	18 Feb 1986	Moldova		28 Nov 1995 a
Gabon	21 Jan 1986		Romania		18 Dec 1990 a
Gambia	23 Oct 1985		Russian Federation	10 Dec 1985	3 Mar 1987
Georgia		26 Oct 1994 a	Saudi Arabia		23 Sep 1997 a
Germany[5,6]	13 Oct 1986	1 Oct 1990	Senegal	4 Feb 1985	21 Aug 1986
Greece	4 Feb 1985	6 Oct 1988	Seychelles		5 May 1992 a

201

Exhibit 79. UNITED NATIONS, MULTILATERAL TREATIES DEPOSITED WITH THE SECRETARY-GENERAL: STATUS AS AT 30 APRIL 1999, at 201 (1999).

UNTS, *LNTS*, and numerous other sources by country, subject, date, and international organization.

The status of Inter–American and European treaties can be determined through the OAS and Council of Europe websites, listed above on page 315, and from the periodically revised guides *Inter-American Treaties and Conventions: Signatures, Ratifications, and Deposits with Explanatory Notes*; and *Chart Showing Signatures and Ratifications of Council of Europe Conventions and Agreements*.

c. Interpretation

Most treaties contain ambiguities which can lead to controversies in interpretation and application. Several documents can assist in understanding the terms of a treaty. Among the most important are court decisions and documents produced during a treaty's drafting and consideration.

Court decisions interpreting a treaty can provide authoritative material for the researcher who seeks information on its meaning or effect. The best approach is probably a full-text online search, because neither Key-Cite nor Shepard's covers citations to treaties. (*Shepard's Federal Statute Citations* includes coverage of treaties in its 1996 volumes, but not in more recent supplements.) The *United States Code Service* includes two useful volumes: *International Agreements*, containing the texts of about two dozen major conventions and treaties, accompanied by research references and case annotations; and *Annotations to Uncodified Laws and Treaties*, which has no treaty texts but provides broader coverage of decisions interpreting U.S. treaties, including sections for treaties

with Native American nations, multilateral treaties (listed by date), and bilateral treaties (listed by country).

For United States treaties, Senate deliberation provides another valuable source of documentation on an agreement's terms and meaning. *Treaty Documents* (until 1980, called *Senate Executive Documents*) contain the text of treaties as they are transmitted to the Senate for its consideration. These documents usually contain messages from the President and the Secretary of State, and also provide an early source for access to the treaty text. The Senate Foreign Relations Committee analyzes treaties, may hold hearings, and issues *Senate Executive Reports* containing its recommendations. Both Treaty Documents and Senate Executive Reports are issued in numbered series which identify the Congress and sequence in which they were issued. Note in Exhibit 78 that one of the sources the *Multilateral Treaty Calendar* lists for the text of the Torture Convention is Treaty Doc. No. 100–20.

The *Legislative Calendar* of the Senate Foreign Relations Committee, the official status table of business before the committee, is perhaps the best list of pending treaties with actions taken thereon, but it is not widely available. *Congressional Index*, CCH's weekly looseleaf service, also includes a table of treaties pending before the Senate, with references to Treaty Documents, Executive Reports, hearings, and ratifications.

Another source available for the interpretation of some multilateral conventions are *travaux preparatoires*, or the documents created during the drafting process such as reports and debates. These are recognized under the 1969

Vienna Convention on Treaties as a source for clarifying ambiguous treaty terms, and U.S. courts frequently rely on such sources. *Travaux* for some conventions have been published, e.g. Marc J. Bossuyt, *Guide to the "Travaux Preparatoires" of the International Covenant on Civil and Political Rights* (1987), or Paul Weis, *The Refugee Convention, 1951: The Travaux Preparatoires Analysed with a Commentary* (1995); but for most treaties they may not be as readily available.

§ 11–4. DISPUTE RESOLUTION

Although most disputes between nations are resolved by direct negotiation between the parties, some are submitted to international tribunals, arbitral bodies, or temporary commissions convened for particular disputes. Adjudications by some international bodies are generally recognized as authoritative, even if they may lack effective enforcement procedures.

Nations are not the only parties to significant international law cases. Courts established by regional organizations resolve disputes between nations and their citizens, and are developing a growing body of international human rights law. Decisions of domestic courts on matters of international law can also be important sources, particularly as evidence of international legal custom, and commercial arbitration is increasingly prevalent in international business.

a. International Courts

The preeminent international tribunal is the International Court of Justice (also known as the World Court), which succeeded the Permanent Court of International Justice of the League of Nations. The ICJ meets at the Hague to settle legal controversies between countries and

to resolve a limited number of other cases involving serious questions of international law.

ICJ decisions are published initially in individual slip opinions and later in the bound volumes of *Reports of Judgments, Advisory Opinions and Orders*. Because the Court's own publication system is rather slow, the best printed source for recent decisions is the American Society of International Law's bimonthly *International Legal Materials*. Exhibit 80 shows the first page of a recent order in a case involving the United States, as published officially by the Court.

The ICJ website <www.icj-cij.org> has recent decisions, basic documents, and information on current docket; a mirror site at Cornell's Legal Information Institute <www.lawschool.cornell.edu/library/cijwww/> may provide quicker access for U.S. researchers. Decisions are also available online through Westlaw.

The most extensive commentary on the work of the ICJ is Shabtai Rosenne, *The Law and Practice of the International Court, 1920–1996* (4 vols., 3d ed. 1997). Rosenne is also the author of a shorter volume, *The World Court: What It Is and How It Works* (5th ed. 1995), and editor of a useful compilation of source material, *Documents on the International Court of Justice* (3d ed. 1991). Arthur Eyffinger, *The International Court of Justice 1946–1996* (1996) is an extensively illustrated overview of the ICJ's procedures and history, with biographies of every judge during its first fifty years.

The annual *Yearbook of the International Court of Justice* contains a summary of the Court's work since 1946, basic information about the Court, and summaries of judgments and opinions issued during the year. Other

426

INTERNATIONAL COURT OF JUSTICE

1998
10 November
General List
No. 99

YEAR 1998

10 November 1998

CASE CONCERNING
THE VIENNA CONVENTION
ON CONSULAR RELATIONS

(PARAGUAY *v.* UNITED STATES OF AMERICA)

ORDER

Present: *Vice-President* WEERAMANTRY, *Acting President; President* SCHWEBEL; *Judges* ODA, BEDJAOUI, GUILLAUME, RANJEVA, HERCZEGH, SHI, FLEISCHHAUER, KOROMA, VERESHCHETIN, HIGGINS, PARRA-ARANGUREN, KOOIJMANS, REZEK; *Registrar* VALENCIA-OSPINA.

The International Court of Justice,

Composed as above,

Having regard to Article 48 of the Statute of the Court and to Article 89 of the Rules of Court,

Having regard to the Application filed in the Registry of the Court on 3 April 1998, whereby the Republic of Paraguay instituted proceedings against the United States of America for "violations of the Vienna Convention on Consular Relations [of 24 April 1963]" allegedly committed by the United States,

Having regard to the request for the indication of provisional measures submitted by Paraguay on 3 April 1998 and to the Order made by the Court on 9 April 1998, by which it indicated provisional measures,

Having regard to the Orders of 9 April 1998 and 8 June 1998, by which

4

Exhibit 80. Case Concerning the Vienna Convention on Consular Relations (Para. v. U.S.), 1998 I.C.J. No. 99 (Nov. 10).

Court publications include *Summaries of Judgments, Advisory Opinions and Orders of the International Court of Justice: 1948–1991* (1992, with a 1997 supplement covering 1992–96); *Pleadings, Oral Arguments and Documents*, containing the briefs and documents submitted by the parties; and an annual *Bibliography of the ICJ* listing books and articles written about the Court.

Similar publications were issued by the Permanent Court of International Justice, the ICJ's predecessor as World Court. An unofficial compilation of PCIJ decisions was published as *World Court Reports*, edited by Manley O. Hudson (4 vols., 1934–43). *International Law Reports* (1956–date), succeeding *Annual Digest and Reports of Public International Law Cases* (1932–55), is a widely used and cited general reporter of international decisions, including all PCIJ and ICJ decisions. It also prints selected decisions of regional and national courts on international law issues.

The ICJ is not the only court of global scope. The United Nations Convention on the Law of the Sea established an International Tribunal for the Law of the Sea (ITLOS), which is based in Hamburg and issued its first judgment in July 1999. Information on ITLOS procedures and cases are available on the Internet at the website for the UN's Division for Ocean Affairs and the Law of the Sea <www.un.org/Depts/los/ITLOS/ITLOSproc.htm>, and the Tribunal's rules and other documents are published in *Basic Texts 1998* (1999).

An International Criminal Court <www.un.org/law/icc/index.htm> with jurisdiction over war crimes, genocide, and crimes against humanity was approved by a United Nations conference in 1998, but it has not yet entered into

force. Background information and documents are available in works such as M. Cherif Bassiouni, ed.,, *The Statute of the International Criminal Court: A Documentary History* (1998), and Roy S. Lee, ed., *The International Criminal Court: The Making of the Rome Statute—Issues, Negotiations, Results* (1999).

Two more focused international criminal courts are currently in operation for violations of international humanitarian law in the former Yugoslavia and in Rwanda. The International Criminal Tribunal for the Former Yugoslavia (ICTY) <www.un.org/icty/> was established in 1993 and meets in the Hague. ICTY has published a *Basic Documents* compilation (1995), a *Yearbook* series, and *Judicial Reports 1994–1995* (1999); these materials are also available on its website. The International Criminal Tribunal for Rwanda (ICTR) <www.ictr.org> was established in 1994 and sits in Arusha, Tanzania. Documents and judgments are available on the ICTR homepage.

Documents and analysis of the criminal courts are also available in secondary sources such as two works by Virginia Morris and Michael P. Scharf, *An Insider's Guide to the International Criminal Tribunal for the Former Yugoslavia: A Documentary History & Analysis* (2 vols., 1995) and *The International Criminal Tribunal for Rwanda* (2 vols., 1998); and their developing case law is summarized in John R.W.D. Jones, *The Practice of the International Criminal Tribunals for the Former Yugoslavia and Rwanda* (2d ed. 2000).

b.   Regional and National Courts

The decisions of the courts of regional organizations have assumed growing importance in international law, as the range of disputes over which they exercise juris-

diction grows. Among the most important of these regional courts are the European Court of Justice, the European Court of Human Rights, and the Inter–American Court of Human Rights.

The European Court of Justice, an organ of the European Union, resolves disputes between EU institutions and member states over the interpretation and application of EU treaties and legislation. A subordinate Court of First Instance was established in 1988 to handle certain classes of cases and reduce the Court of Justice's workload. The official *Reports of Cases Before the Court of Justice and the Court of First Instance* includes decisions from both courts. Commercial publications of these decisions include the CCH *European Union Law Reporter*, described above, and *Common Market Law Reports* (1962–date). All decisions since 1954 are also available online from both Westlaw and Lexis–Nexis, and the ECJ's website <europa.eu.int/cj/en/index.htm> has recent judgments and other information.

The European Commission of Human Rights <www.dhrcommhr.coe.fr> and the European Court of Human Rights <www.echr.coe.int> were created under the European Convention of Human Rights of 1950, which established a system for the international protection of the rights of individuals. Through the Commission a citizen can seek redress against the acts of his or her own government; the Court decides cases referred to it from the Commission. The Commission's decisions are published in *Decisions and Reports*, and the Court's in *Reports of Judgments and Decisions*. Decisions of both the Commission and the Court are also reported commercially in *European Human Rights Reports* (1979–date), available online from Westlaw and Lexis–Nexis; and a

variety of documents and decisions appear in the annual *Yearbook of the European Convention on Human Rights* (1958–date). Cases are summarized in *Human Rights Case Digest* (1990–date, bimonthly), published by the British Institute of Human Rights, and major decisions have been compiled by R.A. Lawson & H.G. Schermers in *Leading Cases of the European Court of Human Rights* (1997).

The Inter–American Commission on Human Rights <www.cidh.oas.org> was created in 1959 and hears complaints of individuals and institutions alleging violations of human rights in the American countries. At least sixteen countries (but not including the United States) have accepted its jurisdiction. The Commission, or a member state, can refer matters to the Inter–American Court of Human Rights <corteidh-oea.nu.or.cr/ci/ HOME_ING.HTM>, created in 1978. The Court's decisions are reported in two series of judgments (advisory opinions in Series A, *Judgments and Opinions*; and contentious cases in Series C, *Decisions and Judgments*), in its annual report, and on its website. The *Inter-American Yearbook on Human Rights* (1985–date) covers the work of both the Commission and the Court and includes selected decisions and other documents. Major texts are published in *Basic Documents Pertaining to Human Rights in the Inter–American System* (1996) and are available on the Internet <www.cidh.oas.org/basic.htm>.

Judicial decisions of national courts on matters of international law are also valuable sources of information. While any U.S. court may be faced with international legal issues, one with a particular expertise is the U.S. Court of International Trade (CIT). Its decisions are reported officially in the *U.S. Court of Interna-*

tional Trade Reports, as well as in the *Federal Supplement* and in BNA's *International Trade Reporter* (1980–date), which also includes cases from other courts (including the Court of Appeals for the Federal Circuit reviewing CIT decisions), administrative agencies, and binational panels under the North American Free Trade Agreement.

Cases from the U.S. and other countries under the Convention on Contracts for the International Sale of Goods are published in a looseleaf reporter, *UNILEX* (1996–date), and are available on the Internet through Pace University's Institute of International Commercial Law <www.cisg.law.pace.edu>. International law cases from some countries are published or summarized in national yearbooks, periodicals, and digests of international law, as well as a few specialized case reporters (such as *British International Law Cases* and *Commonwealth International Law Cases*). As noted earlier, *International Law Reports* includes selected decisions of domestic courts as well as those of international tribunals.

c. Arbitrations

An increasing number of disputes, between nations and between commercial partners, are settled by arbitration. The Hague Peace Conferences of 1899 and 1907 regularized international arbitration and created the Permanent Court of Arbitration and the International Commission of Inquiry. Their decisions were published in the *Hague Court Reports*, edited by James B. Scott (2 vols., 1916–32). This set was continued by the United Nations series, *Reports of International Arbitral Awards* (1948–date), with retrospective coverage back to the end of Scott's reports. The awards now appear in English or French with bilingual headnotes. The UN series includes agree-

ments reached by mediation or conciliation, as well as awards resulting from contested arbitrations, but is limited to disputes in which states are the parties.

Repertory of International Arbitral Jurisprudence (3 vols., 1989–91) collects arbitral decisions from 1794 to 1987 and arranges them by subject, and A.M. Stuyt, ed., *Survey of International Arbitrations, 1794–1989* (3d ed. 1990) provides an extensive digest of decisions.

Several sources cover international arbitrations between private parties, including *Yearbook: Commercial Arbitration* (1975–date) and Hans Smit & Vratislav Pechota, eds., *World Arbitration Reporter* (1986–date). Some coverage is provided in *International Legal Materials*, and selected decisions appear in the *American Review of International Arbitration* (1990–date). Two major current awareness services in this area are BNA's *World Arbitration & Mediation Report* (1990–date, monthly) and Mealey's *International Arbitration Report* (1986–date, monthly).

Other major publications on commercial arbitration include Pieter Sanders, ed., *International Handbook on Commercial Arbitration* (4 vols., 1984–date) and Clive M. Schmitthoff, ed., *International Commercial Arbitration* (5 vols., 1979–date). The leading one-volume treatise in the area is Alan Redfern & Martin Hunter, *Law and Practice of International Commercial Arbitration* (3d ed. 1999); Jack J. Coe, Jr., *International Commercial Arbitration: American Principles and Practice in a Global Context* (1997) provides a U.S. perspective as well as numerous appendices containing the major arbitration treaties and rules.

H.   Smit & V. Pechota, *Commercial Arbitration: An International Bibliography* (2d ed. 1998) provides further research leads, and many of the major documents and secondary sources in the area are now available on *Arbitration CD–ROM: Resources on International Commercial Arbitration* (1998–date, semiannual).

§ 11–5.   SECONDARY SOURCES AND DOCUMENT COLLECTIONS

As in other areas of law, it is often best to begin international law research with a reference work or law review article for background information and for help in analyzing the issues involved. A general treatise, such as Peter Malanczuk, *Akehurst's Modern Introduction to International Law* (7th ed. 1997) or Ian Brownlie, *Principles of Public International Law* (5th ed. 1998), can provide an overview of an area of international law doctrine.

The *Encyclopedia of Public International Law*, edited by Rudolf Bernhardt and published under the auspices of the Max Planck Institute for Comparative Public Law and International Law, provides a comprehensive view of international law issues. Its articles are written by respected authorities, are short but informative, and provide brief bibliographies for further research. The set was originally published in 12 volumes (1981–90), with each volume devoted to one or more specific subjects. It is in the process of being reissued in one alphabetical sequence (1992–date), with some additional articles and addenda. Three volumes covering A through R have been published to date.

To study state practice in international law, it is best to turn to sources summarizing or explaining how a particu-

lar nation has acted in the past. Reference works such as Bruce W. Jentleson & Thomas G. Paterson, eds., *Encyclopedia of U.S. Foreign Relations* (4 vols., 1997), can provide a background understanding, and more detailed discussion of United States practice can be found in a series of encyclopedic digests of international law published by the Department of State. These digests are based on treaties, decisions, statutes and other documents reflecting the U.S. position on major issues of international law, and are essentially official restatements of American international law.

The most current U.S. digest (although long outdated) is Marjorie M. Whiteman's *Digest of International Law* (15 vols., 1963–73), focusing largely on the period from the 1940s to the 1960s. The Whiteman *Digest* is supplemented by a Department of State series called *Digest of United States Practice in International Law*. Annual volumes were issued for 1973 through 1980, and three cumulative volumes covering 1981–88 were published between 1993 and 1995. More current materials are digested in "Contemporary Practice of the United States Relating to International Law," a feature in each quarterly issue of the *American Journal of International Law*.

The earlier digests of international law published by the Department of State, with slight variations in title, were by the following compilers: Francis Wharton (3 vols., 1886; 2d ed. 1887); John Bassett Moore (8 vols., 1906), covering the period 1776 to 1906 and effectively superseding Wharton; and G.H. Hackworth (8 vols., 1940–44), covering the period 1906 to 1939. Since material in Moore and Hackworth is not reprinted in later digests, they retain their research value for the period covered.

More extensive documentation of U.S. practice can be found in *Foreign Relations of the United States* (1861–date), a series prepared by the Historical Office of the Department of State to provide a comprehensive record of material relating to such issues as treaty negotiation and international conflicts. Unfortunately, there is a time lag of more than thirty years between the original (often confidential) issuance of these documents and their publication in this series. A selected series, *American Foreign Policy: Current Documents*, is published on a somewhat more timely basis, after a delay of five to ten years.

The American Law Institute's *Restatement (Third) of the Foreign Relations Law of the United States* (2 vols., 1987) is an unofficial but respected summary of American law and practice in international law and foreign relations. The *Restatement (Second) of Conflict of Laws* (4 vols., 1971–80) covers private international law from an American perspective. Appendices to both Restatements include abstracts of citing court decisions.

The practices of other nations can often be found in annual publications such as the *British Yearbook of International Law* or the *Annuaire Français de Droit International*. Most of these yearbooks also include scholarly articles on international law and reprint selected major documents. Several countries also publish documentary compilations similar to the U.S. foreign relations collections, some as large retrospective collections primarily useful for historical research and others providing continuing series of contemporary documents.

Several collections reprint a variety of important international law documents, usually in specific areas. These include Ian Brownlie, ed., *Basic Documents in Interna-*

tional Law (4th ed. 1994); P.W. Birnie & A.E. Boyle, eds., *Basic Documents on International Law and the Environment* (1995); Richard Plender, ed., *Basic Documents on International Migration Law* (2d ed. 1997); and Chia–Jui Cheng, ed., *Basic Documents on International Trade Law* (3d ed. 1999). An online version of Stephen Zamora & Ronald A. Brand, eds., *Basic Documents of International Economic Law* (2 vols., 1990) is available from both Westlaw and Lexis–Nexis, updated with more recent documents.

§ 11–6. SOURCES FOR FURTHER INFORMATION

The source materials involved in international law issues are often published in diverse, elusive sources, and specialized bibliographies and research guides can be valuable finding aids. One of the most useful sources, and most frequently updated, is the American Society of International Law's web-based *ASIL Guide to Electronic Resources for International Law* <www.asil.org/resource/ Home.htm>, with sections on the United Nations, treaties, and several topical areas.

A number of guides to specific areas have been published in recent years, including several prepared under the auspices of the American Association of Law Libraries: Marylin J. Raisch & Roberta I. Shaffer, eds., *Introduction to Transnational Legal Transactions* (1995); Lyonette Louis–Jacques & Jeanne S. Korman, eds., *Introduction to International Organizations* (1996); Gitelle Seer & Maria I. Smolka–Day, eds., *Introduction to International Business Law: Legal Transactions in the Global Economy* (1996); and Ellen G. Schaffer & Randall

J. Snyder, eds., *Contemporary Practice of Public International Law* (1997). Other recent works include Jeanne Rehberg & Radu D. Popa, eds., *Accidental Tourist on the New Frontier: An Introductory Guide to Global Legal Research* (1998), and the George Washington University Journal of International Law and Economics, *Guide to International Legal Research* (3d ed. 1998). Jack Tobin & Jennifer Green, *Guide to Human Rights Research* (1994) is a bit more dated, but it is available on the Internet <www.law.harvard.edu/Programs/HRP/AboutHRPRG. html> as well as in print.

Several publications focus on new publications in international law. The *Index to Foreign Legal Periodicals* (1960–date, quarterly) is principally an index of journals published in countries outside the common law system, but it also indexes articles on international law in selected American law reviews. An Internet-based German index, RAVE (Rechtsprechung und Aufsätze zum Völker- und Europarecht) (Decisions and Articles in Public International Law and European law) <www.jura.uni-duesseldorf.de/rave/e/englhome.htm> covers recent court decisions and articles in more than 180 legal journals, with links to the full text of articles available on the Internet.

Public International Law: A Current Bibliography of Books and Articles (1975–date, semiannual) is a comprehensive index of the literature in the field. Each issue of the *American Journal of International Law* contains an extensive section reviewing or noting new works in the field, and the *International Journal of Legal Information* regularly publishes bibliographies devoted to specific areas of foreign and international law.

§ 11–7. CONCLUSION

This brief survey of international law highlights the extent and variety of available sources. With the increasingly global nature of business and legal relationships, and the frequent treatment of transnational legal issues by American courts, international law research is no longer an exotic specialty known only to a few practitioners.

In researching international law in this increasingly global age, it is important for American lawyers *not* to limit their research to U.S. sources. Materials from international organizations and other countries can provide new perspectives and present solutions that may not be readily apparent from within the U.S. legal tradition. A facility with other languages assists greatly in broadening the scope of research, but as this chapter has shown there are a large number of English-language resources available for serious international law research.

CHAPTER 12

THE LAW OF OTHER COUNTRIES

---

§ 12–1. INTRODUCTION

Expanded foreign communication, travel, and trade have made the law of other countries increasingly significant to American social and economic life. The law of a foreign country may be relevant in American court proceedings involving international transactions, and American legal scholars and lawmakers use other legal systems as a basis for better understanding and improving our own system. Foreign law sources are also essential to the study of comparative law, by which the differences between the law of diverse countries and systems are analyzed.

The legal systems of most foreign countries can be described as either *common law* or *civil law*. Each system has its own history, its own fundamental principles and procedures, and its own forms of publication for legal sources. Under the common law, as explained in Chapter 1, legal doctrine is derived from specific cases decided by

judges rather than from broad, abstractly articulated codifications. Judicial decisions are traditionally the most important and vital source of new legal rules in a common law system.

The civil law system refers to the legal tradition, arising out of Roman law and the European codes, which characterizes the countries of continental Western Europe, Latin America, and parts of Africa and Asia. There are several distinctive characteristics of the civil law system: the predominance of comprehensive and systematic codes governing large fields of law (civil, criminal, commercial, civil procedure, and criminal procedure); the strong influence of concepts, terms and principles from Roman law; little weight for judicial decisions as legal authority; and great influence of legal scholars who interpret, criticize and develop the law in their writings, particularly through commentaries on the codes.

There are also countries which do not fit clearly into either the civil law or common law systems, but are strongly influenced by customary law or traditional religious systems, particularly Hindu or Islamic law. The law of these countries (e.g. India, Israel, Pakistan and Saudi Arabia) may be a mixture of civil *or* common law and the religious legal system.

The differences between the common law and civil law systems have become less marked in recent years, as each system adopts features of the other. Codes have been enacted in some American jurisdictions, for example, while judicial decisions are being given greater weight in some civil law countries. Nonetheless, basic differences remain in how legal issues are perceived and in how research is conducted.

§ 12–2. ENGLISH AND COMMONWEALTH LAW

The common law system originated in England and spread to its colonies around the world. Most of these nations, now known as the Commonwealth, continue to have legal systems modeled on the English common law. This chapter looks at three major common law jurisdictions: England (which is part of the United Kingdom but has a distinct body of law from Northern Ireland and Scotland), Canada, and Australia.

While related, the legal systems of these countries are quite distinct. The United Kingdom has an "unwritten constitution," meaning that its basic constitutional principles are not found in one specific document. The U.K. has been part of the European Community (now the European Union) since 1973 and is increasingly governed by EU treaties and legislation. The Canadian and Australian systems have federal governments and written constitutions. Canada's Constitution, dating back to 1867, was dramatically changed when the Constitution Act 1982 added an extensive new Charter of Rights and Freedoms. The Australian Constitution has been in effect, with relatively few amendments, since 1901. Further information is available in overviews such as S.H. Bailey & M.J. Gunn, *Smith and Bailey on the Modern English Legal System* (3d ed. 1996); Richard Ward, *Walker & Walker's English Legal System* (8th ed. 1998); Gerald L. Gall, *The Canadian Legal System* (4th ed. 1995); or Gerard B. Carter, *Australian Legal System* (1995).

Although the laws of England and its former colonies have developed separately in recent years, common law countries share a heritage which gives their decisions

more persuasive value in each other's courts than that generally afforded to the law of other countries. English cases have continued to influence American law on issues such as tort causation and contract formation. Similarities in publication and research procedures aid in making developments in legal doctrine more accessible to researchers in the United States and other common law countries.

a. Case Law

Court reports are central to legal research in England and other common law countries, and research is simplified by the relatively small number of published decisions compared to the fifty state jurisdictions and federal system in the United States. England has a relatively simple system of courts, with the House of Lords as the court of last resort. The Canadian and Australian federal court systems are more like that of the United States, although fundamental differences exist. In the U.S., for example, state supreme courts are the final arbiters on issues of state law, while any decision from a Canadian provincial court or an Australian state court is generally subject to review by the highest federal court in its country.

Publication of cases. As in the United States, new decisions in most other common law countries are published first in weekly or monthly advance sheets and later in permanent bound volumes. Both advance sheets and volumes usually include case tables and indexes. Official or authorized series of reports are published, but unofficial commercial reporters often provide quicker access to new cases and may contain more useful headnotes and digests.

English law reporting has had a long and varied history. The recording of cases began with fragmentary reports in the *Plea Rolls*, dating from the reign of Richard I in 1189. The *Year Books*, covering the long period from 1285 to 1537, include both reports of proceedings and brief summaries of decisions. Following the *Year Books* came the *nominate* or *nominative* reports, that is, court reports named for the person who recorded or edited them. The earliest known reporter was probably James Dyer, whose reports were published around 1550. *Plowden's Reports*, first published in 1571, are considered among the finest and most accurate, while the reports of Sir Edward Coke were probably the most influential of the period.

Most nominative reports were cumulated into the *English Reports: Full Reprint*, covering cases from 1220 to 1865 (178 vols., 1900–32). This invaluable set contains about 100,000 decisions originally published in some 275 series of nominative reporters. The volumes are arranged by court and star-paged to the original reporter. There is no subject index, but the set is accompanied by a two-volume alphabetical table of cases. An electronic version published in 1999, available in CD–ROM or by subscription on the Internet <www.jurastat.co.uk>, allows access by case name, date, or keyword. Another compilation of older cases, the *Revised Reports*, covers 1785 to 1866 in 149 volumes and includes some decisions not found in the *English Reports*.

For decisions since 1865, the standard source is the semi-official *Law Reports*, which now consists of four series: *Appeal Cases* (House of Lords and the Judicial Committee of the Privy Council); *Queen's Bench Division*;

Chancery Division; and *Family Division*. Before appearing in these four separate series, new cases are published in *Weekly Law Reports*, which also includes some decisions unreported in the four *Law Reports* series.

All England Law Reports (1936–date) is a commercially published reporter which often issues new cases sooner than the *Weekly Law Reports* and contains some decisions which are not published elsewhere. As in the United States, numerous specialized subject reporters are also published.

English cases since the mid–1940s, including those published in the *Law Reports* and in several other reporters, are available online through both Westlaw and Lexis–Nexis. Some decisions are available free on the Web, including House of Lords judgments since 1996 <www.publications.parliament.uk/pa/ld/ldjudinf.htm>, and subscription-based Internet systems such as Butterworths Direct <www.butterworths.co.uk> and Justis. com <www.justis.com> provide more extensive coverage.

Exhibit 81 shows the *English Reports* text of a decision of the Court of Exchequer (which was abolished in 1875) in *Byrne v. Boadle*, the case famous for establishing the principle of *res ipsa loquitur*. Note that star paging references are included to the original nominative reporter, Hurlstone & Coltman's *Exchequer Reports* (cited as H. & C.).

Canada and Australia both have authorized reports for their federal court of last resort (*Canada Supreme Court Reports*, and *Commonwealth Law Reports* for the High Court of Australia). Both nations also have lower federal courts with trial and appellate jurisdiction, and courts in each province or state. In Canada, the commercially

the defendant in the other action recovered **[722]** judgment against the plaintiff, the
defendants in this action are still liable.   It is said that the plaintiff ought to have
replied specially, but I am of opinion that the defendants ought by their plea to shew
that the judgment in the former action proceeded on a ground which operated as
a discharge of all the joint debtors.

Judgment for the plaintiff.

BYRNE *v.* BOADLE. Nov. 25, 1863.—The plaintiff was walking in a public street
   past the defendant's shop when a barrel of flour fell upon him from a window
   above the shop, and seriously injured him.   Held sufficient primâ facie evidence
   of negligence for the jury, to cast on the defendant the onus of proving that the
   accident was not caused by his negligence.

[S. C. 33 L. J. Ex. 13 ; 12 W. R. 279 ; 9 L. T. 450.   Followed, *Briggs* v. *Oliver*, 1866,
   4 H. & C. 407.   Adopted, *Smith* v. *Great Eastern Railway*, 1866, L. R. 2 C. P. 11.]

Declaration.   For that the defendant, by his servants, so negligently and unskil-
fully managed and lowered certain barrels of flour by means of a certain jigger-hoist
and machinery attached to the shop of the defendant, situated in a certain highway,
along which the plaintiff was then passing, that by and through the negligence of the
defendant, by his said servants, one of the said barrels of flour fell upon and struck
against the plaintiff, whereby the plaintiff was thrown down, wounded, lamed, and
permanently injured, and was prevented from attending to his business for a long
time, to wit, thence hitherto, and incurred great expense for medical attendance, and
suffered great pain and anguish, and was otherwise damnified.

Plea, Not guilty.

At the trial before the learned Assessor of the Court of Passage at Liverpool, the
evidence adduced on the part of the plaintiff was as follows :—A witness named
Critchley said : "On the 18th July, I was in Scotland Road, on the right side going
north, defendant's shop is on that side.   When I was opposite to his shop, a barrel
of flour fell from a window above in defendant's house and shop, and knocked **[723]**
the plaintiff down.   He was carried into an adjoining shop.   A horse and cart came
opposite the defendant's door.   Barrels of flour were in the cart.   I do not think the
barrel was being lowered by a rope.   I cannot say : I did not see the barrel until it
struck the plaintiff.   It was not swinging when it struck the plaintiff.   It struck him
on the shoulder and knocked him towards the shop.   No one called out until after
the accident."   The plaintiff said : "On approaching Scotland Place and defendant's
shop, I lost all recollection.   I felt no blow.   I saw nothing to warn me of danger.
I was taken home in a cab.   I was helpless for a fortnight."   (He then described his
sufferings.)   "I saw the path clear.   I did not see any cart opposite defendant's shop."
Another witness said : "I saw a barrel falling.   I don't know how, but from defendant's."   The only other witness was a surgeon, who described the injury which the
plaintiff had received.   It was admitted that the defendant was a dealer in flour.

It was submitted, on the part of the defendant, that there was no evidence of
negligence for the jury.   The learned Assessor was of that opinion, and nonsuited
the plaintiff, reserving leave to him to move the Court of Exchequer to enter the verdict
for him with 50l. damages, the amount assessed by the jury.

Littler, in the present term, obtained a rule nisi to enter the verdict for the
plaintiff, on the ground of misdirection of the learned Assessor in ruling that there
was no evidence of negligence on the part of the defendant ; against which

Charles Russell now shewed cause.   First, there was no evidence to connect the
defendant or his servants with the occurrence.   It is not suggested that the defendant
himself was present, and it will be argued that upon these pleadings it is not open to
the defendant to contend that his servants were not engaged in lowering the barrel of
flour.   But the **[724]** declaration alleges that the defendant, by his servants, so
negligently lowered the barrel of flour, that by and through the negligence of the
defendant, by his said servants, it fell upon the plaintiff.   That is tantamount to an
allegation that the injury was caused by the defendant's negligence, and it is competent
to him, under the plea of not guilty, to contend that his servants were not concerned
in the act alleged.   The plaintiff could not properly plead to this declaration that his
servants were not guilty of negligence, or that the servants were not his servants.   If it

Exhibit 81.   Byrne v. Boadle, 159 Eng. Rep. 299 (Ex. 1863).

published *National Reporter* contains decisions of the Supreme Court and the Federal Court of Appeal, and *Dominion Law Reports* contains decisions from both federal and provincial courts. The High Court of Australia's decisions are also published in the *Australian Law Reports*, along with lower federal court cases and state court cases on federal issues; *Federal Law Reports* duplicates some of this coverage of lower court decisions. In addition, each country has reporters for the supreme courts of its provinces or states, as well as topical reporters in specialized subject areas.

Lexis–Nexis has selective coverage of cases from Canada and Australia, including the Supreme Court of Canada and the High Court of Australia. The University of Montreal provides Supreme Court of Canada decisions since 1989 <www.droit.umontreal.ca/doc/csc-scc/en/>, and several sites provide links to sources for other Canadian courts. One of the most useful is "Legal Resources" at the University of Toronto Law Library <www.law-lib.utoronto.ca/resources/intro.htm>, which includes annotations explaining content and procedures. More extensive Canadian database systems such as Quicklaw <www.quicklaw.com/en/home.html> and eCarswell <www.carswell.com/ecarswell/> are available by subscription. The Australasian Legal Information Institute <www.austlii.edu.au>, a joint facility of the University of Technology, Sydney, and the University of New South Wales, provides extensive free access to case law and legislation from every Australian jurisdiction, including High Court decisions since 1947 <www.austlii.edu.au/au/cases/cth/high_ct/>.

Case research tools. Many of the same types of tools are available for case research in these other common law

countries as are found in the United States. Digests and encyclopedias are frequently used. *Shepard's Citations* and KeyCite have no direct counterparts in other countries, but there are tools for finding later cases that have considered an earlier decision.

Each country has a major national digest, somewhat similar to the West digest system: *The Digest: Annotated British, Commonwealth and European Cases* (3d ed. 1971–date); the *Canadian Abridgment* (2d ed. 1966–date); and the *Australian Digest* (3d ed. 1988–date). All three sets include consolidated indexes and tables of cases, and each is updated regularly by bound or looseleaf supplements. The Canadian and Australian digests are further updated in the monthly issues of *Canadian Current Law Case Law Digests* and the *Australian Legal Monthly Digest*.

Another English service useful for both finding and updating cases is *Current Law*. Its *Monthly Digest* contains summaries of new court decisions arranged by subject and a table of cases which have been judicially considered. The case summaries cumulate at the end of the year into the *Current Law Year Book*, and the case tables into the *Current Law Case Citator*. The *Case Citator*, which consists of three volumes covering 1947 to 1995 and an annual paperback supplement, lists, by name, cases decided or cited since 1947. (Coverage back to 1977 is available through Westlaw.) For those cases which have been judicially considered, the effect of each later case is indicated with notes such as "Overruled," "Applied," or "Considered."

Updating Canadian and Australian cases is possible through *Canadian Case Citations* and the *Australian*

Case Citator. Like their English counterpart, tables in these works are arranged alphabetically by case name and are useful for finding citations as well as for determining later treatment of cited decisions. *Canadian Current Law* and *Australian Current Law Reporter* update these citators and provide information on recent cases.

b. Statutes and Regulations

Statutes in other common law jurisdictions are published both in session laws and in compilations of statutes in force. The compilations, however, generally reprint acts alphabetically by name or chronologically, rather than by subject. There is no counterpart to the *United States Code*, in which each part of an act is systematically assigned to a title and given a section number as part of a general subject compilation of statutes. Instead, acts are permanently identified by their original name and date of enactment.

The current national session law publications are *Public General Acts* (for Britain), *Statutes of Canada*, and *Acts of the Parliament of the Commonwealth of Australia*; each is published in annual volumes with subject indexes or tables of acts for each year. Statutes of the individual Canadian provinces and Australian states are published in similar annual volumes.

The standard historical collection of English statutes is the *Statutes of the Realm* (11 vols., 1810–22), covering 1235 to 1713. Several other chronological collections were published during the 19th century under the title *Statutes at Large*, extending coverage to the beginning of the modern *Public General Acts* in 1866.

Statutes in Force: Official Revised Edition (1972–date) is the current official compilation of statutes in the United Kingdom, consisting of separate pamphlets for each act, in looseleaf volumes arranged by subject. This is a rather cumbersome set, and the unofficial *Halsbury's Statutes of England and Wales* (4th ed. 1985–date) is much more current and useful for most research. *Halsbury's* is a well-indexed encyclopedic arrangement of acts in force, updated with annual bound supplements and two looseleaf volumes (*Current Statutes Service*, containing annotated versions of new statutes, and *Noter-Up Service*, providing references to developments since the latest annual supplement). A consolidated *Table of Statutes and General Index* is published annually. This is the most convenient subject compilation of English statutes and includes footnote annotations to judicial decisions. Exhibit 82 shows a page from *Halsbury's Statutes* containing sections of a 1797 act still in force; notes summarize court decisions and provide cross-references to related acts.

Current English statutes are also available on Lexis–Nexis, and recent British acts beginning in 1996 are available on the Internet <www.hmso.gov.uk/acts.htm>. The Parliament website <www.parliament.uk> provides information about procedures, debates, and pending legislation.

Current Law Legislation Citator, published as part of the *Current Law* service, consists of a chronological list of British statutes, with each followed by references to later statutes and cases which affect it. Coverage includes any statutes amended, repealed, or considered in judicial decisions since 1947. Three volumes cover 1947 to 1995,

INCITEMENT TO MUTINY ACT 1797

(37 Geo 3 c 70)

An Act for the better Prevention and Punishment of Attempts to seduce Persons serving in His Majesty's Forces by Sea or Land from their Duty and Allegiance to His Majesty, or to incite them to Mutiny or Disobedience [6 June 1797]

The short title was given to this Act by the Short Titles Act 1896.
Northern Ireland. This Act does not apply.

[1] Any person who shall attempt to seduce any sailor or soldier from his duty or incite him to mutiny, etc, to suffer death

From and after the passing of this Act, any person who shall maliciously and advisedly endeavour to seduce any person or persons serving in his Majesty's forces by sea or land from his or their duty and allegiance to his Majesty, or to incite or stir up any such person or persons to commit any act of mutiny, or to make or endeavour to make any mutinous assembly, or to commit any traiterous or mutinous practice whatsoever, shall, on being legally convicted of such offence, be adjudged guilty of felony ...

NOTES

The words omitted were repealed by the SLR Act 1888.

Advisedly. This means knowingly. It is therefore necessary to show that the accused knew that a person he is charged with endeavouring to seduce was a person serving in the royal forces (*R v Fuller* (1797) 2 Leach 790, 1 East PC 92).

Serving. A sailor was held to be serving in the sea forces, although he had been for thirty days in sick hospital, and was therefore not entitled to pay nor liable to be tried by court-martial (*R v Tierney* (1804) Russ & Ry 74).

Mutiny. Ie collective insubordination, collective defiance or disregard of authority, or refusal to obey authority (*R v Grant, Davis, Riley and Topley* [1957] 2 All ER 694, 41 Cr App Rep 173, C-MAC).

Felony. All distinctions between felonies and misdemeanours were abolished by the Criminal Law Act 1967, s 1(1) post, and by s 1(2) of that Act the law and practice in relation to all offences are, in general, to be those previously applicable to misdemeanours. See also, in particular, s 12(5)(a) of that Act concerning the construction of existing references to felony as references to an offence.

Punishment. The punishment of death provided by the repealed part of this section was abolished by the Punishment of Offences Act 1837, s 1 post. Under that section as affected by later enactments the maximum punishment is now imprisonment for life.

Extension. This Act was extended to the Air Force by the Air Force (Application of Enactments) (No 2) Order 1918, SR & O 1918/548 (as amended by the Defence (Transfer of Functions) (No 1) Order 1964, SI 1964/488), which provides that the reference to "his Majesty's forces by land" shall be construed as including a reference to the Air Force.

Further provisions. See now the provisions of the Incitement to Disaffection Act 1934 post. For similar and comparable offences under the enactments relating to the armed forces, see the Naval Discipline Act 1957, ss 9, 94, 97, the Army Act 1955, ss 31(1), (2), 37(1), 39, 192, the Air Force Act 1955, ss 31(1), (2), 37(1), 39, 192, Vol 3, title Armed Forces (Pt 1), and the Reserve Forces Act 1996, s 101, Vol 3, title Armed Forces.

Causing disaffection amongst police officers is punishable under the Police Act 1996, s 91, Vol 33, title Police. In the case of aliens special penalties for incitement to sedition, disaffection or industrial unrest are provided by the Aliens Restriction (Amendment) Act 1919, s 3, Vol 31, title Nationality and Immigration.

2 (*Repealed by the Criminal Law Act 1967, s 10(2), Sch 3, Pt III.*)

3 Persons tried for offences against this Act not to be tried again for the same as high treason or misprision of high treason, etc

Provided always, ... that any person who shall be tried and acquitted or convicted of any offence against this Act shall not be liable to be indicted, prosecuted or tried

with updating provided by annual supplements and monthly coverage in *Current Law Monthly Digest*.

Both Canada and Australia have bound compilations of statutes in force as of specific dates, although neither is very current. In both countries acts are simply arranged alphabetically by title. Neither country has an annotated, regularly updated publication similar to *Halsbury's Statutes*. The most recent compilation of Canadian federal statutes is the *Revised Statutes of Canada 1985*, proclaimed in force in 1988. An index (2d ed. 1991) accompanies the set. The most recent bound compilation of Australian federal acts is *Acts of the Australian Parliament 1901–1973*; since 1979 reprinted acts have also been published in pamphlets filed in looseleaf binders. Subject access is available through the annual *Wicks Subject Index to Commonwealth Legislation*.

Lexis–Nexis provides access to laws from Canada and several of its several provinces, and to all Australian Commonwealth Acts since 1901. The Consolidated Statutes of Canada (a regularly updated electronic version of the *Revised Statutes*) and other documents are also available from the Department of Justice Canada <canada. justice.gc.ca/Loireg/index_en.html>. The Australasian Legal Information Institute has a wealth of legislative information, including Commonwealth Consolidated Acts <www.austlii.edu.au/au/legis/cth/consol_act/>.

A "Table of Public Statutes" in the *Canada Gazette* and on the Department of Justice Canada website lists amendments and repeals since the latest *Revised Statutes of Canada*, and provides information on legislation enacted since the latest revision. Recent legislative activity by both federal and provincial governments is noted in

Canadian Current Law Legislation, and references to citing cases can be found by using *Canadian Statute Citations*.

In Australia, *Commonwealth Statutes Annotations* and *Federal Statutes Annotations* both provide references to amendments and to cases citing federal statutes. Similar works are available for some Australian states, and information on federal and state legislative developments is available in such publications as the *Australian Legal Monthly Digest* and *Australian Current Law Legislation*.

While parliamentary debates and other legislative documents are also published in each of these countries, legislative history materials are generally considered less persuasive than in the United States for purposes of statutory interpretation. Some use of parliamentary materials, however, has now been accepted by courts in most countries. Parliamentary websites (<www.parliament.uk>, <www.parl.gc.ca>, <www.aph.gov.au>) provide information on available sources.

As in the United States, delegated legislation plays a vital role in the legal system of Commonwealth nations. Regulations, the most common form of delegated legislation, are known in Britain as *statutory instruments* and in Australia as *statutory rules*.

The most useful source for research in English statutory instruments is the unofficial *Halsbury's Statutory Instruments* (4th ed. 1978–date). The texts of all statutory instruments of general effect currently in force, including many not printed in *Halsbury's*, are available online from Lexis–Nexis, and instruments since 1997 are on the Web <www.hmso.gov.uk/stat.htm>. *Current Law* lists new instruments and includes them in its subject digests, and

the *Current Law Legislation Citator* contains a "Table of Statutory Instruments Affected" noting amendments or revocations.

Access to Canadian and Australian regulations is similar to that for statutes, with infrequently revised compilations, tables for finding more recent materials, and electronic resources. The latest printed compilation of Canadian federal regulations is the *Consolidated Regulations of Canada 1978*, and new regulations are published biweekly in Part II of the *Canada Gazette*. Access is provided by the "Consolidated Index of Statutory Instruments" in the *Canada Gazette* or the commercially published *Canada Regulations Index*. Australian regulations appear in *Statutory Rules Made Under Acts of Parliament of the Commonwealth of Australia*, published in annual volumes updated by looseleaf pamphlets. Regulations from both countries are also available on the Internet, through the Department of Justice Canada <canada.justice.gc.ca/Loireg/index_en.html> (regularly updated *Consolidated Regulations*) and the Australasian Legal Information Institute <www.austlii.edu.au/au/legis/cth/consol_reg/> (statutory rules, 1989–date), and from Lexis–Nexis.

c. Secondary Sources

The secondary literature of other common law countries parallels that of the United States, with a variety of treatises, practitioners' handbooks, looseleaf services, and other materials. This section examines only a few basic resources.

Encyclopedias. Like *Am. Jur. 2d* and *C.J.S.*, legal encyclopedias in other nations contain concise statements of ruling law and extensive footnote references to primary

sources. Foreign legal encyclopedias may be even more useful than those from one's own country, since they summarize unfamiliar legal doctrines and provide convenient references to materials that might otherwise be difficult to find.

Halsbury's Laws of England (4th ed. 1973–date) is more comprehensive than the American legal encyclopedias, because it covers just one jurisdiction and can encompass statutes and administrative sources as well as case law. Access to the set is provided by a subject index and by tables of cases and statutes cited. The encyclopedia is updated by cumulative annual supplements and Current Service looseleaf volumes, which include a "Monthly Review" summarizing new developments.

While there is no general legal encyclopedia for all of Canada, two regional encyclopedias include coverage of Canadian federal law: *Canadian Encyclopedic Digest (Ontario)* (3d ed. 1973–date), and *Canadian Encyclopedic Digest (Western)* (3d ed. 1979–date). There are now two competing comprehensive Australian legal encyclopedias, *Halsbury's Laws of Australia* (1991–date) and *The Laws of Australia* (1993–date).

Martindale-Hubbell International Law Digest is hardly a substitute for an encyclopedic treatment and original sources, but it provides convenient summaries of major legal principles and references to primary sources for England, Canada, and Australia, as well as each Canadian province, Northern Ireland, Scotland, and several other common law countries.

Periodicals and treatises. No other country has a profusion of legal periodicals to match that in the United States, but the forms of publication are similar. Each

nation has a variety of academic law reviews and professional journals. The major American indexes (*Index to Legal Periodicals* and *Current Law Index/Legal Resource Index*) include coverage of most of the world's major English-language journals, but there are also indexes published in other countries that provide more thorough and specific coverage of legal issues in those countries.

The monthly *Legal Journals Index* (1986–date, available through Westlaw) covers most law journals published in the United Kingdom, and references to recent books and articles also appear in *Current Law*. The most comprehensive Canadian index is *Canadian Legal Literature* (1981–date), covering both books and articles and published as part of the *Canadian Current Law* and *Canadian Abridgment* series. References to recent Australian material appear in the *Australian Legal Monthly Digest* and *Australian Current Law Reporter*.

Dictionaries and research guides. Reference works can help considerably in researching another country's laws. Legal dictionaries ensure that words are understood in their proper context, and foreign research guides contain more detailed and precise discussion than is possible in an American treatment.

The major English legal dictionary is *Jowitt's Dictionary of English Law* (2 vols., 2d ed. 1977, with 1985 supp.); two shorter but useful works are Elizabeth A. Martin, ed., *A Dictionary of Law* (4th ed. 1997), and *Osborn's Concise Law Dictionary* (8th ed. 1993). Daphne A. Dukelow & Betsy Nuse, *The Dictionary of Canadian Law* (2d ed. 1995) is the most substantial treatment of Canadian legal definitions, and Australian legal terms are defined in *Butterworths Australian Legal Dictionary*

(1997). David M. Walker's *Oxford Companion to Law* (1980) is a cross between a dictionary and an encyclopedia, providing concise explanations of basic common and civil law concepts, documents, events, and institutions.

English legal research materials are discussed in Guy Holborn, *Butterworths Legal Research Guide* (1993), and Philip A. Thomas & Catherine Cope, *How to Use a Law Library* (3d ed. 1996). Similar treatment for Canada is offered by Margaret A. Banks & Karen E.H. Foti, *Banks on Using a Law Library* (6th ed. 1994), and Douglass T. MacEllven & Michael J. McGuire, *Legal Research Handbook* (4th ed. 1998). Texts for Australia include Enid Campbell et al., *Legal Research: Materials and Methods* (4th ed. 1996), and *Researching Australian Law* (1997).

§ 12–3. CIVIL LAW

An American lawyer or law student researching the law of a civil law country must be cognizant of the major differences between the civil and common law systems, and the effect of these differences on how legal problems are viewed and how research is conducted. Instead of searching for precedents in factually similar judicial decisions, a civil lawyer looks first to the abstract provisions of the code for a logical and appropriate legal principle. Among the most important sources are extensive article-by-article commentaries on the major codes; the most scholarly and reputable of these commentaries are themselves sources of the law. Other laws, such as legislation, regulations, and decrees, are most often found in official gazettes, which are comparable to but generally broader in scope than the *Federal Register*. Court decisions are published, but they are usually of secondary importance.

Research approaches in civil law vary by country and by topic, and no single procedure will work for all purposes. Because of the difficulty of covering the great variety of sources and procedures in foreign languages and the relative inaccessibility of such sources to most American lawyers, we will focus first on introductory research in English and then briefly treat research in original sources.

a. Research in English

While thorough research on a foreign law problem can only be undertaken in the language of the jurisdiction, English-language materials can provide a working knowledge of the major legal issues. It is usually best to begin with an encyclopedia or treatise for a general introduction to a national legal system, or, if possible, to the specific legal subject in question. A bibliographic guide for the jurisdiction or subject, listing and describing available primary and secondary sources, can help clarify the range of research options. With some understanding of the basic concepts and terminology of the subject matter and a general sense of the publications available in English, one can then begin research in translations and summaries.

Encyclopedias and legal guides. Several encyclopedic works provide coverage of legal topics in various nations. The most comprehensive work in English, the *International Encyclopedia of Comparative Law* (1971–date), is still incomplete after more than thirty years. Most of the encyclopedia covers specific legal topics such as contracts or civil procedure, but volume 1 contains a series of "National Reports" on individual countries, with references to the main sources of law and topical bibliographies for each country. Most of these reports, however, were published in pamphlets in the 1970s and have never

been updated. Depending on the jurisdiction, much of their information may be of historical value only.

Another series of comparative law works, *International Encyclopaedia of Laws*, consists of several sets focusing on specific subjects with separate monographic pamphlets for individual countries. The oldest and most extensive of these works, *International Encyclopaedia for Labour Law and Industrial Relations* (1977–date), covers more than 50 countries. Newer sets covering fewer countries, but still growing, are available in the areas of civil procedure (1994–date), commercial and economic law (1993–date), constitutional law (1992–date), contracts (1993–date), corporations and partnerships (1991–date), criminal law (1993–date), environmental law (1991–date), family and succession law (1997–date), insurance law (1992–date), intellectual property (1997–date), intergovernmental organizations (1996–date), medical law (1993–date), social security law (1994), and transport law (1994–date). These can be excellent scholarly resources, although the chances of finding a specific country covered in a specific subject area are not yet very promising.

Surveys of the legal systems of more than 170 jurisdictions are included in Kenneth R. Redden & Linda L. Schlueter, eds., *Modern Legal Systems Cyclopedia* (1984–date). These vary considerably in length, from three to more than a hundred pages, and in quality. The dates of chapters are not indicated, but some are now clearly obsolete. This set includes a few chapters on legal research methods as well.

A number of guides in English to the legal systems of specific countries or regions are published. These generally explain legal institutions and summarize major

doctrines. A sample of recently published titles includes Gennady M. Danilenko & William Burnham, *Law and Legal System of the Russian Federation* (1999); Anke Freckmann & Thomas Wegerich, *The German Legal System* (1999); Herbert Hausmaninger, *The Austrian Legal System* (1998); Charlotte Villiers, *The Spanish Legal Tradition: An Introduction to the Spanish Law and Legal System* (1999); and Andrew West et al., *The French Legal System* (2d ed. 1998). Two works by Maurice Sheridan and James Cameron, *EC Legal Systems: An Introductory Guide* (1992) and *EFTA Legal Systems: An Introductory Guide* (1993), provide an overview of nineteen countries belonging to the European Union or the European Free Trade Association.

The United States government publishes several useful guides to the legal and business environments in foreign countries. *Country Reports on Economic Policy and Trade Practices*, a biennial report from the Department of State to Congress, summarizes basic trade, investment, and employment laws. Internet resources include the Central Intelligence Agency's *World Factbook* <www.odci.gov/cia/ publications/factbook/>, which has basic demographic and economic information about the countries of the world. More extensive *Country Commercial Guides* are prepared by the embassy staff in each country. Chapters in these guides cover topics such as economic trends, marketing, investment climate, and project financing; and appendices include addresses and telephone numbers for government and business contacts in the country, as well as statistics and lists of published sources on the country's commercial and economic conditions. These guides are available from the International Trade Administration <www.usatrade.

gov/website/ccg.nsf> and from the Department of State <www.state.gov/www/about_state/business/com_guides/>.

Hieros Gamos <www.hg.org> is a website sponsored by Lex Mundi, an international association of law firms. Two of its many features are "World Government Resources" <www.hg.org/govt.html>, with links to information sources by country, and some three dozen legal guides written by Lex Mundi members about their countries <www.hg.org/guides.html>.

Bibliographies and research guides. When starting research in the law of a country other than one's own, it is essential to have some sense of what publications are available and in what sources research is best conducted. A wide variety of bibliographic guides to foreign law are published. Some cover many subjects and many jurisdictions, while others are specialized bibliographic surveys of particular countries, regions, or subjects.

One of the best starting points is Thomas H. Reynolds & Arturo A. Flores, *Foreign Law: Current Sources of Codes and Basic Legislation in Jurisdictions of the World* (6 vols., 1989–date), covering almost every country in the world. A separate section for each country contains a description of its legal system, notes on the major codifications, gazettes, and sources for legislation and court decisions (including those available in English), and a detailed listing of codes and laws covering specific subject areas. Exhibit 83 shows a page from the Costa Rica section of *Foreign Law*, with information about basic primary sources. At the top of the page, an English translation of the Commercial Code is noted.

Claire M. Germain's *Transnational Law Research: A Guide for Attorneys* (1991–date) describes sources in

COSTA RICA

Apr 1964 *(Leyes de Costa Rica anotadas* Tit. 9), replacing the old code of commerce of 1853. The **Commercial Code** (arts. 1–850 of 986 articles) translated, as amended through Ley 7,201 of 10 Oct 1990, in *Commercial laws of the world: Costa Rica.* *

4. Criminal Code
Código penal. Ley 4,573 of 4 May 1970.

5. Code of Criminal Procedure
Código de procedimientos penales. Ley 5,377 of 19 Oct 1973 in *La Gaceta*–20 Nov 1973.

OFFICIAL GAZETTE
La Gaceta, Diario Oficial. Jan 1877– . San José, Imprenta Nacional, 1877– (cited herein as *La Gaceta)* (court decisions are not included in *La Gaceta).*

COMPILIATIONS OR OFFICIAL CODIFICATIONS
Leyes de Costa Rica anotadas. Orford, N.H., Equity Publishing Company, 1977–1978. Titles 1–13 in 5 vols., publication suspended in 1978.

SESSION LAWS
Coleción de leyes, decretos, acuerdos y resoluciones. 1824/26–1979. San José, Imprenta Nacional, 1824–1980 (title and imprint vary: volumes for 1831/32–1867/68 called "tomo 3–17"). Continued by: *Colección de leyes y decretos.* Edición oficial. T. 1– , 1980– . San José, Imprenta Nacional, 1980–

COURT REPORTS
Revista judicial: Corte Suprema de Justicia. No. 1– , 1955– . San Jose, Corte Suprema, 1955– (title varies: 1955–1975, *Boletín informativo de la Corte Suprema de Justicia).*
Sentencias de la Corte de Casación. No. 1– , 1888– . San José, 1888– .

Exhibit 83. Costa Rica: Major Publications, 1 Thomas H. Reynolds & Arturo A. Flores, Foreign Law: Current Sources of Codes and Legislation in Jurisdictions of the World Costa Rica 5, 6 (1996).

international and foreign law, including translations, digests, and current awareness materials. Chapters introducing major procedural and substantive issues are followed by more detailed treatment of sources in more than three dozen subject areas and in seventeen European countries. Most chapters include helpful "where to start" sections listing key resources.

Another source for information on European legal systems is Jules Winterton & Elizabeth M. Moys, eds., *Information Sources in Law* (2d ed. 1997). Its chapters cover more than thirty countries, providing an overview of each legal system and explaining sources for legislation, codes, commentaries, court decisions, secondary sources, and current information sources. More extensive guides for individual countries include Charles Szladits & Claire M. Germain, *Guide to Foreign Legal Materials: French* (2d ed. 1985), and Timothy Kearley & Wolfram Fischer, *Charles Szladits' Guide to Foreign Legal Materials: German* (2d ed. 1990).

Richard A. Danner & Marie–Louise H. Bernal, eds., *Introduction to Foreign Legal Systems* (1994) provides a general introduction to civil law systems and more detailed coverage of the Chinese, French, Ghanaian, Japanese, Mexican, and Taiwanese systems. A chapter by Amber Lee Smith, "Foreign Law in Translation: Problems and Sources," includes an extensive annotated bibliography by jurisdiction of English translations of foreign laws.

One of the most extensive sources is the American Library Association's *Guide to Official Publications of Foreign Countries* (2d ed. 1997), which provides an extensive annotated listing of gazettes, statistical yearbooks, court reports, and other publications for more than 170

countries. Commercially published guides, bibliographies, and directories are included as well as official sources.

The most thorough guide to the vast body of English-language secondary literature on foreign legal systems is *Szladits' A Bibliography on Foreign and Comparative Law: Books and Articles in English* (1955–date), now edited by S. Blair Kauffman, Daniel L. Wade, and Tracy L. Thompson. It is arranged by subject with geographical and author indexes. The bibliography is updated periodically by bound supplements, although there is a time lag of five to seven years between coverage dates and publication. More current coverage of journal articles is available from the standard legal periodical indexes.

Translations and summaries of foreign law. The growing literature on foreign law includes many translations of actual laws, as well as multinational summaries and digests of laws on specific subjects. While translations and summaries cannot substitute for the original sources, they can provide some familiarity with the basic concepts and issues of the foreign law problem.

The simplest and most convenient starting point may be the annual *Martindale-Hubbell International Law Digest*, which has summaries of basic laws and procedures for more than sixty civil law countries. Topics covered include business regulation, foreign trade, family law, property, and taxation. Most national digests are prepared by lawyers in that nation, and include references to codes, laws, and other sources. The *International Law Digest* is available online through Lexis–Nexis.

While civil codes determine private rights and obligations, the basic laws of government structure and indi-

vidual liberties are found in national constitutions. The most current comprehensive collection of constitutions in English translation is the multivolume looseleaf set *Constitutions of the Countries of the World*, edited by Gisbert H. Flanz. For some foreign-language countries, the original text of the constitution is included as well. Robert L. Maddex, *Constitutions of the World* (1995) provides summaries of constitutions and brief constitutional histories for 100 countries. International Constitutional Law at Würzburg University <www.uni-wuerzburg.de/law/> has more than 80 constitutions in English, with introductory pages providing constitutional background and history. The Constitution Finder at the University of Richmond <www.richmond.edu/~jpjones/confinder/>, is even more extensive, with links to constitutions from more than 150 nations, some in more than one language.

Laws affecting international business are the most likely sources to be available in English. Several collections covering specific topics are published, including *Copyright Laws and Treaties of the World* (1956–date), *Digest of Commercial Laws of the World* (1966–date), *Investment Laws of the World* (1973–date), and *International Securities Regulation* (1986–date). Foreign Tax Law, Inc. publishes two extensive series, *Commercial Laws of the World* (1976–date) and *Tax Laws of the World* (1964–date), each covering more than 100 countries. The International Bureau of Fiscal Documentation publishes several series covering taxation laws throughout the world, including *African Tax Systems* (1970–date), *Guides to European Taxation* (1963–date), *Taxation in Latin America* (1970–date), *Taxes and Investment in Asia and the Pacific* (1978–date), and *Taxes and Investment in the Middle East* (1977–date).

Online access to foreign laws in English is not very extensive. Among the exceptions available from Westlaw and Lexis–Nexis are databases containing commercial laws of China, Russia, and Central and Eastern European countries. ENFLEX databases, available through both systems, contain English translations of environmental, health and safety regulations from Brazil, France, Indonesia, Italy, Mexico, and Spain. On the Internet, the German Law Archive <iecl.iuscomp.org/gla/> has numerous sources in English including statutes, court decisions, secondary sources, and bibliographies. Several law school libraries provide links to sites for laws in other countries, in translation and in their original languages. Timothy F. Mulligan's "Foreign Primary Law on the Web" <www.law.uh.edu/librarians/tmulligan/foreignlaw.html> lists sites for almost 100 countries.

b. Research in Original Sources

Translations and summaries of foreign law in English may be quite helpful, but translated texts of legal materials are no substitute for the original documents. The most effective research in any legal system is likely to be in the language of the country being studied.

Introductory study in an encyclopedia, treatise, or journal article may provide leads to original sources. The next step is to consult the relevant code (preferably in an edition accompanied by extensive commentary) or other statutes applicable to the problem. One should then find administrative orders and judicial decisions implementing or interpreting the legislative norms. It bears repeating that research usually begins with the code itself, and almost never, as in the United States, with a review of judicial decisions.

Basic legal sources. Most countries in the civil law system have several separately published codes. These include the basic general codes (civil, criminal, commercial, civil procedure and criminal procedure), and minor codes which are often simply statutory compilations on specific subjects (such as taxation, labor law, and family law). The codes are usually published in frequent unannotated editions, and also in larger editions with scholarly commentary, annotations, and other aids.

In many countries, daily or weekly official gazettes contain the texts of new laws, decrees and administrative orders. These comprehensive gazettes are the official sources for new legislation, but in many countries they are poorly or infrequently indexed. Research is conducted instead in commercially published periodicals or with more thorough and timely indexing.

Because judicial decisions carry less weight in civil law countries, most jurisdictions have fewer official reports of such decisions and less developed means for finding cases by subject. In many countries, legal periodicals publish court decisions in addition to articles and other legal news. Tracking down these decisions can be difficult, but leads are provided by code commentaries and other sources.

Most larger civil law countries have both free and subscription-based legal databases similar to those available in the United States. Among the leading free sites are Legifrance <www.legifrance.gouv.fr/>, with codes, the *Journal Officiel*, and cases from several French courts; and Würzburg University's collection of German case law <www.uni-wuerzburg.de/glaw/>. Two of the most extensive listings of links to sites by country are Emory

University's "Laws of Other Countries" <www.law.emory. edu/LAW/refdesk/country/foreign/> and Cornell University's "Law by Source: Global" <www.law.cornell.edu/ world/>. Both provide access to constitutions, government websites, and other resources.

Materials from a few countries are available through U.S. online systems. Lexis–Nexis has extensive libraries of French and Mexican materials, in both instances including codes, other laws, official gazettes, and case law; and more selective coverage of material from Argentina and Italy. Westlaw's foreign-language coverage is less broad, but it too has Mexican materials.

Secondary materials. Under the civil law system, scholarly commentaries and treatises by recognized experts have considerable weight as persuasive authority. They are discussed as "secondary materials" here in keeping with our own notion of authority, but in many instances they have greater weight than judicial decisions. The range of available texts, as in common law countries, is quite broad in both subject and quality. There are comprehensive scholarly treatises, highly specialized monographs on narrow topics, pragmatic manuals and guides for the practitioner, and simplified texts for students and popular use. For those with the necessary language skills, these works offer considerable help in legal research. Information about the literature available on specific topics can be found in legal bibliographies and guides published for particular countries, or in the general bibliographies discussed above on page 360-63.

Foreign legal encyclopedias, particularly the French *répertoires* published by Dalloz, are often of higher quality and reputation than those in this country. Their

articles are frequently written by leading legal scholars. Except for major publications such as these, however, many foreign legal sources are difficult to find outside their home countries. The American Association of Law Libraries' *Directory of Foreign Law Collections in Selected Law Libraries* (1991) may be of assistance in identifying possible holding libraries.

Civil law countries have a multitude of periodicals covering legal developments and often printing primary sources. In France, for example, the leading legal periodicals, *Recueil Dalloz* (1808–date) and *La Semaine Juridique* (1927–date), provide both legislative texts and judicial decisions, as well as scholarly articles. The *Index to Foreign Legal Periodicals* (1960–date, quarterly; available through Westlaw) covers nearly 500 journals from more than seventy countries, as well as *festschriften* and other collections of essays. There are also periodical indexes published in some foreign countries, limited to the literature of these countries. Like foreign encyclopedias, however, these indexes—and the journals they cover—may be hard to obtain in this country.

Reference aids. Part of the difficulty of doing legal research in the civil law system stems from differences in language. Bilingual legal dictionaries can help somewhat, although a dictionary alone can provide only a superficial sense of the differences in meaning and usage.

Numerous bilingual dictionaries are available for assistance in translating foreign terms into English. Two of these, *Dahl's Law Dictionary: Spanish to English / English to Spanish* (3d ed. 1999) and *Dahl's Law Dictionary: French to English / English to French* (1995) are also available through Lexis–Nexis. Several multilingual law

dictionaries are also published. The standard work in English, French, and German is Robert Herbst & Alan G. Readett, *Dictionary of Commercial, Financial and Legal Terms* (3 vols., 4th ed. 1985–date). *West's Law and Commercial Dictionary in Five Languages* (2 vols., 1985) adds Italian and Spanish as well.

Citation forms for foreign legal materials can be very confusing for American lawyers. The *Bluebook* (16th ed. 1996) includes citation information for fifteen civil law countries, providing coverage of the most frequently cited sources. More in-depth coverage is available from *World Dictionary of Legal Abbreviations* (4 vols., 1991–date), which has separate sections for abbreviations in French, German, Hebrew, Italian, Portuguese, and Spanish.

§ 12–4. CONCLUSION

Any serious legal problem involving another jurisdiction will require consultation with a lawyer trained and licensed in that jurisdiction. The resources discussed in this chapter, however, can provide a solid starting point for the American researcher.

Other than availability of materials, there is little hindrance to research in English, Canadian, or Australian law. These countries have legal research resources that are quite similar to our own and are easily accessible to American legal researchers, either for comparative study or for analysis of legal problems arising in those nations.

In researching the law of civil law countries, lawyers limited to English-language materials will be seriously handicapped. However, the increasing availability of secondary sources in English and translations now allow

preliminary study of most foreign legal problems. Such study may help the American lawyer to determine the general nature of a problem, and can facilitate communication with the foreign law specialist who may be called in to assist.

APPENDIX A

SOURCES FOR STATE APPELLATE COURT CASES

Most state appellate court cases are published in both official reports and the National Reporter System, but there are significant exceptions. Most regional reporters did not begin publication until the 1880s, and several states have discontinued official reports in recent decades.

This table shows major published and electronic sources for the decisions of state courts of last resort and intermediate appellate courts. Electronic coverage, which of course is subject to change, is current as of April 2000. Internet sites are listed if they provide free access to cases and maintain archives for more than just a few weeks or months. Most of the sites listed are official state sites, but commercial sites are included if they provide searching enhancements or other features unavailable from the official site.

In some instances, listings include earlier courts with similar functions to the current courts listed. Some court systems have changed dramatically under new state constitutions, e.g., New York in 1846 and South Carolina in 1868, but the earlier courts are not listed separately. For more precise information it may be necessary to turn to a state legal research guide (see Appendix B).

The Bluebook: A Uniform System of Citation (16th ed. 1996, pp. 170-225) has listings of state nominative reports (with abbreviations); and Cohen, Berring & Olson, *How to Find the Law* (9th ed. 1989, Appendix B) includes more

extensive coverage of nominative reports, miscellaneous reports, and sources for state trial court cases.

ALABAMA

Supreme Court

Nominative reports, 1820-39
1-295 *Alabama Reports*, 1840-1976
Southern Reporter, 1887 [80 Ala.]-date
Westlaw, 1820-date
Lexis-Nexis, 1840-date
<www.wallacejordan.com/decision.htm>, 1998-date

Court of Civil Appeals

1-57 *Alabama Appellate Court Reports*, 1911-76
Southern Reporter, 1911 [1 Ala. App.]-date
Westlaw and Lexis-Nexis, 1911-date

Court of Criminal Appeals

1-57 *Alabama Appellate Court Reports*, 1911-76
Southern Reporter, 1911 [1 Ala. App.]-date
Westlaw and Lexis-Nexis, 1911-date

ALASKA

Supreme Court

Pacific Reporter, 1959-date
Westlaw and Lexis-Nexis, 1959-date
<www.touchngo.com/sp/sp.htm>, 1991-date

Court of Appeals

Pacific Reporter, 1980-date
Westlaw and Lexis-Nexis, 1980-date
<www.touchngo.com/ap/ap.htm>, 1991-date

ARIZONA

Supreme Court

Arizona Reports, 1866-date
Pacific Reporter, 1866 [1 Ariz.]-date
Westlaw and Lexis-Nexis, 1866-date
<www.supreme.state.az.us/opin/>, 1997-date

Court of Appeals

1-27 *Arizona Appeals Reports*, 1965-76
Arizona Reports, 1976-date
Pacific Reporter, 1965 [1 Ariz. App.]-date
Westlaw and Lexis-Nexis, 1965-date

ARKANSAS

Supreme Court

Arkansas Reports, 1837-date
South Western Reporter, 1887 [47 Ark.]-date
Westlaw and Lexis-Nexis, 1837-date
<courts.state.ar.us/opinions/opmain.htm>, 1994-date

Court of Appeals

Arkansas Appellate Reports, 1979-date (bound with *Arkansas Reports*)
South Western Reporter, 1979 [1 Ark. App.]-date
Westlaw and Lexis-Nexis, 1979-date
<courts.state.ar.us/opinions/opmain.htm>, 1994-date

CALIFORNIA

Supreme Court

California Reports, 1850-date
Pacific Reporter, 1883 [64 Cal.]-date)
California Reporter, 1960 [53 Cal. 2d]-date)

Westlaw and Lexis-Nexis, 1850-date
<california.findlaw.com/CA02_caselaw/slip.html>,
 1996-date

Courts of Appeal

California Appellate Reports, 1905-date
Pacific Reporter, 1905 [1 Cal. App.]-1959 [175 Cal.
 App. 2d]
California Reporter, 1960 [176 Cal. App. 2d]-date
Westlaw and Lexis-Nexis, 1905-date
<california.findlaw.com/CA02_caselaw/slip.html>,
 1996-date

COLORADO

Supreme Court

1-200 *Colorado Reports*, 1864-1980
Pacific Reporter, 1884 [7 Colo.]-date
Westlaw and Lexis-Nexis, 1864-date

Court of Appeals

1-44 *Colorado Court of Appeals Reports*, 1891-1915,
 1970-80
Pacific Reporter, 1891 [1 Colo. App.]-1915, 1970-date
Westlaw and Lexis-Nexis, 1891-1915, 1970-date

CONNECTICUT

Supreme Court

Nominative reports, 1786-1813
Connecticut Reports, 1814-date
Atlantic Reporter, 1886 [53 Conn.]-date
Westlaw, 1786-date
Lexis-Nexis, 1814-date

Appellate Court

Connecticut Appellate Reports, 1983-date
Atlantic Reporter, 1983 [1 Conn. App.]-date
Westlaw and Lexis-Nexis, 1983-date

DELAWARE

Supreme Court

1-3 *Delaware Cases*, 1792-1830
1-59 *Delaware Reports*, 1832-1966
Atlantic Reporter, 1886 [12 Del.]-date
Westlaw, 1792-date
Lexis-Nexis, 1832-date
<courts.state.de.us/supreme/ordsops/list.htm>, 1998-date

DISTRICT OF COLUMBIA

Court of Appeals

Atlantic Reporter, 1942-date
Westlaw and Lexis-Nexis, 1942-date
<www.dcbar.org/dcca/opinions.html>, 1998-date

FLORIDA

Supreme Court

1-160 *Florida Reports*, 1846-1948
Southern Reporter, 1887 [22 Fla.]-date
Westlaw and Lexis-Nexis, 1846-date
<www.law.ufl.edu/opinions/supreme/>, 1995-date

District Courts of Appeal

Southern Reporter, 1957-date
Westlaw and Lexis-Nexis, 1957-date

GEORGIA

Supreme Court

Georgia Reports, 1846-date
South Eastern Reporter, 1887 [77 Ga.]-date
Westlaw and Lexis-Nexis, 1846-date

Court of Appeals

Georgia Appeals Reports, 1907-date
South Eastern Reporter, 1907 [1 Ga. App.]-date
Westlaw and Lexis-Nexis, 1907-date

HAWAI'I

Supreme Court

Hawai'i Reports, 1847-date
Pacific Reporter, 1884 [43 Haw.]-date
Westlaw and Lexis-Nexis, 1847-date
<www.hsba.org/index/court/CASELAW.HTM>, 1989-date
<www.state.hi.us/jud/ctops.htm>, 1998-date

Intermediate Court of Appeals

1-10 *Hawai'i Appellate Reports*, 1980-94
Hawai'i Reports, 1994-date
Pacific Reporter, 1980 [1 Haw. App.]-date
Westlaw and Lexis-Nexis, 1980-date
<www.hsba.org/index/court/CASELAW.HTM>, 1989-date
<www.state.hi.us/jud/ctops.htm>, 1998-date

IDAHO

Supreme Court

Idaho Reports, 1866-date
Pacific Reporter, 1881 [2 Idaho]-date
Westlaw and Lexis-Nexis, 1866-date

Court of Appeals

Idaho Reports, 1982-date
Pacific Reporter, 1982 [102 Idaho]-date
Westlaw and Lexis-Nexis, 1982-date

ILLINOIS

Supreme Court

Illinois Reports, 1819-date
North Eastern Reporter, 1884 [112 Ill.]-date
Westlaw and Lexis-Nexis, 1819-date
<www.state.il.us/court/>, 1996-date

Appellate Court

Illinois Appellate Reports, 1877-date
North Eastern Reporter, 1936 [284 Ill. App.]-date
Westlaw and Lexis-Nexis, 1877-date
<www.state.il.us/court/>, 1996-date

INDIANA

Supreme Court

Nominative reports, 1817-47
1-275 *Indiana Reports*, 1848-1981
North Eastern Reporter, 1885 [102 Ind.]-date
Westlaw, 1817-date
Lexis-Nexis, 1848-date

Court of Appeals

1-182 *Indiana Court of Appeals Reports*, 1891-1979
North Eastern Reporter, 1891 [1 Ind. App.]-date
Westlaw and Lexis-Nexis, 1891-date

IOWA

Supreme Court

Nominative reports, 1839-54
1-261 *Iowa Reports*, 1855-1968
North Western Reporter, 1879 [51 Iowa]-date
Westlaw, 1839-date
Lexis-Nexis, 1855-date
<www.judicial.state.ia.us/decisions/>, 1998-date

Court of Appeals

North Western Reporter, 1977-date
Westlaw and Lexis-Nexis, 1977-date
<www.judicial.state.ia.us/decisions/>, 1998-date

KANSAS

Supreme Court

Nominative reports, 1858-61
Kansas Reports, 1862-date
Pacific Reporter, 1883 [30 Kan.]-date
Westlaw, 1858-date
Lexis-Nexis, 1862-date
<www.kscourts.org/kscases/>, 1996-date

Court of Appeals

Kansas Court of Appeals Reports, 1895-1901, 1977-
date

Pacific Reporter, 1895 [1 Kan. App.]-1901, 1977-date
Westlaw and Lexis-Nexis, 1895-1901, 1977-date
<www.kscourts.org/kscases/>, 1996-date

KENTUCKY

Supreme Court

1-314 *Kentucky Reports*, 1785-1951
South Western Reporter, 1886 [84 Ky.]-date
Westlaw and Lexis-Nexis, 1785-date

Court of Appeals

South Western Reporter, 1976-date
Westlaw and Lexis-Nexis, 1976-date

LOUISIANA

Supreme Court

Nominative reports, 1813-30, 1841-46
1-19 *Louisiana Reports*, 1830-41
1-52 *Louisiana Annual Reports*, 1846-1900
104-263 *Louisiana Reports*, 1900-72
Southern Reporter, 1887 [39 La. Ann.]-date
Westlaw, 1813-date
Lexis-Nexis, 1841-date
<www.lasc.org/documents.html>, 1996-date

Courts of Appeal

Nominative reports, 1881-85, 1903-23
1-19 *Louisiana Courts of Appeals Reports*, 1924-32
Southern Reporter, 1928 [9 La. App.]-date
Westlaw and Lexis-Nexis, 1928-date

MAINE

Supreme Judicial Court

1-161 *Maine Reports*, 1820-1965
Atlantic Reporter, 1886 [77 Me.]-date
Westlaw and Lexis-Nexis, 1820-date
<www.courts.state.me.us/mescopin.home.html>,
   1997-date

MARYLAND

Court of Appeals

Nominative reports, 1787-1851
Maryland Reports, 1851-date
Atlantic Reporter, 1886 [63 Md.]-date
Westlaw, 1787-date
Lexis-Nexis, 1851-date
<www.courts.state.md.us/opinions.html>, 1995-date

Court of Special Appeals

Maryland Appellate Reports, 1967-date
Atlantic Reporter, 1967 [1 Md. App.]-date
Westlaw and Lexis-Nexis, 1967-date
<www.courts.state.md.us/opinions.html>, 1995-date

MASSACHUSETTS

Supreme Judicial Court

Massachusetts Reports, 1804-date
North Eastern Reporter, 1885 [139 Mass.]-date
Westlaw and Lexis-Nexis, 1804-date
<www.lawyersweekly.com/sjc.htm>, 1997-date

Appeals Court

Massachusetts Appeals Court Reports, 1972-date
North Eastern Reporter, 1972 [1 Mass. App.]-date

Westlaw and Lexis-Nexis, 1972-date
<www.lawyersweekly.com/mapps.htm>, 1997-date

MICHIGAN

Supreme Court

Nominative reports, 1838-47
Michigan Reports, 1847-date
North Western Reporter, 1879 [41 Mich.]-date
Westlaw, 1838-date
Lexis-Nexis, 1847-date
<www.icle.org/michlaw/>, 1995-date
<www.lawyersweekly.com/misct.htm>, 1996-date

Court of Appeals

Michigan Appeals Reports, 1965-date
North Western Reporter, 1965 [1 Mich. App.]-date
Westlaw and Lexis-Nexis, 1965-date
<www.icle.org/michlaw/>, 1996-date
<www.lawyersweekly.com/micoa.htm>, 1996-date

MINNESOTA

Supreme Court

1-312 *Minnesota Reports*, 1851-1977
North Western Reporter, 1879 [26 Minn.]-date
Westlaw and Lexis-Nexis, 1851-date
<www.courts.state.mn.us/library/archive/>, 1996-date

Court of Appeals

North Western Reporter, 1983-date
Westlaw and Lexis-Nexis, 1983-date
<www.courts.state.mn.us/library/archive/>, 1996-date

MISSISSIPPI

Supreme Court

1-254 *Mississippi Reports*, 1818-1966
Southern Reporter, 1887 [64 Miss.]-date
Westlaw and Lexis-Nexis, 1818-date
<www.mssc.state.ms.us/decisions/>, 1996-date

Court of Appeals

Southern Reporter, 1995-date
Westlaw and Lexis-Nexis, 1995-date
<www.mssc.state.ms.us/decisions/>, 1996-date

MISSOURI

Supreme Court

1-365 *Missouri Reports*, 1821-1956
South Western Reporter, 1886 [89 Mo.]-date
Westlaw and Lexis-Nexis, 1821-date
<www.osca.state.mo.us>, 1997-date

Courts of Appeals

1-241 *Missouri Appeal Reports*, 1876-1952
South Western Reporter, 1902 [93 Mo. App.]-date
Westlaw and Lexis-Nexis, 1876-date
<www.osca.state.mo.us>, 1997-date

MONTANA

Supreme Court

Montana Reports, 1868-date
Pacific Reporter, 1884 [4 Mont.]-date
Westlaw, 1868-date
Lexis-Nexis, 1964-date
<www.lawlibrary.state.mt.us>, 1997-date

NEBRASKA

Supreme Court

Nebraska Reports, 1860-date
North Western Reporter, 1879 [8 Neb.]-date
Westlaw, 1860-date
Lexis-Nexis, 1871-date

Court of Appeals

Nebraska Appellate Reports, 1992-date
North Western Reporter, 1992 [1 Neb. App.]-date
Westlaw and Lexis-Nexis, 1992-date

NEVADA

Supreme Court

Nevada Reports, 1865-date
Pacific Reporter, 1884 [17 Nev.]-date
Westlaw and Lexis-Nexis, 1865-date

NEW HAMPSHIRE

Supreme Court

Nominative reports, 1803-16
New Hampshire Reports, 1816-date
Atlantic Reporter, 1886 [63 N.H.]-date
Westlaw and Lexis-Nexis, 1816-date
<www.state.nh.us/courts/supreme/opinions.htm>,
   1995-date

NEW JERSEY

Supreme Court

1-137 *New Jersey Law Reports*, 1789-1948
1-142 *New Jersey Equity Reports*, 1830-1948
New Jersey Reports, 1948-date

Atlantic Reporter, 1885 [47 N.J. Law, 40 N.J. Eq.]-
date
Westlaw and Lexis-Nexis, 1789-date
<lawlibrary.rutgers.edu/search.shtml>, 1994-date

Superior Court, Appellate Division

New Jersey Superior Court Reports, 1948-date
Atlantic Reporter, 1948 [1 N.J. Super.]-date
Westlaw and Lexis-Nexis, 1948-date
<lawlibrary.rutgers.edu/search.shtml>, 1995-date

NEW MEXICO

Supreme Court

New Mexico Reports, 1852-date
Pacific Reporter, 1883 [3 N.M.]-date
Westlaw and Lexis-Nexis, 1852-date

Court of Appeals

New Mexico Reports, 1966-date
Pacific Reporter, 1966 [78 N.M.]-date
Westlaw and Lexis-Nexis, 1966-date

NEW YORK

Court of Appeals

Nominative reports, 1791-1847
New York Reports, 1847-date
North Eastern Reporter, 1885 [99 N.Y.]-date
New York Supplement, 1956 [1 N.Y.2d]-date
Westlaw, 1791-date
Lexis-Nexis, 1847-date
<www.law.cornell.edu/ny/ctap/>, 1992-date

Supreme Court, Appellate Division

Nominative reports, 1821-95
Appellate Division Reports, 1896-date
New York Supplement, 1896 [1 App. Div.]-date
Westlaw, 1821-date
Lexis-Nexis, 1896-date

NORTH CAROLINA

Supreme Court

North Carolina Reports, 1778-date
South Eastern Reporter, 1884 [96 N.C.]-date
Westlaw and Lexis-Nexis, 1778-date
<www.ncinsider.com/insider/supreme/supco.html>,
   1994-date
<www.aoc.state.nc.us/www/public/html/opinions.
   htm>, 1997-date

Court of Appeals

North Carolina Court of Appeals Reports, 1968-date
South Eastern Reporter, 1968 [1 N.C. App.]-date
Westlaw and Lexis-Nexis, 1968-date
<www.ncinsider.com/insider/appeals/appeals.html>,
   1994-date
<www.aoc.state.nc.us/www/public/html/opinions.
   htm>, 1996-date

NORTH DAKOTA

Supreme Court

1-6 *Dakota Reports*, 1867-89
1-79 *North Dakota Reports*, 1890-1953
North Western Reporter, 1867 [1 Dak.]-date
Westlaw, 1867-date

Lexis-Nexis, 1926-date
<www.court.state.nd.us/court/opinions.htm>, 1993-date

Court of Appeals

North Western Reporter, 1987-date
Westlaw and Lexis-Nexis, 1987-date

OHIO

Supreme Court

1-20 *Ohio Reports*, 1821-52
Ohio State Reports, 1852-date
North Eastern Reporter, 1885 [43 Ohio St.]-date
Westlaw and Lexis-Nexis, 1821-date
<www.sconet.state.oh.us/rod/Opinions/List.asp>, 1992-date
<www.lawyersweekly.com/ohsc.htm>, 1997-date

Courts of Appeals

Ohio Appellate Reports, 1913-date
North Eastern Reporter, 1923 [20 Ohio App.]-date
Lexis-Nexis, 1913-date
Westlaw, 1923-date

OKLAHOMA

Supreme Court

1-208 *Oklahoma Reports*, 1890-1953
Pacific Reporter, 1890 [1 Okla.]-date
Westlaw and Lexis-Nexis, 1890-date
<www.onenet.net/oklegal/sample.basic.html>, 1936-date
<www.oscn.net>, 1952-date

Court of Criminal Appeals

1-97 *Oklahoma Criminal Reports*, 1908-53
Pacific Reporter, 1980 [1 Okla. Crim.]-date
Westlaw and Lexis-Nexis, 1908-date
<www.occa.state.ok.us>, 1936-date
<www.oscn.net>, 1943-date
<www.onenet.net/oklegal/sample.basic.html>, 1995-date

Court of Civil Appeals

Pacific Reporter, 1968-date
Westlaw and Lexis-Nexis, 1968-date
<www.oscn.net>, 1968-date
<www.onenet.net/oklegal/sample.basic.html>, 1968-date

OREGON

Supreme Court

Oregon Reports, 1853-date
Pacific Reporter, 1884 [11 Or.]-date
Westlaw and Lexis-Nexis, 1853-date
<www.publications.ojd.state.or.us/supreme.htm>, 1998-date

Court of Appeal

Oregon Reports, Court of Appeal, 1969-date
Pacific Reporter, 1969 [1 Or. App.]-date
Westlaw and Lexis-Nexis, 1969-date
<www.publications.ojd.state.or.us/appeals.htm>, 1998-date

PENNSYLVANIA

Supreme Court

Nominative reports, 1754-1845
Pennsylvania State Reports, 1845-date
Atlantic Reporter, 1886 [108 Pa. St.]-date
Westlaw, 1791-date
Lexis-Nexis, 1845-date

Superior Court

Pennsylvania Superior Court Reports, 1895-date
Atlantic Reporter, 1930 [102 Pa. Super.]-date
Westlaw and Lexis-Nexis, 1895-date

Commonwealth Court

1-168 *Pennsylvania Commonwealth Court Reports*,
1970-94
Atlantic Reporter, 1970 [1 Pa. Commw.]-date
Westlaw and Lexis-Nexis, 1970-date

PUERTO RICO

Tribunal Supremo

1-100 *Puerto Rico Reports*, 1899-1972
Decisiones de Puerto Rico, 1899-date
Westlaw and Lexis-Nexis, 1899-date

Tribunal Circuito de Apelaciones

Lexis-Nexis, 1995-date

RHODE ISLAND

Supreme Court

1-122 *Rhode Island Reports*, 1828-1980
Atlantic Reporter, 1886 [15 R.I.]-date
Westlaw and Lexis-Nexis, 1828-date

SOUTH CAROLINA

Supreme Court

Nominative reports, 1783-1868
South Carolina Reports, 1868-date
South Eastern Reporter, 1886 [25 S.C.]-date
Westlaw, 1783-date
Lexis-Nexis, 1868-date
<www.law.sc.edu/opinions/opinions.htm>, 1996-date

Court of Appeals

South Carolina Reports, 1983-date
South Eastern Reporter, 1983-date
Westlaw and Lexis-Nexis, 1983-date
<www.law.sc.edu/ctapp/scctapp.htm>, 1999-date

SOUTH DAKOTA

Supreme Court

1-6 *Dakota Reports*, 1867-89
1-90 *South Dakota Reports*, 1890-1976
North Western Reporter, 1867 [1 Dak.]-date
Westlaw, 1867-date
Lexis-Nexis, 1966-date
<www.sdbar.org/opinions/sdindex.htm>, 1996-date

TENNESSEE

Supreme Court

1-225 *Tennessee Reports*, 1791-1971
South Western Reporter, 1886 [85 Tenn.]-date
Westlaw and Lexis-Nexis, 1791-date
<www.tsc.state.tn.us/intertst.htm>, 1995-date

Court of Appeals

1-63 *Tennessee Appeals Reports*, 1925-71
South Western Reporter, 1932 [16 Tenn. App.]-date
Westlaw and Lexis-Nexis, 1925-date
<www.tsc.state.tn.us/intertst.htm>, 1995-date

Court of Criminal Appeals

1-4 *Tennessee Criminal Appeals Reports*, 1967-71
South Western Reporter, 1967 [1 Tenn. Crim. App.]-
   date
Westlaw and Lexis-Nexis, 1967-date
<www.tsc.state.tn.us/intertst.htm>, 1995-date

TEXAS

Supreme Court

Nominative reports, 1840-45
1-163 *Texas Reports*, 1846-1963
South Western Reporter, 1886 [66 Tex.]-date
Westlaw and Lexis-Nexis, 1840-date
<www.supreme.courts.state.tx.us/scopn.htm>, 1997-
   date

Court of Criminal Appeals

1-30 *Texas Court of Appeals Cases*, 1876-92
31-172 *Texas Criminal Reports*, 1892-1963
South Western Reporter, 1886 [21 Tex. App.]-date
Westlaw and Lexis-Nexis, 1876-date
<www.cca.courts.state.tx.us>, 1998-date

Courts of Appeals

1-63 *Texas Civil Appeals Reports*, 1892-1911
South Western Reporter, 1892 [1 Tex. Civ. App.]-date
Westlaw and Lexis-Nexis, 1892-date

UTAH

Supreme Court

1-123, 1-30 2d *Utah Reports*, 1861-1974
Pacific Reporter, 1884 [3 Utah]-date
Westlaw and Lexis-Nexis, 1861-date
<courtlink.utcourts.gov/opinions/>, 1996-date

Court of Appeals

Pacific Reporter, 1987-date
Westlaw and Lexis-Nexis, 1987-date
<courtlink.utcourts.gov/opinions/>, 1997-date

VERMONT

Supreme Court

Nominative reports, 1789-1826
Vermont Reports, 1826-date
Atlantic Reporter, 1885 [58 Vt.]-date
Westlaw, 1789-date

Lexis-Nexis, 1826-date
<dol.state.vt.us/wwwroot/000000/html/supct.html,
  1993-date

VIRGINIA

Supreme Court

Virginia Reports, 1790-date
South Eastern Reporter, 1887 [82 Va.]-date
Westlaw and Lexis-Nexis, 1790-date
<www.courts.state.va.us/opin.htm>, 1995-date
<www.lawyersweekly.com/vasc.htm>, 1998-date

Court of Appeals

Virginia Court of Appeals Reports, 1985-date
South Eastern Reporter, 1985 [1 Va. App.]-date
Westlaw and Lexis-Nexis, 1985-date
<www.courts.state.va.us/opin.htm>, 1995-date
<www.lawyersweekly.com/vacoa.htm>, 1997-date

WASHINGTON

Supreme Court

1-3 *Washington Territory Reports*, 1854-89
Washington Reports, 1889-date
Pacific Reports, 1884 [2 Wash. Terr.]-date
Westlaw, 1854-date
Lexis-Nexis, 1889-date

Court of Appeals

Washington Appellate Reports, 1969-date
Pacific Reporter, 1969 [1 Wash. App.]-date
Westlaw and Lexis-Nexis, 1969-date

WEST VIRGINIA

Supreme Court of Appeals

West Virginia Reports, 1864-date
South Eastern Reporter, 1884 [29 W. Va.]-date
Westlaw and Lexis-Nexis, 1864-date
<www.state.wv.us/wvsca/opinions.htm>, 1991-date

WISCONSIN

Supreme Court

Nominative reports, 1839-53
Wisconsin Reports, 1853-date
North Western Reporter, 1879 [46 Wis.]-date
Westlaw, 1839-date
Lexis-Nexis, 1847-date
<www.courts.state.wi.us/WCS/scsearch.html>, 1995-date
<www.wisbar.org/Wis/>, 1995-date

Court of Appeals

Wisconsin Reports, 1978-date
North Western Reporter, 1978 [85 Wis. 2d]-date
Westlaw and Lexis-Nexis, 1978-date
<www.courts.state.wi.us/WCS/casearch.html>, 1995-date
<www.wisbar.org/WisCtApp/>, 1995-date

WYOMING

Supreme Court

1-80 *Wyoming Reports*, 1870-1959
Pacific Reporter, 1884 [3 Wyo.]-date
Westlaw and Lexis-Nexis, 1870-date
<courts.state.wy.us/newopn.htm>, 1996-date

APPENDIX B

STATE RESEARCH GUIDES

Because of variations in legal materials from state to state, a general research guide like this *Nutshell* cannot provide the necessary detail for specific state sources. These guides are therefore suggested for further information on the materials of individual states. The list includes some journal articles discussing state practice materials and research methods, and several short but useful guides to state materials or government documents issued by the American Association of Law Libraries. These materials are generally listed here only if no other recent guide is available for that state.

Nancy Adams Deel & Barbara G. James, "An Annotated Bibliography of State Legal Research Guides," 14 Legal Reference Services Q., nos. 1/2, at 23 (1994) provides a more extensive, well-annotated list of state guides. The "State Legal Publications and Information Sources" chapter of Kendall F. Svengalis's annual *Legal Information Buyer's Guide & Reference Manual* lists research guides as well as other basic resources for each state.

Alabama	Hazel L. Johnson & Timothy L. Coggins, *Guide to Alabama State Documents and Selected Law–Related Materials* (1993); Lynne B. Kitchens & Timothy A. Lewis, "Alabama Practice Materials: A Selected Annotated Bibliography," 82 Law Libr. J. 703 (1990).

Alaska	Aimee Ruzicka, *Alaska Legal and Law–Related Publications: A Guide for Law Librarians* (1984).
Arizona	Kathy Shimpock–Vieweg & Marianne Sidorski Alcorn, *Arizona Legal Research Guide* (1992).
Arkansas	Kathryn C. Fitzhugh, "Arkansas Practice Materials II: A Selective Annotated Bibliography," 21 U. Ark. Little Rock L.J. 363 (1999).
California	Larry D. Dershem, *California Legal Research Handbook* (1997); John K. Hanft, *Legal Research in California* (3d ed. 1999); Daniel W. Martin, *Henke's California Law Guide* (4th ed. 1998).
Colorado	Mitch Fontenot, "Colorado Practice Materials: A Selective Annotated Bibliography," 88 Law Libr. J. 427 (1996).
Connecticut	Shirley Bysiewicz, *Sources of Connecticut Law* (1987); Lawrence G. Cheeseman & Arlene C. Bielefeld, *The Connecticut Legal Research Handbook* (1992); Jonathan Saxon, "Connecticut Practice Materials: A Selective Annotated Bibliography," 91 Law Libr. J. 139 (1999).
Delaware	Patrick J. Charles & David K. King, "Delaware Practice Materials: A Selective Annotated Bibliography," 89 Law Libr. J. 349 (1997).
District of Columbia	Leah F. Chanin, "Legal Research in the District of Columbia," in *Legal Research in the District of Columbia, Maryland and Virginia* (1995).
Florida	Suzanne E. Rowe et al., *Florida Legal Research: Sources, Process, and Analysis* (1998); Betsy L. Stupski, *Guide to Florida Legal Research* (5th ed. 1998).

Georgia	Leah F. Chanin & Suzanne L. Cassidy, *Guide to Georgia Legal Research and Legal History* (1990); Nancy P. Johnson & Nancy Adams Deel, "Researching Georgia Law (1998 Edition)," 14 Ga. St. U. L. Rev. 545 (1998).
Hawaii	Richard F. Kahle, Jr., *How to Research Constitutional, Legislative, and Statutory History in Hawaii* (rev. ed. 1997).
Idaho	Lemaala R. Seeger, "Idaho Practice Materials: A Selective Annotated Bibliography," 87 Law Libr. J. 534 (1995).
Illinois	Frank G. Houdek & Jean McKnight, "An Annotated Bibliography of Legal Research Tools," 16 S. Ill. U. L.J. 767 (1992); Laurel Wendt, *Illinois Legal Research Manual* (1988).
Indiana	Linda K. Fariss & Keith A. Buckley, *An Introduction to Indiana State Publications for the Law Librarian* (1982).
Iowa	Angela K. Secrest, *Iowa Legal Documents Bibliography* (1990).
Kansas	Joseph A. Custer, ed., *Kansas Legal Research and Reference Guide* (2d ed. 1997).
Kentucky	Kurt X. Metzmeier, "Kentucky Legal Research on the Internet," 86 Ky. L.J. 971 (1997–98); Arturo L. Torres, "Kentucky Practice Materials: A Selective, Annotated Bibliography," 84 Law Libr. J. 509 (1992).
Louisiana	Win–Shin S. Chiang, *Louisiana Legal Research* (2d ed. 1990).
Maine	William W. Wells, *Maine Legal Research Guide* (1989).

Maryland	Pamela J. Gregory, "Legal Research in Maryland," in *Legal Research in the District of Columbia, Maryland and Virginia* (1995).
Massachusetts	Virginia Wise, ed., *How to Do Massachusetts Legal Research* (1998).
Michigan	Richard L. Beer & Judith J. Field, *Michigan Legal Literature: An Annotated Guide* (2d ed. 1991); Nancy L. Bosh, *The Research Edge: Finding Law and Facts Fast* (1993).
Minnesota	Arlette M. Soderberg & Barbara L. Golden, *Minnesota Legal Research Guide* (1985).
Mississippi	Ben Cole, *Mississippi Legal Documents and Related Publications: A Selected Annotated Bibliography* (1987).
Missouri	Mary Ann Nelson, *Guide to Missouri State Documents and Selected Law–Related Materials* (1991).
Montana	Stephen R. Jordan, *A Guide to Montana Legal Research* (6th ed. 1999).
Nebraska	Partrick J. Charles et al., *Lexis Publishing's Research Guide to Nebraska Law* (2d ed. 1999).
Nevada	G. LeGrande Fletcher, "Nevada Practice Materials: A Selective Annotated Bibliography," 91 Law Libr. J. 313 (1999).
New Jersey	Cameron Allen, *A Guide to New Jersey Legal Bibliography and Legal History* (1984); Paul Axel–Lute, *New Jersey Legal Research Handbook* (4th ed. 1998).
New Mexico	Patricia Wagner & Mary Woodward, *Guide to New Mexico State Publications* (2d ed. 1991); Mary A. Woodward, "New Mexico Practice Materials: A Selective Annotated Bibliography," 84 Law Libr. J. 93 (1992).

New York	Ellen M. Gibson, *New York Legal Research Guide* (2d ed. 1998).
North Carolina	Jean Sinclair McKnight, *North Carolina Legal Research Guide* (1994).
Ohio	James Leonard, "A Select, Annotated Bibliography of Ohio Practice Materials," 17 Ohio N.U. L. Rev. 265 (1990); Melanie K. Putnam & Susan Schaefgen, *Ohio Legal Research Guide* (1997).
Oklahoma	Marilyn K. Nicely, *Oklahoma Legal and Law–Related Documents and Publications: A Selected Bibliography* (2d ed. 1997).
Oregon	Karen S. Beck, "Oregon Practice Materials: A Selective Annotated Bibliography," 88 Law Libr. J. 288 (1996).
Pennsylvania	Joel Fishman, *Bibliography of Pennsylvania Law: Secondary Sources* (1992); Joel Fishman, *An Introduction to Pennsylvania State Publications for the Law Librarian* (1985).
Puerto Rico	Carlos I. Gorrín Peralta, *Fuentes y Proceso de Investigación Jurídica* (1991); Luis Muñiz Argüelles & Migdalia Fraticelli Migdalia, *La Investigación Jurídica en el Derecho Puertorriqueño: Fuentes Puertorriqueñas, Norteamericanas y Españolas* (2d ed. 1995).
Rhode Island	Colleen McConaghy, *Selective Bibliography for the State of Rhode Island: State Documents and Law–Related Materials* (1993).
South Carolina	Paula Gail Benson & Deborah Ann Davis, *A Guide to South Carolina Legal Research and Citation* (1991).
South Dakota	Delores A. Jorgensen, *South Dakota Legal Research Guide* (2d ed. 1999).

Tennessee	Lewis L. Laska, *Tennessee Legal Research Handbook* (1977); D. Cheryn Picquet & Reba A. Best, *Law and Government Publications of the State of Tennessee: A Bibliographic Guide* (1988).
Texas	Lydia M.V. Brandt, *Texas Legal Research: An Essential Lawyering Skill* (1995); Karl T. Gruben & James E. Hambleton, eds., *A Reference Guide to Texas Law and Legal History: Sources and Documentation* (2d ed. 1987); Pamela R. Tepper & Peggy N. Kerley, *Texas Legal Research* (2d ed. 1997).
Utah	Kory D. Staheli, "Utah Practice Materials: A Selective Annotated Bibliography," 87 Law Libr. J. 28 (1995).
Vermont	Wise, *A Bibliographical Guide to the Vermont Legal System* (2d ed. 1991).
Virginia	John D. Eure & Robert D. Murphy, Jr., eds., *A Guide to Legal Research in Virginia* (3d ed. 1999); Sarah K. Wiant, "Legal Research in Virginia," in *Legal Research in the District of Columbia, Maryland and Virginia* (1995).
Washington	Penny A. Hazelton et al., *Washington Legal Researcher's Deskbook 2d* (1996).
West Virginia	Sandra Stemple et al., *West Virginia Legal Bibliography* (1990).
Wisconsin	Richard A. Danner, *Legal Research in Wisconsin* (1980); Ellen J. Platt & Mary J. Koshollek, "Wisconsin Practice Materials: A Selective, Annotated Bibliography," 90 Law Libr. J. 219 (1998).
Wyoming	Nancy S. Greene, *Wyoming State Legal Documents: An Annotated Bibliography* (1985).

APPENDIX C

TOPICAL LOOSELEAF AND ELECTRONIC SERVICES

This is a selective list of topical services useful in legal research. Most services are available in numerous formats, including print, CD–ROM, and online versions, sometimes with slight variations in name. Electronic options are indicated in brackets, and italic type indicates services available only electronically. The basic criteria for inclusion are frequent supplementation (at least monthly); publication of primary documents (either abstracts or full texts); and availability in law libraries. Electronic services change frequently, so this list must be used with some caution. For regularly updated and more comprehensive listings, see publisher websites or the annual *Legal Looseleafs in Print*.

Abbreviation	Publisher
BNA	Bureau of National Affairs <www.bna.com>
CCH	CCH Inc. <www.cch.com>
IHS	IHS Regulatory Products <www.ihs.com>
LRP	LRP Publications <www.lrp.com>
RIA	Research Institute of America <www.riatax.com>
Thompson	Thompson Publishing Group, Inc. <www.thompson.com>
WGL	Warren, Gorham & Lamont <www.wgl.com>

Accounting

Cost Accounting Standards Guide (CCH) *[CD, Internet]*

Aviation

Aviation Law Reports (CCH) *[CD, Internet]*

Banking

Banking Report (BNA) *[Internet, Lexis, Westlaw]*

Banking Library (IHS) *[CD, Internet]*

Federal Banking Law Reports (CCH) *[CD, Internet, Lexis, Westlaw]*

Federal Reserve Regulatory Service (Federal Reserve System) *[CD]*

Bankruptcy

Bankruptcy Law Reporter (BNA) *[Internet]*

Bankruptcy Law Reports (CCH)

Commercial Law

Consumer Credit Guide (CCH) *[CD, Internet, Lexis, Westlaw]*

RICO Business Disputes Guide (CCH) *[CD, Internet]*

Secured Transactions Guide (CCH) *[CD, Internet]*

Communications

Communications Regulation (Pike & Fischer) *[CD, Lexis]*

Media Law Reporter (BNA)

Computers

Electronic Commerce & Law Report (BNA) *[Internet]*

Guide to Computer Law (CCH) *[CD, Internet]*

Corporations

Capital Changes Reports (CCH) *[CD, Internet]*

Corporate Practice Series (BNA) *[Internet]*

Corporate Secretary's Guide (CCH)

Corporation (Aspen Law & Business) *[CD]*

Mergers & Acquisitions Law Report (BNA)

Criminal Law

Criminal Law Reporter (BNA) *[Internet]*

Disabilities

ADA Compliance Guide (Thompson)

Accommodating Disabilities: Business Management Guide (CCH) *[Lexis]*

AIDS Law & Litigation Reporter (University Publishing Group)

Americans with Disabilities Act Manual (BNA) *[CD, Westlaw]*

Individuals with Disabilities Education Law Reporter (LRP) *[CD, Westlaw]*

National Disability Law Reporter (LRP) *[CD, Westlaw]*

Elections

Federal Election Campaign Financing Guide (CCH)

Employment Practices

Employment and Training Reporter (MII Publications)

Employment Discrimination Coordinator (West) *[CD]*

Employment Practices Guide (CCH) *[CD, Internet, Lexis]*

Employment Testing: Law and Policy Reporter (University Publications of America) *[Lexis]*

Fair Employment Practices (BNA) *[CD, Internet, Lexis, Westlaw]*

Family and Medical Leave Handbook (Thompson)

Energy

Energy Management and Federal Energy Guidelines (CCH)

Nuclear Regulation Reports (CCH)

Utilities Law Reports (CCH)

Environment

Chemical Regulation Reporter (BNA) *[CD, Internet, Lexis, Westlaw]*

ENFLEX *(IHS) [CD, Internet, Lexis, Westlaw]*

Environment Reporter (BNA) *[CD, Internet, Lexis, Westlaw]*

Environmental Due Diligence Guide (BNA)

Environmental Law Reporter (Environmental Law Institute) *[CD, Internet, Lexis, Westlaw]*

International Environment Reporter (BNA) *[Internet, Lexis]*

Right–to–Know Planning Guide (BNA) *[Internet]*

Toxics Law Reporter (BNA) *[Internet, Lexis]*

Underground Storage Tank Guide (Thompson)

Estate Planning and Taxation

Estate Planning & Taxation Coordinator (RIA) *[CD]*

Federal Estate and Gift Tax Reports (CCH) *[CD, Internet, Lexis, Westlaw]*

Financial and Estate Planning (CCH) *[CD, Internet, Lexis, Westlaw]*

Inheritance, Estate and Gift Tax Reports: State (CCH)

United States Tax Reporter: Estate and Gift Taxes (RIA) *[CD, Internet, Lexis]*

Excise Taxation

Federal Excise Tax Reports (CCH) *[CD, Internet, Lexis, Westlaw]*

United States Tax Reporter: Excise Taxes (RIA) *[CD, Internet, Lexis]*

Family Law

Family Law Reporter (BNA) *[Internet]*

Family Law Tax Guide (CCH)

Federal Taxation (General and Income)

Federal Tax Service (CCH) *[CD, Internet, Lexis, Westlaw]*

Federal Tax Coordinator 2d (RIA) *[CD, Internet, Lexis, Westlaw]*

Federal Tax Guide (CCH) *[CD, Internet, Westlaw]*

Kleinrock's TaxExpert (Kleinrock Publishing) *[CD]*

Standard Federal Tax Reports (CCH) *[CD, Internet, Lexis, Westlaw]*

Tax Analysts OneDisc/ TaxBase (Tax Analysts, Inc.) *[CD, Internet]*

Tax Management Portfolios (BNA) *[CD, Internet, Lexis, Westlaw]*

United States Tax Reporter (RIA) *[CD, Internet, Lexis, Westlaw]*

Food and Drug

Food & Drug Library (IHS) *[CD, Internet]*

Food Drug Cosmetic Law Reports (CCH)

Medical Devices Library (IHS) *[CD, Internet]*

Medical Devices Reports (CCH)

Foundations and Charities

Charitable Giving and Solicitation (WGL)

Exempt Organizations Reports (CCH) *[CD, Internet, Lexis, Westlaw]*

Tax Exempt Organizations (RIA)

Franchises

Business Franchise Guide (CCH) *[CD, Internet, Lexis, Westlaw]*

Government Contracts

Federal Contracts Report (BNA) *[Internet, Lexis, Westlaw]*

Federal Grants Management Handbook (Thompson)

Government Contracts Reports (CCH) *[CD, Internet, Lexis]*

Health Care

BioLaw (University Publications of America)

Health Care Policy Report (BNA) *[Internet, Lexis, Westlaw]*

Health Law & Business Series (BNA) *[CD, Internet]*

Health Law Reporter (BNA) *[CD, Internet, Lexis, Westlaw]*

Healthcare Facilities Library (IHS) *[CD, Internet]*

Managed Care Reporter (BNA) *[Internet]*

Medicare and Medicaid Guide (CCH) *[CD, Internet]*

Medicare/Medicaid Library (IHS) *[CD, Internet]*

Medicare Report (BNA) *[CD, Internet, Lexis, Westlaw]*

Housing and Real Estate

Fair Housing / Fair Lending (Aspen Law & Business)

Housing and Development Reporter (West) *[CD]*

Real Estate Coordinator (RIA)

Insurance

INSource (NILS Publishing Co.) *[CD, Internet]*

Intellectual Property

Patent, Trademark & Copyright Journal (BNA) *[Internet, Lexis, Westlaw]*

Copyright Law Reports (CCH)

United States Patents Quarterly (BNA) *[CD, Lexis, Westlaw]*

International Business and Taxation

International Trade Reporter (BNA) *[CD, Internet, Lexis, Westlaw]*

U.S. Taxation of International Operations (WGL)

Labor Relations

Collective Bargaining Negotiations and Contracts (BNA)

Employment Coordinator (West) *[CD]*

Government Employee Relations Report (BNA) *[Internet, Lexis, Westlaw]*

Human Resources Management (CCH) *[CD, Internet]*

Labor Arbitration Information System (LRP)

Labor Law Reports (CCH) *[CD, Internet]*

Labor Relations Reporter (BNA) *[CD, Lexis, Westlaw]*

Policy and Practice Series (BNA) *[CD]*

Lawyers and Legal Ethics

ABA/BNA Lawyer's Manual on Professional Conduct *[Internet, Westlaw]*

Ethics in Government Reporter (CCH Washington Service Bureau)

National Reporter on Legal Ethics and Professional Responsibility (University Publications of America) *[Lexis]*

Legislation

CIS/Index (Congressional Information Service) *[CD, Internet, Lexis]*

Congressional Index (CCH)

Native Americans

Indian Law Reporter (American Indian Lawyer Training Program)

Occupational Safety and Health

Employment Safety and Health Guide (CCH) *[CD, Internet, Lexis]*

Occupational Safety & Health Reporter (BNA) *[CD, Internet, Lexis]*

Partnerships and S Corporations

Partnership Tax Planning & Practice (CCH)

S Corporations Guide (CCH)

Pensions and Compensation

Compliance Guide for Plan Administrators (CCH) *[CD, Internet, Lexis, Westlaw]*

Employee Benefits Compliance Coordinator (RIA)

Employee Benefits Management (CCH) *[CD, Internet, Lexis, Westlaw]*

Executive Compensation & Taxation Coordinator (RIA)

Fringe Benefits Tax Guide (CCH) *[CD, Internet, Lexis, Westlaw]*

Individual Retirement Plans Guide (CCH) *[Lexis]*

Payroll Management Guide (CCH) *[CD, Internet, Lexis, Westlaw]*

Pension & Benefits Reporter (BNA) *[CD, Internet, Lexis, Westlaw]*

Pension and Profit Sharing (RIA) *[CD]*

Pension Coordinator (RIA) *[CD]*

Pension Plan Guide (CCH) *[CD, Internet, Lexis, Westlaw]*

Products Liability and Consumer Safety

Consumer Product Safety Guide (CCH)

Product Safety & Liability Reporter (BNA) *[Internet]*

Products Liability Reports (CCH) *[CD, Internet]*

Securities and Commodities

Blue Sky Law Reports (CCH) *[CD, Internet, Lexis, Westlaw]*

Commodity Futures Law Reports (CCH) *[CD, Internet, Lexis, Westlaw]*

Federal Securities Law Reports (CCH) *[CD, Internet, Lexis]*

SEC Compliance: Financial Reporting and Forms (WGL) *[CD, Internet]*

Securities Regulation & Law Report (BNA) *[Internet, Lexis, Westlaw]*

Securities Regulation (WGL)

Securities Regulatory Library (IHS) *[CD, Internet]*

State and Local Taxation

All States Tax Guide (RIA) *[CD, Internet]*

State and Local Taxes (RIA) (for each state) *[CD, Internet]*

State Tax Guide (CCH) *[CD, Internet, Lexis, Westlaw]*

State Tax Reports (CCH) (for each state) *[CD, Internet, Lexis, Westlaw]*

Supreme Court

United States Law Week (BNA) *[Internet, Lexis, Westlaw]*

Taxation

See specific headings

Trade Regulation

Antitrust & Trade Regulation Report (BNA) *[Internet, Lexis, Westlaw]*

Trade Regulation Reports (CCH) *[CD, Internet, Lexis, Westlaw]*

Transportation

Federal Carriers Reports (CCH)

Shipping Regulation (Pike & Fischer)

Unemployment Insurance / Social Security

Unemployment Insurance Reports (CCH) *[CD, Internet, Lexis]*

Workers' Compensation

Workers' Compensation: Business Management Guide
(CCH) *[CD, Internet]*

*

SUBJECT INDEX

References are to pages

Boldface references are to exhibits

413

*

TITLE INDEX

References are to pages

Boldface references are to exhibits

427